The Royal Tennis Court

A History of Tennis at Hampton Court Palace

HER MAJESTY QUEEN ELIZABETH II

PATRON OF THE ROYAL TENNIS COURT

The Royal Tennis Court

A History of Tennis at Hampton Court Palace

David Best

Ironbark
Ronaldson Publications

To
Joy

First published in 2002 by Ronaldson Publications

13A Linkside Avenue, Oxford, OX2 8HY

Copyright David Best

British Library Cataloguing in Publication Data

Best, David

Tennis
1 Court Tennis
Title

ISBN   1 – 899804 – 10 – 2 (leather bound)
ISBN   1 – 899804 – 11 – 0 (cloth bound)

Printed by Alden Press
Osney Mead
Oxford OX2 0EF

Bound by Green Street Bindery
Green Street
Oxford OX4 1YB

CONTENTS

APPENDICES

ILLUSTRATIONS

Dust Jacket   Designed by Julie Smith
(Standard edition only)   Rear photograph by Les Jones — Cover Shots, Toronto

----oooO0Oooo----

HIS ROYAL HIGHNESS THE PRINCE EDWARD, EARL OF WESSEX, CVO

BAGSHOT PARK

One of my earliest encounters with David Best was in the mid-1990s, when we were paired to play a friendly match at the Royal Tennis Court, Hampton Court Palace. A combative game ensued, in which David's longer experience was balanced by my more youthful court coverage, but towards the end of our allotted hour, a difficult ball took a ricochet off the top of my racket and gave me a black eye. As you might expect everyone, especially the press, had a field day speculating on the cause, including a tiff with my girlfriend and future bride, Sophie, who shares my passion for Tennis and membership of this historic club.

Apart from this close brush with an appointment at Her Majesty's Palace and Fortress, David has been a wonderful servant of the Royal Tennis Court. As Honorary Treasurer for the dozen years since 1990, he has guided the club's finances from the austere times of national recession to a position from which, at the start of the new millennium, the funding of a new Tennis court at Hampton Court was viable. No less heroically, he has now completed a history of the most famous Tennis venue in the world, from Cardinal Wolsey's tenure almost five centuries ago to the machinations of bureaucracy over the issue of a twenty-first century court.

Aside from sports such as hunting, fishing and archery, Tennis has one of the longest and most impressive pedigrees. From its humble origins as a street game to its lofty status as the Sport of Kings, the sport and its courts regularly provides amusing and often tragic footnotes in a variety of history books. In David Best's book, the central character is our own magnificent court whose story is compellingly brought to life.

David's research has been conducted in a variety of London's sources over a period of nine years. Long hours have been spent poring over obscure and sometimes misleading documents for connections with the ancient and royal game of Tennis. The result is a fascinating and highly readable volume that bears the stamp of an author writing on his favourite subject.

Edward

His Royal Highness The Earl of Wessex, CVO

2002

INTRODUCTION

The Royal Tennis Court is a Club within a Court of the same name, which lies inside the walls of Hampton Court Palace. Its history, and that of Tennis at the Palace, has been continually evolving ever since Cardinal Wolsey built the first Tennis Court there in the early part of the sixteenth century. Several of the Country's monarchs have spent many enjoyable hours at Hampton Court participating in this most pleasurable of pastimes.

For the last hundred years Tennis has had to take a back seat while its recent offspring, Lawn Tennis, has caught the public imagination. A major problem faced by the older game is that the courts in which it is played are horrendously expensive to build and therefore not normally an economic proposition. This is the main reason that there are less than 30 active courts in the British Isles and only around 50 worldwide. Traditionally they have been built by royalty, the nobility or wealthy individuals, leading universities and schools, and by a few exclusive clubs. As a result, courts are often found in interesting locations and these days most have members' clubs operating from them. Several have had their histories published, but until now a major omission from that list has been the Court with the greatest story of all to tell: The Royal Tennis Court at Hampton Court Palace.

From the start it was envisaged that the main interest in this book would come from two groups, the tennis-playing community and those interested in the Palace. I must therefore apologise to the tennis enthusiast for repeating some material that appears in standard tennis works. However, these books can be expensive and rare, and newcomers to the game may be unfamiliar with its long and interesting heritage. For those whose main interest is the Palace, or who have little knowledge of Tennis, it would perhaps be advisable initially to spend a few moments referring to the first two Appendices, in order to gain an insight into the intricacies of this ancient game.

The first part of the book introduces the setting, which encompasses the whole story: the Palace itself. There follows a synopsis of the game's evolution and its royal pedigree. Subsequent chapters deal with the construction of, and modifications to, the various Tennis Courts at Hampton Court. They work through the Tudor, Elizabethan, Stuart, Hanoverian, Victorian and Edwardian periods, the formation of a Members' Club, and on past the upheavals of the twentieth century up to the present day. The peripheral buildings associated with the Courts are dealt with in a separate chapter, as are the careers of the succession of Masters, Markers and Professionals. A later chapter guides the reader through the tortuous negotiations with the Palace authorities, as the Club has attempted to build a second tennis court within the confines of the Palace.

As the Palace belongs to the nation a large part of the research had to be undertaken at the Public Records Office in London. Other major sources of information have been the British Library in Central London and the British Library's Newspaper Library at Colindale. Of the published works, the most useful have been: *The History of the King's Works* by Sir Howard Colvin; Ernest Law's *History of Hampton Court Palace*; and the classic tennis volumes, the *Annals of Tennis* by Julian Marshall; *A History of Tennis* by Noel and Clark; *Tennis and Rackets* by Lord Aberdare; and *Tennis, The Development of the European Ball Game* by Roger Morgan.

Not all of the building records have survived. Of most help have been the Exchequer account books that cover the period immediately following Henry VIII's acquisition of Hampton Court, which are available up until 1538. Here, for example, there is a considerable amount of detail concerning the building of Henry VIII's enclosed Tennis Court, but sadly nothing about Cardinal Wolsey's earlier open one, because originally the Palace was not a royal residence. Also invaluable have been the monthly account books of the Office of the King's Works, and its successive departments, which survive from the start of Charles II's reign in 1660 until the end of William III's in 1702. They resume in 1778 and continue until 1814. As for the missing records, of most concern is the early Stuart period when there was intensive tennis activity at both the Palace and in the country at large. Fortunately, the Declared Annual Accounts of the Exchequer and Audit Office in the form of Pipe Rolls, which give sporadic details of works in the royal palaces, have survived throughout and have helped to fill in some of the gaps. Treasury files and those of the Lord Chamberlain's Office have also been useful. Many relevant entries from these manuscripts have been transcribed into the Appendix and, for those interested, there are comprehensive notes listing reference sources.

Inevitably with the research spanning several centuries, the investigation becomes easier as one draws closer to the present day, with the amount of material available ever increasing. For this reason it has been a constant struggle trying to avoid loading the later chapters. As with any project of this nature where basic research has to be carried out, that research often follows on from previous historians work: the validity of the deductions made and conclusions reached are for others to decide.

Three different methods of dating were encountered. Sometimes documents would be dated by the Regnal Year – the number of years a monarch had reigned, for example: 'January 45 Elizabeth I' is January 1603, Elizabeth I having come to the throne in November 1558; and 'August 1 James I' is August 1603, because James I succeeded Elizabeth I in March 1603. The Julian calendar was in official use until 1752 with its New Year on 25th March, leading to documents issued between the 1st January and the 25th March carrying the date of the preceding year. After that the Gregorian calendar became compulsory with its New Year on 1st January. In Stuart times both calendars were in common use. Where dates are recorded they have been converted to the Gregorian style used today.

Throughout the text various costs have been shown. It is not a precise science trying to gauge the value in today's terms but, as a rough guide, £1 in Tudor times corresponded to about £330 at the turn of the Millennium, and the same pound in the Stuart and Victorian eras equated to £70 and £30, respectively. Almost all the figures quoted are pre-decimal, when there were 12 pence to a shilling and 20 shillings in the pound.

I am indebted to many people who have been only too happy to give me specialist help when called upon. At the Palace these have included Dr. Simon Thurley, the former Curator, Jonathan Foyle, Clare Murphy, Suzanne Groom and Sarah Parker. I would also like to convey my thanks to Gerard J. Belliveau, Jr., the Librarian at the Racquet & Tennis Club, New York, Thierry Bernard-Tambour, Cees de Bondt, Saul David, Paul Elkins, Michael Garnett, Tina Gibbens, Stephen Green, the Curator at Lord's, Louis Jebb, Kathryn McNicoll, Bruce Ronaldson, Manfred Schotten, John Stanley Rogers, Andrew Steven and Dr. Michael Turner of English Heritage. Likewise, several club members have been most helpful, particularly Lord Aberdare, Derek Allen, Michael Banks, Pat Barker, John Clark, Stephen de Laszlo, Betty Evans, Nicki Faircloth, David Frost, Murray Glover, Jamie Ingham, Henry Macintosh, Mike Milne-Home, Michael Morton, Richard Oldham, Derek Steel, Richard Stocks, Ronald Swash, Jane Vaughan, Ray Wigger, Peter Wordie and John Yarnall. Sue Marley, a great-great-great-granddaughter of the Club's first Professional, John Case, very kindly provided me with a wealth of material on three generations of Cases who worked at Hampton Court. Equally the Professionals, Peter Ashford who supplied details of his father's career and Derek Barrett who helped with his own. A few have sadly passed away in the years between conception and completion: Tony Negretti and Lord Butterfield, and Henry Johns with whom I spent many happy hours listening to his wonderful stories and discussing his involvement with the Royal Tennis Court. Those who kindly supplied me with pictures and photographs are acknowledged in the list of illustrations and some other gratitudes are expressed in the notes section.

Had it not been for the enthusiasm of the indefatigable former Honorary Secretary of the Royal Tennis Court, John Edwards, I might never have started the project. His advice on the overall perspective has been most useful. For sharing his wealth of tennis knowledge, I am most grateful to club member Brian Rich: on many occasions he has prevented me from falling into unforeseen traps. In addition, he was only too willing to undertake time-consuming investigations to solve particular problems, and the years of research for this work coincided with his invaluable cataloguing of the Tennis articles in *The Field, The Country Gentleman's Newspaper*, which shed light on much of Hampton Court's tennis history during the latter half of the Victorian era and the first three decades of the twentieth century. I am extremely appreciative of the time Daphne Ford, the Palace's former Archaeological Recorder, gave me helping to decipher the small scraps of information that have led to a better understanding of the development of the Tennis Courts at Hampton Court. Roger Morgan has helped to solve some of the problems that arose regarding the early features of the Courts, often supplying a vital piece of the jigsaw. I am very grateful to Hilda Forster, for her many patient hours of initial proof reading, which saved me some embarrassment, to John Partridge for the final exhaustive editing and proof reading, and to Martin Bronstein who patiently reset the text into a camera-ready state prior to printing.

I would particularly like to thank Chris and Lesley Ronaldson for their help and encouragement throughout. Finally I must especially thank my wife Joy, who has not only helped with matters of style and phraseology during the writing of the book, but has also been totally supportive over the nine years it has taken to bring this volume to publication.

David Best
Walton on Thames

August 2002

CHAPTER 1

HAMPTON COURT PALACE

The silvery Thames embraces
Hampton Court's wide open spaces
Of Park and Lawn and Garden fair
And Tilt Yard kept in good repair.
Hard by the stream stands Wolsey's pile,
With Gothic arch in Tudor Style;
Wren's ruddy brickwork in the east
Gives architects a varied feast.

The Palace at Hampton Court lies along the north bank of a beautiful section of the River Thames some 12 miles south-west of Central London. There is an early reference in the *Domesday Book* of 1086 to 'Hamntone in the County of Middlesex', when a value of £39 was put on the land. That land was then owned by Walter de St Valerie and later passed to Henry de St Albans before a crusading order, the Knights Hospitallers of St John of Jerusalem, acquired it in 1236. They used the land as a centre for their agricultural estates, which helped to fund the headquarters of the branch at Clerkenwell, which in turn supported their overseas activities. They later built a manor house on the land.

Henry VII in 1503 was the first king to stay at the house as a guest of the Abbots of the Order of St John and it was his Lord Chamberlain, Lord Daubeney, who took over the lease some two years later.

In 1514 Thomas Wolsey gained possession and importantly his 99-year lease allowed him to redevelop the land and even to pull down the manor house.

Wolsey was an ambitious clergyman who rose quickly through the church's ranks to become a royal chaplain, where he soon became involved in diplomatic affairs. Within a year he was elevated to Cardinal on the personal recommendation of Henry VIII to the Pope. Wolsey, now starting to accrue enormous wealth, began building a magnificent palace in place of the old manor house. The King first visited the Palace at an early stage of its development in 1516 with his Queen, Catherine of Aragon. Two years later Wolsey had become the most powerful cleric in the country, dealing with all the King's diplomatic and foreign business. So close were the two that Henry even supported his attempts to be elected Pope; he was, though, thwarted by the Holy Roman Emperor Charles V, the King of Germany and Spain, who was at the time all-powerful as the ruler of much of Western Europe.

Wolsey's Palace now had 1,000 rooms with some 500 staff. It was surrounded by a moat, one of the last in this country, which was used more for drainage than defence. Much of the old Tudor Palace one sees today was built by the Cardinal, including the Chapel and the West Front. When their rooms were ready in 1525 Henry and Catherine again stayed there.

Wolsey had some years earlier unwisely incurred the displeasure of Anne Boleyn, who was now the King's mistress. Catherine, the first queen, had failed to produce a male heir, so Henry was seeking to dissolve the marriage in order to marry Anne. The King sought the help of Wolsey and when the Cardinal failed to bring about the divorce he began to fall out of favour. In an attempt to re-establish himself Wolsey invited the King to use the Palace as a court whenever he wished to do so; Wolsey was subsequently allowed by Henry to reside there for another three or four years and it was during this time that his many enemies, including Anne Boleyn, plotted his downfall. He was accused of asserting papal jurisdiction over the authority of his country, a crime for which he was found guilty and stripped of his Great Seal of Office and much of his property. He left the Palace in disgrace in July 1529 for Esher and later York, where he was further charged with being in league with foreign powers. On his way back to London, bound for the Tower and probable execution, he was to die, passing away at Leicester on the 29th November 1530.

After his acquisition of Hampton Court, Henry embarked on a major expansion programme. His first projects were new privy lodgings for himself and a massive extension to the Great Kitchen. Many subsidiary kitchen office buildings, larders, storage areas and specialist kitchens were also built. Once these works had been completed the King started to build the Great Hall and, for his leisure, a new closed tennis court. The Court was located in the north-east part of the Palace, an area Henry had set aside for his sporting pursuits. Apart from the Tennis Court the area included a bowling alley, the tiltyard with its five spectator towers, and facilities for archery. The surrounding parkland also provided opportunities for his favourite pastime, hunting.

While these works were proceeding the King had finally divorced Catherine in 1533 allowing him to marry Anne. Their first child was a girl, Elizabeth. This caused violent arguments with the disappointed king, and when their second child, a son, was stillborn, Henry, whose attention had already begun to wander, looked for his pleasure elsewhere. His eye had caught that of Jane Seymour, one of the young ladies of the Queen's court. A trumped-up charge of adultery was then brought against Anne, who was found guilty and beheaded at the Tower of London on the 19th May 1536, allowing Jane to become his new Queen. Jane was soon pregnant and a son Edward was born, but the joy quickly turned to sorrow as it became clear that the Queen was seriously ill with complications following the birth. She died twelve days later.

With the arrival of a son, new lodgings were needed and these were built for him next to the 'Close' Tennis Court as it was called. At about the same time, lodgings that had been intended for his late mother were nearing completion.

1.　HAMPTON COURT PALACE

2. THE WEST FRONT OF THE PALACE

The first sight of the Palace for most visitors.

Each new queen had occupied a new suite of rooms up to this date. Another major project of this period was also finished, the magnificent Close Bowling Alley, which was also located in the sporting area.

Henry was to marry three more times. Firstly there was Anne of Cleves. The King had chosen her from a Holbein portrait but was disappointed with the reality and the marriage was quickly annulled on the grounds that it was never consummated. His next queen was Catherine Howard. Like Anne Boleyn, who ironically was Catherine's cousin, she was charged with adultery and suffered the same fate on the executioner's block. It is said that the ghost of Catherine runs through the Haunted Gallery at the Palace, still protesting her innocence to this very day. Catherine Parr became his sixth and last wife. Henry, by now obese and with ulcerated legs, left Hampton Court for the last time in 1546 and died at Whitehall early the following year. All three of his surviving children were to become monarchs and were to live in the Palace from time to time.

Edward VI acceded to the throne at the age of nine; he had spent much of his youth at Hampton Court and continued to live there as King. He was popular, particularly locally, when he reopened Hampton Court Chase. This was an area that included East and West Molesey, Walton, Weybridge, Shepperton, Hersham, Byfleet, Wisley, Cobham, Esher and Thames Ditton, which his father had enclosed for hunting in the latter part of his reign. Because of his youth, his uncle, Lord Hertford, became Lord Protector and was created Duke of Somerset.

He gradually reduced the King's role to insignificance, at the same time enriching himself at the expense of the people. This encouraged his enemies to plot against him leading to the issue of a proclamation in the King's name calling on his subjects to defend the Palace. It was suggested that if Somerset were to fall the King's life would be in danger. The Palace was fortified for the first and only time in its history. Five hundred servants and attendants were issued with suits of armour to assist the resident soldiers and the moat was filled. The local population, whose support had been sought, showed little enthusiasm for the task, so Somerset and the King fled to the more secure Windsor Castle. The crisis was defused with Somerset being sent to the Tower, allowing Edward to return to his beloved Hampton Court. Never physically strong, he was last in residence there in September 1552 and died of tuberculosis the following July, at the tender age of fifteen.

Next came Queen Mary, Catherine of Aragon's daughter. She was married to the unpopular Philip of Spain who was never crowned king. They spent their honeymoon at Hampton Court in the autumn of 1554. Like her late half-brother, she was frail and subject to illness, dying childless in 1558 at the age of 42.

Elizabeth I spent much of her time at the Palace enjoying short periods of rest and quiet. She particularly liked to spend her Christmases at Hampton Court and was very fond of the gardens. The Queen also entertained many of her suitors there but she was never to marry. The only addition during her reign was a new privy kitchen, the remaining portion of which can be seen in Tennis Court Lane. Elizabeth nearly died of smallpox while at Hampton Court in 1562; however, she recovered and lived another 40 years, last staying there in the summer of 1599 and finally passing away at Richmond Palace three and a half years later.

As all three of Henry VIII's children remained childless, the House of Tudor came to an end and the pre-planned Union of the Crowns came to pass. That brought James VI of Scotland to the English throne as James I. His queen was Anne of Denmark. It was during the celebrations of his accession, much of which took place at Hampton Court, that Shakespeare's Company performed plays there before the King and his guests. James I did not add to the Palace but, as other monarchs had done before him, he found it a useful refuge from the many plagues that often hit London. He hosted the Hampton Court Conference in 1604, a religious discussion called to settle the differences between the Puritans and the Church of England, a result of which was the publication of the Authorized Version of the Bible. James was not an athletic man; however, his two sons Henry and Charles were and in the summer of that year Prince Henry was to be found at Hampton Court enjoying all the sporting facilities including, of course, tennis. The Queen was to die while staying at the Palace in 1619 and six years later James followed, having spent every September there during his reign.

James was succeeded by his younger son Charles I, Prince Henry the heir having died in 1612. Charles married Henrietta Maria, daughter of Henri IV, the

The Royal Palace of Hampton Court. ——————— Le Palais Royale de Hampton Court.
Printed for Jo.s Bowles & Son at the Black Horse in Cornhill London.

3. AN EARLY 18th CENTURY VIEW OF WREN'S SOUTH & EAST FRONTS
OF THE PALACE

The Stuart Tennis Court can be seen in the distance.

King of France, and they honeymooned at Hampton Court. Charles, who also used the Palace to escape the plagues, did very little by way of building works, apart from a new tennis court and the creation of an eleven-mile channel cut from the River Colne, to supply water to his ponds and fountains, which became the Longford River. Continually in confrontation with Parliament, he fled the Palace in 1642 after attempting to arrest five of its Members, retreating firstly to Windsor and then to Oxford. Five years later he was brought back to Hampton Court as a prisoner of Cromwell. He later escaped to the Isle of Wight, where he was again arrested and imprisoned, this time at Carisbrooke Castle. He was returned to London in 1649 and executed outside his own Banqueting House in the Palace of Whitehall.

During the period of the Commonwealth an inventory was prepared of the contents of Hampton Court with the intention of selling everything. A price of £7,777 13s. 5d. was even put on the Palace. In the event, there was only a partial sale and the Palace itself was not sold, as Oliver Cromwell had taken a liking to it, moving into a suite of rooms and treating it as his country house.

After the 1660 Restoration, Charles II, who had already been King of Scotland for ten years, did very little by way of improvements. He did however, refurbish the Tennis Court and carry out extensive work in the gardens. In 1662 he

6

brought his new bride, Catherine of Braganza, to Hampton Court. He was, though, remembered more for his many mistresses resulting in him becoming known as the Merry Monarch. He provided a suite of rooms at the Palace for his principal mistress, Barbara Palmer (Lady Castlemaine). In later life he used the Palace very little and his brother James II, on coming to the throne, used it even less. James had two daughters from his first marriage, but a son from his second marriage was brought up as a Catholic, which caused uproar amongst the Protestant population. William of Orange was invited to invade England by virtue of his marriage to Mary, the King's elder daughter, forcing James to flee to France. William also had a claim to the English throne as a grandson of Charles I and at the time he was third in line.

William and Mary came to Hampton Court at the start of their reign early in 1689 for the clean air, as the new king was in poor health and asthmatic. They quickly fell in love with the place but found the old Tudor buildings not to their liking, preferring a palace more like that of Louis XIV's Versailles. Their joint sovereignty also required two sets of state rooms, so Sir Christopher Wren was called in to design and build a new palace. His initial idea was to knock down the whole of the old Tudor Palace; however this never came about, leaving the curious mix of architectural styles one sees today. Mary was to die of smallpox in 1694 and the distressed King then stopped all work at Hampton Court and moved to London. That could have spelt the end for the Palace, but fate took a hand when a major fire at Whitehall in 1698 destroyed the palace there. William at once ordered work to restart at Hampton Court with his own apartments given priority. Fine craftsmen were employed; Grinling Gibbons carved much of the ornamental woodwork and Antonio Verrio painted the ceilings and murals. The gardens were completely redesigned under the direction of Henry Wise. The works also included the creation of the Maze, the Wilderness and the Privy Garden; the delightful Banqueting House near the river was another addition.

William died in 1702, following a riding accident in the surrounding park, bringing Mary's sister Anne to the throne. Naturally she set about completing the construction of the Queen's apartments for her own use, these having been neglected by her late brother-in-law. By now the King's and Queen's State Apartments had the new east and south facades that dominate the view from the rear gardens. Anne used the Palace occasionally and at times held Privy Council meetings in the Cartoon Gallery. Married to Prince George of Denmark she endured eighteen pregnancies, most of which resulted in stillborn babies. Only a son William, who was born at Hampton Court, lived for any length of time. He though was never to become king, dying at the age of eleven, predeceasing his mother.

After the Queen had died, the throne passed to the House of Hanover, as William III's Act of Settlement had ensured the Protestant succession. So in 1714 George I became the new king. He was a dull man, German-speaking with very little English and unpopular. However, he was to use Hampton Court regularly and among his first acts were to dismiss Sir Christopher Wren and to commission Sir James Thornhill to paint the ceiling in the Queen's bedchamber. Some insight into life at the Palace at this time will be seen in Chapter 5.

George I was to die of apoplexy in 1727, which brought his son to the throne as George II. He was an equally dull man preferring Hanover to England. He did, however, come to Hampton Court every summer for two months where he carried out further works, the Queen's Presence and Guard Chambers being completed. The last alterations to the Palace were carried out in George II's reign when the apartments for the Duke of Cumberland were finished in 1732. Five years later, the Queen died and the King rarely used the Palace after that.

In 1753 the first bridge across the River Thames at Hampton Court was built as a toll bridge. It was rebuilt in 1778 and again in 1865.

George II was the last monarch to live at Hampton Court. He died in 1760, but his son Frederick had died before him, so it was Frederick's son who became the new king and reigned as George III. He hated the Palace because of the brutal childhood his grandfather had inflicted upon him there: so he refused to use it, although he did maintain it. Capability Brown, the famous garden designer, was put in charge of the gardens but resisted the temptation to remodel them. Notable happenings during this reign were the planting of the Great Vine, which is still producing grapes today, the reduction of Wolsey's Great Gatehouse on the West Front by two storeys due to its unsafe condition and the creation of the Grace-and-Favour Apartments.

George IV, both as Prince Regent and King, neglected the Palace except for the Royal Stud, which benefited from his passion for horses. At this time there was a resident housekeeper, who was allowed to charge visitors one shilling. William IV thought that these visitors should get more for their money so he scoured his other palaces for pictures that could be hung at Hampton Court. During his ten-year reign he also restored the King's Staircase and the Astronomical Clock.

The Palace was opened to the public, free of charge, in 1838 by Queen Victoria. It was during her reign that the ugly old sash windows in the old West Front were replaced with ones of the original type, and most of the plain Georgian chimneys were rebuilt in the tall Tudor style with wonderfully patterned brickwork.

With the coming of the railway to Hampton Court in 1849, many more visitors came and the Palace became the first public building to be opened on a Sunday. This caused an outcry amongst traditionalists that raged for many years. Wolsey's Gatehouse, the splendid western entrance to the Palace, was refurbished in 1882, when the original wooden gates were discovered, restored and rehung. Unfortunately, some refacing of the brickwork was carried out using wrongly coloured bricks, the result of which is still there for all to see. That same year there was a major fire with the unfortunate death of a servant in whose room it had started. Eight rooms were badly damaged and as a result fire alarms were installed and a form of central heating replaced the old coke stoves in the State Rooms. A more serious fire, in terms of damage to the Palace, broke out some four years later. This time 40 rooms were affected, mainly in the old Tudor apartments of Prince Edward at the eastern end of Tennis Court Lane, and this resulted in a system of hydrants being installed throughout the building.

In 1901 Queen Victoria was succeeded by her eldest son Edward VII. At the time of Edward's death in 1910, part of the moat by the Wolsey Gatehouse was being excavated revealing the old Tudor stone bridge. In 1924, during George V's reign, the old tiltyards which had been a vegetable plot for many a year were converted into the Rose Garden and the surviving tower into tea-rooms.

George VI saw the Palace survive the Second World War, being bombed only once, details of which will be dealt with in Chapter 8. Shortly after the war the charge of one shilling was reintroduced for visitors wishing to see the State Rooms; however, the gardens remained free of charge.

Various members of the Royal Family continue to visit the Palace for official functions and at other times informally to see friends. One such official visit occurred in 1982 when Queen Elizabeth II was entertained by Queen Beatrix of the Netherlands, who was staying at Hampton Court, necessitating the closure of the Palace to the public.

Four years later in 1986 the Queen was horrified when she witnessed the devastation caused by another fire, again with loss of life, this time a Grace-and-Favour resident. The fire badly damaged the King's State Apartments, which took six years to restore at a cost of £11 million. The rooms were reopened to the public in 1992.

The last major works of the twentieth century were carried out in 1995 when William III's charming Privy Garden on the south side of the Palace was restored to its former glory. However, this was not done without controversy as it involved felling yew trees planted by the former king nearly 300 years earlier.

The Palace currently has half a million paying visitors a year and hosts a major music festival in the summer, attracting some of the world's leading classical performers. There is also the Hampton Court Flower Show, held in the adjacent Home Park, which is now rivalling Chelsea as the country's premier horticultural event. It has become the largest flower show in the world.

This then is the setting wherein the ancient game of Tennis continues to be played with great enthusiasm.

CHAPTER 2

THE ROYAL GAME OF TENNIS

Here within this Court of Hampton
By the broad walk that you've trampt on,
There's another Court still standing,
Tribute at your hands demanding.
It is King Henry's Tennis Court
For sport of Kings and King of Sport.

The game of Tennis played in the Royal Tennis Court at Hampton Court Palace today has evolved over the centuries, from a simple hand-ball game played in open spaces into a game of great skill, involving the mind as well as the body. It has been played in a form similar to that of the present day for some 700 years, and it should not be confused with the modern game of Lawn Tennis, which is only a little over 100 years old and played to different rules. However, because of the immense popularity of Lawn Tennis, it has become universally known as *Tennis*, forcing the old game to adopt the prefix *Real*. In America it is known as *Court Tennis*, in Australia *Royal Tennis* and in France as *Jeu de Paume*, the game of the palm (hand).

The game is the head of a family of about twenty forms of tennis still being played in Europe, all of which use a four-point scoring system, generally 15, 30, 45 (often simplified to 40), and game (60). Sixty was 'the whole' in mediaeval times. These games are all played with one or more opponents facing each other across a net, cord, or sometimes just a line on the ground. Most of them still have the unique feature known as a *chase*, a point held in abeyance and played for later in the game (see Appendix 2).

Recent research by Dr. Roger Morgan for his work *Tennis, The Development of the European Ball Game*, has suggested that the court configuration (Appendix 1) can be traced back to the time the game moved from the countryside into the towns during the thirteenth century. The walls reflect the enclosed nature of the streets and the penthouses originate from the small sloping roofs on the fronts of the shops under which the traders displayed their wares. It seems the galleries below the penthouses were probably developed during the sixteenth century in order to accommodate spectators. The roof of the court is for the comfort of the players — early courts were usually open. Previously it had been thought that the features of a Tennis Court had their origins in the monastic cloisters of the Middle Ages.

Two styles of court developed, *jeu quarré* and *jeu à dedans*. However, as the centuries passed, the dedans courts began to dominate, this process being virtually complete by the end of the eighteenth century. In general the difference between the two is that a quarré court has only two penthouses, along the service and grille walls, whereas a dedans court has a third penthouse, which houses another spectator enclosure known as the dedans. Quarré courts have no tambour, but do have apertures that vary in size, shape and number, located in the end walls. They are known as a *trou*, or *lunes*, and are winning openings. Sometimes there is an *ais*, a long thin vertical board mounted behind the server in the corner of the end wall. When hit, this is also a winning shot. Only one quarré court survives today, an open one, at Falkland Palace.

In early times, these games were played with the hand but, as the years passed, balls became harder and more painful to strike. This led to players' hands being bandaged for protection. Gloves were then used, which were later reinforced, before the introduction of simple rackets that caused the balls to be propelled even further and faster. The form of racket often depended on the type of tennis being played. Even today some games still use the hand. Through the centuries improvements have resulted in a strung racket with a wooden frame and asymmetric head — the introduction of graphite or metallic frames as used in Lawn Tennis is still being strongly resisted.

As rackets and balls improved so courts needed to be bigger. Hampton Court provides such an example for whereas Henry VIII's closed court was 83 feet by 27 feet, only ninety years later Charles I required a court nearly 111 feet by 40 feet (actual size 110 feet 11 inches x 39 feet 7 inches).[1]

Enclosed courts were expensive structures to put up, so they were at first only available to royalty and the nobility, indeed the game was to become associated with many of the royal houses of Europe, from Spain through to Russia. In the meantime, the townsfolk continued to play the game in the streets in ever-increasing numbers. So alarmed did the authorities become, that tennis was often added to the list of games and pastimes that were subject to prohibition in the hope that the active men would turn their attention to more useful pursuits. These bans were common throughout Europe; the first mention of them in England came during the reign of Edward III in 1365. They were often reconfirmed by subsequent monarchs over the next 250 years. However, the bans were usually ignored.

The game's greatest period ran from the end of the fifteenth century until the end of the seventeenth. During this time, there were courts in most of the major European towns; however, it was in France that tennis took hold most strongly. Courts sprang up all over the country; there were several in châteaux along the Loire and as many as 60 in the city of Orléans. Paris was thought to have had at least 250 courts, although some exaggerated reports talk of as many as 1,800. Certain streets in the capital were almost entirely devoted to tennis: for example, there were ten courts along the *Rue des Boucheries* during the sixteenth century and the *Rue Mazarine* had up to 15, prompting Julian Marshall to dub it 'this street of *tripots*' in his authoritative *Annals of Tennis*. The French word *tripot*, meaning 'gambling house', became synonymous with tennis as gambling was always associated with the game. Loans were available for the erection of new courts in those days, so the game must have been a profitable business.

French monarchs were particularly fond of Tennis. Philip IV was known to have had a court of his own in 1308 and since then 17 of the last 25 Kings of France played the game at some time during their lives. The great French palaces had several courts. Three were built at The Louvre and two at Fontainebleau, the second of which is still in use. Other courts were built at Compiègne, St Germain, Vincennes and Versailles. The latter, which was erected outside the palace walls, was destined to make its mark in French history. On 20th June 1789 the National Assembly was denied access to the Palace so they looked for a suitable building in which to hold a meeting and the nearby Tennis Court suited their purpose. There they vowed 'never to dissolve and to meet whenever circumstances demanded until the Constitution of the Realm was established on solid foundations'. This was the famous *Tennis Court Oath*, acknowledged as the start of the French Revolution. The Court at Versailles is now a museum dedicated to that event.

Tennis went into serious decline during the eighteenth century when courts were being lost at an alarming rate and many were converted into theatres, at first for a few hours a day, then for weeks at a time and finally, some permanently. Several of these conversions suffered serious fires, so losing any chance of restoration and by 1783 there were only 54 courts left in France, 13 of them in Paris. But it was the Revolution that almost caused the game's complete demise. With most of the aristocracy lost to the guillotine, Paris emerged in 1800 with only one court still in play. Since then the capital has only ever had one or two courts in use at any one time; a few more were built in other parts of the country but numbers have again fallen back. Today only three remain in play, Fontainebleau, Bordeaux and one of the two *Rue Lauriston* courts in Paris. All other courts on continental Europe have been lost to play.

The history of the game in the British Isles followed a similar pattern. At first, courts appeared in Scotland in the thirteenth century, probably due to the Flemish influence, and Wales and Ireland have had several, but it was in England where they flourished.

Henry VII was the first English king known to have played, taking up the game seriously in about 1494, at the age of 37. He had courts at many of his residences and at his Palace at Richmond in Surrey, formerly Sheen Palace, rebuilt and renamed after a disastrous fire, he set aside a large area devoted to sporting activities. This recreational part of the Palace included tennis courts, bowling alleys and other of the usual activities associated with Tudor sporting excellence. The concept was modelled on similar complexes Henry had seen while exiled in northern Europe, built by the Dukes of Burgundy.[2]

When Henry VIII acceded to the throne in 1509 he immediately set about adding to his late father's stock of tennis courts. During his reign, new courts were built at Bridewell Palace at Blackfriars, Beaulieu in Essex[3] and at Hampton Court. After the downfall of Cardinal Wolsey, he gained many more properties, notably York House, which he transformed into the Palace of Whitehall. Here, as his father had done at Richmond, Henry built a mixed sports area that included tiltyards, bowling alleys, the Cockpit for cockfighting and four tennis courts, two open and two closed. Another acquisition from Wolsey was The More in Hertfordshire. This house already possessed its own court and it is known that the King played on it.

4. THE ROYAL TENNIS COURT FROM THE PALACE GARDEN

Henry VIII continued to play into his mid-forties, when increasing weight began to affect his mobility. For exercise during his remaining years he turned to hunting. After his death in 1547, no other member of the Royal Family was known to have played during the remainder of the sixteenth century.

As part of his education, Edward VI had been taught to play tennis. However, as soon as he was able to decide his priorities for himself he dropped active sports in favour of his first loves, music and dancing.[4] Edward though might have been responsible for one of the country's most famous courts, the Brake at Whitehall; a fifth court was built there during his reign.[5] Edward's half-sister, Elizabeth I, was a keen spectator and she made sure the royal courts were regularly maintained. There are many well-documented tennis anecdotes involving her and her courtiers. Perhaps the most quoted is the instance in which a scuffle broke out in the Queen's presence during a game between Lord Norfolk and Robert Dudley, the Earl of Leicester. There was some intimacy between Dudley and the Queen, and he had the audacity to take a napkin out of her hand to wipe his face after he had become overheated. Norfolk was incensed and threatened to strike Dudley in the face with his racket. The ensuing rumpus upset the Queen

5.   HENRY VIII

Henry VIII built a magnificent enclosed Tennis Court at Hampton Court.

who then blamed Norfolk for overreacting. Ernest Law, the author of the definitive history of the Palace, thought the incident probably occurred at Hampton Court, which might well have been the case as Dudley had a suite of rooms there.

Following the Union of the Crowns, James I's sons, the Princes Henry and Charles, were encouraged to play tennis by their father. James, who acceded to the Scottish Throne as James VI when only one year old, had been taught the game during his schooldays and continued to play as a young man; [6] however his favoured sport was hunting. He did though erect a new Court at his house at Newmarket and another was built at his Queen's London residence, Denmark House, now Somerset House. Major works were carried out

6. CHARLES I

Charles I rebuilt the Open Court at
Hampton Court and enclosed it.

on the Brake Court at Whitehall, Falkland Palace and Hampton Court. The elder son, Prince Henry, was a very active player and built himself a new Court at his

7. CHARLES II

One of Charles II's first acts as King was to
refurbish the Tennis Court at Hampton Court.

principal residence, Richmond Palace. However, he did not live to be king and it was Charles I who succeeded his father in 1625. Also a keen player, he promptly rebuilt the Open Court at Hampton Court and later built a replacement Court at Somerset House, the first having been converted into a chapel.[7] It is said that Charles I was the best of the English tennis-playing monarchs: he played a great deal in the Court at St James, which he had built when Prince of Wales.[8] During the Civil War, Charles was forced to run his affairs from Oxford. His tennis though did not suffer, for it is known that he used the Oriel Street Court with his nephew, Prince Rupert. Here we learn a little about his appearance on court, when he ordered from London '4 yards of taby, 2 ells and

¼ of taffety to be a tennis-suit, and 2 pairs of garters and roses with silk buttons and other necessaries for making up of the said suit.' [9]

Following the capture and subsequent execution of Charles, the new Commonwealth was administered by Oliver Cromwell. Unfortunately, he did not approve of Tennis and the famous Brake Court at Whitehall was one of the casualties of this period.

Whitehall though did not have to wait long for a replacement. Following the Restoration, Charles II built a new Court on the old Brake site, as soon as he had completed the refurbishment of the present Stuart Court at Hampton Court. Later in his reign, he constructed another Court at Windsor Castle. The King did not restrict himself to playing only on royal courts, for he and his younger brother, James, Duke of York (later James II), often used one of the Haymarket Courts.[10] After Charles's death and his brother's forced exile to France, royal interest continued with William III. William, a tennis player himself,[11] ordered a major renovation of the Court at Hampton Court, whilst he was having the Palace itself partially rebuilt.

8. WILLIAM III

William III commissioned Sir Christopher Wren to carry out a major renovation of the Tennis Court at Hampton Court.

A decline in the popularity of the game had begun during the latter part of the seventeenth century, mirrored as has been seen throughout Europe. Courts were lost to theatres and some were even used as boxing arenas.[12] Exercise was not fashionable during the early Hanoverian period, but one of the young royal princes began to take an interest. He was George II's first son, Frederick, Prince of Wales. The heir to the Throne died in 1751, it is said of a burst abscess in his side due to a blow received at tennis or cricket some years earlier. Two of Frederick's sons followed in their father's footsteps and took up the game, William, Duke of Gloucester and Henry, Duke of Cumberland. In 1789, the Duke of Cumberland, who was in temporary residence at Hampton Court, sustained a serious injury when playing. He was hit in the eye by a ball: it was reported that he bore the pain well but was upset by a comment from the Prince of Wales, who hoped his uncle 'would not have a black eye, as people would be apt to say that his wife had beat him'.[13] This Prince of Wales acceded to the Throne as George IV in 1820 and he may have been the only Hanoverian monarch to have played tennis. Although his whole outlook on life would suggest sport was the last thing on his mind, he did occasionally play cricket and there is circumstantial evidence which leaves very little doubt that played tennis as well.

In the Prince's circle were several keen tennis players; apart from his aforementioned uncles, the Duke's of Gloucester and Cumberland, there was his brother Frederick, the Duke of York, whom he was extremely fond of, Charles James Fox and Richard Meyler. The strongest evidence can be found in a *Morning Post* article in 1788, where it said of the Duke of York: 'On the whole he is superior to his brother, the PRINCE, and in a few months will probably be able to give him the odds of nearly half a game.' [14] At that time whenever there was a newspaper reference to 'the PRINCE' (in capital letters) it meant the Prince of Wales and not one of George III's other sons. Another indication of a possible interest came in the 1790s when he was renting a house in the Hampshire village of Crawley. His presence there encouraged Richard Meyler, who owned the Crawley Court estate, to build a Tennis Court in the grounds of his house for the 'delectation of the Prince of Wales and the Duke of Gloucester'.[15] When the Prince came to build the Brighton Pavilion, he included a Tennis Court, but unfortunately before its completion he decided to convert it into stables.[16] There would seem to be very little chance of proving that the Prince played through any surviving tennis account, as he had a very relaxed attitude towards money, which is illustrated by his exasperated Treasurer's response to his command to prepare a statement of his debts for transmission to the King: 'Every day brought on some change in every department which I could not account for nor control.' [17]

As for his brother Frederick, Duke of York, he was a tennis fanatic, and was often to be found at the Haymarket Court in 1788, and in the first half of the following year he was said to have played every day, prompting *The Times* to comment on his neglect of his military duties: 'The Tennis Court now takes up more of the Duke of York's time, than the Parade; his Royal Highness paying more respect to the top of the ball than the step of the soldier.' [18] Even after his famous duel with Colonel Lennox, he calmly left the scene to play a game. He was a serious gambler when it came to tennis: in just one week in 1789 he won £1,500, but he was said to be 'the dupe of every designing sharper', and that year ran up a debt of over £60,000.[19]

The popularity of the game has always been cyclic and a revival of sorts occurred in the middle of the eighteenth century when three new public courts were opened in London (see Chapter 2, Note 10). This was followed by the reawakening of royal interest just referred to, but towards the end of the century *The Times* commented: 'The once fashionable game of Tennis is very much upon the decline. The Court in the Haymarket seems to be now entirely forlorn.' *The Times* was referring to the James Street Court.[20]

Royal interest was not rekindled until Victorian times when the Queen's Consort, Prince Albert, started to play. He played on the Duke of Bedford's Woburn Abbey Court, and on the one at Strathfield Saye belonging to the Duke of Wellington. He also came once to Hampton Court.

Victoria's eldest son, Albert Edward, the Prince of Wales and later Edward VII, was much more enthusiastic. He learned to play tennis at Hampton Court and became a member of the Club, and of the Prince's Club in Knightsbridge where he had the choice of two courts. He also used both the Oriel and Merton Street Courts in Oxford, as well as two of the old Cambridge Courts, Wellington and Pembroke. It is thought he last played the game on the private Court of Sir Robert Loder, at Whittlebury in Buckinghamshire.

9. ALBERT EDWARD, PRINCE OF WALES

Taken soon after he started to play
tennis at Hampton Court.

His two surviving sons played: Prince Albert Victor, Duke of Clarence, and Prince George of Wales. Prince George, who due to the early death of his older brother became George V, occasionally played either at the Prince's Club, at Hampton Court, or on the Duke of Fife's Court at Sheen. It was said that he showed great promise, but affairs of State did not permit him to devote very much time to it.[21]

Outside royal circles, the Victorian aristocracy became the game's saviour. They built many courts attached to their large houses. Nearly half of those in use today came from that period. Club courts began to appear: Brighton (1836), Lord's (1838, rebuilt in 1900), Leamington (1846), Prince's (1854, re-sited closer to Hyde Park in 1888), Manchester (1880) and Queen's (1888). In 1893 the Brighton Club forged a link with the Prince's Club and from then on it was known as the Prince's Club, Brighton. All this activity resulted in an increase from some ten courts in play at the start of the century to about 30 at its close.

The university cities of Oxford and Cambridge have had many courts over the centuries. However, it was not until 1859 that the first Varsity Match was played at James Street. When that Court was closed seven years later, the fixture was transferred to Lord's along with the James Street Racquet, which became the MCC Gold Racquet, the winner of which was considered to be the amateur champion. Lord's at that time was the headquarters of the game until the two new Courts at The Queen's Club were opened.

The World Championship of Tennis is the oldest of any sport. It dates back to 1740 when the first holder was a Frenchman named Clerge (Appendix 14). Since then, there have been only 24 champions, including two outstanding Frenchmen, J. Edmond Barre and Pierre Etchebaster who held the title for 33 and 27 years, respectively. Two of them were professionals at the Royal Tennis Court, George Lambert in Victorian times and Chris Ronaldson in the 1980s. Wayne Davies, the first Australian to become world champion, was for a while an assistant at Hampton Court.

The game was introduced into Australia during the second half of the nineteenth century. Today it is played with great enthusiasm in Melbourne, Sydney, Hobart, Ballarat and Romsey. At about the same time, the first American court, of which anything is known, was built in the City of Boston, the first of four to be constructed there. However, it would seem that a form of the game may have arrived in America some 200 years earlier, for tennis was included in a prohibition order issued in 1659 by Peter Stuyvesant, the Director of New Netherland, which included New Amsterdam, and later became New York.[22] New York, though, definitely had two courts by the end of the nineteenth century and Chicago and Newport, Rhode Island, had one apiece. Several private courts were built around the turn of the century, to be followed by a superb new club court in Philadelphia in 1907. The New York Racquet & Tennis Club relocated in 1918 to a sumptuous new home on Park Avenue and the new building, like its predecessor, included two tennis courts. Today this magnificent five-storey building stands proudly alongside its gigantic skyscraper neighbours.

Meanwhile, back in Britain, the Victorian revival spilled over into the early part of the twentieth century and included, for the first time in over 300 years, a new court in Scotland. This was the court in Troon, Ayrshire, built in 1905 by J.O.M. Clark, co-author of *A History of Tennis*.

This period saw the founding of the Tennis & Rackets Association (T&RA), which administers the game in Great Britain. Originally the Association also administered Fives and Squash Rackets. Rackets has historically been linked with Tennis. The game originated in the debtors' prisons of the eighteenth century when some of those imprisoned for debt took their tennis rackets with them to pass the time – hitting balls against the prison walls led to the game of Rackets. Nowadays a few clubs have both tennis and rackets courts and some of the World Tennis Champions have also held the Rackets title. Both games featured in the Olympic Games of 1908, which were held in London. The American Jay Gould became the Tennis Gold Medallist, with the leading English amateur, E.H. Miles, taking the Silver. The other co-author of *A History of Tennis*, E.B. Noel, won the Olympic Rackets Gold Medal. These competitions were all held at The Queen's Club. Gould was later to become the first American – and the first amateur – to win the World Championship.

The two World Wars were to have a devastating effect on the game in Great Britain. Most of the courts remained open during the First World War, but, with

10. THREE PATRONS OF THE ROYAL TENNIS COURT

King Edward VII with his son George, Prince of Wales (later George V), and
his grandson Prince Edward of Wales (later Edward VIII) c. 1909 taken on
board the Royal Yacht.

many of the players abroad fighting for their country, there was very little play
and sadly many players did not return. Between the wars Britain suffered from a
severe economic depression and several courts were lost. Many courts were used
for purposes other than tennis during the Second World War, to assist the war
effort. It has been a slow painstaking process returning courts to play since then.
In recent years the Court at Newmarket has been restored, having been lost to

tennis for 75 years; another is the Hyde House Court at Bridport, which had been out of use for at least as long; the latest to be recovered is the second Clare and Trinity Court at Cambridge — this Court had been lost before the war when squash courts were erected within it. In the last few years no less than six new courts have been constructed: one at The Oratory School near Reading (1990), the first new court in London for over 100 years at the Harbour Club in Fulham (1993), one at Bristol (1998), two at Prested Hall near Feering in Essex (1998), and most recently one at Middlesex University in Hendon.

In recent years the Princes Charles and Edward learned to play the game whilst studying at Cambridge University. Prince Charles did not take to the game. However, his younger brother continues the royal tradition, having become a keen player and enthusiastic supporter. Prince Edward, The Earl of Wessex, has played on most of the British courts and on many of those abroad. He participated in the 450th Anniversary Tournament at Falkland Palace in 1989, attended the reopening of Fontainebleau a year later and officially opened the Harbour Club Court in 1993, both Bristol and Bridport in 1998, and the Millennium Court at Middlesex University in January 2000. In his work as a producer, he has made television programmes about the game, helping to bring its delights to a wider audience.

Today tennis is in a healthy state. Most of the clubs in Great Britain, America and Australia have high levels of activity. Only in France is the game languishing. New courts in Washington D.C. and Australia, in Sydney and Romsey, have recently been completed and there is an active Dutch Real Tennis Association which hopes to build the first new court in Holland for several hundred years.

A later chapter deals with the serious attempt made by the Club during the nineteen-nineties to build a second court inside the walls of Hampton Court Palace.

CHAPTER 3

THE TUDOR TENNIS PLAYS

Perchance a parallel we'll find
Betwixt this game and Henry's mind,
For in affairs of state he'd get
His rivals tangled in a net.

Two Tennis Courts were built at Hampton Court during its Tudor period. Cardinal Wolsey erected the first, an open one, and the second was a magnificent enclosed Court constructed by Henry VIII. When these Courts were first put up, they were known as *Tenys, Tennys* or *Tenes Playes* and it was not until the Elizabethan period that they began to be referred to as *Courtes*. Neither of these courts is now in existence.

THE OPEN PLAY

Exactly when the first Tennis Court was built at Hampton Court cannot be accurately determined because detailed accounts of the building works there only survive from April 1529. This was the date when Henry VIII took control of these works, following the downfall of Cardinal Wolsey.[1] The accounts, which are known as the *Chapter House Accounts*, clearly show that there was an Open Court in existence before that date. Wolsey therefore must have built it. As no plans or drawings of Wolsey's Play have come down to us through the passage of time, it is only by analysing the building accounts of the associated structures that we can attempt to establish its location. These are (A) the chambers (or lodgings) built in 1529 and (B) a gallery erected between the Open Play and the new Close (enclosed) Play between 1533 and 1534.

(A) There were two chambers under construction by April 1529 which were clearly intended for the King's use whenever he wished to play tennis. They were situated next to the Open Tennis Play and described as 'belonging unto it.' [2] Therefore if the position of these chambers can be established, then so can the site of the Tennis Play.

(B) The other important factor is the gallery that was built for the specific purpose of linking the Open Play to the King's new Close Play. There are a few clues in the accounts to suggest that at least part of this gallery ran east to west. One entry states that there was a double door at its east end and another door at the west end.[3] Further confirmation of its alignment comes with the description of ironwork for the windows on the north side.[4] This prompts the question: Did this gallery run west of the new Close Play, or did it go east? The following analysis would seem to favour the east.

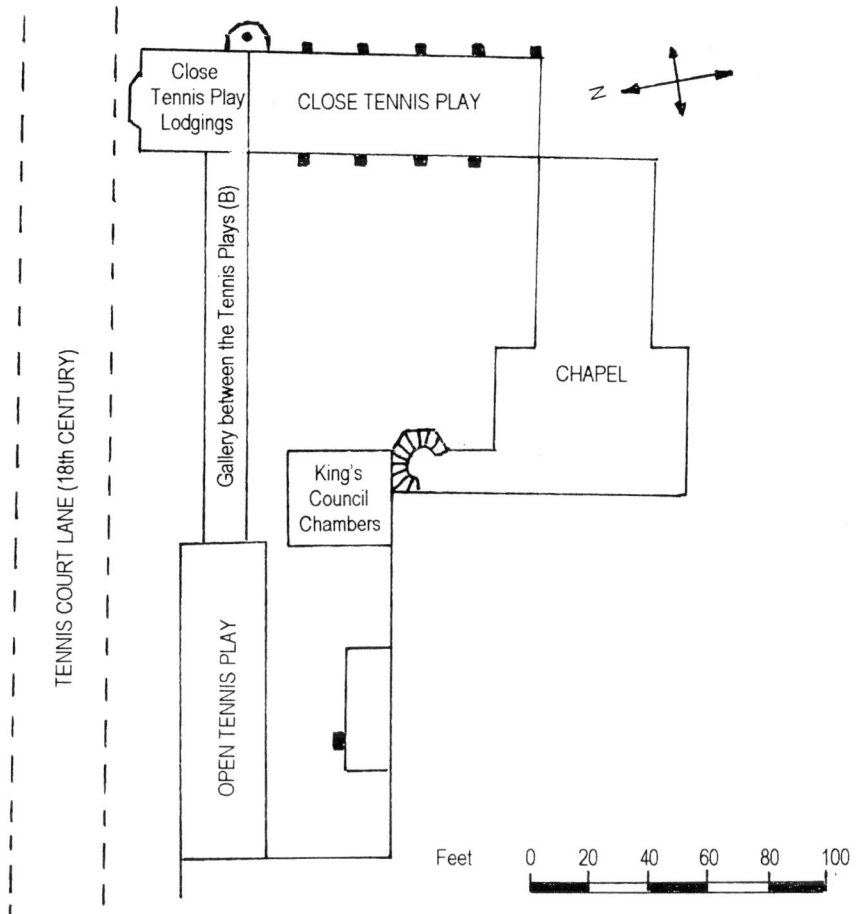

11. GALLERY TO THE WEST?

This plan shows the relationship of the two Tennis Plays if the gallery between them
had run to the west. The Open Play is shown here on the site of the Privy Kitchen.

If the gallery between the tennis plays (B) had run as one continuous passage
to the west of the Close Play, the only space available that could have
accommodated the Open Play was the site later used for Elizabeth I's Privy
Kitchen (figure 11). This creates a problem, as the Open Play would had to have
been pulled down to make way for the kitchen in 1567 and rebuilt elsewhere.
This can be said with confidence as the accounts show there were two courts in
use during the latter part of the Elizabethan era after the erection of the Privy
Kitchen. For example, the 1596-97 account details three items of repairs to
Tennis Courts, one of which is identified as 'the little Tenes Court' to set it apart
from the larger Close Tennis Court. Further proof of the continued existence of
an Open Court comes at the start of James I's reign in 1603, with the entry
'takeinge downe and newe alteringe the Tennys Courte.'[5] This has to refer to the
Open Court, because the Close Court remained in use unaltered until the second
half of the seventeenth century. Another problem with the western site is that
the only chambers close by were the ones known as the 'King's Council
Chambers', and they were not really near enough to be described as 'next to' or

23

'besides' the Tennis Play and therefore do not properly fulfil the requirement of
(A). And most significantly, there is no evidence to suggest that Elizabeth I ever
built a tennis court at Hampton Court during her reign (1558-1603).

There are also problems in trying to prove that the gallery ran east of the new
Close Play as there was only a short distance from the Play itself and the
boundary wall (figure 12). There is, though, an entry in the accounts mentioning
the gilding of four vanes.[6] These are heraldic plates fixed to pinnacles and the
spacing needed to accommodate four vanes equates closely to the gallery length if
it had run to the east. There is archaeological evidence to suggest that there was
a gallery running from the Close Play to the boundary wall.[7]

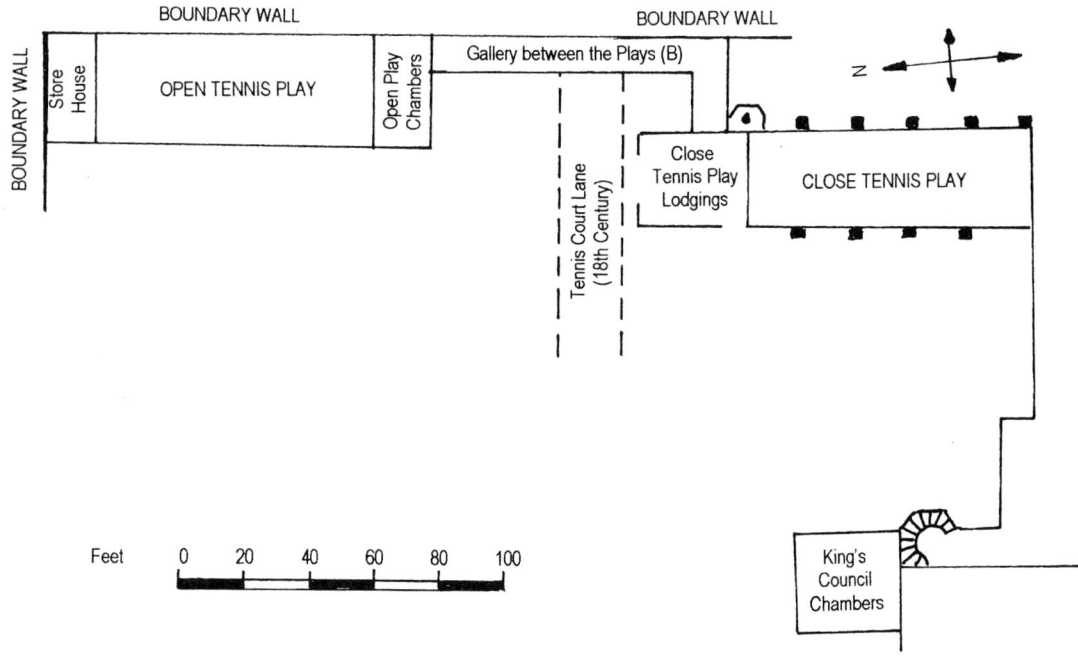

12.   GALLERY TO THE EAST?

This Plan shows the relationship of the two Tennis Plays
if the gallery between them had run to the east.

However, the Open Play could not have been at the point where the gallery
would have joined the boundary wall, as the Queen's Long Gallery was built
there in 1537 and extended a long way southwards, so it would have to have run
to the north. Wolsey was very fond of galleries and may well have had one
running along the inside of his boundary wall, into which the new east-west
section could have linked, thereby completing a gallery between the Tennis
Plays. Alternatively, if no such boundary wall gallery existed, a new one could
have been built. In either circumstance, Wolsey's Open Play would have been on,
or close to, the site of the present Stuart Court.

The final piece of the jigsaw is the storehouse that was known to have been
next to the Open Play.[8] If the Play was in the position outlined above, one would

24

expect to arrive at the changing facilities first (the 1529 chambers), then the Play itself, which would leave the storehouse at the other end, in the corner of the boundary walls. The logical place for a garden storehouse, which may have pre-dated the Open Play, would have been in a corner.

The balance of probabilities would therefore suggest that Wolsey's Play was on the site of the present Stuart Court. This conclusion also fits well with lodgings being described as 'between the gallery and the Tenys playe', and the fact that there was a bowling alley 'betwixt the tenys playes' in 1534.[9]

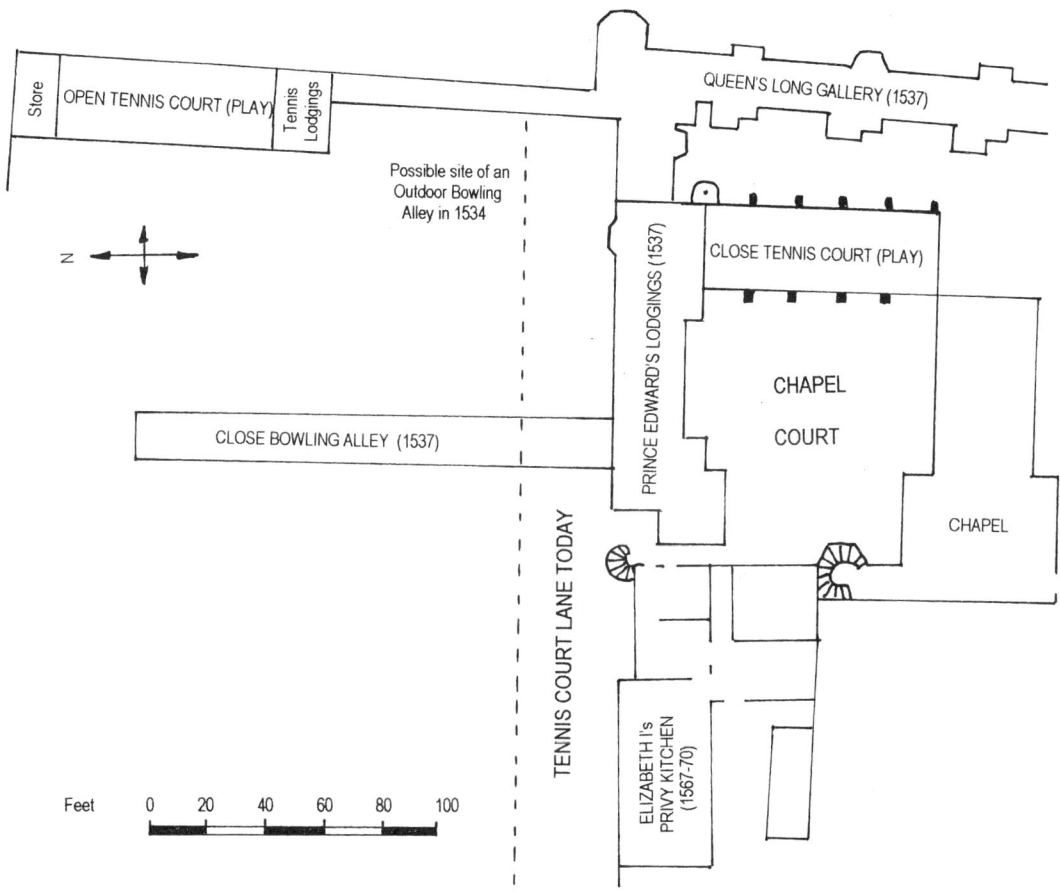

13.   THE SPORTS AREA OF THE PALACE

At the end of the sixteenth century

With the limited information available, it has not been possible to verify what materials were used to construct the Open Court's walls. What is known is that at least one wall was brick and that wall had glazed windows.[10] These were probably for the illumination of the gallery beneath the side penthouse, so making it the service wall. There is some evidence that this was the eastern boundary wall. Nothing is known for certain about the form of construction of the other three walls. References in the Stuart era, which will be discussed in the next chapter, suggest that part of the Court was made of timber. Whether this Court made use of any of the walls of the adjacent buildings, such as the storehouse, or later, the lodgings, must also remain a mystery.

The date when Wolsey built his Court can only be a matter of conjecture. He was an ambitious man, always eager to impress and please his king. Henry VIII was, of course, a keen sportsman and, as we know, he was particularly fond of tennis in his younger days, so it would have been only natural for the Cardinal to have provided him with the means of play whenever he entertained him. The King though, was not the only person for whom a Tennis Court might have been needed, for Wolsey's palace had 280 guest bedrooms, all kept in constant readiness.[11] He was always entertaining ambassadors, and other foreign and local dignitaries, and some of these might have enjoyed a game during their stay.

Present knowledge suggests that the Open Play could have been built at any time between June 1514, when Wolsey acquired the lease, and April 1529, when we first learn of its existence. Henry and his Queen were first invited to Hampton Court in the spring of 1516 and according to Cavendish, Wolsey's biographer, the King was an occasional visitor over the following years. However, it is more likely that it was built after the boundary wall had been erected. The brick typology of this wall matches that of the Chapel, so dating it 1526-29. This, of course, was also the very time that Wolsey was desperate to ingratiate himself with the King.

While the Cardinal was busy providing tennis facilities at Hampton Court, he was actively issuing proclamations prohibiting the majority of the population from enjoying the same game. His major concern was the neglect by the King's subjects of developing skill at the longbow, still seen as a most effective weapon for the defence of the realm. Some of the population had acquired crossbows, or even handguns, and these were being blamed for the increase in felony, and for the depletion of game in the forests. Their increased use, and the playing of unlawful games including tennis, was perceived as contributing to the decline in the practice of archery. Wolsey's zeal for issuing these proclamations prompted the sixteenth-century chronicler Edward Hall, in 1550, to comment in his *The Union of the Two and Illustrious Families of Lancaster and York* that 'the people murmured against the Cardinal saying he grudged at every man's pleasure saving his own'. One proclamation issued by Wolsey in 1528 forced the keepers of hostelries, inns and alehouses to allow persons authorized by the King 'to take and burn the said tables, dice, cards, bowls, closhes, tennis balls and all other things pertaining to the said unlawful games'. While the penalties for refusing to surrender handguns and crossbows were draconian — in this proclamation death — those for allowing or taking part in unlawful games were less so, at worst imprisonment, but usually a heavy fine or a day in the stocks.[12]

These proclamations of course did not apply to the nobility, but for them a game of tennis with their Sovereign was potentially a very expensive affair, for the King was a heavy gambler. Although only his losses seem to have been recorded, the amounts involved were staggering. In 1519, when he lost to an opponent, it cost him two shillings a game. By 1530 this had escalated to 30 shillings, and a year later he was found paying out the enormous sum, for those days, of £30 for fifteen games lost.[13] Some of these losses were recorded in his Privy Purse Expenses and it is here that we find another interesting payment involving a game on Wolsey's Play.

The entry for 15th December 1531 reads: 'paied to one that served on the King's side at Tennes, at hampton-courte, in Rewarde .... vs.'[14] This reference to a paid 'server' has been thought to be the origin of the word 'service'. Although this may be the correct interpretation, it is possible that the server here was a 'stopper', employed to stop the ball making a short chase (see Appendix 2).[15] Stoppers were commonplace in those days and at times it was a job undertaken by some quite eminent people. There is the well-documented

14. CARDINAL WOLSEY

The Cardinal built the first
Tennis Court at the Palace.

event at Blackfriars in 1522, when Henry, partnered by Emperor Charles V, against the Prince of Orange and the Marquis of Brandenburg, used stoppers. On this occasion, the stoppers were the Earl of Devon and Lord Edmund (Howard).[16]

For an insight into Henry, the tennis player, some of the reports of Venetian diplomats are useful. Sebastian Giustiniani, the Ambassador, in his *Report of England*, before returning home in 1519, wrote of the King, who was then in his late twenties: 'He is much handsomer than any other Sovereign a great deal handsomer than the King of France'. He continues: 'It was the prettiest thing in the world to see him play; his fair skin glowing through a shirt of the finest texture.'[17] Eight years later, we learn of a tennis injury, through the Venetian Secretary, Gasparo Spinelli. Writing to his brother he recalls the occasion when the King arrived at a function: 'Behind the King 4 couple of noblemen (*signori*), all masked and all wearing velvet slippers on their feet, this being done, lest the King should be distinguished from the others, as from the hurt which he received lately on his left foot when playing tennis (*allo palla*) he wears a black velvet slipper.'[18] When he was able to play, we know the King used felt-soled tennis shoes and wore specially-designed 'tenes cotes' of blue and black velvet, presumably for use before and after play.[19]

An incident occurred on this Play in 1543 that shows that at times the game was still being played with the hand. A sonnet written by the Earl of Surrey describes the distraction he suffered when the fair Geraldine, the recipient of his affections, sat watching him play:

'The palm-play, where, despoiled for the game,
With dazed eyes oft we by gleams of love,
Have missed the ball, and got sight of our dame,
To bait her eyes, which kept the leads above.' [20]

After that, the Court remained in play until at least the end of the century, as Elizabeth I made sure it was properly maintained. One of the two courts in use during her reign was repaved between 1576 and 1578.[21] It would seem more likely to have been the Open Court, as it was the older one and was exposed to the weather.

At the start of the Stuart era the Court was 'taken down'. This may signal its demolition, or it could indicate a complete refurbishment, in which case, it would then have continued in play until 1625.

THE CLOSE TENNIS PLAY   (THE HENRICAN COURT)

Henry VIII's new Close Tennis Play at Hampton Court was virtually identical to the Great Close Tennis Play at Whitehall, where there were four new courts under construction at the same time. Of all Henry's works at the Palace, the new Play was the largest single structure he built, except for the Great Hall. When completed, it abutted the north-east corner of the Chapel and was aligned north to south.

Exactly when the project started is difficult to determine, as the surviving accounts do not detail the progress of the work. Payments to bricklayers, masons and carpenters were generally for day work, and cannot be separated out from other works that were going on at the same time, most notably, the construction of the Great Hall. The programme of the building work can therefore only be retraced through the accounts of the specialist trades.

Construction of the Play was under the control of four men: James Nedeham, the Clerk (or Surveyor) of the King's Works, John Moulton, the King's Master Mason, Christopher Dickenson, who supervised the bricklaying, and the King's Master Carpenter, William Clement.[22] The last three were paid at the rate of 12d. a day.[23] So many workmen were needed at the Palace for these works that many had to be pressed into service. There are several charges in the accounts for riding out to various parts of the country to round up skilled tradesmen. Bricks for the new Play were supplied from kilns that had been set up in the surrounding park. Prior to 1530, bricks for the Palace had been supplied by a London-based company for 3s. 4d. per thousand. The new local kilns were able to supply at 2s. 10d. per thousand.[24] Most of the stonework for windows and doors came from quarries in the Cotswolds — much of it was preformed in moulds at the quarry site. The finished stone was then transported by cart across country to wharves on the Thames, near Abingdon in Oxfordshire, and then sent by barge to Hampton Court. Most of the timber also came by river, from an estate at

Sonning, in Berkshire. Transportation costs, as a proportion of total building costs, were very much higher centuries ago than they are today.

The first reference to the new Play in the account books comes with the supply of four pairs of stone hooks, in October 1532.[25] These were iron hooks that were fixed into stonework for door hinges. The following month, there was a delivery of 4,100 paving tiles for the new Play costing 16 shillings per thousand.[26] That quantity of tiles would suggest each one would have been quite small, perhaps nine inches square. One cannot be sure they were square — some tennis courts of the period used rectangular tiles. However, Tudor tiles elsewhere in the Palace, although glazed, were square and about the same size. The tiles would have been brick, which was usual for that time. The later Stuart Court also had a brick floor until the end of the next century. Brick was also the material used when the Royal Court at Woodstock was repaved in 1541.[27] There would not have been any chase lines, but there may have been two lines across the court adjacent to the end galleries. These lines were incorporated into later court floors, as will be seen shortly. The provision of the above items towards the end of the year could indicate that work on the building itself had been under way for some time. It had probably started earlier in the summer.

By March of the following year the smith, John van Guylders, was busy making ironwork for the windows. Dozens of staybars, standards, lockets and soudelets were turned out for the Play and its adjoining lodgings.[28] The *staybars* were horizontal bars set into the window jamb or mullion. If the bars had eyes to fit round the upright *standards* they were known as *lockets* and the *soudelets* were small bars onto which the glazing was soldered or wired. Those lodgings, located at the northern end of the Play, were thought to have been for the Keeper of the King's Tennis Play, or possibly for his Marker.[29] They were two storeys high and linked by a *vice* (a staircase turret) on the north-east corner of the Play.[30]

April saw the digging out of the foundations for a new gallery, built for the specific purpose of linking the new Close Play to the old Open one (the gallery mentioned earlier).[31] The following month, a gang of six plasterers was busy plastering the walls. Seven gagers assisted them, and it was their job to prepare the plaster. The plasterers received 7d. a day and the gagers 5d., nine hours being the normal working day.[32] The walls were later blacked. A recent survey of this building (which still stands today), has shown that the plasterwork was coated with a white lime wash on top of which were fragmentary remains of a black wash.[33] During that month and the following, there were payments to wyre drawers, who were engaged in making wire grills for the protection of the glazed windows.[34] Glazing of windows in the Tudor tennis courts of royal palaces seems to have been the normal practice. The Court at Greenwich had glazed windows, as did the two Closed Courts at Whitehall.[35] However, tennis courts generally were not glazed until the nineteenth century. The wyre drawers received 8d. a day, with the Master Wyre Drawer, William Heyton, getting twice that amount. These wire grills and the other window ironwork were painted red, which was usual in royal tennis courts at that time.[36]

The King's glazier, the Dutchman, Galyon Hone, glazed the windows, and it is his bill that appears in the November accounts for work probably carried out earlier in 1533 (figure 16).[37]   The account tells us a lot about the appearance of the building.   There were eleven large windows and each one had three lights, the outer pair being 36 square feet and the central section 39 square feet.   They were set some 21 feet off the ground, five on each side and one in the end wall. There was a smaller three-light window of 50 square feet.   It is not clear where this was: it may have been in the south wall above the penthouse, but it is more likely that it was below the large window in the north wall at first floor level to

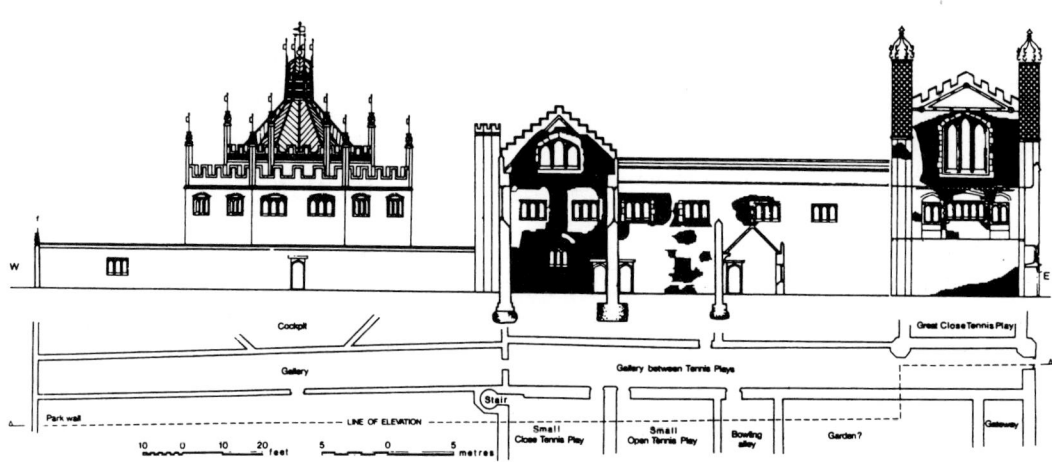

15.   THE COCKPIT GALLERY AT WHITEHALL

This gallery ran between three of the Tudor Tennis Plays at Whitehall and shows
the first floor window that looked into the Great Close Tennis Play. A similar window
was probably incorporated into Henry VIII's Close Tennis Play at Hampton Court.

allow viewing from the adjacent lodgings.   The Great Close Tennis Play at Whitehall had windows in this position, for the spectators to watch from the gallery between the Tennis Plays there (figure 15).[38]   For all these windows, Galyon Hone charged £26 14s. 4d.   Following excavation and research at Whitehall in 1960-62, a reconstruction of that Court was produced, showing low-level irregularly placed windows for the illumination of the penthouse gallery (figure 17).   Although there is no record of their existence, it seems likely that Hampton Court had similar windows.

The completed Play can be seen, to the east of the Great Hall, in the 1558 Wyngaerde view of the Palace from the north-east (figure 18). This drawing confirms that the larger window was in the north wall.

16. GALYON HONE'S GLAZING ACCOUNT

The account was submitted by Galyon Hone for the installation
of the main windows in HenryVIII's Close Tennis Play at Hampton Court.

Galyon Hone was one of the leaders of the large foreign community that resided in Southwark, across the river from the City of London, and as such had spent some time in prison. Trouble often flared between the foreign workers and the old established London guild of glaziers. Hone was, though, generally protected by his powerful friends. Many of the tradesmen working at the Palace came from the Southwark community. Apart from Hampton Court, Hone also worked on Whitehall Palace, King's College Chapel, Cambridge and Eton College.[39]

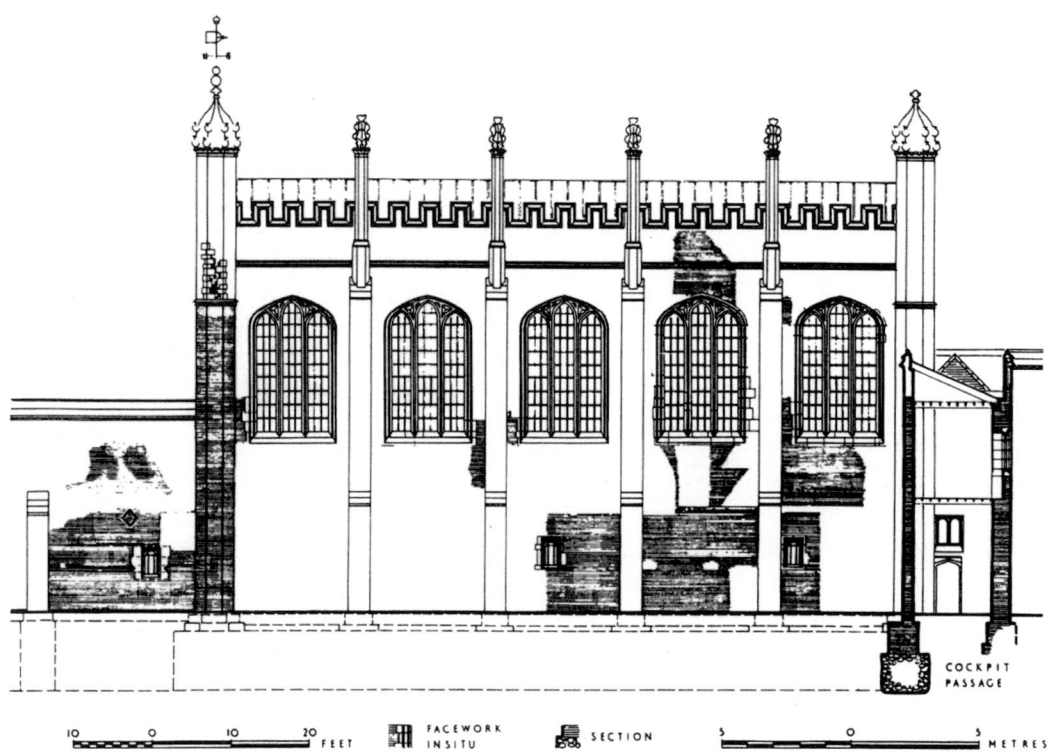

17. HENRY VIII'S GREAT CLOSE TENNIS PLAY AT WHITEHALL

This building, shown here reconstructed, was almost identical to
the King's Close Tennis Play at Hampton Court.

Midsummer 1533 saw Thomas Acon, the King's sergeant plumber, covering the roof with lead and installing the new pipework and guttering.[40] By the autumn, the decorative vanes were being set up on the stone types (domical caps) at gable ends[41] and that November, 'vente and creest' for the crenellations was being delivered from the Barrington Quarry in the Cotswolds. Vent and crest is the stonework that forms the embattled parapet on top of the Palace walls. The vents are spaces between the crests.[42]

At the same time the bricklayers were busy painting the external walls with red ochre to hide the cracks and blemishes.[43] Work on the building then seems to have slowed right down in the following year – maybe other palace projects had priority. The only recorded works were the gilding of the vanes with the King's Arms that April,[44] and the completion of the gallery between the Plays at about the same time.

It is possible that a boarded ceiling was installed during the year. In the sixteenth century ceilings were 'in play'. The reason no records of any such work exist is possibly because, as mentioned before, the carpenters were usually paid on a day-work basis. The supply of the boards would then have been lost in the account for the general supply of wood for the whole of the Palace works, along with their labour costs.

Early in 1535, there was a flurry of activity to prepare the Play for the King's use. Over a two-day period in March, fifteen carpenters were brought in. Some were paid 8d. a day, others 7d. for 'makyng the hasserdes in the Close tennys play a gaynst the Kyngs cumyng'.[45] That was probably for the construction of the penthouses, as it is difficult to see what type of hazard would take so many carpenters two days to complete. The accounts also show that John Yerlye, of Kingston, supplied and delivered 100 seasoned boards for the new Play, shortly before.[46] The supply of so much timber virtually confirms that it was the penthouses that were being constructed. The standard measurement of a sixteenth-century board was 10 feet x 18 inches.[47] Surviving floorboards from the Tudor period at the Palace vary in width from 9 to 12 inches. Assuming these boards were the standard length, then the area of timber was between 750 and 1,500 square feet, more than enough for the penthouse roofs, even if they were boarded underneath as well.

It has not been possible to determine which style of penthouse was installed in this Play. The absence of bricklayers and stonemasons at this time would suggest an all-timber construction. When the Play was erected the evolution of the penthouse was at an early stage – in the previous century simple sloping roofs with nothing underneath were much more common. In those days, if one wished to observe a game one would either have had to do so from underneath the roof, where if hit by a ball a chase would be marked, or watch through windows from outside the court walls. By the early part of the sixteenth century some tennis courts had penthouses with planked front faces, and usually had apertures sawn out to create crude viewing openings. But, this being a royal court, and with Henry VIII an avid tennis enthusiast, it is likely that viewing facilities were of some importance and therefore a much more elaborate system of galleries would have been installed. The configuration could have been similar in style to that seen today, except there would have been no gallery nets. These were not introduced into the game until the next century, but there would have been ledges on top of the battery walls for spectators to lean on. Another possible arrangement might have involved 'pillared galleries', similar to those seen in some contemporary French courts. Roger Morgan has investigated courts of this type and his conclusions have recently been published in his *Tudor Tennis, A Miscellany*. Suffice it to say here that in this type of court, pillars supported the penthouse roof directly from the floor. Usually the galleries so formed, whether along a side or an end wall, extended into the corners of the court occupying the entire length of the wall. In some of these courts low battery walls were inserted between the pillars.[48] If Henry's Close Tennis Play had battery walls, then the likelihood is that it would have had two entry points into the playing area. These 'doors' would have been positioned between the first and second galleries in each half of the court. Two markers were usually employed to mark the chases in those days, with the one at the service end keeping the score.[49]

With the King's anticipated arrival, mats were ordered from Nicholas Homys of Richmond and laid on the floors of the galleries and adjoining lodgings.[50]

18. NORTH-EAST VIEW OF THE PALACE IN 1558 BY ANTHONIS WYNGAERDE

The Close Tennis Play is the chapel-like building with the three-light windows in its end wall and a turret on the left. The curious buildings in the foreground are the tiltyard towers.

The last entry in the accounts relating to work on the Play comes at the end of the year, when locks and hinges were made for two doors in the south wall leading out to the Chapel stairs.[51]   If the Play had penthouses of the type in use today, then the south wall was probably the grille wall, as all the available evidence points to the Play being a quarré type with only one end penthouse. The walls, although much altered, still exist, and enough of the original remains to suggest there was no tambour. The internal section of wall, where any tambour would have been, was finished with the same brick face as the remainder of the Play and was the same width.[52] There are no surviving plans of Hampton Court or Whitehall that show any signs of a thickening of the wall that would indicate the presence of a tambour in either of these Plays. The recent excavation of the Great Close Tennis Play at Whitehall did not find any evidence of a tambour or a dedans penthouse.

More evidence supporting the *jeu quarré* theory comes when one compares the internal wall measurements at Whitehall with the corresponding floor measurements there, 83 feet 6 inches x 26 feet and 78 feet x 22 feet,

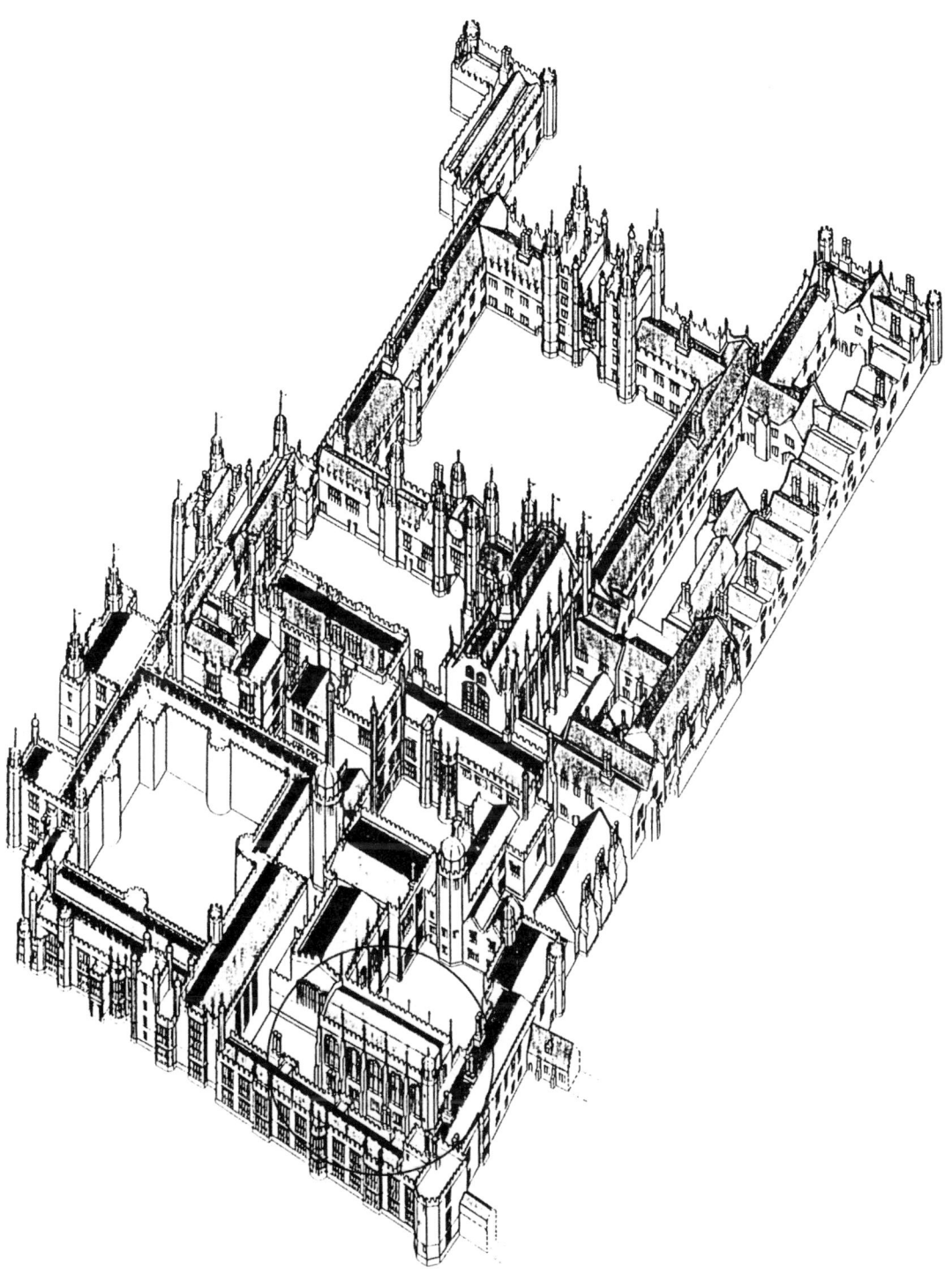

19. HAMPTON COURT PALACE AT THE END OF THE SIXTEENTH CENTURY

In this axonometric reconstruction of the Palace
the Close Tennis Play can be seen circled.

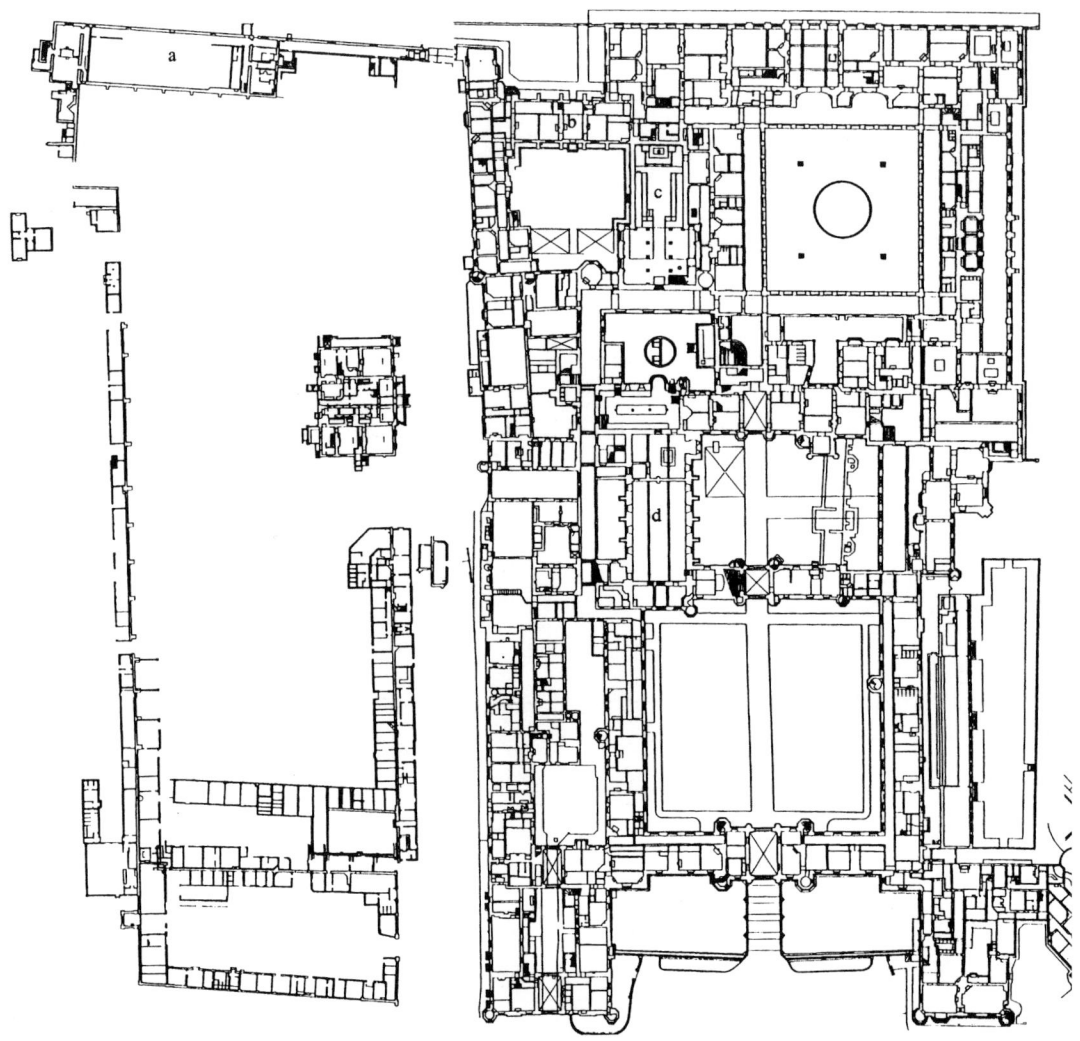

20. A PLAN OF THE PALACE AS IT IS TODAY

- *a.*   The Stuart Tennis Court
- *b.*   The remains of the old Henrican Court
- *c.*   The Chapel
- *d.*   The Great Hall

respectively.[53] Although one must not place too much reliance on these measurements, if they are close to the truth then the Whitehall Play would have had two penthouses and not three. The internal measurements of the Close Play at Hampton Court were almost identical, 83 feet x 27 feet. Another interesting observation is that when James V of Scotland built his Court at Falkland Palace in 1539, he also chose the quarré format. Dedans courts were still at an early stage of development at this time.

Unfortunately, no record has so far come to light that gives us any clue as to how much use Henry made of his splendid new Play. It is thought that his physical condition probably would have forced him to give up the game soon after its completion.

In 1537 the new lodgings for the infant Prince Edward were constructed, running west, away from the Close Play's lodgings, so enclosing Chapel Court. To the east, a wider structure replaced the earlier gallery between the Play and the boundary wall, thereby linking the Queen's Long Gallery to the new Prince's apartments (figure 13). Access was therefore through the Tennis Play's lodgings, which may have been lost at that time. The small court formed to the east of the Close Play was then covered with 'pybbylles' (pebbles) from Epsom Common.[54] At about the same time, new lodgings were being constructed for the new queen, Jane Seymour. These extended to the south wall of the Close Play. Sadly, she was never to occupy them.

Like the old Open Play, the Close Play continued to be used after Henry's death, with only minor repairs being necessary during the remainder of the sixteenth century. James I kept it in good repair for his sons to use. He had the floor repaved in 1606-07, the roof retiled in 1614-15, and new wire grills were made for the windows in 1621-22.[55]

When Charles I came to the throne in 1625, he had the Court renovated for his own use. John Decreate, his sergeant painter, was ordered to redecorate it;[56] it is likely that this Court was still in regular use, as it was the one with a roof.

After the Restoration, Charles II would use this Court when he came down to check on the progress of the refurbishment of the Stuart one, which took nearly a year to complete. During the winter of 1660-61 he used to ride from Whitehall to Hampton Court and back in the same day, taking some exercise on the Henrican Court in the mornings. This king was a very early riser, often to be found playing tennis for an hour or two at the unearthly hour of 5 o'clock in the morning.[57] The Stuart Court referred to here was built by Charles I in 1625. Details of its construction and subsequent alterations will be dealt with in Chapter 4.

When the Stuart Court had been restored, the Henrican Court became known as the 'ould' and then the 'disused' Tennis Court, and by 1666 the windows were boarded up and the inside partitioned for other uses.[58] Three years later, the decision was taken to convert it into new lodgings for the Duke and Duchess of York. The estimate for the work came to £3,000, but the Treasury only released two-thirds of the money, delaying the balance until 1674, due to the financial pressures of the day.[59]

There are, therefore, two extraordinary accounts covering this conversion. The first for the period, February 1670 to June 1673, is of interest because it includes the removal of the remaining tennis features.[60] Particularly useful is the confirmation that the Court did have penthouses — unfortunately, there is no record of how many. The old floor tiles were carefully lifted and stored for later use. The rest of the 'rubbish' was dumped in the old moat. An extra floor was inserted and an additional storey built. At this time the old Court lost its distinctive large three-light windows.

Once completed, only the Duchess seems to have moved in, the Duke being accommodated elsewhere. By coincidence, the sister Court at Whitehall was also lost to tennis at about the same time; it was converted into lodgings for the Duke of Monmouth. There were further alterations at Hampton Court in 1716-18 to accommodate the young Hanoverian Princesses.

Today, both the side walls of the Henrican Court and its buttresses can still be seen. The west side forms the east side of Chapel Court, and the other side can be seen from the palace gardens with its original turret (figure 21).

It is interesting to note that Ernest Law in his *History of Hampton Court Palace*, published in three volumes 1885-1891, did not recognise the building as a Tennis Court. This oversight perpetuated the myth that the present Stuart Court was built by Henry VIII. This mistake was not rectified until research by Sir Howard Colvin, for his mammoth *History of the King's Works, 1962-83*, correctly identified the building.[61]

21.   THE HENRICAN COURT TODAY

Top: The east view from the public gardens
Bottom: The west wall that now forms part of Chapel Court

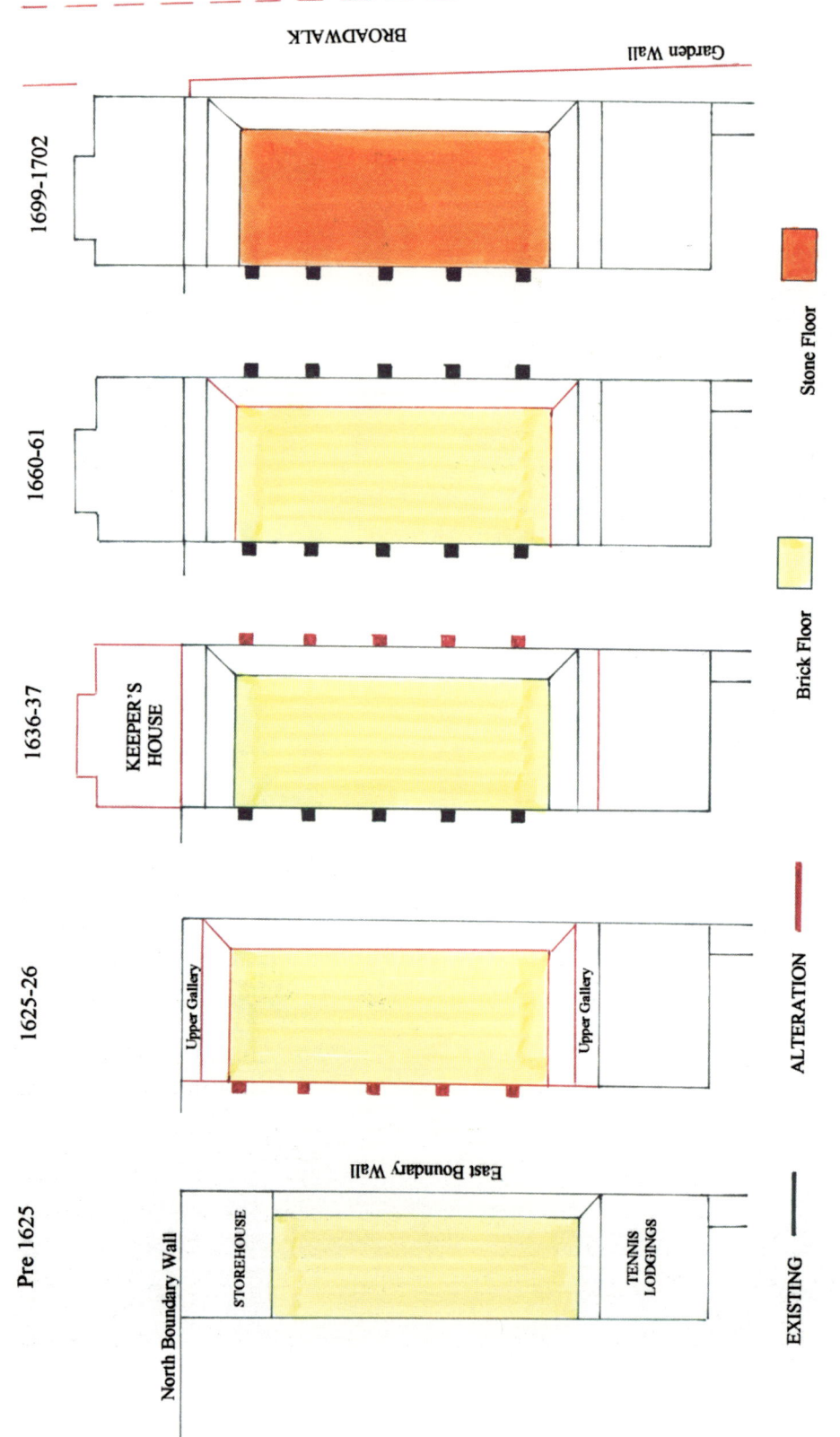

22. SEVENTEENTH-CENTURY IMPROVEMENTS

Over the next hundred years there were many alterations to the Open Court, which slowly transformed it into the Court in use today. These floor plans show the extent of each change and support the analysis in the forthcoming chapter.

CHAPTER 4

THE STUART COURTS

These through various hazards chased,
By definite defeat were faced.
With skill he served them all the same
And loss of head oft marked the game.

This Chapter seeks to establish a link between Wolsey's old Open Court and the present Stuart Court, in so far as they both may have used the original Palace boundary wall as the service wall. If this can be proved, both courts would have occupied the same site: it would therefore follow that the latter was a replacement for the former.

As one moves into the Stuart era the two Tudor Courts were still in play, but there is a period of uncertainty concerning the Open Court. Only the declared annual works accounts are available until the reign of Charles II and these contain very little information. The first three Stuart monarchs all carried out major alterations to the old Open Court. In order to minimise any confusion, this Court will be referred to by the name of the reigning monarch. As far as the Henrican Court is concerned, it has already been seen that there were no further structural changes and that after 1661 it had fallen into disuse.

As James I's reign gets under way, the entry mentioned earlier appears in the accounts for 'takeing downe and newe alteringe the tennys courte'.[1] It has not been possible to determine whether this is a reference to the court walls or just to the penthouses. What is known is that James I's Court (previously referred to as Wolsey's Open Court) was smaller than the present one, but on the same site. This is obvious from the 1625 accounts at the start of Charles I's reign, where an entry exists: 'Ripping and taking downe the bourded walles round about the Tennis courte, and bringing upp a brickewall there for the inlargement of the same.'[2]

From this wording it is clear that some wooden boarding was used for part of James I's Court. It would therefore seem likely that Wolsey's Court was also built the same way. If the Cardinal's Court had been all brick, James surely would not have used an inferior material for the walls, had he rebuilt them in 1603. In fact the reverse would have been more likely, a point that suggests the 'takeing downe' may have referred only to the penthouses and that Wolsey's Court could have survived until 1625.

The walls of the new Open Court that Charles I built in 1625 are those that are still in use today. However, there is a clue as to the size and position of James I's earlier Court to be found when one examines the service wall. Abram Booth, an envoy of the Dutch East India Company — who was a competent

23. THE EAST FAÇADE OF THE PALACE IN 1630 BY ABRAM BOOTH

The Open Tennis Court can be seen at the end of the boundary wall on the right. The two windows
that allow light into the side penthouse gallery can clearly be seen. The pitched roofs that appear to
be on top of the Tennis Court are in fact buildings along what is now Tennis Court Lane.

artist — sketched the east side of the Palace during his travels through
southern England in 1630 (figure 23).[3]   This shows the east boundary wall,
including the section that formed the service wall of the Tennis Court, with two
small windows illuminating the gallery beneath the side penthouse.   These
windows were bricked up in 1636-37, but their remains are still visible today.
Inside the Court they appear as two recesses in the external wall of the passage
under the service penthouse and it is clear that they do not line up with the
galleries of the present Court (figure 24). They must have been in existence
before 1625, for it would have been inconceivable that they would have been
placed in those positions in Charles I's new Court. The window at the service end
would have been a serious distraction for the player at that end. Making the
reasonable assumption that they would have been central to the gallery system of
the earlier Court, it can be deduced that tennis players in the time of James I
were using a Court no more than 90 feet in length and that the service wall was
again Wolsey's old boundary wall. This all fits well with the idea that the old
Tudor storehouse was to the north of the Open Court. Its demolition would then
have allowed for the 1625 enlargement (figure 22).

All this adds weight to the conclusion that the east boundary wall was common also to Wolsey's Court and has therefore been in continuous use as the service wall from at least 1529 to the present day. It is interesting to note that the Stuart brickwork used to fill in each of those old windows measures about 3 feet x 2 feet, which is the same size as the glass that was supplied for Wolsey's Court in 1531.[4]

Penthouse Gallery Windows seen on the 1630 View

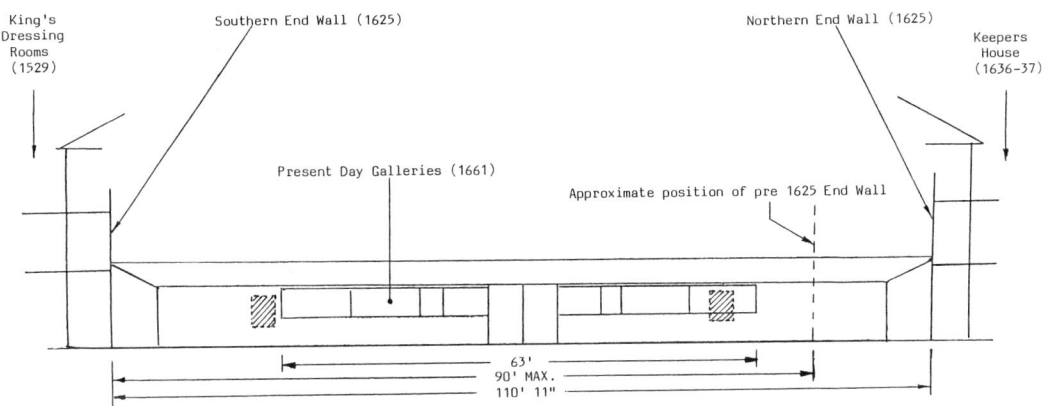

24. SIDE ELEVATION OF THE STUART COURT

This drawing shows the relationship between the
present Stuart Court and the pre-1625 Open Court.

It may at first seem strange that a tennis court could have some walls built of brick and others of timber. Certainly, in the sixteenth century, courts of mixed construction existed. The court at St John's College, Cambridge, made use of the brick wall of the adjoining orchard as an end wall, the others being made of wood.[5] Another was the Clothworkers' Court in Fenchurch Street, London, where the garden wall of the neighbouring Ironmongers Company was used. Here, wooden boards were used to extend its height.[6] Even though Wolsey was expending vast amounts of money on his new Palace, one would not necessarily expect him to have erected an all-brick tennis court, because wooden-walled ones were commonplace during his lifetime. The Royal Court at Greenwich for instance was a timber one.[7] During the latter part of the sixteenth, and in the seventeenth century, many of the old timber-built courts were rebuilt using brick or masonry, so it is reasonable to suppose that this also happened at Hampton Court.

Returning to the start of James I's reign, both his refurbished Open Court and the Henrican Closed Court would have been available to those who took part in the celebrations of his accession. These festivities took place over the Christmas period of 1603-04 at Hampton Court.[8] Whether James, then aged 37, ever ventured onto the Tennis Courts remains a mystery. He was never an athletic man and was not known to have played Tennis in later life. In any case he had always preferred hunting. After the King and Queen left, Prince Henry their eldest son moved into the Palace for about eight months.[9] Although he was only ten at the time he had shown an interest in tennis from an early age and may well have used the two Courts.

In 1606 King Christian IV of Denmark visited Hampton Court and is said to have played a tennis match there with James I. That the fun-loving King enjoyed playing tennis is not in dispute, but surviving records of the visit offer no evidence to prove any such match took place at Hampton Court. The Danish King had sailed up the Thames to Greenwich where he was greeted by James. He used Greenwich as a base during this visit and while there it is known that he played tennis, but there is no confirmation that his opponent was James. From Greenwich he visited the City of London, Whitehall Palace and the King's houses at Eltham and Theobalds near Waltham Cross. After a few days rest, the two monarchs set off on a three-day trip taking in Richmond, Hampton Court and Windsor. All three royal residences offered tennis-playing facilities if he had the opportunity to play, but little spare time seemed to be available to him. For instance, the day he visited Hampton Court, August 8th 1606, he went hunting with James in the parkland that surrounds the Palace, dined there and watched a play put on in his honour by the King's Company of players, which almost certainly included Shakespeare. The following morning he left for Windsor. Whilst it not possible to dismiss completely the idea of the two kings pitting themselves against each other on the Tennis Court at Hampton Court, it must be treated with extreme caution.[10]

Henry's early death had led to the crowning of his brother Charles as King. When he rebuilt his father's Court, the new end wall on the service side was placed just in front of Wolsey's old north boundary wall, while the hazard end wall was erected equidistant from the lodgings at the southern end. It would seem that this was done so as to provide viewing galleries over the end walls, as there are today (figure 22). There would appear to be no other reason for not utilising the old north boundary wall, which was intact at the time, as an end wall in a similar way to the use of the east one, as the service wall.

The 1625 accounts also record the 'squareing, and woorkeing of blackstone for the hazard of the Tennis courte' and the 'setting of a stone in the middle of the sayd courte and yoltinge of an jron hooke into it for to hould the lyne there.' [11] *Yolting* or *yotting* means setting an object in place using molten lead. The use of blackstone for the hazard, refers to the floor line by the end gallery on the hazard side (this gallery was not known as the 'winning gallery' until the eighteenth century). There would have been a corresponding line on the floor by the last gallery on the service side. The blackstone was probably marble — certainly later ones were made of that material. They were not chase lines, as these were not introduced into the game until the next century. Recent research has raised the possibility that these lines were the original base lines of tennis courts and hence, any ball landing beyond them on the second bounce would have been 'out'.[12] The floor in use today, although early eighteenth century, still has two black marble lines in these positions.

The 'lyne', for which an iron hook was provided, was the cord used to hold the net across the court. The term is still used today to record chases close to the net. Whether Charles I's Court ever had a net as we know it is uncertain. Early tennis courts just had a cord strung across the playing area: its original purpose was thought to be to prevent players encroaching into their opponents half of the court. Later, fringed cords were used before the modern net was introduced.

It is not known whether the new Open Court was of the *jeu quarré* or the *jeu à dedans* type, and major alterations carried out in 1636-37 and 1660-61 do not help to solve the mystery. In 1661 a tambour was built and an old dedans replaced. The construction of a tambour seems to suggest that one was not included in 1625 unless it was poorly built or in some way inadequate for use a generation on. Whether the dedans was installed in 1625, or added in 1637, cannot be determined. This of course was the era of transition from *quarré* to *dedans* courts.

The lodgings that can be seen in the Booth drawing at the southern end of the Court, may have been those built by Henry VIII in 1529 (figure 23). Between the lodgings and the old Queen's Long Gallery, in the Palace proper, there is a further stretch of boundary wall, behind which was the gallery linking the two Courts. In Stuart times this gallery was known as the 'Whispering Gallery'. Today this passage links the Court to Tennis Court Lane and has residential accommodation above it.

Although Charles I used the Palace a great deal in his early years, by 1632 he rarely visited it. However, after a gap of some four years he was back in June 1636 following an outbreak of the plague in London and he remained until the Christmas of that year.[13] It was during this time that he decided to enclose the Court. The east boundary (service) wall was buttressed to support the new roof; the buttresses on the west (main) wall had formed part of that wall when it was erected in 1625. The southern end lodgings were partially rebuilt and both the lodgings, which were again used as the King's dressing rooms, and the Whispering Gallery, had new pitched roofs. A section of the northern boundary wall was taken down to allow for a new Keeper's House at the other end. This house was specifically for the Master or Keeper of His Majesty's Tennis Courts. The inner walls of the two dwellings had a dual purpose: they also supported the roof of the Court.

The 1636-37 account tells of James Carver 'turning twoe Piramides' and of James Bayes 'woorkeing and setting upp the firste Pyramides and taking them downe againe from the topp of Teniscourte.' [14] These two *pyramides* were the decorative pinnacles on top of the roof. This is the only reference to work on the roof that has so far come to light. It illustrates the problem one has when trying to interpret the information in the declared annual works accounts. Only a small amount of detail on any project is ever recorded and very often it is not the most relevant aspect. Fortunately, a picture of this Court survives (figure 25).[15]

25. THE STUART COURT BETWEEN 1637 AND 1660

This picture drawn by an unknown artist between 1558 and 1660
shows the roof and window structure that Charles I erected on top
of his Open Court. The buildings to the right are tiltyard towers.

This view of Charles I's Roofed Court was drawn between 1658 and 1660 at the
end of the Commonwealth period. Although many of the perspectives are wrong,
the unknown artist has gone into a great amount of detail on the Court itself that
can be relied upon. The new pitched roof had simple gable ends and was covered
in lead sheeting. On top of the gable ends, the two pyramids, described in the accounts, can be seen. The windows were taller than those of today and were not glazed. They were reduced in height when the walls were raised in 1660. Huge nets were drawn across the openings, their purpose being to catch the balls. Beyond those nets that are shown tied back, there can be seen a series of upright posts. These appear to have been part of an internal upper gallery. This would explain the curiously angled pieces of wood at the bases of the main window up-rights, which might have been part of a cantilever support for the internal gallery. This system of support would have avoided the need for any brackets under the gallery itself, which would have interfered with play off the side walls (figure 26). Galleries, whether inside or outside, were obviously needed for the marker to adjust the nets and to collect stray balls.

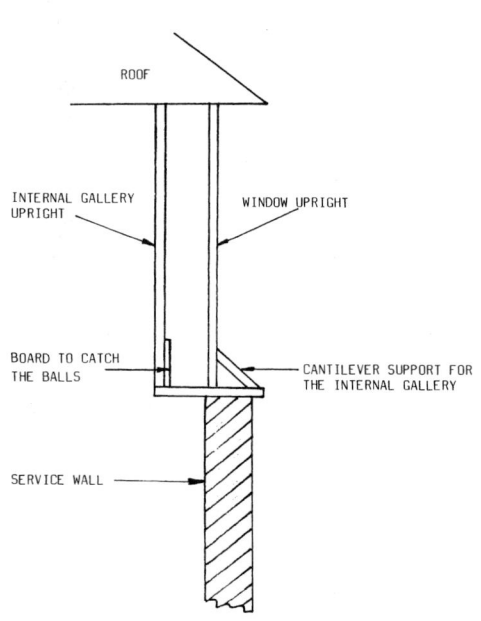

26. THE INTERNAL GALLERY

Cross-section of the cantilever system
thought to have supported the
high-level internal side wall galleries.

46

After the King's defeat by Cromwell's army in 1645, Parliament took control of the Palace and Charles was brought back there as a prisoner in August 1647. He was allowed a measure of freedom and during that time played much tennis. It is said that he last played there later that same year, the day before he escaped to the Isle of Wight.[16]

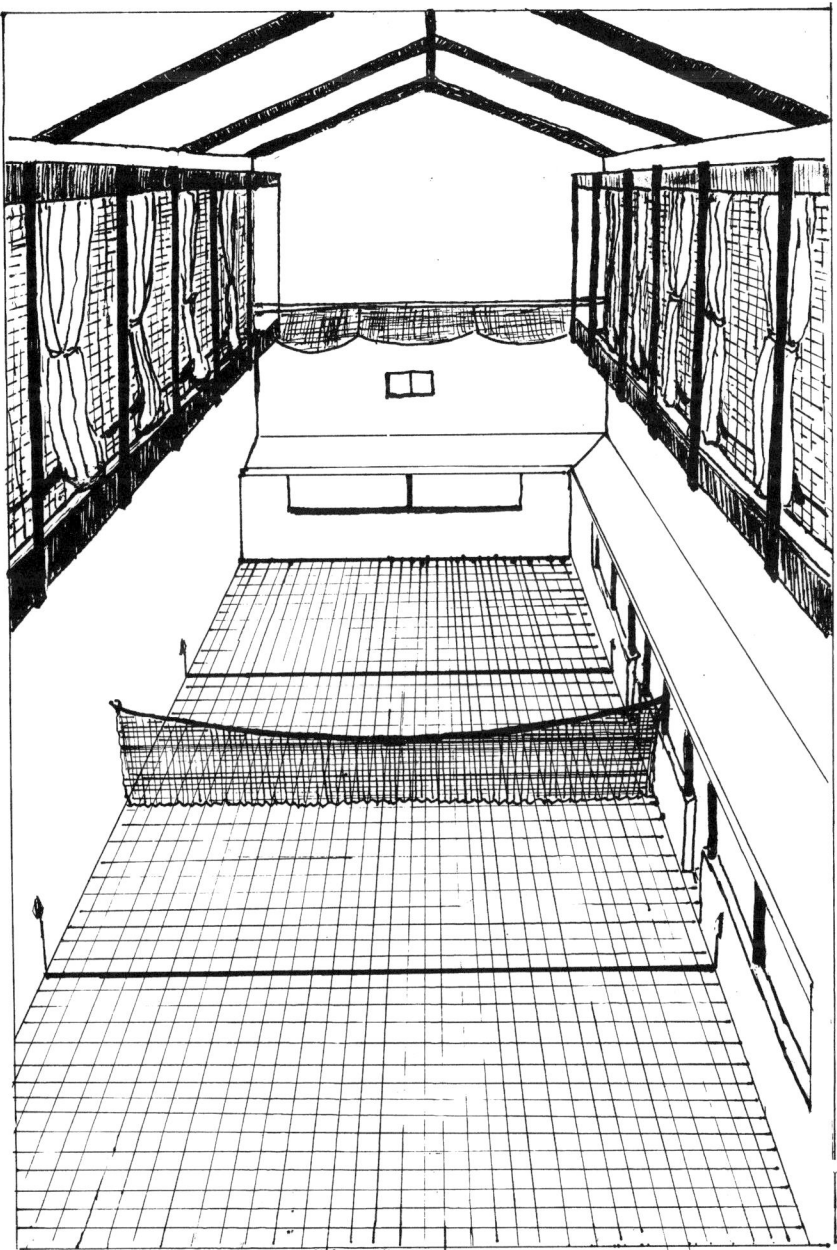

27.   ARTIST'S IMPRESSION OF THE INSIDE OF CHARLES I's COURT

This drawing not only shows a rabat net above the dedans penthouse, it
also dramatically illustrates the dominance of the upper internal galleries.

There is a dearth of information in the surviving accounts in the first half of the century, while there is a mass of detail available following the Restoration of the Monarchy. Nearly all of the comprehensive monthly account books of the *Board of the King's Works* have survived between 1660 and 1702. These are particularly useful in tracing the history of the Court as they cover two important renovations, the first by Charles II, and the second by William III.

The first renovation was extensive and was carried out by Charles II in 1660-61 at the start of his reign. It took almost a year to complete. The works accounts list many of the tradesmen and their apprentices who worked on the Court, and their rates of pay. The masons, carpenters and plasterers, were paid between 22d. and 30d. a day, but the bricklayers, who were paid at the same rate elsewhere in the Palace, received three shillings a day when working on the Tennis Court. Robert Long, the King's Marker, was employed to supervise the work, for which he was paid five shillings a day.[17]

This renovation was in fact a major rebuilding project, which began when the lead sheeting was stripped off the roof and the gable ends and roof timbers altered to form the hipped roof that is seen today. The 1625 brick floor tiles were taken up and the penthouses demolished, including the battery walls (the portion of the wall between the openings and the floor).[18] As mentioned earlier a tambour was built — there are several payments to the masons for its construction over the first few months of 1661. The four masons who built the tambour were John Ashlee, William Fitch, Moses Bramton and Giles Fines.[19]

The monthly accounts open in October 1660 with payments to Long for 'paveing tiles' and 'for money by him laid out for sands and his charges for workemen.'[20] The paving tiles and other materials for the project were delivered by barges along the River Thames. As in Tudor times, the Thames was the principal route for the delivery of goods to the Palace.

Scaffolding was erected so that work could start on reshaping the roof in November 1660.[21] Once the alterations to the structure had been completed, a team of bricklayers under the direction of Izak Corner carried out the tiling at a cost of £63 12s. 11d.[22] This was the first time a Tennis Court at the Palace had had a tiled roof, all previous ones being lead. At the same time, as mentioned earlier, the brick wall on the park side (service wall) was raised by about 1½ feet and the main wall was brought up to the same height the following month.[23] The park side buttresses were repaired early the next year.[24]

Work on the inside of the Court started once the roof was finished and the men could work in the dry. The penthouse at the hazard end was renewed in February 1661, when the accounts detail: 'Takinge downe the gallery att the Tennis Courte and the roofe of the end gallerie where the hazard is; plaininge all the timbers; and settinge them upp againe.'[25] The carpenters and bricklayers then slowly worked their way round to the dedans, which was completed by July.[26] As so often when investigating the history of Tennis at the Palace, it is a demolition account which tells one more about a court than the original construction details. For example, as mentioned before, it is only from the 1661 accounts that confirmation is found of the existence of a dedans in Charles I's

Court. Throughout these accounts the words *indan* or *judan* are used to describe the dedans.

The gallery posts were made by the turner, John Phillipps. Simon Basill, the Clerk of the Works, delivered the raw timber (deal) to Phillipps at his Hampton Wick workshop for turning and collected them when they were ready. Phillipps charged sixpence each for them.[27] Today's players will notice that the two gallery posts nearest to the net have been replaced by metal rods; the reasons for this will be discussed later.

Towards the end of the penthouse construction carpenters were being paid for 'settinge upp bourds in the galleries and the judan to leane on: 90fo: in length.' As previously mentioned, gallery nets were not used in those days, so the spectators would lean on the gallery ledges to watch play. Once the deal boards were in place the job was completed with the making of 'two coubourds to laie racketts and balles in.'[28]

Meanwhile, throughout the first six months of 1661 the floor tiles were being laid by the bricklayers.[29] As before, the masons made up two new black marble floor lines that were inserted by the end galleries.[30] The floor tiles, which cost 32s. 6d. a hundred, were brick and one foot square.[31] They must have been poor-wearing and uneven, as forty years later they had to be replaced with stone.

By April the masons had finished the new tambour and the grille aperture was cut out in readiness for the carpenters.[32] At the same time the upper walls were plastered.[33] The surfaces of the end walls below the bandeau (the junction of the penthouse wall and its sloping roof) were stone and not plastered. It was therefore the masons who rebuilt the dedans wall and not the bricklayers.[34] The lower seven feet of the main wall were also stone.[35] This happens to be the same height as the bandeau and supports the recent theory, put forward by Dr. Roger Morgan, that the bandeau may originally have been the *dead ball line*, effectively the line limiting play. There appears to be a wooden beam running the whole length of the main wall above the stonework, which can still be seen, and could easily have been painted to indicate such a line.[36]

June 1661 saw the carpenters 'puttinge upp of bourds on topp of the wale on both sides the Tennis Courte: to keepe in the balles cout.' These boards collected the balls caught by the nets covering windows, which were not glazed, so preventing them from falling back into the playing area — they would have been part of the upper galleries. From later seventeenth century views of the Court, it would appear that outside galleries were erected at this time, replacing the previous internal arrangement. The carpenters completed their work the following month when they fitted the boards ('like deskes') on top of the upper end gallery walls, finished the grille and made the dedans door.[37]

There is a strange reference in June to 'putting upp of poles att each end of the Tennis Court; to carrey the blackcloth.'[38] It is not clear what this refers to. Although there has been no way of confirming it, the most likely explanation is that they were for *rabat* nets suspended above each of the end penthouses. Their purpose would have been to catch balls rising steeply off the penthouses before they hit the roof, thereby sending them back into play. The roof at this time was not boarded and therefore balls hitting it would have been subject to deflections off the beams. The use of a black material would have helped in keeping sight of the ball. 'Black-hair cloth' was also supplied for Charles II's new Court at Windsor some seventeen years later.[39] The supporting poles were probably the four 'colloumes' costing 12d. each, which were made by the turner at the same time as the gallery posts. Julian Marshall in his *Annals of Tennis*, published in 1878, suspected as much when he tells us 'there was a trace of the rabat at Hampton Court.'[40] What he was referring to is still there today. It is the curved edge of the wooden board that now forms the play line on each of the end walls. Rabat nets had not been used in any court for nearly a hundred years until the Harbour Club Court, with its low ceiling, reintroduced them in 1993.

Once the plastering of the walls had been completed, they were blackened. This task was carried out by the plasterers in July 1661 and it needed to be done 'twice over.' They were also responsible for the finishing touches, when they were paid for 'redding the nett that goes cross ye Court' and for the 'making of ye Marks and Figures in the Court.'[41] The dedans too, was blackened and finished off with the supply of two seven-foot seats of 'Crimson velvet & garnished wth gilt nails, a foote cushion and a small turkey worke Carpett.'[42]

While these works were progressing, the smith John Miles was busy making new 'great long courtaine rodds' and 'great iron thimbles' for them.[43] It seems, though, that the Court did not get its first set of curtains until the summer of 1663, although nets were fitted immediately after the restoration. It was then that the Lord Chamberlain issued a warrant to the Master of the Great Wardrobe 'to provide and deliver unto Thomas Cooke Master of all his Majesty's Tennis Courts', the following items for Hampton Court: 'Foure hundred seaventy foure yards of Canvas for Curtaines, fifty five pounds of Brass rings, Six dozen and Six Buckles and Strapps and Sixty leathers for them, twenty two whitelynes for ye Curtaines, Tenn pounds of wyre, Seaventy Eight pound of fine rope, Thirty foure yards and a halfe more of canvas One thousand of Broadheaded nayles, 24 lynes More, Six Dozen of Blocks and five hundred of hookes.'[44] The opening and closing of these huge curtains was part of the daily duties of the Marker. The curtains and nets were subject to frequent damage due to their exposed position and there were regular warrants issued for their replacement. Some years later, when curtains and accessories came to be ordered for the Courts at Whitehall and Windsor, the warrants always stated that they should be furnished 'as Hampton Court'.

There are several pictures of Charles II's Court and some are quite misleading: the number of windows often varies, as does their shape. They are variously shown as oblong, oval or even diamond-shaped. The most famous, thought to have been commissioned by Samuel Pepys, shows them as oval (figure 28). The answer to this confusion may lie with the practice of the artists drawing a rough sketch on site and then completing the work in the studio at a later date. This

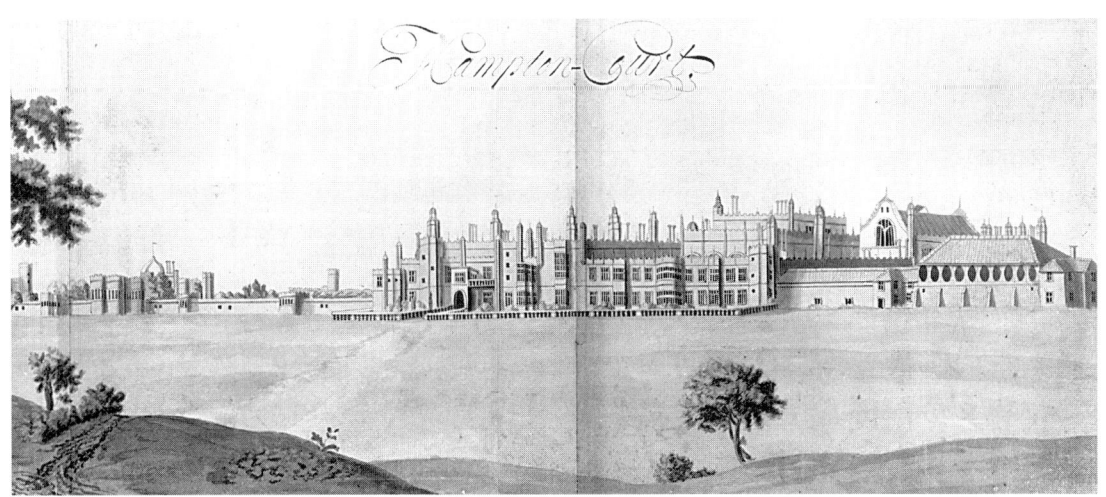

28.   PROGRESSIVE DISTORTIONS OF THE STUART COURT

Top: Pepys's original commission
Middle: Pye's engraving
Bottom: A copy of Pye's engraving distorting the Court even further

often caused problems with accuracy, especially if there was any delay in completing the work. Another problem is that all of these views of the Court were only part of a more general scene, where the Palace itself was the more important subject. Even Johannes Kip, with his well-known c1705 bird's eye view from the south-west, whilst meticulous with the Palace detail, was somewhat careless when he came to the Tennis Court (figure 32). As previously noted, the Court's new windows were not glazed: they had nets to catch the balls and large curtains to keep out the weather and control the admission of light. These heavy curtains were made of canvas and when tied back they created, from a distance, an oval appearance to the window. As the artist who worked for Pepys sketched the view from a position several hundred yards from the Court, he mistook the pulled back curtains for oval windows. There is no evidence in the works accounts to suggest that the windows were ever oval. The picture was erroneously attributed to Wenceslaus Hollar by J. Pye, when he engraved it for the Society of Antiquaries, *Vetusta Monumenta* series, in 1769. Entries in Pepys's *Diary* give rise to the possibility that it was painted by Hendrik Danckerts, though there even is some doubt about this. Pepys had commissioned Danckerts in 1669 to paint 'the four houses of the King, Whitehall, Hampton Court, Greenwich and Windsor' to hang in his dining room. He was unhappy with the Hampton Court picture and chose a Danckerts view of Rome in its place.[45] The situation is further complicated by Pye's addition of the caption 'A VIEW of HAMPTON COVRT as finished by K. HENRY VIII'. That is clearly wrong as far as the Tennis Court is concerned. A print of Pye's engraving was presented to the Royal Tennis Court by Julian Marshall towards the end of the nineteenth century and still hangs in the clubrooms today. The best representation of the restored Court is the 1662 picture by Willem Schellinks (figure 29).[46]

When the King commissioned Thomas Cooke to build his new Court on the old Brake site at Whitehall,[47] Robert Long was entrusted with the job of supervising the building work. There are many entries in the Lord Chamberlain's accounts through the winter of 1662-63 for payments to Long for his charges in going to Hampton Court with several workmen 'to take demencon of some parte of the Tennis Courte there'.[48] Marshall says: 'We may, therefore, take it for granted that this was a reproduction of the old Court at Hampton Court.' [49] The well known c1670 plan of Whitehall [50] shows the Court there as having two doors in the 'door gallery' positions (figure 30). Contradicting this, there is another plan drawn up by John Soane (afterwards Sir John) in 1793, shortly before the Court's demolition — this shows that the Court was virtually identical to Hampton Court, albeit slightly smaller, but access to the playing area was through the marker's box at the centre of the galleries. There were still two doors though, but now they were side by side (figure 31). At Hampton Court, the door on the hazard side is still there, but long since sealed up. The Soane plan is useful as it shows the measurements of the Court, including the lengths of the side galleries.[51] The error on the c1670 plan probably occurred because the plan was concerned with the whole of Whitehall Palace, the Tennis Court being a minor detail, and the interior guessed at. Courts with doors in the 'door gallery' positions were commonplace in those days.

This does however raise the question of when the change from the two-door to the central-access format was made at Hampton Court. The galleries, wooden posts and ledges in use today appear to be those that were installed in 1661 — their arrangement does not seem to have altered since. The earliest surviving plan of the Court, thought to have been drawn by Thomas Fort, the Clerk of the Works from 1715 to 1745, shows the Court with a central entrance through the marker's box (figure 35).[52] This, coupled with the fact that the Soane plan of Whitehall shows the same arrangement, means it can be safely assumed that the gallery configuration in use today is the one Charles II put in. The mid-seventeenth century was early for a central entrance, although it does seem that England may have led the way — in the important Haymarket Court in James Street (c1673) players entered the court through the marker's box by the net.[53] The French though, seem to have been slower to change: as late as 1767, Francois de Garsault in his *L'Art du Paumier-Raquetier et de la Paume (The Art of the Tennis-Racket-Maker and of Tennis)* wrote that the standard French court of his time was a two-door one.[54] The King's preference for a central entry into the Court may have been the reason that the penthouse and galleries, including the battery walls, were rebuilt. If that were the case, it would follow that all the earlier Courts in the Palace were of the two-door variety.

29.   THE EAST FRONT OF THE PALACE

A 1662 view by Willem Schellinks

The dwellings at each end of the Court were also renovated at this time. The Keeper's House at the northern end, by now occupied by Thomas Cooke, had its roof reconstructed and tiled. New windows and floors were put into the King's Dressing Rooms at the other end.[55] Although the Keeper was provided for, the Marker, Robert Long, was not normally accommodated at Hampton Court. His apartments were at Whitehall.

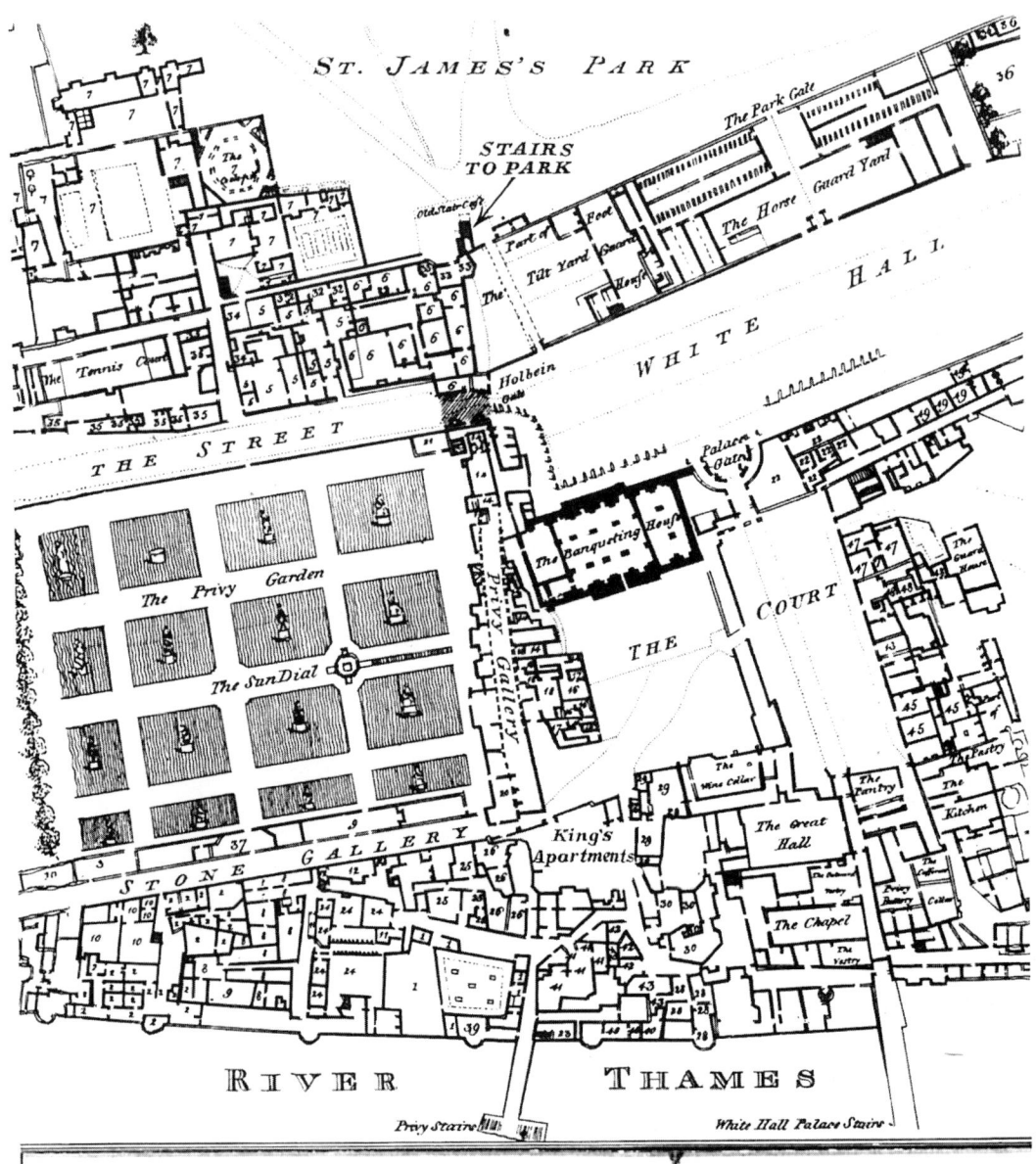

30. PLAN OF WHITEHALL c1670

The rooms marked '35' around Charles II's Tennis Court were occupied by the Master of the King's Tennis Courts and those marked '5' are on the site of Henry VIII's Great Close Tennis Play.

Apart from his penchant for early morning play, a further insight into Charles, the tennis player, comes from the recollections of Samuel Pepys. His *Diary* tells of the King playing well at Whitehall with Sir Arthur Slingsby against Lord Suffolk and Lord Chesterfield. On another occasion he describes how: 'The King's play was extolled without any cause at all, was a loathsome sight, though sometimes endeed he did play very well and deserved to be commended; but such open flattery is beastly.' The King was also concerned about his weight. After a game partnered by Prince Rupert against Thomas Cooke and Bab May (the Keeper of the Privy Purse), he had a steel yard carried to him, to weigh himself.

On enquiry, Pepys was told 'the King's curiosity, which he usually hath, of weighing himself before and after his play, to see how much he loses in weight by playing, and this day he lost 4½lb.' [56] From the accounts of the Master and Gentleman of the Wardrobe, we know the makers and suppliers of some of his tennis apparel. His 'taffata drawers' were made by Robert Graham at a cost of 30d. each, from material supplied by Nicholas Townes, and his 'tennis shoos' were made by John Pate.[57] Perfume too was supplied to the tennis courts.[58] Charles played tennis virtually all his life and as late as 1683, only 15 months before he died, Lady Charworth wrote to her brother the Duke of Rutland: 'The King is very well and plays much Tennis. Lord Feversham and his Majestie and Lord Churchill with Mr. Godolphin all so excellent players that if one beat the other 'tis alternatively.' [59]

In its first winter, the renovated Court, along with other parts of the Palace, suffered severe storm damage. Roof tiles on both the Court and the Keeper's House had to be replaced and the window net frames repaired.[60]

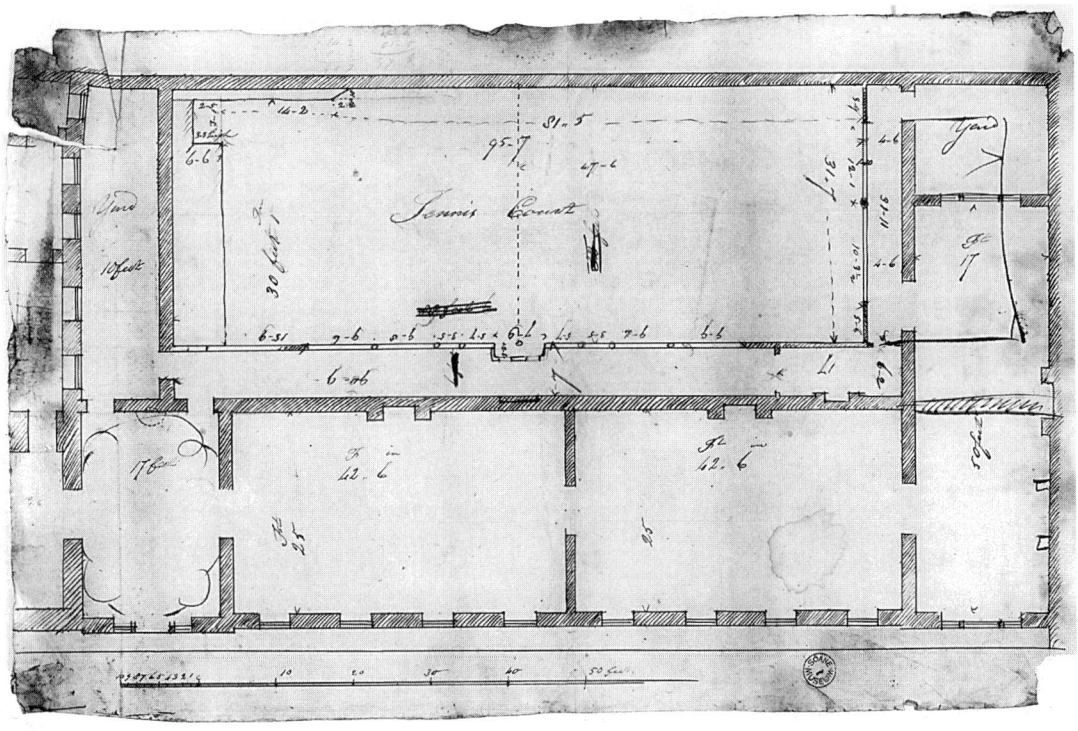

31. THE SOANE PLAN OF THE STUART COURT AT WHITEHALL

This plan was drawn in 1793 when John Soane was redeveloping a large part of Whitehall. It confirms that Charles II's Court there was virtually identical to the Stuart Court at Hampton Court.

The following spring saw the erection of a guardhouse, some 50 feet long x 20 feet wide, with beds for soldiers, set up against the side of the Court. It was in use for 17 years before being pulled down in 1679.[61] It must have been against the west wall as it does not appear in any of the late seventeenth-century views.

Robert Long continued to be in charge of the Court's maintenance and there are many warrants for payments to him throughout the 1660s for minor works. Other warrants make it clear that he was paid extra for his attendance upon the King whenever he played. He was succeeded as the King's marker by his son (also Robert) after his death.

After Charles II's death in 1685, his brother the Duke of York became King James II. During his short reign very little is recorded about the Court except that in July 1687 the roof seems to have been under some threat. Carpenters were employed in 'putting upp 2 stout beams to hold upp a purlin in the roofe in the upper end of the tennis courte.' [62] Nothing is known of the use James made of the Court, either as Duke of York or as King. It is possible he played when he visited his father, Charles I, when he was detained at the Palace by Cromwell, in 1647. Further opportunity for tennis came when he had his own apartments at Hampton Court after the Restoration in 1660.

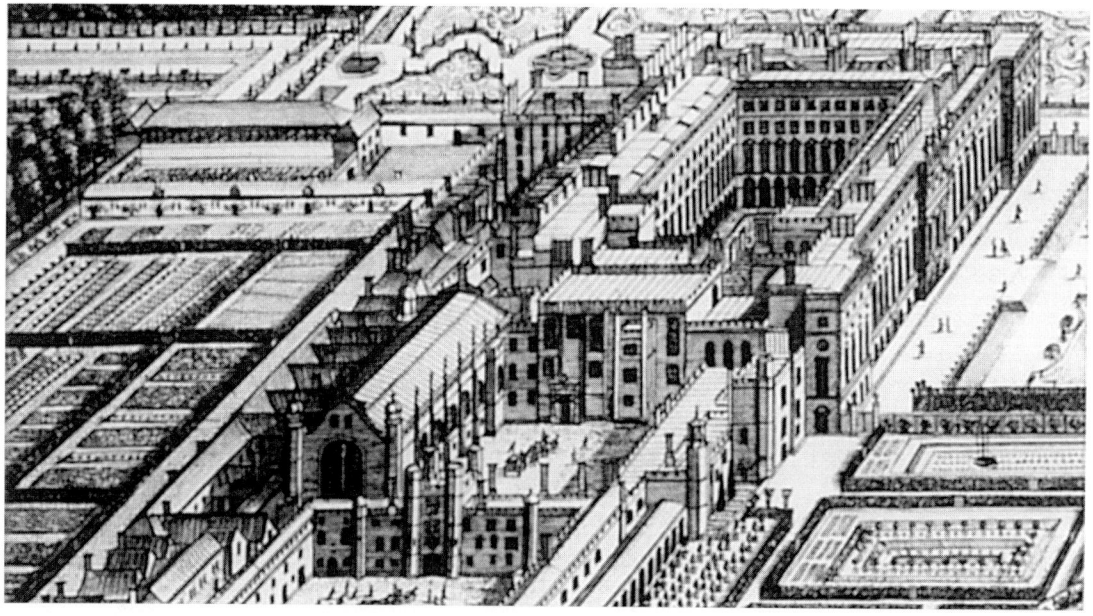

32.   JOHANNES KIP'S c1705 VIEW OF THE STUART COURT

Henry VIII's Close Bowling Alley can be seen in the foreground.

Very few names of people who played at Hampton Court during the Stuart era are known. But one who almost certainly did was Tobias Rustat, the Under-Houskeeper at the Palace from 1660 until his death in 1694. Evidence of his tennis involvement comes from the fact that amongst his goods and chattels when he died were three pairs of tennis socks. A trusted courtier, Rustat, was believed to have helped the Duke of Buckingham and Lord Holland engineer the escape of Charles I from Hampton Court in 1647. After Charles's execution, which family legend says he witnessed, he served Charles II in exile as his valet. He was appointed Yeoman of the Robes, which enabled him to amass a considerable fortune from fees acquired for granting knighthoods and other honours. However, coming from a religious background he became a philanthropist — he was the largest private contributor to the Chelsea Hospital. The post of Under Housekeeper at Hampton Court would have been another reward for his loyalty. He was quite likely to have played tennis with Charles II and the Duke of York (later James II) when they were in residence at the Palace and it is interesting to speculate further as to whether he was one of Charles I's playing partners, on that day in 1647 when the King escaped. Incidentally, one of Rustat's co-lateral descendants is today's leading British lawn tennis player, Tim Henman.[63]

When William and Mary came to the throne, they embarked on the rebuilding of the Palace. Sir Christopher Wren was put in charge of the works and one of his first acts was to commandeer the Tennis Court for the storage of timber. In May 1689, a bricklayer was despatched to cut a 'way in the Tennis cour(t) wall for three windows, and making good the Jams and head againe.'[64] This may have been the time when the two wooden posts nearest the net were removed, to be replaced later when play resumed, with the metal rods seen today. They would certainly have impeded the movement of timber in and out of the Court.

The following month, the first of thousands of boards were being transferred from barges on the Thames to the Court.[65] For the next three years until the Queen's death, when work stopped, there were constant payments to the Clerk of the Works and others for the movement of timber from the river to the Court. Whenever a barge arrived at the quay much of the palace workforce would be diverted to unload it. There are also many smaller payments recorded for the distribution of this timber from the Court to other parts of the Palace. Not only was the Court used for the storage of new timber, but wainscot (oak wall panelling) that had been stripped out of the old Tudor Palace was also stored there until a new use for it could be found. Pebbles and even 'mould' for Wren's garden were kept there too.[66]

Following the resumption of the Palace rebuilding programme in 1697, the Court continued to be used for storage.[67] However, from a tennis point of view, there were some encouraging signs in the August of 1699.

CHAPTER 5

THE EIGHTEENTH CENTURY

And other Kings and Queens they say
Were good at love games in their day
Within these Courts; Ah! Who can tell
How love set in those hearts could dwell.

With the completion of the new East Front of the Palace, the Tennis Court at the northern end must have looked somewhat dilapidated after ten years of use as a timber store, so the King ordered its restoration. In August 1699 work started on the external features of the building: an old portico was pulled down, along with the buttresses on the park side[1] — those on the west wall remain to this day. The position of the portico has never been established, although it might refer to the section of the southern end lodgings that projected out from Wolsey's old boundary wall into the park, which was demolished to allow for a new garden wall. The new high wall can be seen today; it runs north from Wren's east facade alongside Broadwalk. It matches one to the south.

Wren was not a tennis player and had no real idea of what was required within a modern tennis court. He even advised the King that the old uneven brick paved floor should be repaired and that the Court could be returned to play for only £200. He did however turn to the Master of the King's Tennis Courts, Horatio Moore, for some expert advice in early January 1700. A copy of Moore's estimate to the Treasury survives amongst the correspondence now held in the Public Records Office in London (figure 33). It reads:

'May it please your Lordships,

'His Majesty having commanded Sir Christopher Wren to make an Estimate of ye repairs of Hampton Court Tennis Court in ye State it now is and report ye same to your Honours and Sir Christopher haveing accordingly given his report with mending the brick paveing and makeing it usefull, it will amount to £200.

'But Sir Christopher haveing declared his being unaquainted with Tennis Play has consulted Mee (who have ye honor to be Master of his Majesty's Tennis Courts) and desired mee to give him my Estimate which accordingly I have done, viz a Stone floor without which no Ball can give a true bound: a boarded Ceiling altogether necessary not only for Play but preservation of ye Roof; Curtain Rodds, Rings, hooks & c: a Penthouse frame for Netts, Plaister of paris, blacking and figureing which will for ye Court only in the whole amount to £365.

'The Lodgings at each end of ye Court ye one being ye Keeper's apartment, the other for the Players, are much out of repair, and will cost £160 to make them good: the Totall for yᵉ Court and Lodgings will come to £525 which I conceive will be yᵉ utmost.

'I am My Lords your Lordships most humble Servant Horatio Moore' [2]

The estimate was passed over to the Officers of the Works for their consideration, but in the meantime the King had intervened, forcing the following reply to the Treasury:

'In pursuance of your Lordship's reference upon the Memoriall of Captain Horatio Moore and in obedience to his Majesty's verball direcion concerning yᵉ Tennis Court at Hampton Court that hee would have yᵉ same repaired with brick paveing, not considering at present yᵉ Repairs to yᵉ houses. Wee humbly Certify that by reason yᵉ persons concerned can best direct what is necessary to be done to make yᵉ Court convenient for their use; Your Lordship's may allow Captain Moore yᵉ sume of £200 to make yᵉ Court itself usefull with brick paveing & all other necessary repairs and yᵉ officers of yᵉ Works may observe that yᵉ money be expended; all which is humbly submitted by.....' [3]

This letter, signed by the Board, which included Wren as Surveyor and William Talman as Comptroller of His Majesty's Works, authorized only work on the court itself. The floor was to be repaired and not replaced, nothing was to be spent on the lodgings and only £200 was proposed for the whole project. Further debate ensued, of which no correspondence has survived, but Moore obviously got his own way in the end, as a Treasury estimate in the May for various works about the Palace included the item:

'To repair the Tennis Court £300' [4]

and the Office of Works accounts go on to detail the laying of a new floor using Ketton Stone.

Moore's other requests were also significant. With the installation of new gallery nets, spectators would no longer have to avoid balls being hit into the side galleries, thereby reducing the risk of injury. The boarding of the ceiling, being 'altogether necessary not only for play', is an interesting confirmation that the ceilings were still in play in 1700 and raises the question of when the rules were changed. In France the ceilings were in play until at least 1800, as Pierre Barcellon tells us in his *Règles et Principes de Paume*. [5] However, in Lukin's *Treatise on Tennis* which contains the first published rules in England only twenty years later, he states quite categorically that the ceiling was not in play.[6] Marshall thought the rules in this country changed about 1800.[7]

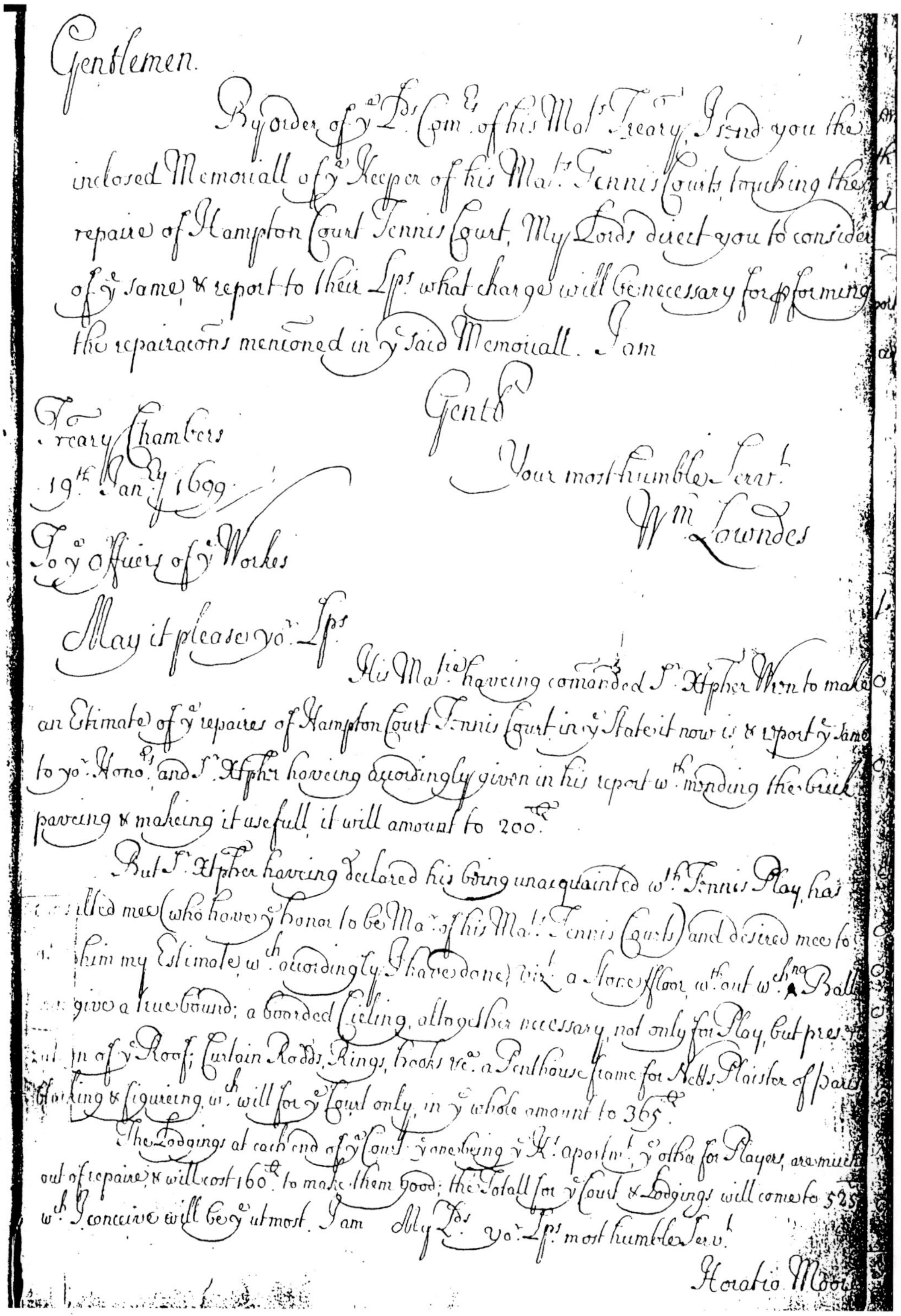

Gentlemen.

By order of y[e] L[ds] Com[rs] of his Ma[ts] Treas[ry] I send you the inclosed Memoriall of y[e] Keeper of his Ma[ts] Tennis Courts, touching the repaire of Hampton Court Tennis Court, My Lords direct you to consider of y[e] same, & report to their L[ps] what charge will be necessary for p[er]forming the reparacons mencioned in y[e] said Memoriall. I am

Gent[l]

Your most humble Serv[t]

W[m] Lowndes

Treas[ry] Chambers
19[th] Jan[ry] 1699.

To y[e] Officers of y[e] Workes

May it please yo[r] L[ps] His Ma[tie] haveing comanded S[r] X[pho]er Wren to make an Estimate of y[e] repaires of Hampton Court Tennis Court in y[e] State it now is & report y[e] same to yo[r] Hono[rs] and S[r] X[pho]er haveing accordingly given in his report wth mending the bric[k] paveing & makeing it usefull, it will amount to 200[li]

But S[r] X[pho]er haveing declared his being unacquainted w[th] Tennis Play, has referred mee (who have y[e] honor to be Ma[ster] of his Ma[ts] Tennis Courts) and desired mee to give him my Estimate w[ch] accordingly I have done, viz[t]. a stone floor, w[th]out w[ch] no Ball can give a true bound; a boarded Ceiling, altogether necessary not only for Play, but preservacon of y[e] Roof; Curtain Rodds, Rings, hooks &c[a], a Penthouse frame for Netts, Plaister of paris, boarding & figureing w[ch] will for y[e] Court only, in y[e] whole amount to 365[li]

The Lodgings at each end of y[e] Court, y[e] one being y[e] K[s] apartm[t] y[e] other for Players, are much out of repaire, & will cost 160[li] to make them good; the Totall for y[e] Court & Lodgings will come to 525[li] w[ch] I conceive will be y[e] utmost. I am obly[ged] L[ps] yo[r] L[ps] most humble serv[t].

Horatio Moore

33.   HORATIO MOORE'S 1700 ESTIMATE AND RECOMMENDATIONS

However, the restoration far exceeded the budget, the work inside the court alone costing nearly twice the original estimate. The floor came to nearly £200, the repairs to the walls £130, ceiling work £72, and at least £100 was spent on nets and curtains. Then there were numerous minor payments for other services. This may explain why the renovation took nearly two years to complete.[8]

In fact, work had started in March 1700, when the gallery net frames were made and the old brick floor was taken up.[9] Over the next two months, the King's Master Mason, Thomas Hill, was busy laying the new Ketton Stone floor into which the old black marble floor lines were reinserted in their usual place, centred on the end galleries. In the event only a third of the salvaged marble was reusable and Hill was paid £2 2s. 0d. for 42 feet more to finish the job.[10]

Once the new floor was down, scaffolding was erected to allow the plasterers to carry out the lathing and plastering of the more seriously damaged sections of the walls. The remainder was washed, stopped and pointed, before blacking of the playing area and whiting of the walls above the play line was carried out.[11] In the meantime, Lord Jersey, the Lord Chamberlain, issued a warrant to the Master of His Majesty's Great Wardrobe, the Earl of Montague, for the supply of new 'Canvas Curtains, Netts, Curtain Rings, Staples', plus 'a line and Nett to reach across yᵉ middle of yᵉ Court.'[12] Despite the King's reluctance, repairs were carried out to the Keeper's House and the players' rooms at the other end.[13]

Work then stopped for eight months, resuming in February 1701, when two thousand tiles on the roof were replaced.[14] This work must have damaged the finished walls, for in May, John Grove, the Master Plasterer, was again employed to clean and black them, for which he received £20 14s. 6d.[15] In the same month Thomas Hill laid 1,723 square feet of Purbeck paving in the yard leading to the Court.[16] This was in front of the Keeper's House.

Another warrant was issued in July 1701 by the Lord Chamberlain, this time to Sir Christopher Wren for 'ceiling yᵉ Tennis Court att Hampton Court with Slit deal.'[17] By October the Master Carpenter, James Grove, was busy implementing the order, so fulfilling the last major requirement of Moore. For this he was paid £29 18s. 0d., and a further £26 18s. 2d. for flooring above the ceiling.[18] All the ceiling works must have damaged the walls yet again, as John Grove was brought back for a third time to black the lower walls again and repaint the upper ones white, receiving this time £46 10s. 9d. for the court, and £3 13s. 8d. for the gallery.[19]

Whether the two Groves ever received these amounts is questionable, for many of the craftsmen who worked at the Palace had to wait for up to ten years for payment, often causing financial problems when paying their own employees. This failure by the Crown to recompense these loyal servants properly also extended to Sir Christopher Wren himself, who after his dismissal by George I in 1718 at the great age of 86, was still owed £341 3s. 4d., several years back salary.[20]

The redecoration of the court was completed when the King's sergeant painter, Robert Streeter, painted the woodwork with 'flatt colour', receiving £4 10s. 9d. for the gallery posts and trays, five shillings for ten casements, and five shillings and sixpence for eleven windows on both sides of the court.[21] Streeter's task included the monogram of William III: he was paid £3 10s. 0d. for three ciphers and crowns, an amount that also included the gold supplied.[22] It is a popular misconception that this monogram, which still remains in the centre of the main wall today, is that of William and Mary. In fact Mary had died eight years earlier.

34. THE MONOGRAMS OF WILLIAM III

The left-hand monogram is that of William and Mary
and the right-hand one of William III alone.

Mention should be made here of the Neapolitan artist Antonio Verrio. Verrio was at this time busy painting the ceilings and walls of the King's new apartments. There is though some evidence that he also worked in the Tennis Court. Robert Streeter's bill for the court included the painting black of a cupboard and frames for Mr Verrio. Unfortunately, Verrio's bill does not survive and it cannot be determined what these items were.

The final task was to set up the nets and curtains. The curtains were made from the 540 yards of canvas supplied. Stretched across the outside of the windows along the entire length of the court were two nets, four yards deep.[23] These nets caught the badly struck balls, which could then be retrieved by the marker. The new side gallery nets were hung and Josiah Key, the smith, was called in to make a wire grill which was to be mounted across the whole of the dedans to protect the King.[24]

Externally, the completion of the Court coincided with the completion of the gardens. The Royal Gardener, Henry Wise, planted 65 fruit trees of various species outside the Court. They must have been an attractive sight in the springtime with their subtle shades of pink blossom.[25]

It is doubtful whether William III ever played on his refurbished court, for he was by now suffering not only from asthma but also from severely swollen legs. His only regular exercise was stag hunting. He had though played tennis earlier in his life. At the age of thirteen he had been taught the game in his native Holland[26] and there is some evidence that he was still playing when he acceded to the English throne in 1689. One of the *Harleian Manuscripts* in the British Library lists items that had to be available each time the King played tennis. They were three *manchets* (small loaves), along with a bottle of claret and a bottle of Spanish wine.[27] Some maintain that the Spanish wine was for washing the King's feet after he played. This arises because the same manuscript mentions that a bottle had to be provided for this purpose once a week. However, there is no evidence to suggest the bottle at the Tennis Court was for anything other than refreshment.

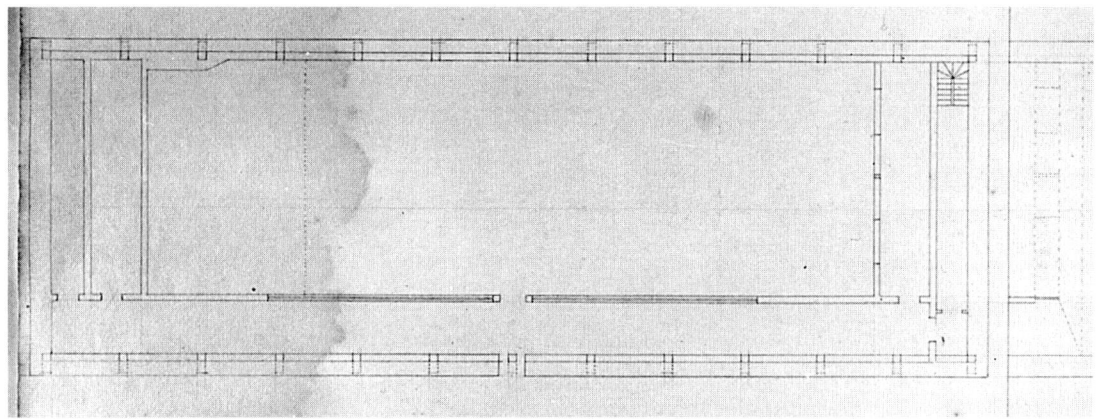

35. THE EARLIEST KNOWN FLOOR PLAN OF THE STUART COURT

It is thought that this plan was drawn by Thomas Fort,
the Clerk of the Works from 1715 to 1745.

The Court was of course available to William between February and May in his first year as King, before its conversion into a timber store. He was in residence at the Palace during that time. The King certainly enjoyed watching the game, even at times risking his own personal safety, as can be seen in a letter from one James Kelly to Mr Vernon, the Principal Secretary of State. He wrote: 'His Majesty is in great danger when he exposes himself so much amongst papists. One Hugh Dicconson, one Blout, one Lane, and one Manors, are sent for perpetually to play at tennis before him.' Kelly goes on to say that these men are agents of the King of France. As this letter was dated Ash Wednesday 1698 the men could not have been playing at Hampton Court. They might have been at Whitehall, but the Palace there had been destroyed by fire the previous month, although the Tennis Court survived. It is more likely that they were at Windsor.[28] He obviously continued to enjoy watching the game after Hampton Court had been restored, as the installation of the protective wire grill across the dedans shows.

It was in fact a hunting accident that indirectly led to William's death. While riding in one of the parks near the Palace, his horse stumbled over a molehill, dislodging the King and causing his shoulder to break. It was reset that day, but

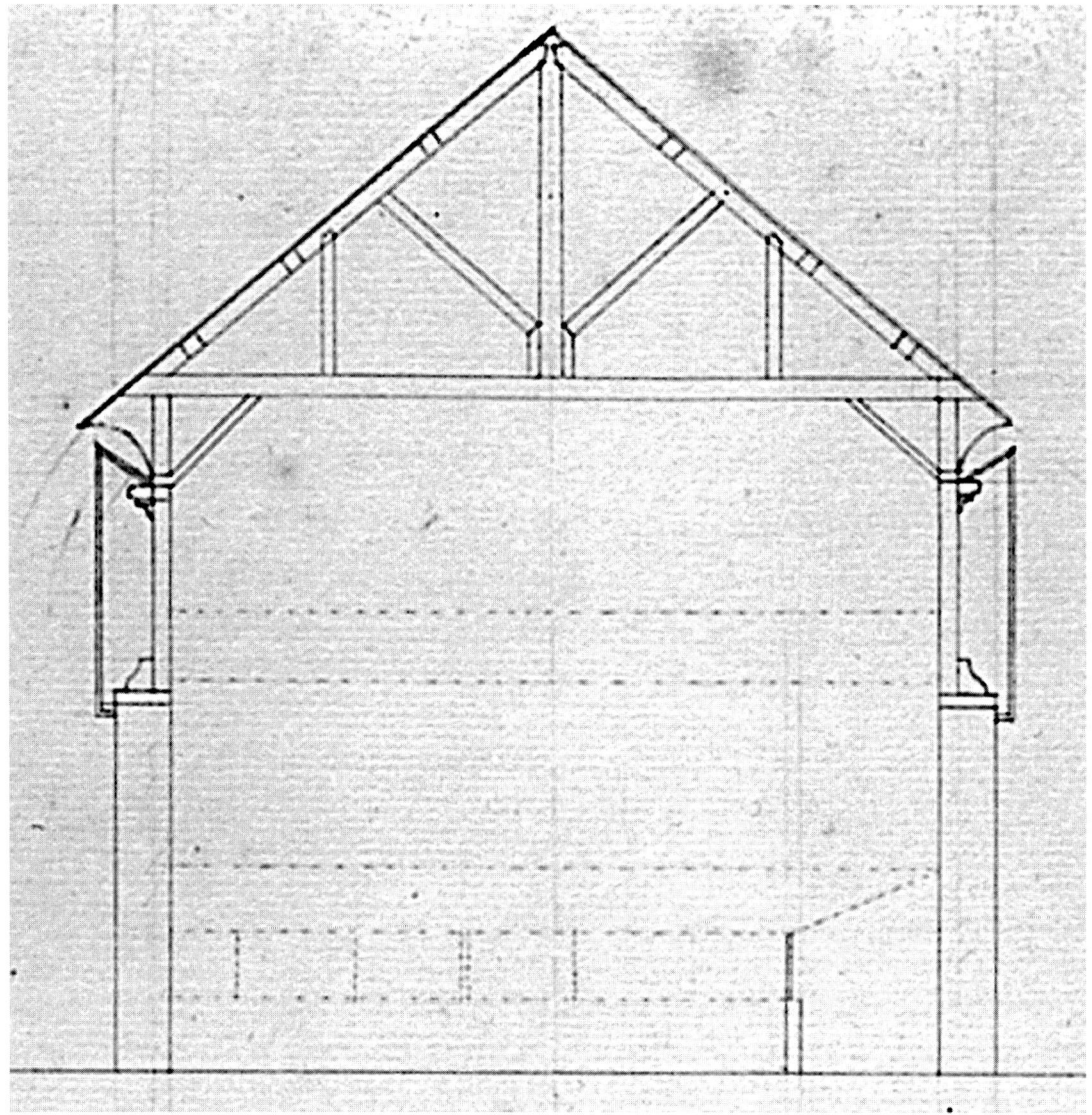

36.   18th CENTURY CROSS-SECTION OF THE STUART COURT

Drawing attributed to Thomas Fort

his health quickly deteriorated and he passed away three weeks later, on 18th March 1702.

Very little is known about the Court during the twelve-year reign of Queen Anne. That it remained in play is evident from the fact that a new set of curtain rods was delivered to Thomas Chaplin in 1709.[29] Chaplin was the new Master of Her Majesty's Tennis Courts, having been appointed on the death of Horatio Moore a year earlier. In 1712, Thomas Highmore submitted an account for repainting the Court.[30] Highmore, the Queen's sergeant painter, was another of those tradesmen who had great difficulty in getting paid by the Crown.[31]

An event occurred early in the next reign that almost caused the demise of the Court. Within three years of his accession, the first of the Hanoverian monarchs,

George I, who was not a popular king, found himself in dispute with his son. The Prince (later George II) and Princess of Wales were, at the time, held in high esteem by the general public and the King saw this as a political threat. To counter it, he decided he must make himself more accessible to his subjects. During his four-month stay at Hampton Court, from August 1718, this manifested itself in the conversion of the Great Hall into a theatre, the King's dining in public, and his holding assemblies every evening in either the Cartoon Gallery or the Tennis Court.[32] In fact the King had issued a warrant four months earlier for the Tennis Court to be 'fitted up as a Drawing Room' for this very purpose.[33]

Plasterers were ordered into the court to scrape all the black off the walls and to repair and repaint them white. At the same time carpenters were busy making a gallery within the court for musicians to perform.[34] A billiard-table was set up for the King's use. The Treasury warrant for this tells us that it was to be covered with fine broad green cloth, to have green silk pocket nets, ivory balls and round irons. The round irons, a feature of the game at the time, were similar to the hoops used in croquet, a game with which billiards has an affinity although it was originally developed from closh.[35] It seems that the floor was boarded and part of the court partitioned.[36]

Just when the Court was returned to play is not clear. The immensely useful monthly account books between 1703 and 1778 have not survived. Again one is left with only the annual declared accounts with very little detail, limited inter-departmental correspondence and the warrant books, as the main information sources for tracing the history through this period. One possible indication of a restoration to play comes with the order to Thomas Fort, the Clerk of the Works, for 'a new doore to be made against the Tennis Court and the breach there be made good.'[37] This order was issued in April 1720, the date that coincided with the patching up of the quarrel between the King and the Prince.

All the available evidence would suggest that the walls remained white for over seventy years. It is not until 1790 that we find a payment to the King's plasterer, John Dillman Engleheart, for 'blacking walls at ye Tennis Court 788½ yds. of blacking done twice in lamb black and double size.' For this, he was paid £13 2s. 9¼d.[38] The reference to *lamb* black is an error of the scribe, *lamp* black being a usual component part of the mix used to colour court walls in those days.

The last major work on the Court during George I's reign was the complete replacement of the roof tiles in 1724.[39] Nothing of importance occurred during George II's reign. Like his father, he did not play the game. Of the other members of the Hanoverian Royal Family, the most prominent tennis player at that time was George II's son, Frederick, Prince of Wales. He had a suite of rooms at Hampton Court before he moved to Kew in 1737, following a serious argument with his parents, where it is said he continued to arrange cricket and tennis matches.[40] As there was no court at Kew, he must have either travelled back to Hampton Court, or up to Whitehall or Haymarket, to play.

37. CHARLES JAMES FOX

One of the most prominent politicians of his day, Charles James Fox, was involved in his youth in an extraordinary game of tennis at Hampton Court. The incident, which probably occurred in the 1770s, saw Fox, who played tennis well, agreeing to take part in a match for a large wager, completely naked! It is recorded that he won. Nobody knows whether this was a childish prank or a calculated insult to the King, George III, for Fox, a great-great-grandson of Charles II, opposed the influence of the Crown for most of his political life. As a young man he was described as an 'outrageous fop'. A reckless gambler, he seldom went to bed before 5 am or rose before 2 pm. At the age of 25, his father, Lord Holland (the first Baron) had to settle his gambling debts amounting to an incredible £140,000. However his addiction continued and 20 years later he had to be rescued again, when his friends subscribed £70,000. He entered Parliament in 1768 at the age of 19, having been returned for Midhurst in Sussex, and he later represented Westminster. At first he was a Tory, but he later switched his allegiance to the Whigs. It was during this transition that he became very popular in the country at large and a duel with a political opponent, during which he suffered a slight stomach wound, confirmed him as 'the Man of the People'. He led the 'Foxite' faction of the Whig party and spent 40 years in the House of Commons serving in several administrations, at times as Foreign Secretary. He was at odds with George III over most of the great foreign issues of the time, the King's policy on the American colonies, Ireland, India and the French Revolution. The rift was widened further when he befriended George's son, the extravagant Prince of Wales. As for his tennis-playing, little else is known. He was playing at the age of fifteen while at Eton – the Earl of Carlisle recorded that he and Fox were whipped for 'stealing out of Church, to play at Tennis'. They would almost certainly have played on Charles II's Windsor Castle court, to which the Eton boys had access. He was still playing 30 years later at Woburn, when he wrote to a friend bemoaning the fact that the Duke of Bedford had just beaten him, whereas a year earlier he could give him fifteen. Whether his change of fortune was due to his increasing obesity, or an improvement on the part of the Duke, who had recently built the court, was not mentioned.[41]

With the Office of Works monthly account books again available from 1778, it becomes clear that the Court must have been in regular use, for there are endless entries for minor repairs of both the Court and the Keeper's House, now occupied by Richard Beresford. An interesting entry in March 1781 relates to the covering of the penthouses with strong canvas.[42] It should be remembered that the Court at that time was still not glazed, so the penthouses would have got soaked during a heavy rainstorm. Once covered, they were painted by Elizabeth Betts.[43] This lady was in charge of the painters at the Palace for the greater part of George III's reign and her name is often to be found in the accounts charging for small jobs on or about the court.

Seven years later, in August 1788, the Court must have been in a very poor state. The Lord Chamberlain wrote to the Office of Works requiring an estimate for 'repairing and putting the said court into a proper state so that any of the Royal Family may occasionally play tennis therein.'[44] The Office of Works reported back that £253 3s. 9d. would be needed for repairs.[45] On consideration, the Lord Chamberlain ordered that only the floor should be re-laid that year, 'the rest of the repairs to be laid over till next spring.'[46] The re-laying of the floor was carried out by the mason, John Vidler, and it is clear from the money expended that the 90-year-old Ketton Stone was reused and this remains the floor in use today.[47]

This renovation was carried out as a consequence of William, the Duke of Gloucester, having to move into apartments inside the Palace while his Pavilion was being restored. Although The Pavilions in the House Park were only three-quarters of a mile from the Palace, it does suggest the Duke made little or no use of the Tennis Court before this time.[48] It may have been that he was caught up in

38. EXTRACT FROM *THE TIMES*

4th August 1788

His Royal Highnefs the Duke of Gloucefter has apartments at prefent in Hampton Court, during the repairs of his pavillion. The Tennis-court at that place is, in confequence, fitted up, and much reforted to, by not only the Duke and his fuite; but the Duke of York, and feveral of the neighbouring gentlemen.

the enthusiasm of his nephew, George III's second son, Frederick, Duke of York, who became a frequent visitor to the Court in 1788. From the columns of *The Times* one learns that Frederick would often play with Lord Darnley and the Marquis of Titchfield, and one gets an insight into his demeanour on court. His play was said at times to be 'too hot and passionate' and that he 'leaps over the net with great agility.' When he played, he wore a 'dress of flannel — stockings, breeches and shirt, all joined together which is put on and off in a moment.'[49] It is clear from a *Morning Post* article a few months earlier that he was playing the game regularly at this time, when they reported that he was often at the James Street Court in the Haymarket.[50] This was the Duke of York who was later immortalised as 'The Grand Old Duke of York' by the nursery rhyme that lampooned his military ability. Eventually though, he gained a great deal of respect for his concern over the welfare of the soldiers under his command and for the reforms he introduced.

It would seem that the remaining works were in fact delayed for two years, when, as mentioned earlier, Engleheart was to be found blacking the walls again. The only other major work during the remainder of the century was another retiling of the roof, after the winter of 1791-92.[51]

Within a few years of the start of the nineteenth century, the status of the Royal Court at Hampton Court was about to change. On the 26th January 1818,

39. FREDERICK, DUKE OF YORK

a letter of some importance arrived at the Office of Works (figure 40). The letter was sent from the Royal Pavilion at Brighton by Benjamin Bloomfield, the Prince Regent's Private Secretary. It read:

'I am commanded by The Prince Regent to desire that the Tennis Court at Hampton Court be put into a fit state for use.'[52]

Following this command, responsibility for internal repairs was transferred from the Office of Works to the Keeper and a Committee of Players. Effectively this was the birth of the Club known as THE ROYAL TENNIS COURT.

40. THE PRINCE REGENT'S COMMAND

CHAPTER 6

THE MEMBERS TAKE OVER

Yes tribute asking at your hands
To strike a ball in the Dedans,
Or in the Grille, or lay a chase,
Or play upon the Tambour's face.

The word 'Club' will now be used to describe the Royal Tennis Court membership, although as Tony Negretti, Honorary Secretary and Treasurer from 1947 to 1973 and President from 1973 to 1987, was at pains to point out, 'We are more a society for the preservation of tennis at Hampton Court Palace than a club.'

From the very start of the new arrangement the Palace attempted to draw a clear line between internal (including all aspects of play) and external responsibilities. This policy, at first strictly enforced, was to cause severe financial difficulties for the Club.

Following the Prince Regent's command in January 1818, Thomas Hardwick, the Clerk of the Works, drew up an estimate for the necessary repairs. These included: repairing the roof timbers, another retiling of the roof, repairing the boarded ceiling, a complete repainting of the court and colouring of the walls. Hardwick's estimate for this work amounted to £835. He also added: 'There is a House adjoining, belonging to the Master of the Tennis Court, which is out of Repair, but this is not taken into consideration in the Estimate.' [1] The response of the Office of Works was to sanction only those repairs needed to keep the building 'weathertight', so leaving all the internal works to the new committee.[2]

The first known committee-appointed marker was John Case, who started around 1820. There are indications that he was only employed on a part-time basis at first, but as the court got busier he needed help and his son Henry was taken on as an assistant. When Henry left in 1843 John was joined by his nephew Joseph Case.[3] In Victorian times these assistants were referred to as 'boys'. The term *marker* was used at the Royal Court throughout this century: it was not until early in the next that the Club fell into line with other courts and the markers became known as *professionals*. In 1843 Case's terms of employment changed: he was no longer a salaried employee, but engaged on an annual contract and acted more as a manager.

As the Club became more active many London-based members would set aside a whole day for play, travelling down by rail to Surbiton (then the end of the line) and walking to the ferry at Ditton to cross the Thames to the Palace. Luncheon was usually supplied by Case, who was said to serve 'excellent crusty rolls and ale,' or the players could dine at The Mitre, opposite the Trophy Gate entrance on the West Front. For those not wishing to sample Case's beer there was the excellent water that flowed from a spring in Coombe Wood, some three miles away, through conduits laid down by Cardinal Wolsey.[4]

One man who would have been familiar with the new Club was Edward Hughes Ball-Hughes, known as the 'Golden Ball'. A Regency dandy and notorious gambler, he inherited an immense fortune on coming of age in 1819, and was reputed at the time to be the richest commoner in the land. In 1824 he purchased the Oatlands Estate, on which was situated Oatlands House, a large mansion on the southern side of the Thames, five miles upstream of Hampton Court. The estate, which comprised over 3,200 acres, included much of present-day Walton, Weybridge and Byfleet. A gifted sportsman, the very first thing he did at Oatlands House was to demolish part of the stables and erect a Tennis Court. Reckless, in both his spending and his gambling, by 1829 he was broke. In an attempt to evade his creditors Ball-Hughes fled to France. The estate was put up for sale in lots, but the house failed to reach the reserve, so was subsequently let to Lord Francis Leveson-Gower in 1830. The stables were a third of a mile from the house, which Lord Leveson-Gower found inconvenient, so he had a new yard set up closer to the house. Unfortunately, he did not require the Tennis Court, which was pulled down along with the old stables, thereby making it a candidate for the tennis court with the shortest life: it only stood for five or six years. Ball-Hughes continued to play tennis in Paris.

41. EDWARD HUGHES BALL-HUGHES

The Regency dandy who built
the Court at Oatlands House.

There is a certain irony in the fact that it was Ball-Hughes who built the tennis court at Oatlands, and not one of the two enthusiastic royal tennis players who had lived there previously. Perhaps the close proximity of the tennis facilities at Hampton Court Palace would explain it. The first owner of Oatlands had been Henry VIII who built a Palace there in 1537. This Palace fell into disrepair and was finally pulled down during the Commonwealth. After the Restoration the land returned to the Crown and Oatlands House was erected on the same site. In 1789, the Duke of York purchased the property and expanded the estate. This was at the very time the Duke was said to have played tennis virtually every day. His career as a soldier did not allow him to spend much time at Oatlands, and after the Duchess died in 1820 the house and the estate was put up for sale — after a protracted negotiation the new owner was Edward Hughes Ball-Hughes.[5]

42.   J. EDMOND BARRE

On several occasions the Royal Tennis Court was visited by leading French players, the most notable of these being Edmond Barre, one of the game's greatest world champions who held the crown from 1829 to 1862. Another was M. Antoine Mosneron, the world's leading amateur. Louis Labbé was another. Sir Spencer Ponsonby-Fane, who later became the President of Club, remembered these three as early as 1835. He described Labbé as 'a little fat man, with a red handkerchief tied round his protuberant belly, and another round his head.'[6] He was obviously one of the game's great eccentrics. He was said to have distinguished himself when he once played Ball-Hughes in Paris using a boot-jack instead of a racket. On other occasions he played a match with a marker on his back, for a large wager, and with a donkey fastened to him. It is said he won both matches.

Barre once played an exhibition match at Hampton Court with Labbé, Mosneron and Cox, in the presence of William IV's Queen Adelaide.[7] The play was described as brilliant, but which Cox this was is uncertain. Philip Cox, known as 'Old Cox', had been the lessee of the Haymarket Court and was the World Champion until deprived of it by Barre. One of Cox's sons, William, was also a fine player.

Sir Spencer Ponsonby-Fane was one of a series of members who were to give outstanding service to the Club, often travelling down by gig from London with his brother Frederick (later Lord Bessborough) to spend the whole day playing. At times they would meet up with Charles Taylor, the leading amateur, who would travel from Southampton twice a week. Others were Frederic Micklethwaite, James Wilde (later Lord Penzance) and Edward 'Popes' Bligh, a former winner of the Haymarket Gold Racquet.[8] The Duke of Wellington was often at Hampton Court, visiting his mother Lady Mornington who had a Grace-and-Favour apartment there, so it is more than likely that he used the Court.[9] The Duke was a keen tennis player and had his own court at his family home, Strathfield Saye; by coincidence, part of his mother's apartment extended into the southern end of the old Henrican Court and the garden between the old

Court's east wall and Broadwalk is still known today as 'Lady Mornington's Garden'.

Henry Case continued as assistant marker until 1843, when he moved to take charge of the new court at the Marquess of Salisbury's Hatfield House. He was to return to Hampton Court, as Head Marker, five years later, on the death of his father.[10] 1843 was also the year that the windows on the west side of the Court were glazed to prevent the driving rain from entering. This was some 200 years after the roof had been put on. However those on the east side were to remain open for a further 40 years.[11] The glazing costs were met by a special appeal to the members.

Apart from the new windows, little is known of the condition of the Court in the early days of the nineteenth century. Ponsonby-Fane described it as 'a good deal neglected,' even though play was flourishing. A Committee Minute Book that goes back to 1844 contains a great deal of useful information covering over 100 years of the Club's history and it shows there were regular surpluses in the annual accounts during the eighteen-forties.

A committee meeting was held on 13th April 1844 when four members were present: Lieutenant-General Sir Edward Bowater, Mr Charles Bayley, Captain Charles Corkran and Captain James Cuthbert. They reported a balance of £74 1s. 3½d., and it was decided, because of heavy expenditure, to enforce the original rule that no person, except Officers quartered in the neighbourhood, should be allowed to subscribe less than the sum of £3 3s. 0d. This payment of three guineas was not an annual subscription: it appears to have entitled the subscriber to life membership. The Officers were allowed to join for one guinea.

About this time John Arthur Lambert became the Honorary Treasurer, the first person known to have fulfilled the role. He was the first of several members who were to give exceptional service to the Club. A life-long soldier, he joined the Grenadier Guards in 1835 as an eighteen-year-old Ensign. As was the practice at the time he purchased his first three commissions, but in 1854 he was promoted to Colonel on merit. Further advancement followed, and he reached the rank of General in 1877. Three years later he was appointed Honorary Colonel of the 89th Princess Victoria's (Royal Irish Fusiliers). He was also a local Justice of the Peace, and resided at Thames Ditton where he owned Weston House on the Green. General Lambert was the Treasurer of the Royal Tennis Court for over 40 years

43. CAPTAIN JAMES CUTHBERT

44. GENERAL JOHN ARTHUR LAMBERT

Honorary Treasurer 1844-1887

and never missed a committee meeting between 1851 and 1885, forty-five in all; he finally stepped down in 1887, a few months before he passed away.

John Lambert must have been a respectable player, as he would often partner Charles Taylor on court. Taylor, who gave up playing singles early in his career, was a magnificent cricketer and billiards player, as well as being the amateur champion of English tennis from about 1843 to 1859. He was, though, never quite as good as his great French rival, Antoine Mosneron. At one time, for a wager, Taylor took a pony onto the court at Hampton Court and rode it to a three-set victory against a weaker opponent playing conventionally.[12]

The Keeper of the Tennis Court, Major William Beresford, who had been appointed in 1815, was to be the last person to hold this ancient office and he, as his predecessors had done, occupied the Keeper's House and also had control of the apartments at the southern end. Here the players were using a dressing room, which in those days was on the first floor. In 1848 Beresford applied for permission to transfer it to the ground floor. His official request read: 'The Room below is at present floored with stone, which will not suit the use of Men heated with play and I have agreed to go to the expense of having it refloored with planks and the Walls battened and put in order.' No objection was raised by the Board of Works so long as Beresford paid for works himself; the new changing room he created is the one in use today.[13]

45. CHARLES TAYLOR

He once played a match
riding on a pony.

46. PRINCE ALBERT

A photograph taken in 1848,
the year he came to Hampton Court.

It was soon after the work was completed that Queen Victoria's Consort, Prince Albert, came to play. A brass plaque (figure 47) was fixed to a locker set aside for his use — sadly he only came the once. The Committee Minutes record a payment to: 'Winden for engraving a brass plate, 8s. 6d.' Years later, Ponsonby-Fane recalled: 'Some flannel garments and a racket remained for many years until moth and corruption eventually consumed them.'[14]

Another leading French player came that same year, 1848. He was Charles Delahaye, better known as 'Biboche', a flamboyant man and second only to the great Barre. He came over to play a match at the Royal Court against the leading English player, 'Peter' Edmund Tompkins, the Marker at the Brighton Court. The Frenchman won on level terms.[15]

The following year saw the return of Henry Case to Hampton Court and the departure of Joseph Case to Leamington.[16] Henry Case also acted as a manager, with his father's annual contract being adapted for his employment. In 1850 the Club employed a new assistant marker, who was to become one of the game's longest-serving professionals. His name was Thomas Stone, and he stayed with Case for nine years before moving to the James Street Court. His tennis career spanned 74 years, most of them spent in Australia. Henry Case married into the famous Tompkins tennis family; his wife, Martha, was the daughter of the above-mentioned 'Peter'.[17]

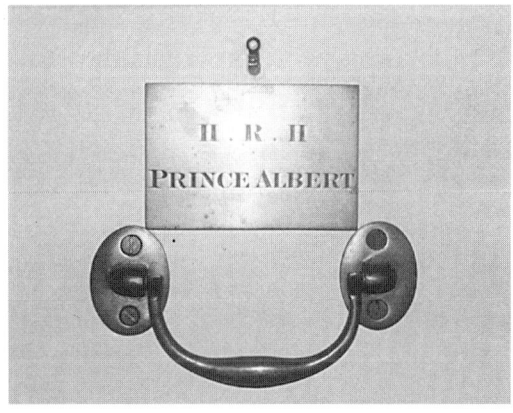

47. PRINCE ALBERT'S PLAQUE

This plaque is still fixed to the
locker in the changing room.

Elaborate plans were drawn up late in 1857 to increase the amount of natural light in the court (figure 49). Six huge skylights, each twenty feet long and four feet wide, three on each side, were to be inserted into the roof. Boxed shafts were then to transmit the light through apertures in the boarded ceiling onto the playing area below. At the same time new outside galleries were to be erected.[18] Many newspaper reports of the day referred to shadows that appeared under the gallery walls which caused severe difficulties to players unfamiliar with the court. It was always suggested that the solution would be the installation of skylights. It might have been the imminent arrival of the Prince of Wales (who was to be taught the game), that prompted the preparation of these plans. Beresford certainly seized the opportunity and attempted to get the east side windows glazed. Using subtle pressure, he wrote: 'I have apprehensions that in cold weather, particularly with an easterly wind, H.R.H. when heated with the exertion of the game may probably catch cold, and I consider that every precaution ought to be adopted to prevent it' (figure 50).[19] The Board agreed and a provision of £170 was entered into the Estimates for 1859-60. This figure though was struck out the following year, for reasons unknown, but it could have been that the Prince by then was playing most of his tennis in the courts at Oxford and Cambridge. The plans for the skylights and those to replace the outside galleries also came to nothing.[20]

48. CHARLES DELAHAYE

Better known as 'Biboche'

It was to Henry Case that the honour fell of teaching the heir to the Throne to play. According to Beresford, the Prince at first came to the Court two or three times a week, and a surviving letter from White Lodge, Richmond Park, the Prince's residence, shows he paid a three-guinea subscription to become a member of the Club.[21] Thomas Stone was later to recall that he came many times to Hampton Court during 1858, always playing a four-handed game, usually taking him (Stone) as his partner against Major Teesdale, his equerry, and Mr Case. They always had lunch in the dedans, brought in a hamper down Tennis Court Lane to the door by the dressing room, which was firmly locked to all and sundry. The only time this rule was relaxed was when Princess Mary of Cambridge came with other ladies to watch the Prince play.[22] The Prince also settled the accounts of other tennis players, the names of Major Lindsay, Mr Tarver and Mr Gibbs appearing on the invoice from Case (figure 51).

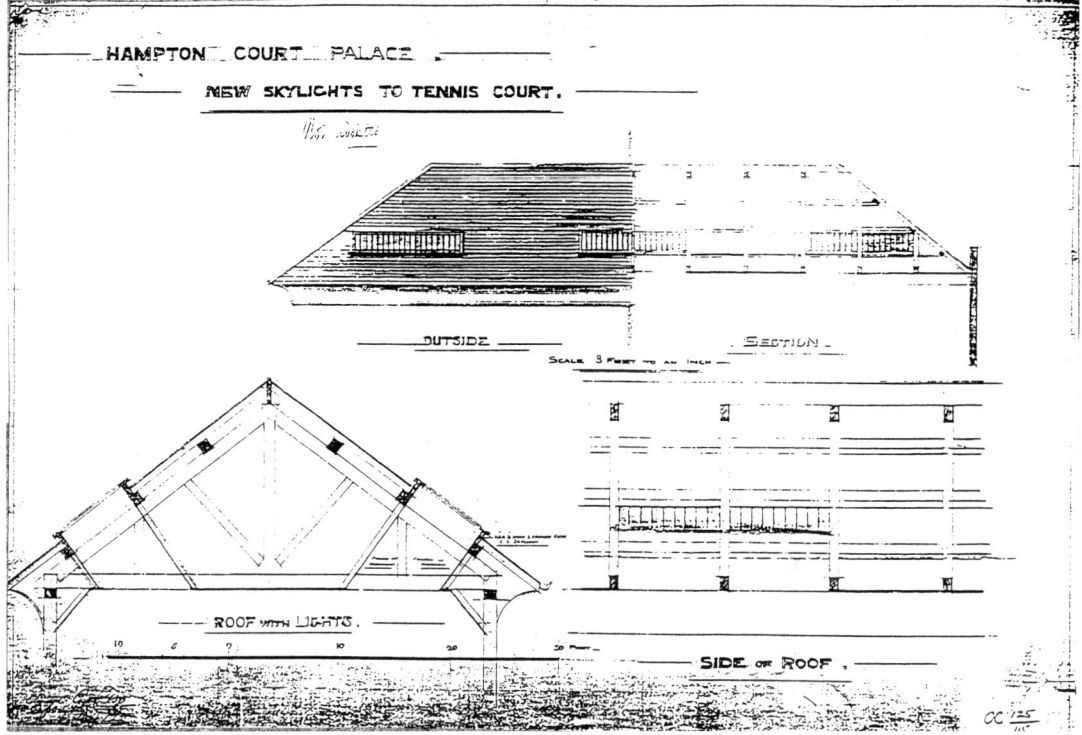

49. PROPOSED SKYLIGHTS

Plans drawn up in 1857 to increase the amount of natural light in the court.

This was a period of relative financial stability, but there was very little play and the Committee felt obliged to pay Case a gratuity each year as compensation. The amount varied from £10 to £30. However, the Club still managed to maintain a balance of over £200 throughout the eighteen-fifties. This was held at the bank, Messrs Shrubsole in Kingston.[23] The Club's reserves though were eroded by the high cost of internal maintenance. In 1862 the Committee attempted to get the Palace to pay the £12 needed to re-board the penthouses. This was rejected, as was another request four years later, for help with repairs to the walls, floor and curtains.[24] More serious was the Board's refusal to repair the outside galleries.

With the 1857 plans for new galleries not implemented, they were in a very poor state by 1870. This prompted Beresford to write to the Palace, warning of the danger to the marker, who had to walk on them daily to discharge his duties. Mr Starie, the Clerk of the Works, who seemed to be no friend of the Club, stated that in his opinion the galleries, which would cost £20 to repair, were 'for the purpose of arranging the large canvas blinds for regulating the admission of light during the play of Tennis' and therefore did not form any part of the main building. The Board decided they should not be repaired at public expense.

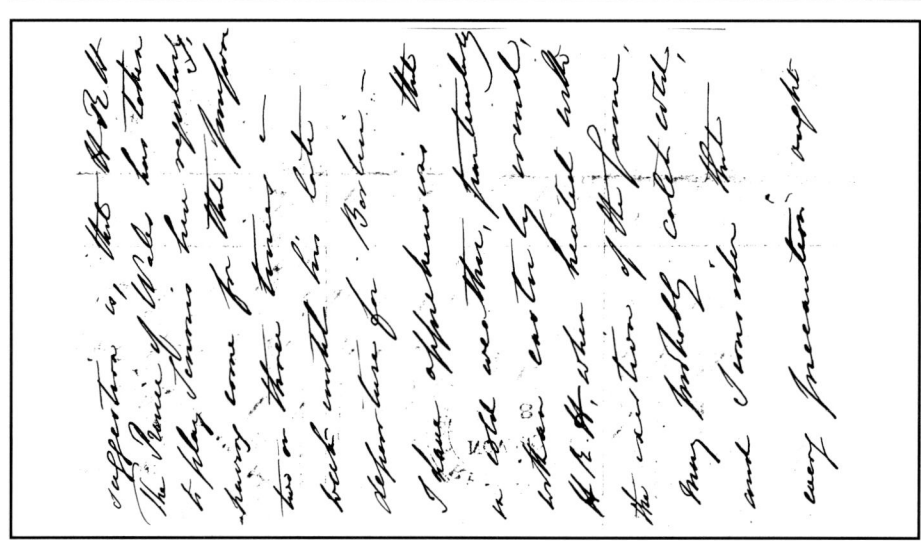

50. WILLIAM BERESFORD'S LETTER

Beresford was furious. In a sharp letter, he informed the Board that the galleries were part of the building, they had always repaired them and he would take no responsibility for them falling down into the public gardens. After a long internal debate, with Starie standing firm, the Board again refused to carry out the repairs. The galleries therefore continued to decay.[25]

Serious losses occurred every year from 1868, and by 1874 the Club was insolvent. Only a loan from the Honorary Treasurer, Lieutenant-General Lambert, kept it going. Letters from Lambert and Beresford were sent to the First Commissioner of Works, begging him to consider accepting responsibility for the interior of the Court. Attached to Lambert's letter was a long list of repairs that were needed — they amounted to a complete refurbishment.[26] After two years of protracted discussion, the Board relented. At public expense the roof and walls were repaired and repainted, the western side windows were reglazed and all the gallery and window nets were repaired or renewed. The dedans and dressing room were also redecorated and, at last, the eastern external gallery was replaced.[27] One peculiarity which was corrected at this time was the lop-sided net. Julian Marshall's *Annals of Tennis*, which were at the time being published as a series of articles in *The Field*, revealed that the net was 4 feet 11 inches high at the net post and 5 feet 5 inches high at the net hook. The problem was solved by the net hook on the main wall being lowered to the same height as the hole in the net post. This enabled Marshall to record as much, when *The Field* sponsored and published his whole work in book form shortly after.[28]

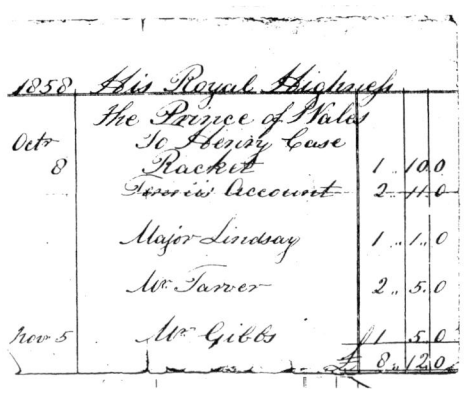

51. PRINCE OF WALES'S TENNIS ACCOUNT

In the meantime there had been several changes of marker. Henry Case died in 1864 and was replaced by John Nightingale who remained for three years with Case's son, Henry John, as his assistant. George Lambert (a future world champion) succeeded Nightingale and looked after the Court for just under two years. He then moved to Lord's, leaving his brother William in charge for the next eleven years, before he too went to Lord's. Another assistant at that time, who, over the years became a highly respected professional, was Edward (Ted) Johnson. He later went to Sir Ivor Guest's new Canford Court, again via Lord's. Tom White took over in 1880 and during his time the assistants included his son Alfred, his grandson Harold, his nephew John, Stanley Lambert (the son of William), John McCann and Henry John Case who returned to the Royal Court for a short spell.

It is possible that one of the game's great champions, Edmund Tompkins (son of 'Peter'), may have worked for a short time at the Royal Court. Following the closure of the James Street Court in 1866 he was known to have been living just across the river in Molesey before he took the lease of the Merton Street Court in Oxford.[29] He was staying with his sister Martha, Henry Case's widow. There is a reference to him as a professional at Hampton Court in an article in *The Field* on the occasion of the 400th Anniversary of the Court in 1929.

The 1876 court restoration had taken four months to complete and had caused severe financial hardship to the marker, William Lambert. On March 3rd 1877, several of the top players took part in a benefit match for him. John Tompkins (the Brighton marker) played in a three-handed match against William and his brother Charles (the Hatfield marker). Tompkins was the victor giving odds of half-fifteen for a bisque. This exchange of odds was common practice in times past. The match was followed by a singles between George Lambert, the champion, and Mr C.E. Boyle, a leading amateur, who received half-thirty but lost by three sets to love. At the end of this match the dedans proposed a fourth set, with Lambert giving Mr Boyle half-thirty and a bisque; this Mr Boyle won 6-4. The days entertainment concluded with a four-handed match, the Rev. F.C. de Crespigny and William Lambert defeating Mr Balfour and Charles Lambert.[30]

The Reverend Frederick J. Champion de Crespigny gave a lot of his time to the Royal Tennis Court, serving on the Committee for 21 years. He came from a wealthy family with a strong naval tradition, his father serving under Nelson and Collingwood. He, though, did not follow that path, but went into the church and became Vicar of The Church of St. John the Baptist at Hampton Wick. After his death his widow made an endowment to the church and provided funds for a stained glass window in his memory, which is now set above the vestry door.

George Lambert played several more matches at Hampton Court over the following two years, the results of which are listed below.

21st April 1877	- against Mr Boyle (rec. ½ 30) - Lambert won 3-1.
21st July 1877	- against Edmund Tompkins (rec. 15 for a bisque) Lambert won 2-1.
28th September 1878	- against John Tompkins (rec. 15 for a bisque) Tompkins won 3-0.
1st November 1879	- against William Lambert and Ted Johnson (rec. 15 for a bisque) - George Lambert lost.
	- against William Lambert (rec. 15 and the dedans) 2-1 to George Lambert.

The *bisque* (a point that can be taken at any time during a set) has sadly in recent years become a casualty of the modern handicapping system. Its value is difficult to quantify mathematically, as its worth varies with the guile of its possessor.

The change of heart by the authorities in 1876 had finally acknowledged that a few tennis players could not be expected to maintain a building of such historic national importance, so when another estimate for internal repairs was submitted in 1883, which included £110 for glazing the east side windows, it was accepted, and the Court was finally enclosed in 1884. At the same time the Committee agreed to meet the cost of new wire grills on both sides of the court to protect the glass.[31]

With the windows glazed, no longer did the Court have to be closed during severe weather. An early playbook highlighted the sort of problems the Club used to have. An entry dated January 18th 1881 read: 'Snow all over tennis court floor two inches deep.' [32] Unfortunately, when one problem is solved another often arises — in this case there were two! Firstly, with the loss of the huge canvas curtains, there was no means of controlling the admission of sunlight. Initially, the windows were stippled with a white paint, but this was not satisfactory and in 1898 blinds were put up.[33] Secondly, condensation, which had in the past occasionally caused the court to sweat, became more of a problem. The solution to this will be dealt with in a later chapter.

After the shutdown for the installation of the east-side windows, the Court was reopened on the 14th June 1884 with an afternoon of exhibition matches. First on court was Mr Akroyd who played a three-handed match against Julian Marshall and George Lambert, which they won. The main match though, was between the Hon. Alfred Lyttelton and Thomas Pettitt, who won by three sets to two giving odds of half-fifteen.[34] Pettitt was the hard-hitting unorthodox young professional attached to the Buckingham Street Court in Boston, Massachusetts. He was in fact an Englishman having been born in Beckenham, Kent, but had emigrated from England to America when he was a young lad of seventeen.

The next problem exercising the Committee's mind was the colour of the floor. The natural stone is a beige hue and caused the players difficulty when trying to keep a good sight of the ball. Their solution was to stain it with ink and the Palace agreed to this so long as the Club paid for it. But when the scheme went to the Lord Chamberlain's Office for approval, Sir Spencer Ponsonby-Fane (who was obviously not party to the proposal) was horrified and stopped it at once. He was concerned that 'colouring the floor with ink or other material containing acids of any kind might destroy the surface of the stone or the cement fixings.' Sir Spencer was at the time Comptroller of Her Majesty's Household (part of the Lord Chamberlain's department) and as such was responsible for the Court. The Committee then turned to him to use his influence to allow the floor to be flooded with bullock's blood in order to darken it. There was no objection to this, as it was the accepted method of darkening tennis court floors and had been employed many times before at Hampton Court.[35]

With the new windows in place, the floor darkened and other repairs completed, the Court was in perfect condition in May 1885 for the first World Championship match ever to be played on it. The match was between the holder, George Lambert, who had been World Champion since 1871, and Tom Pettitt. Pettitt, an Englishman, was no stranger to the court. As has been seen, he came over the year before and played a match against the leading amateur of the day, the Hon. Alfred Lyttelton. The World Championship was the first to be contested using the modern format of the best of thirteen sets, played over three days. One hundred and forty spectators a day were accommodated. As well as the dedans, there were another two rows of seating in each of the upper end galleries and one in the side gallery. Half of those in the side gallery on the service side were allotted to professionals and half to ladies. A feature during matches at Hampton Court in Victorian times was always the large number of ladies who came to watch. Lambert who was 43 years of age and 18 years older than Pettitt, lost by seven sets to five.[36] A detailed account of this match can be found in Appendix 12. Pettitt returned to the Royal Court two years later, again to play Alfred Lyttelton. This time he gave his opponent half-fifteen and a bisque, but the result was the same, three sets to two to Pettitt.

The Honourable Alfred Lyttelton was a great supporter of the game and of the Club. The youngest of four famous brothers, he was a gifted sportsman who represented Cambridge at five different sports — athletics, cricket, association football, tennis and rackets. He played both football and cricket for England. His tennis record is impressive: he won the MCC Gold Racquet twelve times between 1882 and 1895. At cricket his role was that of a wicket-keeper who could be relied upon to make a few runs. Perhaps his most remarkable achievement came in 1884 when England was playing Australia at The Oval. Australia was in a commanding position with 532 for six wickets. Every other member of the team had been asked to bowl, when in desperation Lord Harris finally turned to Lyttelton. Without removing his pads, he bowled a series of lobs and got the last four Australian batsmen out in

52. THE HONOURABLE
ALFRED LYTTELTON

eight overs, for only eight runs. He also had a political career as the Liberal Unionist MP for Warwick and Leamington from 1895 to 1906. In 1903 he was appointed Colonial Secretary.[37]

Following his world championship victory, Pettitt made some extraordinary accusations against George Lambert. Difficulties were arising between Pettitt and Charles Saunders, the challenger, during negotiations for his first defence of the title. Pettitt was insisting that the match should take place at the Boston Athletic Association Court (then his home court) and that American balls be used. To justify this stance, Pettitt implied that he had had to play at Hampton Court to gain the title — effectively Lambert's home court — and had to play with unfamiliar English balls. He further made the unsubstantiated allegation that Lambert had been secretly training at the Royal Court for four months prior to

the match. In fact Lambert had not played at Hampton Court for 17 years, with the exception of perhaps half a dozen exhibition matches. Their respective backers had agreed that the match be played on one of two neutral courts, Manchester or the Royal Court. The choice between the two was decided by the toss of a coin in the MCC committee-room, in the presence of Mr Perkins (the Secretary of the Club), and Julian Marshall and J.M. Heathcote, acting for Pettitt and Lambert, respectively. The negotiations for the match, which were conducted through the columns of *The Field*, became so heated that the newspaper had to warn Pettitt that they would cease to publish his letters unless he moderated his language. The outcome of all Pettitt's paranoia was that the world championship match of 1890 was played in the most peculiar circumstances. The venue, a neutral one, was the new St. Stephen's Green Court attached to the Dublin home of Sir Edward Guinness. This court was unique in having black marble walls and floor, with the walls polished. It also had a low play line. The balls were French and there was no practice allowed before the match —

53. THOMAS PETTITT AND GEORGE LAMBERT

not even a 'knock up'! These demands nearly cost Pettitt dear, for he went three sets to one down on the first day, before he recovered to retain the Championship on the third day.[38]

The Club's finances had improved by 1887 when General Lambert stepped down, leaving a balance of £144. The following resolution was carried at a committee meeting on January 8th 1887:

'The committee wish to record their grateful thanks to Gen. Lambert for the benefit he has conferred on the tennis players at Hampton Court by his unremitting care for the well-being of the court, supervision of the

54. 1885 WORLD CHAMPIONSHIP GROUP

l to r: Top row: General John Lambert, Alfred Tompkins, Ben Peggs, Bill Holden (marker),
~~~~~~~, ~~~~~~~~, Tom White, George Frederick Savage and James Fennel.

Seated: John Tompkins, Charles Saunders, Tom Pettitt, Edmund Tompkins
(*former World Champion*), George Lambert and J. Alfred Tompkins.

markers and the accurate accounts kept for a period exceeding 40 years.   They consider that the prosperity of the tennis court at the present time is largely owing to his kind exertions and regret much that he finds himself compelled to retire.' [39]

Edward Rutter succeeded General Lambert as Treasurer, and like his predecessor he was effectively in full control of the Club because the Treasurer's duties still embraced those that are now carried out by the Honorary Secretaries. Rutter had joined the Committee in 1882 and was to serve for 26 years, of which nine were as Treasurer. He was a triplet, and he and his two brothers were something of a curiosity during their schooldays at Rugby, which is where his great passion for cricket blossomed. After his education he became a civil engineer and worked in the rapidly expanding railway industry, spending several years of his early working life in the United States. He developed into a first-class cricketer playing for Middlesex for eight years as a bowler, when the County was based at the old Princes Club in Hans Place. In 1865 he played his first match for the Free Foresters, a wandering cricket club, and became their Secretary five years later, a role he fulfilled for 40 years. He was also a member of the MCC Committee and his love of cricket led to him publishing his semi-autobiographical *Cricket Memories* in 1925.

A series of benefit matches was arranged in the summer of 1889 for the marker Tom White, to celebrate his 50th birthday. Before the introduction of artificial lighting, the main tennis season ran from the start of April to the end of July. Three matches were arranged, the first played on May 25th. This was between the English champion, Charles Saunders, and the Hon. Alfred Lyttelton, who received half-fifteen and a bisque and won by three sets to one. During this match, there was an incident involving a lady watching from the upper gallery at the hazard end. She narrowly avoided being struck by a ball, following a hard misdirected force from Mr Lyttelton. This had the distressed amateur apologising profusely for the 'attempt on her life'! The second match was between Tom White's son, Alf, and the up-and-coming future world champion, Peter Latham. The match on June 22nd was played on level terms and won by White, but because of poor advertising not many tennis enthusiasts pre-booked seats, and as

55. EDWARD RUTTER

Honorary Treasurer 1887-1896

the match took place on a very hot day, few of the visitors could be tempted off the Palace lawns. The poor attendance therefore badly affected the amount of money that was raised for White senior. He suffered similar problems when the third and last of these matches took place on July 26th. On that occasion he took to the court himself, against the leading amateur, Mr Russell D. Walker.[40]

The floor continued to cause concern, and in 1891 paint was applied. This was not successful because the successive applications of bullock's blood had made it greasy and marble-like. So in 1896 the Committee sent five samples of treated stone to the Palace for examination, with a request to 'rub off' a sixteenth of an inch of the court floor to enable the selected agent to bond properly. The samples were mainly branded products already in general use on tennis and rackets court floors, but included was a strange concoction of logwood and copperas, vinegar, bruised nut falls and tincture of iron — all these were to be applied hot! Sensibly, the Committee's choice was a red rackets court paint. However, all the products were rejected, again for fear of damage, so the floor had to wait until 1903 before it was ground down and stained, using Bickley paint.[41]

Joseph Bickley was a man with an enormous amount of experience of the requirements for playing surfaces. He was responsible for building most of the tennis and rackets courts around the turn of the century. Tennis players today are still playing on Bickley surfaces in about half of the courts in use in England and America.

There had been a surge in play in 1886 when the old Prince's courts closed. There were no other Central London clubs to play in, except for Lord's, and to play there one had to be a member of the Marylebone Cricket Club. This busy period lasted only until 1888, when The Queen's Club opened its two new courts and allowed Prince's members to use them — a year later the new Prince's Club opened. E.B. Noel states that the Royal Court at this time was awash with celebrated players: J.M. Heathcote (a seventeen-times winner of the MCC Gold Racquet), his brother C.G. Heathcote, Julian Marshall, the Hon. Alfred Lyttelton, Sir Courtenay Boyle, R.D. Walker, Lord Wimborne (owner of the Canford court) and the former world rackets champion, Sir William Hart Dyke, to name but a few.[42]

There followed a serious decline in the amount of play and associated income. The only regular source of income the Club had was a court fee of sixpence a set.[43] Golf and motoring were having an effect, as they were attracting the affluent away from tennis. By 1895 the Club was again facing bankruptcy and a meeting was convened at Lord's, with Sir Spencer Ponsonby-Fane in the Chair, where it was decided that an annual subscription should be introduced. The amount proposed was a £1 a year, which was to be collected by banker's order. A circular was sent to members explaining the situation and the recommended solution (figure 57).

At a meeting of the Committee held on January 20th 1896, Ponsonby-Fane reported, in response to the circular which he had issued to old subscribers inviting an annual subscription of £1, that:

> 'Fifty-five had agreed to the proposal; fourteen had refused for various reasons, but raised no objections to the proposal; and more than 130 had not replied. The Committee considered this to be a general acquiescence to the scheme, and resolved "That the Royal Tennis Club cannot be carried on its present form, and that it shall be reconstituted on the following conditions: First, old subscribers of £3 3s. who consent to an Annual Subscription of £1, to be Members of the New Club and to have the privilege of playing in the Court at 1s. 6d. for first hour and 1s. for second hour or part of it; Second. Old subscribers of 3 Guineas who decline to subscribe annually, or who have not replied to the Circular, to lose the privilege of Membership — but to be eligible at any time to resume, on the payment of £1 annually; Third, New Members who join after January 1896 to pay an Entrance Fee of £2 and a Subscription of £1 annually; Fourth, Officers of the Regiment stationed at Hounslow and Hampton Court to be admitted to the privileges of Members for a year on payment of £1; Fifth, Members to give a Bankers Order for their subscriptions, to the Treasurer of the

Club, payable on 1st Jan in each year." A new Committee was nominated to consist of the following: President, Sir Spencer Ponsonby-Fane, Treasurer and Secretary, Mr. J.J. Freeman; Committee — Sir C.E. Boyle, Col. S. Corkran, W.A. Cockerell, A. Kennedy, E. Law, B. Paget, E. Rutter, Gen. Lord W. Seymour and A. Vesey, with power to frame the rules of the Court and deal generally with the affairs and funds of the Club. At a meeting of the new Committee, held on January 27th, the above resolutions were adopted, and it was resolved that a summary of them be sent to all old subscribers who had consented to pay the annual subscription.'

56. SIR SPENCER PONSONBY-FANE

President of The Royal Tennis Court
1896-1915

J.J. Freeman was instructed to open an account at Coutts & Co., in London's Strand, for members to make their payments into.

Sir Spencer Ponsonby-Fane was the first President of the Royal Tennis Court, holding office from 1896 to 1915. The sixth son of the fourth Earl of Bessborough, Sir Spencer was born in London in 1824 and adopted his full title on inheriting Lady Georgina Fane's estate of Brympton d'Evercy in Somerset in 1875. His lifetime overlapped with the reign of five British monarchs. He progressed to many important posts in the Foreign Office, including that of private secretary to Lord Palmerston. He brought back from Paris the treaty ending the Crimean war. As well as becoming Comptroller of the Accounts of the Lord Chamberlain, he was Gentleman Usher to Queen Victoria and was much involved in affairs at Court. Sir Spencer's great passion was cricket where he always refused to wear pads. After playing for the MCC as a teenager, he was elected to membership in 1840. For about half of his 74 years' membership, then a record, he was MCC's Honorary Treasurer and was several times invited to become President, but declined. He was a Trustee from 1900 until his death in 1915. Sir Spencer was responsible for starting the collection of pictures in the Long Room at Lord's, which he began to assemble in 1864. He was a keen amateur actor and said to be the most charming and courteous of men. From 1890 until his death Sir Spencer was President of Somerset County Cricket Club. In 1845 he was one of four founder members of I Zingari ('the gypsies'), perhaps the most famous of nomadic cricket clubs, which survives to this day. From its inception it was decreed that 'the entrance fee be nothing and that the annual subscription do not exceed the entrance fee'. Membership was limited to 45 and Sir Spencer was appointed the first 'Governor' of I Zingari.[44]

John Joseph Freeman was another of those who worked tirelessly on behalf of the members. A resident of nearby Shepperton, he lived at Halliford House (now Halliford School). By day he was a solicitor, practising across the river in Walton on Thames. His interest in the legal system led to him becoming a Justice of the Peace and subsequently the Chairman of the local Spelthorne bench of magistrates. He was later to run the Club almost single-handedly for many years, often bearing a large part of the costs himself.[45] In 1913, he retired as Honorary Secretary, but remained Treasurer for two more years before succeeding Sir Spencer Ponsonby-Fane as President. He was a good player, renowned for his ability consistently to achieve short chases, and he regularly turned out for club matches until he was well over 70 years of age — then he was often four times older than some of his opponents. He was one of the first to be invited by the Duke of Fife to serve on the Committee of the Sheen Tennis Court Club, when the Duke agreed to his court becoming a private members' club. It was through the generosity of J.J. Freeman that one of the famous *David and Bathsheba* pictures, which are of such interest to tennis enthusiasts, now hangs in the MCC Museum at Lord's. The picture had been part of Julian Marshall's collection and was purchased by Freeman shortly after his death in 1903. There are eleven of these pictures, which are mainly attributed to sixteenth-century artists, and central to them all is a tennis court with a game in progress, although each artist brings an individual interpretation to his work.[46] His son, T. Freeman, was also a member of the Club. A good player, he represented Oxford University in 1914, but sadly he lost his life in the First World War.[47]

The early ledgers containing the Club's accounts in the Bank's archives read like a *Who's Who* of the tennis world.[48] Heading the list of subscribers was H.R.H. The Prince of Wales. He continued to contribute until he acceded as Edward VII in 1901, when he increased the amount from his Privy Purse to £5 a year. His son continued to support the Club when he became King George V in 1910, sending the same amount until he died in 1936 (except for the duration of the First World War). Other notable members were: The Duke of Wellington (the third Duke), who had the court at Strathfield Saye, the Duke of Fife (owner of the Sheen court), Lord Windsor the Earl of Plymouth, who owned the court at Hewell Grange, the Hon. Alfred Lyttelton, Samuel Heilbut, who built a court at his house at Holyport, Julian Marshall, H.E. Crawley (a future amateur champion) and C.G. Heathcote. J.M. Heathcote was a member of the Club, but surprisingly decided not to contribute to the new scheme. The names of those on the new Committee of course appear and some other keen supporters were: Sir Godfrey Lushington, His Honour Judge Vernon Lushington, Sir E.B. Medlycott, Sir Augustus Paget, Sir Charles Pontifex, Sir R.E. Webster, General Sir Henry Ewart and Spencer Gore (the first Wimbledon Lawn Tennis Champion). The man that Gore defeated in that first ever Wimbledon final in 1877, William C. Marshall, was also a member. He was a fine tennis player, the best at Cambridge during his university days, following which he became an architect and designed several tennis courts, including those at The Queen's Club. Out of the 22

ROYAL TENNIS COURT CLUB.

HAMPTON COURT PALACE.

Lord Chamberlain's Office,

St. James's Palace, S.W.

I regret to inform you that there is a very serious prospect of this old Club coming to an end.

The Tennis Court was granted to the Club in the early part of the Century and is structurally maintained by the Office of Works. Of later years a Residence for the Marker has also been granted to the Club.

The Club has been carried on by a payment of £3 on entrance of New Members, and a charge of 6d. a set for Play in the Court. In the last 3 years the entrance of New Members has dwindled to 5 or 6 annually, and the receipts for Play in the Court have very considerably diminished. The Expenses may be set down at about £100 a year including the wages of the Marker and a boy, and the average cost of Balls, Nets, Linen, Coals and other necessary expenses.

The Receipts have fallen in the same period to about £70 a year, and the excess of Expenditure has been met hitherto from a reserve fund, which is now all but exhausted.

It would certainly be a calamity if this Royal Grant of the enjoyment and using of the Tennis Court was allowed to lapse, for it is extremely doubtful if it could ever again be renewed under present conditions with regard to the maintenance of the Palace by the Office of Works.

At a meeting of some members of the Managing Committee held at Lords on the 29th July, it was resolved to appeal to the Members of the Club to consent to pay a small annual subscription of say £1, to meet the annual expenditure and to re-establish the Reserve Fund which is now practically exhausted.

I am aware that many members of the Club have ceased to play at Hampton Court, and may perhaps consider that their original Entrance Fee should free them from further charge; but I venture to appeal to them from the interest which they have formerly taken in the Game there, to assist the Committee to resuscitate the Club, and to preserve the Grant to them from the Crown of this fine old Historic Court.

Will you kindly inform me if you are willing to consent to this proposal.

Yours very faithfully,

SPENCER PONSONBY FANE.

(President of the Club.)

57. 1895 MEMBERS CIRCULAR

entrants for that first Wimbledon, over a third were members of the Royal Tennis Court. Sir Godfrey Lushington was a good tennis player, the winner of the Oxford Gold Racket in 1853; he loved the game and continued to play until a great age.[49]

Although the eighteen-nineties were desperate times for the Club financially, royal interest revived. Prince George of Wales (later George V) played several times, most controversially on 22nd June 1894, the day before his first child, the future Edward VIII, was born. The Prince's brothers-in-law, the Princes Adolphus and Francis of Teck also played at Hampton Court, as did Prince Philippe, duc d'Orléans, who as the eldest great-grandson of Louis Philippe I, the last King of France, had the strongest claim to the former French throne.[50]

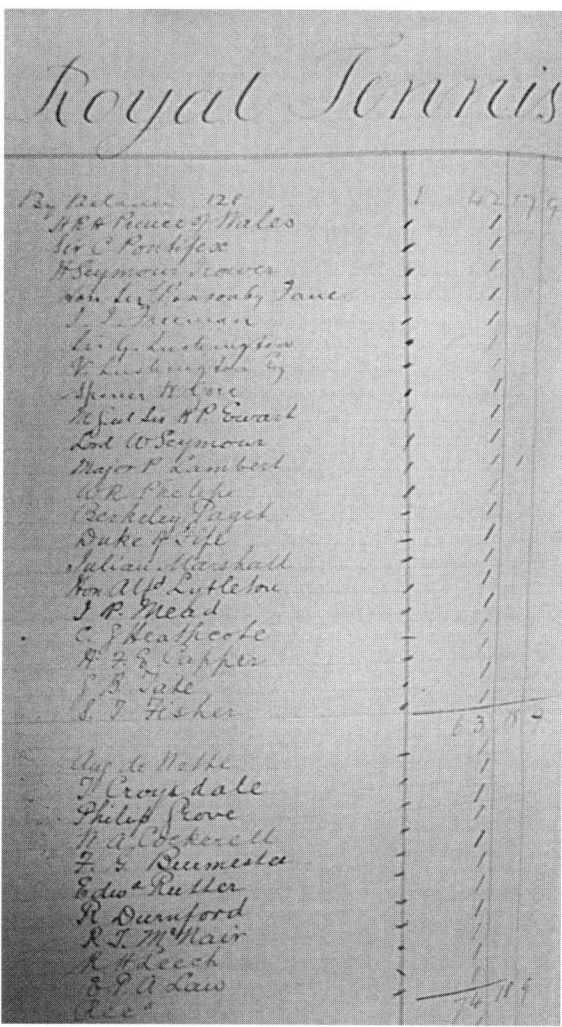

Court usage remained low until the end of the century, when there was for a short time, another surge in play. This occurred when the old tennis court at Lord's was pulled down and replaced by the current one. During the rebuilding, the Committee at Hampton Court decided that members of the MCC would be treated as Honorary Members of the Royal Court. MCC members then had three courts at their disposal, as Queen's also allowed them to use their two. The Court was at this time in superb condition as it had been thoroughly renovated in the summer of 1898.[51] It will be seen shortly that it would not be long before Lord's was to come to the rescue of the Royal Court.

58. COUTTS BANK LEDGER 1897

An unusual day's play was organised in October 1898 to introduce the young John White, nephew and pupil of Tom, to public exhibition matches. The young assistant marker was first pitted against the formidable Cecil 'Punch' Fairs, a player who would eventually reach the pinnacle of the game. Fairs only gave him fifteen — not enough, as he thrashed young White by two sets to love, twelve games to one.

Sensing the ease of his task Fairs decided to experiment with his game by copying Pettitt's style of play. Despite his emphatic win, it was reported that he showed how a railroad service 'should not be done'; and his hard-straight forces would have 'added to the reputation of a Spanish gunner for wild shooting'. The youngster played better in a second match, gaining victory over his cousin, Alf White, by two sets to love, again receiving fifteen.[52]

Before this chapter concludes there needs to be some mention of a few of the other influential Victorians who served on the Committee.

Amongst them during the 1840s was General Sir Edward Bowater. He was a life-long soldier who had seen service at Waterloo and became equerry to William IV, Prince Albert, and Groom-in-Waiting in Ordinary to Queen Victoria. He served on the Committee of the Royal Tennis Court for at least 16 years. Another who gave a great deal of his time to the Club was Captain James Cuthbert, equerry to the Duke of Cambridge. A chubby man, who seems to have been quite a character, often wearing a nightcap when he played. After his death, his widow set up the 'Cuthbert Fund' for the benefit of the poor of Hampton Court. The Duke of Wellington's second son, Lord Charles Wellesley, was on the Committee from 1846 to 1850. He was a Major-General in the British Army and later Chief Equerry and Clerk Marshall to Queen Victoria. He also served as a Member of Parliament, at first for South Hants and then Windsor. The Third and Fourth Dukes of Wellington were his sons. Towards the end of the eighteen-forties Vice Admiral Henry Seymour joined them.

Another military man of note, General Sir Henry Ponsonby, joined the Committee in the late eighteen-fifties. A distinguished soldier who served in the Crimean War, he became equerry to Prince Albert, and after the death of the Consort, Private Secretary to Queen Victoria, a post held for 25 years. Sir Henry was Keeper of the Privy Purse, and Lord Lieutenant of Ireland. His brother Frederick was a fine tennis player, who represented Oxford in 1859 and 1860, and won the University's Silver Racket in 1859. Seven years later, the Reverend F.J. Ponsonby was appointed Chaplain of the Chapel Royal in the Palace. He served on the RTC Committee for 22 years. These two Ponsonbys were cousins of Sir Spencer Ponsonby-Fane.

Towards the end of the century Sir Courtenay Boyle joined the Committee, serving for nine years from 1887 to 1896. He was a career Civil Servant and accepted authority on Irish affairs, which culminated in his appointment in 1892 as the Permanent Secretary to the Board of Trade. His childhood was spent at Hampton Court Palace where his parents had a Grace-and-Favour apartment. He was an extremely good tennis player, winner of the MCC Silver Racquet in 1878 and 1879, only denied Gold by the legendary J.M. Heathcote. Cricket was another of his passions, at which he was a superb fielder. This led to his developing the skill of playing tennis with his hands, catching and throwing the ball back to his opponent. Contemporary reports speak of his ability to beat anyone encumbered with a racket, including the best professionals of the day. So good at this skill was Mr Boyle (as he was in 1877), that a match was arranged at Lord's against the world champion George Lambert. The match was played at evens, despite the fact that Lambert could give Mr Boyle half-30 when he played with a racket. The three-set match was over in 45 minutes with Lambert only able to secure two games. Mr Boyle then gave Lambert the marker Ted Johnson as a partner, to play another set three-handed, but it made little difference with Mr Boyle winning by six games to one. The apartment his parents occupied in the Palace was adjacent to the Haunted Gallery, and Ernest Law recorded an instance when Sir Courtenay's mother, Mrs Cavendish Boyle, heard in the middle of the night 'a loud and most unearthly shriek, proceeding from that quarter, followed immediately by perfect stillness'. Fearful of fuelling rumours of Catherine Howard's ghost, she kept it quiet for a number of years, only revealing it when a friend said, she too had heard it when staying overnight.

And then there was Ernest Law! A man who loved everything about the Palace, who had been brought up in a Grace-and-Favour apartment that had been granted to his mother, on the death of his grandmother Lady Montgomery. For 34 years until his death in 1930 he lived in another Grace-and-Favour residence, the last remaining Pavilion in Home Park (see Chapter 5 note 48). He extended the Pavilion, with the creation of a new library and by adding extra bedrooms.

As a young man he was called to the Bar, but soon gave up the legal profession because of ill health. He became Comptroller and Secretary of the Provident Institution Savings Bank, and in later life developed an interest in the burgeoning electrical industry and became an Associate Member of the Institution of Electrical Engineers and a Director of the Metropolitan District Railway (now part of the London Underground), and of the London General Omnibus Company.

A Shakespearean scholar and prolific author, he published several books on the Bard and other subjects, including Kensington Palace, and Vandyke's and Holbein's pictures at Windsor Castle. He wrote several guidebooks on various aspects of Hampton Court Palace, but his greatest work was the *History of Hampton Court Palace* published in three volumes between 1885 and 1891.

He was responsible for the re-creation of the knot garden based on old Tudor plans, but he upset many people because of his propensity to claim credit for other palace improvements. In this he was notorious; he had the habit of writing to *The Times* with suggestions knowing full well that they had already been approved, thereby appearing to be the originator. This was all too much for Edwin Chart, the Clerk of the Works, who in 1908 had initiated the excavation of the moat at the West Front, when he discovered that Ernest Law had written an article in *Country Life* claiming credit! Mr Chart immediately disclosed the contents of a memorandum written by a senior officer of the Office of Works, which noted: 'Ernest Law was coming to believe that he had built Hampton Court himself.' Queen Victoria disliked him, and personally intervened to prevent him becoming Curator of the Palace, but after her death he was appointed Surveyor of Pictures.

He not only upset those in high places, but he was also unpopular with local people when he absorbed part of the barge walk (the river towpath) into his garden and followed that up by enclosing over three acres of Home Park for his own use. Unusually, he served two terms on the RTC Committee, from 1896 to 1898 and from 1925 to 1927.

There is no doubt that, without his contribution to the recorded history of the Palace, this present work would be the poorer.[53]

CHAPTER 7

MASTERS AND KEEPERS

For over 350 years Tennis at Hampton Court Palace was under the control of the Master of the King's (or Queen's) Tennis Courts. This post, which embraced all of the sovereign's courts, was one of royal patronage. The Masters had the rights to run the royal courts and received fees for doing so — a few had to pay a token rent for the privilege. They were, however, able to derive additional income from court fees, from the provision of marker's services and by renting out surplus accommodation. Their duties included the maintenance of the courts and their associated lodgings, not only the maintenance of the fabric of the buildings but also the furnishings. In some cases, they even built courts. They were also responsible for keeping the accounts, arranging their sovereign's tennis, and that of other members of the royal family and their guests, and attending the court whenever required. At times, that attendance involved playing themselves, and occasionally instructing, so blurring the distinction between the Masters and the Markers. The Royal Markers on the other hand were normally only concerned with aspects of play, such as the provision of rackets and balls, the cleaning of the courts, marking and teaching.

Some courts had their own Keeper; Whitehall and St James's Palace are examples. Where this occurred the individual court Keeper was answerable to the Master of the King's Tennis Courts. During Queen Anne's reign, the word 'Keeper' was added to the official title, by which time only three royal courts remained — Whitehall, Windsor and Hampton Court.

From Tudor times until the early part of the nineteenth century the fee the Masters received was 8d. a day. To this was added, by the Prince of Wales in 1621, a further £120 a year. From the latter part of the seventeenth century these payments can be traced in their entirety through the surviving Treasury files at the Public Record Office.

The Masters who had direct responsibility for Hampton Court were:

Oliver Kelly	c1540 - 1543	
Thomas Johns	1543 - 1584	
William Hope	1584 - 1591	
Edward Stone	1591 - 1604	
Jehu Webb	1604 - c1621	
John Webb	c1621 - 1656	(jointly with Gedeon Lozier)
Ralph Bird	1656 - 1660	
Thomas Cooke	1660 - 1689	
Henry Villiers	1689 - 1697	
Horatio Moore	1697 - 1708	
Thomas Chaplin	1708 - 1728	
Charles FitzRoy	1728 - 1762	
Richard Beresford	1762 - 1764	

William Chetwynd	1764 - 1765
Richard Beresford (again)	1765 - 1791
Charles Meynell	1791 - 1815
William Beresford	1815 - 1883

The name of Anthony Ansley crops up several times in the King's Privy Purse tennis expenses between 1528 and 1532.[1] It is not clear whether Ansley was the Royal Marker, or the Master of the King's Tennis Courts. In 1528, and again the following year, he was paid 6s. 8d. a quarter, and one entry describes him as a 'Tennis Play Keeper'. It is possible he combined both roles, for he certainly seemed to be in attendance whenever the King played. His daily attendance fee was, curiously, the same amount, 6s. 8d; this may seem a high figure when one considers a skilled tradesman of the time earned 7d. to 8d. a day.[2] However, Ansley also supplied balls, so his fee may have reflected the cost of these. A major supplier of tennis balls from 1460 to 1535 was the Ironmongers' Company and in 1529 they were charging 12d. per dozen.[3]

On balance, it seems more likely that Ansley was the Royal Marker. It was not he who was appointed Keeper of the King's new Tennis Plays at Whitehall in 1533, but the Keeper of the Palace there, Thomas Alvard.[4] When Alvard's successor, Anthony Denny (later Sir Anthony) took over in 1536, the Tennis Plays were again specifically mentioned.[5] Another Keeper comes to light amongst the manuscripts kept at Longleat. One of them lists payments in 1561 by Lord Robert Dudley to: Thomas Whitely, Keeper of the Tennis Court at Whitehall £8 10s. 6d.; the Marker there (whose name is unfortunately missing), 12d; and to two stoppers ten shillings.[6]

Yet an office of 'Master of all the King's Tennis Plays within the Palace of Westminster and elsewhere in England' existed at the same time! Westminster in this case meant Whitehall.[7] The first person known to have held the post was Oliver Kelly. When he was appointed has not been established, but he died in office in 1543.

Kelly was succeeded by Thomas Johns, a page of the Chamber, who was appointed on 9th December 1543.[8] Over a period of 41 years Johns served four monarchs: Henry VIII, Edward VI, Mary I and Elizabeth I. With his appointment comes the first mention of a fee of 8d. a day. Thomas Johns died in 1584.

The next to hold the Office was William Hope, from 22nd April 1584.[9] He died seven years later and was replaced by one of Queen Elizabeth I's footmen, Edward Stone. Stone's Letters Patent are dated 21st December 1592, but his term ran from Michaelmas 1591.[10] Letters Patent were written on open sheets of parchment and conferred a patent or privilege.

The first of the Stuart Masters was Jehu Webb, appointed on 7th February 1604, following the death of Edward Stone (figure 59).[11] He seems to have been favoured by the King. For example, when he was reconfirmed in the Office in 1607 he was additionally granted a moiety of £1,600 of old debts due to the

Crown, which he was then entitled to recover.[12] However, all did not go smoothly for Webb, for two years later he found himself embroiled in a court case. Some of the influential residents of Whitehall, including the Keeper of the Palace Lord Knyvet, along with John Freeburne and Roger Rolles, tried to deprive him of his rights as Master there. They did not succeed and Webb continued to enjoy the benefits of Whitehall.[13]

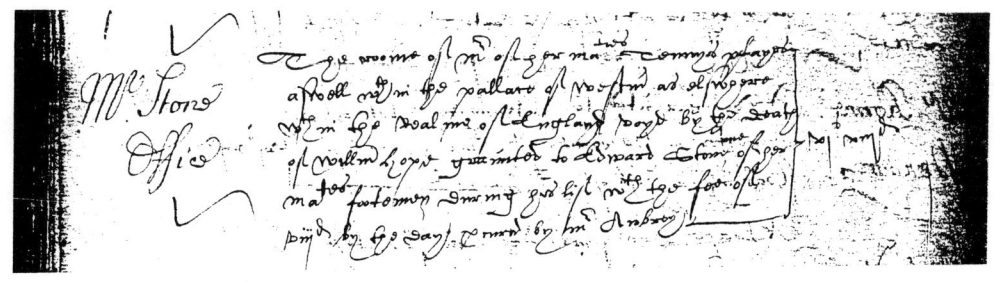

59. EDWARD STONE'S APPOINTMENT

James I entrusted Webb with teaching his son Charles, Duke of York (later Charles I), to play tennis and to provide him with rackets and balls. For this he was paid £20 a year. The first mention of such a payment comes in 1610 when the future king was only ten years old.[14] In 1621 he was granted an annuity of £120 by Charles — by then the Prince of Wales — which was consolidated into the fee structure paid to all of the following Masters.[15] He died shortly afterwards.

In January 1618, John Webb, possibly Jehu's son, and Gedeon Lozier had been granted Letters Patent to succeed jointly to the Office of Master after Jehu Webb's death.[16] In both cases the appointment was for life. They therefore acceded to the Office together around 1621.

John Webb was also a tennis instructor to the Prince of Wales. An original manuscript authorising a payment of £20 to Webb in 1623 came up for auction in the United States in the 1970s. An American member of the RTC bought it and kindly donated it to the club; it is currently on loan to the Wimbledon Lawn Tennis Museum (figure 60). John Webb was the first Master to have the use of the new Keeper's House next to the Tennis Court at Hampton Court when it was built in 1637, but his principal residence was Whitehall. When it came to getting paid Webb had trouble; Charles I seems to have been somewhat tardy when it came to paying for his tennis. After the King's execution in 1649, Webb was owed a considerable sum, £3,308 6s. 4d., some of which was for improvements at Whitehall. He was unable to recover this money when Cromwell came to power, but he did manage to remain Master until his death in 1656. His widow, Anne, then had to wait four years for the Restoration before she could petition Charles II for the monies owed to her late husband.[17]

Although Gedeon Lozier had been appointed joint Master with John Webb, his primary responsibility was the court at St James's Palace. The court there was built by Lozier between 1617 and 1619.[18] It was located opposite the main entrance to St James's Palace in the south-west corner of St James's Field, at its junction with St James's Street and Cleveland Row (part of the old highway linking Charing Cross to Hyde Park). Once the court was operational, Lozier was granted a 31-year lease at 13s. 4d. a year. Although the court at St James's Palace had a house attached, Lozier's main home was in Staines, in the County of Middlesex. After his death in 1631 the lease passed to his wife Mary, but she immediately assigned it to Thomas Hooker. This was probably not Gedeon Lozier's first wish, for in his Will he left the lease of the court to his son Henry Duncumb (possibly an adopted or illegitimate son) if his wife were to die before him. Thomas Hooker suffered from the same problem as John Webb, in that he had great difficulty getting paid by Charles I, who continued to play there regularly.[19] The lease appears to have remained with the Hooker family — after the death of Thomas, his wife took over, their son John claimed it in Cromwell's time, and following the Restoration, Gideon Hooker was the lessee.[20] By 1663 the lease of the court and the adjacent house had passed to Martha Barker who sub-let the tennis court and part of the house to Robert Havercampe.[21] During the Commonwealth, the court was used to garrison troops. After the Restoration, Pall Mall was laid down in 1661, slightly to the north of the old highway, which left the tennis court obstructing its western end. The court was pulled down

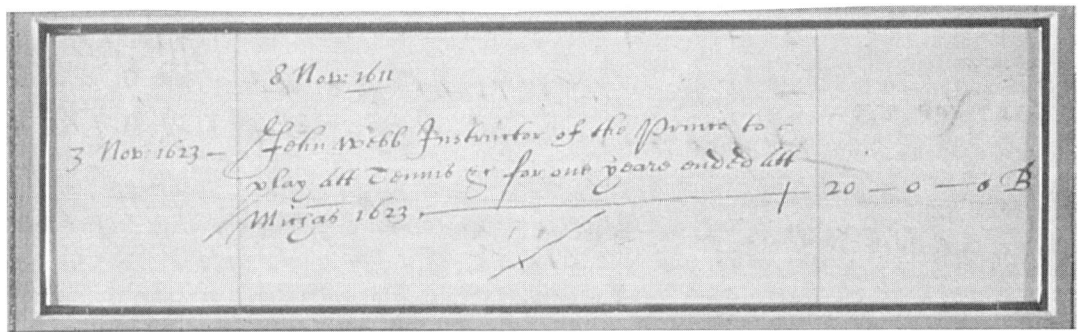

60. PAYMENT TO JOHN WEBB IN 1623

around 1679 and the bricks used as foundation for the road.[22] Technically, Lozier could have taken on Hampton Court and the other royal courts as well, had he not pre-deceased his co-master John Webb. The Hookers do not appear to have had any responsibility for other royal courts.

The Lord Protector, Oliver Cromwell, only had cause to appoint one Master, Ralph Bird. This occurred in 1656 following the death of John Webb. Bird was granted the 'Roome of the Office of Master of Our Tennis Courts' on 8th March 1656.[23] Nothing else is known about him; he probably had no purposeful role knowing Cromwell's distaste for tennis. He did not survive the Restoration. Whether that was because he had died, or was seriously out of favour with Charles II, is not known.

Only one man held the Office of Master during the reigns of Charles II and James II, and he was Captain Thomas Cooke. The date of his appointment is unknown, but it is likely that it followed soon after the Restoration. Before he was granted the position, he had to fight off a challenge from Simon Smith, who had married John Webb's widow. Smith used the marriage as the basis of his claim. As compensation, Smith was granted the office of Master of the Otter Hounds. In his petition to the King for this latter appointment, he expressed his disappointment at not getting the place as Master of the Tennis Courts.[24] That was in August 1660, which would indicate that Cooke had already been appointed. Cooke's name first appears in the surviving documents of the Exchequer in March 1663, when he was paid for erecting the new court at Whitehall on the Brake site[25] — he does not seem to have had any involvement in the 1660-61 refurbishment of Hampton Court, the first warrant with his name on it being dated June 1663.[26]

In 1675 Cooke surrendered his rights at Whitehall to Charles Cornwallis for £1,500, the same amount he had been paid to erect the court there. The Crown then gave Cornwallis a 21-year lease.[27] Thomas Cooke continued to administer Hampton Court, and he and John Hall were granted permission, jointly or separately, to build a new court at Windsor.[28] It is Cooke's name that appears on all the subsequent warrants for the supply of goods to Windsor — which was always to be furnished in the same way as the court at Hampton Court as was, incidentally, Whitehall. By 1689, Cooke was unable to continue in the post because of poor health and was replaced.

Another dispute then broke out between two claimants, Horatio Moore and Henry Villiers. Moore, whose claim was probably the stronger, lost out to Villiers, who was appointed by William III on 4th June 1689.[29] The appointment, though, was only for the natural life of Thomas Cooke. Moore's claim was based on the fact that he had been granted Letters Patent in May 1675, to succeed to the Office of Master on the death of Thomas Cooke, or on the determination of the 21-year lease granted to Charles Cornwallis. The grant had the additional clause requiring an annual payment of 6s. 8d. to the Crown and excluded the benefit of the court that was to be built at Windsor.[30]

The Villiers family were the custodians of Tynemouth Castle and lighthouse in Northumberland. Henry Villiers, who was born in 1658, was the garrison commander there, having been made Captain of his father's company in 1681. The company was absorbed into Colonel Cornwall's Regiment of Foot (later the Norfolk Regiment) in 1687 and he was officially commissioned a captain. By 1702 he had become a colonel in the regiment having purchased the rank, which was the normal practice at the time. The Castle's primary function was the protection of Newcastle, something that became more difficult when the King removed the guns in 1688, causing Villiers to express concern about his company's ability to cope should foreign ships attempt to enter. He was though able to benefit from the substantial income generated by the lighthouse tolls. It was a month to the day after becoming Master of the King's Tennis Courts, that he was appointed Governor of Tynemouth Castle following the death of his father Sir Edward Villiers. His new responsibility may explain the need to have had a deputy to look after his tennis interests. The deputy was John Wright, to whom his fees were assigned in 1690. In 1706, in an extraordinary turn of events, Henry Villiers was charged with smuggling. He was accused of bringing in brandy, claret, white wine, pepper, linen, doeskins and Scottish plaid. He was found guilty and fined a substantial amount, £536. However, this did not seem to affect his status in the community, as he remained Governor at Tynemouth until his death a year later.[31]

Henry Villiers was probably able to overturn Horatio Moore's right to succeed as Tennis Master because of his family's close links to the royal family. His father was an active royalist during the Civil War and was rewarded with Tynemouth immediately after the Restoration; Charles II additionally appointed him Keeper of the Closet. His mother acted as governess to James II's two daughters, the princesses Mary and Anne, both of whom became Queens of England. Henry's elder brother Edward was attached to Mary's court at The Hague when she was the Princess of Orange, and was later created the first Earl of the Island of Jersey and subsequently appointed Lord Chamberlain. A sister, Elizabeth, was a Maid of Honour to Queen Mary, and was a mistress of the Queen's husband, William III. One of his first cousins was the notorious Barbara Villiers (Palmer), a mistress of Charles II, and an earlier cousin, George Villiers, the first Duke of Buckingham, was a particular favourite of James I, to whom he was 'Steenie'.[32]

Henry Villiers' tenure on the office of Master of the King's Tennis Courts was terminated when Thomas Cooke died on the 14th December 1697. Horatio Moore immediately staked his claim, but was challenged yet again, not this time by Villiers, but by Henry Baker, a Treasury solicitor. At a hearing before the Lords of the Treasury, Moore's counsel argued that he had merit, because he had 'carried in a Troop to the King's service'. Moore held the rank of captain, but there is no surviving record confirming him as a commissioned officer, which raises the possibility that the troop in question may have been one of the private militias that were still prevalent at this time. The strength of his claim won through and his appointment was confirmed on 23rd August 1698, with his fees backdated to Michaelmas 1697.[33]

Moore, as seen earlier, acted as a consultant to Sir Christopher Wren during the 1700-02 restoration of the Tennis Court at Hampton Court. When William III died in 1702, Moore had not received his fee for two and a half years, so he petitioned Queen Anne for the arrears. Instead of claiming the usual amount, 8d. a day plus £120 a year, which would have resulted in a claim of £330   8s. 4d., eight shillings was substituted for the eight pence enabling £665 to be entered.[34] The error was presumably discovered as Treasury records show Moore's fee resumed at the annual rate of £132   3s. 4d. (8d. a day with the £120 a year added).

Before becoming Master, Horatio Moore had an interest in and may have been partly responsible for the construction of the Tennis Court in Portugal Street, Lincoln's Inn Fields. In 1656 Moore, in partnership with James Hooker, was developing part of the southern side of the Fields — building houses and selling off leases. That year Hooker and Anne Tyler applied to the Honourable Society of Lincoln's Inn for permission to build a second tennis court in the Fields, in Portugal Street — the other there was known as the Gibbons Tennis court, which was located to the west, in Bear Yard. Moore, who lived in the Fields, made sure he retained the right-of-way into the new tennis court when he sold the lease of the house next to his. The Portugal Street court only remained in play for five years before being converted into a theatre. It was restored to tennis in 1674, but reverted back to a theatre in 1694 and was lost forever. The same fate had overtaken the Gibbons Court in 1660 — that court was eventually consumed by fire.[35]

Moore continued as Master during the early years of Queen Anne's reign, serving until he died in 1708. Until then the Office of Master of the King's Tennis Courts had been granted by royal warrant, and was for life. The only exception had been Henry Villiers who had been granted the Office when Thomas Cooke had become bedridden, and in his case it expired when Cooke died. With the appointment of Thomas Chaplin came a change. Not only was the title altered to include the word 'Keeper', but also the appointment was embodied in Letters Patent under the Great Seal and granted during pleasure. This was during the pleasure of the reigning monarch, who was therefore able to dismiss the Master at any time; the other consequence of the change was that the Letters Patent were determined on the death of the monarch.[36]

Thomas Chaplin was appointed as 'Master or Keeper of Her Majesty's Tennis Courts' on 9th February 1708. He still had to pay the six shillings and eight pence a year for the Office, but the exclusion of the court at Windsor Castle was no longer mentioned.[37] Chaplin immediately found himself fighting a court case trying to preserve his rental income. His ability to charge rents for the properties at Whitehall occupied by the Duke of Monmouth and the Earl of Rochester was challenged, and he lost.[38] Monmouth and Rochester occupied apartments that had been associated with the earlier Tudor Tennis Plays; one may recall that the Great Close Tennis Play was actually converted in 1663 for the benefit of the first Duke of Monmouth. Chaplin was however, allowed to retain the income from other properties at Whitehall, perhaps the best known being the Tennis Court Coffee House, which was adjacent to the grille wall of the Tennis Court — a popular meeting place for the greater part of the eighteenth century.[39] The extent of the property originally granted to Thomas Cooke in 1662, can be seen (marked 35 on figure 30) on the c1670 plan of Whitehall — property from which Villiers and Moore subsequently derived benefit. The court ruling did not affect his ability to collect rents at Hampton Court.

With the new style of appointment, Chaplin's tenure in office lapsed in 1714 when George I came to the throne. He was obviously acceptable to the new King as he was re-granted the office in January 1715; however, when George II acceded to the throne in 1727, Charles Fitzroy was appointed in his place.[40]

The Honourable Charles FitzRoy was sworn into office in February 1728 by the Lord Chamberlain, his cousin the 2nd Duke of Grafton, who may have been instrumental in securing his appointment (figure 61).[41] He was also a distant cousin of the earlier Master, Henry Villiers. As well as his duties as Master of the King's Tennis Courts he had other responsibilities; he was, for instance, appointed George II's Groomporter in 1743. There his principal function was to regulate all matters concerned with gaming, a position from which he granted licences for various activities including the common tennis courts in the Cities of London and Westminster, and the Borough of Southwark.[42] Later in life he assumed the additional title of Scudamore after he married the Honourable Frances Scudamore, the daughter and heir of Sir James Scudamore, the third Viscount Scudamore. His Letters Patent relating to his place as Master of the Tennis Courts were revoked soon after George III came to the throne, as were those for his role as Groomporter. He died in 1782. Charles FitzRoy was a grandson of Charles II. He was the second son of Charles FitzRoy, the 1st Duke of Cleveland, who was the first of Charles II's illegitimate children by Barbara Palmer (afterwards the Duchess of Cleveland).[43]

61. CHARLES FITZROY'S APPOINTMENT

Charles FitzRoy Scudamore's replacement was Richard Beresford. As one of the Beresfords of Fenny Bentley in Derbyshire, he inherited large estates in the Dovedale area to the north of Ashbourne. However, he preferred the excitement of the town, rather than the more remote life at the family seat, so he chose to live in a large house in the centre of Ashbourne. Born in 1731, Richard Beresford was appointed to a number of important posts in his late twenties and early thirties. He became Sergeant-at-Arms to the City of London in 1759 (the last person to hold the office, which was abolished in 1782), Deputy Lieutenant for the County of Derby in March 1762 and in June of the same year, Master of the King's Tennis Courts. He was also a Justice of the Peace. Mysteriously, he was replaced as Tennis Master two years later by William Chetwynd, but returned to office in October 1765 and continued until his death in September 1790.[44] When he passed away, he was described as 'Sir Richard'. He was buried alongside his ancestors at Fenny Bentley, where his memorial is in St. Edmunds Church.

William Chetwynd was appointed Master in May 1764.[45] A member of a prominent Staffordshire family, he was born in 1721 the son of William, the third Viscount Chetwynd of Bearhaven, who held the lucrative position of Master of the Mint for over 40 years. William the Younger served in Parliament as a Whig for the Borough of Stockbridge between 1747 and 1754, and was Equerry to George II during the last two years of the King's life. He was only Master of the George III's Tennis Courts for a year and a half; it is not known why. He succeeded as the fourth Viscount Chetwynd in 1770, taking his seat in the House of Lords three years later. He died in 1791.[46]

62. RICHARD BERESFORD'S APPOINTMENT

This was the Grant received by the Signet Office directly from the King when he appointed Richard Beresford to the post of Master of the King's Tennis Courts. They would attach the Signet Seal to a warrant, which was then passed to the Keeper of the Privy Seal and finally the Keeper of the Great Seal who was the authority for affixing the Great Seal to the Grant.

The next Master was Charles Meynell[47]. Like Richard Beresford he came from Ashbourne, where he lived in a large country house two miles to the east of the town and owned large estates in the surrounding area. He also possessed many dwelling houses and tenements in the City of London.

The Meynell family, who were closely associated with fox-hunting, can trace their ancestry back to the time of William the Conqueror, having descended from powerful Norman barons. Charles Meynell was by all accounts an excellent horseman, on one occasion the winner of a great 16-mile steeplechase in Leicestershire. His father, Hugo, was the High Sheriff of the County of Derby, and he was the first man to breed hounds fast enough to catch foxes in open countryside, and is therefore considered to be the founder of modern fox-hunting in Britain. His grandfather, Littleton Poyntz Meynell, was an interesting character; he incurred the displeasure of the celebrated eighteenth-century writer Samuel Johnson when he lent Frederick, Prince of Wales, £10,000 in return for a bond for £30,000 and a peerage, which was to be honoured when Frederick became king. Unfortunately for Littleton Meynell, that never came to pass. Frederick, who Dr. Johnson described as a scoundrel for having entered into the arrangement, died before his father and therefore never acceded to the throne, ironically, as seen earlier, the result of a tennis injury.

Charles Meynell was appointed Master of the King's Tennis Courts in 1791; but this was not the only responsibility he had in common with Richard Beresford, for they both served as the Steward of the Ashbourne Assemblies. Here they were charged with organising three or four assemblies each winter, which took place in the large mansions in and around Ashbourne, consisting of an evening ball with formal set dances and card games played on side tables.[48] It would therefore seem implausible to think, especially as they were both leading members of Derbyshire's Georgian society, that it was not the influence of Meynell's neighbour that led to him being appointed as his successor.

The court at Windsor had been lost during Beresford's time and at the end of 1793 Whitehall went as well. Charles Meynell immediately put in a claim for compensation. At the time he received £200 from the tennis courts, £35 from Hampton Court and £165 from Whitehall. The Treasury agreed to meet his losses, but instructed the Lord Chamberlain that the compensation was to be for the life of the present Keeper only.[49] He continued to look after the Tennis Court at Hampton Court until his death on 10th April 1815, staying in the Keeper's House on his visits.

The last Master was by far and away the longest-serving. For 68 years the Right Honourable Major William Beresford ruled the Royal Tennis Court with a 'rod of iron'!

There is a family link between Richard Beresford, the earlier Master, and William, but one has to go back four centuries to find it — back in fact to Thomas Beresford whose father fought at Agincourt in 1415. Richard Beresford was descended from Thomas's third son Hugh, while from the sixth son Humphrey came the Irish Beresfords and William.[50] It was therefore not the family connection that gave him a claim to the Office — it is more likely that he secured the post through the influence of his widowed mother who lived in the Clerk of the Spiceries Lodgings, a Grace-and-Favour apartment at the Palace.[51]

The Irish Beresfords were a powerful political family based in County Waterford. William, the second son of Lord Marcus and Lady Frances Beresford, was born in 1797, educated at Eton and Oxford, and appointed Master of His Majesty's Tennis Courts at the age of eighteen. In 1818 he secured the additional appointment of Groom of the Privy Chamber, a position he held for five years.[52]

Beresford was obviously a thorn in the side of the Committee — it was said that he was a tremendous autocrat, always interfering and putting petty difficulties in the way.[53] His officious nature could explain why he was given the job of Tory Whip soon after he became a Member of Parliament following his military career. As a soldier, he was best remembered for leading an expeditionary force from Hounslow to Portugal, where he was the first cavalry officer to land at Lisbon.[54]

63. THE RIGHT HONOURABLE MAJOR WILLIAM BERESFORD

The last Master of the King's Tennis Courts

Beresford's presence at Hounslow could explain why officers from the barracks there were bracketed with those stationed at Hampton Court Palace and given concessionary membership rates by the Royal Tennis Court. He was commissioned a Captain in 1826 and became a Major in 1835. After serving eleven years in the 9th and 12th Lancers, he unsuccessfully contested Waterford in 1837, before entering Parliament in 1841 as one of two Tory Members for Harwich. Although not implicated, he suffered badly from a corruption scandal involving the other member and was deserted by most of his friends — his name was not entered for the 1847 election. Instead he fought and was returned for North Essex which he held until defeated in 1865.[55] He was appointed Secretary at War in Lord Derby's Administration in January 1852 and remained in office for eleven months. The same year he was made a Privy Councillor.

William Beresford was a wealthy man and had a house in County Wicklow, Ireland, where he attended to the duties of country gentleman and magistrate. After his election to Parliament he lived in Oxford, but soon moved to London, residing first in fashionable Eaton Square and then in St. James's. As Master of the Queen's Tennis Courts he was entitled to the Keeper's House at Hampton Court, but until 1849 he rented it out. A year later he successfully negotiated with the Palace to lease the large walled garden west of the Tennis Court (now the club's garden). This was part of an upgrading of the property prior to him taking up permanent residence, which it will be seen later included major building works that he paid for personally.[56]

No record of a reappointment following the death of a sovereign during Beresford's time as Master has so far come to light, and he served under four: George III, George IV, William IV and Queen Victoria. The reason may lie in the fact that he was originally appointed at a time George III was unfit to rule, and it was therefore the Prince Regent who granted him the office, making it unnecessary for the grant to be reconfirmed when he came to the throne in 1820.

When the Regent acceded as George IV he reigned for ten years, at the end of which time another change in the status of the office took place.

It was an Act of Parliament in 1831, soon after William IV's accession, which sealed the fate of the old office of Master of the King's Tennis Courts when legislation transferred the Master's fee from the Civil List to the Consolidated Fund with the proviso that it was for the life of the present incumbent only. At the same time, Beresford's fee was cut from the time honoured £132 3s. 4d. (8d. a day plus £120 a year) to just £83 per annum.[57] One wonders whether it dawned on the Treasury that by this time the last Master only had one royal court to look after. Another possibility is the fact that a members' committee now shared responsibility for the Court.

In 1883, the Treasury carried out a review of 'Various ancient and miscellaneous payments charged on the Consolidated Fund with a view to their extinction by commutation or otherwise; and that their attention had been called to the annual payment made to the Keeper of the Tennis Court at Hampton Court Palace.' As Beresford still retained the office there was no immediate question at issue, but they required confirmation that 'there is no necessity for continuing the appointment in any form, after the present Keeper'. The following reply was sent from the Palace:

> 'There is no reason why the office of Keeper of the Tennis Court at
> Hampton Court Palace should be renewed if a vacancy occurs therein.'[58]

Within two months Beresford was dead.

With William Beresford's death on 6th October 1883, the ancient office of Master of the King's Tennis Courts passed into history.

105

THE MEMBER FOR HARWICH,

OR,

THE BERESFORD LAMENT!

SHOWING HOW HIS FRIENDS DESERTED HIM, AND WENT OVER TO
KING JOHN.

Ah! woe is me!
That I live to see
These symptoms of dire miscarriage!
I begin to quake,
And my knees to shake,
In my place as the Member for Harwich.

Six years ago
We baffled the foe,
By a scheme both wise and witty :
King John, they said,
Was twenty a-head :—
But we bribed King John's committee!

Six years I've fought,
As a statesman ought,
For the benefit of the nation.
In the *lobster* cause
I earned applause,
And excited a great sensation.

My speeches all,
With great and small,
Have golden opinions won me :
O'Connell, Dan,
The big beggar-man,
His benison passed upon me.

But this renegade set
The past forget,
And my services all disparage :
I plainly see
'Tis time for me
To cease to be Member for Harwich.

For one by one
My friends are gone,
To the enemy's camp deserting :
And he, the while,
With a bow and a smile,
My interest is subverting.

With dinner and fête
Their hook they bait,
Try every mode to cheat us :
But, worst of all,
They are giving a *ball* :
That *ball* is my *quietus!*

So now 'tis o'er,
And I no more
Shall drive to the House in my carriage ;
But plod along
In the vulgar throng,
No longer the Member for Harwich.

Yet if this were all,
I could bear my fall
With tranquil resignation :
But it raises my bile,
To see the while
Such a traitorous defalcation.

For my chaplain too,
Who ought to be true,
Is one of the worst of sinners ;
With a solemn face
He pronounces the grace
And blesses them at their dinners.

So, like Cæsar of old,
My mantle I fold,
And fall like an ancient Roman :
For Brutus's steel
Has made me feel
'Tis better to trust in no man.

But ere I go,
Here's a health to my foe!
His merits I wont disparage :—
So adieu! King John,
And when I am gone,
May'st *thou* be the Member for Harwich.

64.   BERESFORD'S LAMENT

This lament recalls his fall from grace and the loss of his Parliamentary Seat at Harwich.

CHAPTER 8

TWO WARS AND A REVOLUTION

Four hundred years its walls four square
Have stood 'gainst Time for Tennis here,
And most tenacious in its hold,
Has cast from out its sterner mould
A game that's played with softer balls
In open space without its walls.

Soon after the dawn of the Twentieth Century the Prince of Wales acceded to the throne as King Edward VII, and on July 9th 1903 he agreed to become Patron of the Club. Since then, all of our subsequent Monarchs have honoured the Club in this way, including our present Queen.[1] It is not known whether George IV, William IV or Queen Victoria granted patronage. Edward VII always held the Club in great affection and used to tell the then Club President Sir Spencer Ponsonby-Fane: 'It was there that I first learned to play tennis.'[2]

With the sealing of the building, following the glazing of the east windows in 1884, the court began to suffer badly from condensation. This phenomenon in tennis courts is known as 'sweating', and it presented a continual problem during the first half of the twentieth century. The court often had to be shut for many weeks of the year when the water running down the walls formed large puddles on the floor. This was forever causing damage to both the walls and the floor. There was one occasion when a team from Oxford University came to play a match and the players had to put socks over their tennis shoes in order to get a foothold when the court started to sweat.[3] The Committee sought permission to paint the affected areas with Bickley paint. A letter from Sir Spencer Ponsonby-Fane was sent to Lord Windsor, the First Commissioner of Works, requesting that the lower walls and floor be painted. At the same time he asked for a stove to be installed in the dressing room to provide piped hot water for the bath, and for the conversion of the old workshop by the garden entrance into a second dressing room. A sympathetic Lord Windsor agreed to all the works being carried out at public expense including, for the first time, the floor, arguing that it was too important and should not be left to the chance of the club committee being in funds.[4] Lord Windsor had first-hand knowledge of the problems inside tennis courts as he owned his own, Hewell Grange at Tardebigge, Worcestershire.

Mentioned earlier was the possibility of there having been *rabat* nets in the court. What is certain is that early in this century there was a wing net. This net was stretched across the end windows above the tambour and any ball hitting it was still in play. Strangely, at Hampton Court the post holding the net was regarded as not being in play, whereas the same post in the old Lord's court was. The wing net was fitted at Hampton Court because many of the more modern courts had raised walls and higher play-lines above the end penthouses, thereby reducing the risk of balls going out of play. For the same reason, the three windows in each of the other three corners were also in play.[5] One major problem with the wing net was that a ball hitting it would often fall dead, leaving the striker at the hazard end with no possibility of a decent return, so penalising him for his opponent's poor shot! It was finally taken down in 1934.

In 1905 the Committee discussed the possibility of allowing a lady to become a member. It was decided that there was no rule to the contrary. The lady in question may have been the formidable the Honourable Judith Blunt, who married the Hon. N.S. Lytton and later inherited the title Baroness Wentworth. Neville Lytton later built a court of his own at Crabbet Park. Lady Wentworth's name is one of two ladies listed as members in the first published Members' Handbook, in 1921. Many years later, she was the subject of an amusing anecdote involving the Club's Honorary Secretary and Treasurer, Tony Negretti. On a visit to Crabbet towards the end of the Second World War, she invited him to play squash. Clad in her customary long black smock-like dress, she entered the squash court, which was also black — only the ball was white. She then proceeded to move in front of him every time she served, obscuring his view of the ball. Needless to say, he was somewhat embarrassed to have to admit to being beaten by a woman over 70 years old! Negretti perhaps should have considered himself fortunate. During the First World War Canadian officers had been stationed at Crabbet, and three of the officers in succession broke their ankles playing squash against her. This resulted in Lady Wentworth being declared 'out of bounds' until the unit left.[6]

Towards the end of the first decade of the new century, court use was dropping drastically. There were no more than half a dozen regular players and the financial position was becoming precarious. Tom White was by now in poor health and unable to play, which was adding to the club's problems. His son Alfred could not offer any assistance because he had accepted an appointment at Harvard; however Alfred left his son Harold to help out. The Committee was unhappy with that arrangement and suggested that another assistant should be engaged; the problem was solved by the return, after many years at Holyport, of John McCann. The Club approached both Lord's and Prince's, asking them to put up notices in their clubs, inviting honorary membership of the Royal Court on payment of a registration fee of five shillings. Both clubs agreed, and in 1909 Lord's generously offered an annual subscription of £20 for the next five years.[7]

However, there was some relief from the gloom in June 1908, when Jay Gould came over from the United States to defend his Amateur Championship and to take part in the Olympic Games. His private professional, Frank Forester, accompanied him. A series of matches was arranged at Hampton Court, all involving the World Champion Cecil 'Punch' Fairs. Fairs gave a handicap of fifteen to all three of his opponents. In the first match on Saturday 6th June, he beat Forester by two sets to one. On the following Monday, he defeated Alf White by three sets to love, and on the Wednesday, he comfortably won against Gould by three sets to one.[8] This was only Gould's second visit to the court. He had played on it the previous year, but this time he had trouble finding the winning openings. Despite his defeat by Fairs, Jay Gould went on to retain the Amateur Championship and win the Olympic Gold Medal.

Tom White died in 1910 and Alfred White returned to take over as Head Marker. He was allowed to re-employ his son Harold as his assistant and was

later joined by a second son. Court usage was still very low, lower than any other club court in the country — only 154 hours of court time taken in the whole of 1911. Inter-club matches were organised in an attempt to boost play. Matches were arranged with Lord's, Prince's, Queen's, Oxford, Cambridge, Manchester, Brighton, Hatfield and Newmarket. By 1914 court usage had risen to over 300 hours per annum.[9] Compare this to over 5,000 a year today!

Sir Spencer continued as President until his death in 1915. J.J. Freeman, who had resigned as Honorary Secretary two years earlier, but had remained Treasurer, succeeded him. C.T. Agar, who had been appointed Secretary, then assumed the role of Honorary Treasurer as well.

65. JAY GOULD

World Champion 1915-16
and member of the Royal Tennis Court

Charles Talbot Agar, a barrister by profession, was another member who gave long and dedicated service to the Club. He was a good all-round sportsman. At school (Westminster) he won the Fives Cup three years running, and turned out for the cricket XI. Because he was short in stature, and during his university days only weighed a little over seven stone, he was the ideal candidate to cox the Cambridge eight in 1893. Unfortunately for him, they lost to Oxford by just over a length. In later life he concentrated on tennis and golf, entering the Amateur Tennis Championships six times between 1914 and 1927, and the MCC Prizes in 1925.

In 1913, at the invitation of Lionel Earle, the new First Commissioner of Works, a list of repairs was drawn up. These included again: repairs to the damp floor, the roof, new gallery nets and a request to paint the ceiling white. Earle agreed to all the works at public expense, except for the gallery nets — these the club had to pay for. Hampton Court was the last court in the country to have a black ceiling and it absorbed too much light, often making play impossible in the winter. The court had to be closed for a month while the ceiling was being painted, at a cost of £40. In his letter of thanks to Earle, Agar wrote: 'Mr.

Freeman, who has been secretary and treasurer for the last 17 years, tells me he has never been able to follow the flight of the ball so well. The floor at that time was black. [10]

These were troubled times in Britain. Women were pressing for the vote, and the more militant of them joined the Suffragette movement. They were causing concern at the Palace, and Agar became alarmed about the possibility of the suffragettes planting a bomb in the Court. In May 1913 he wrote to the authorities requesting that the public be kept out by locking the door from the gardens and this was agreed. Not only was Agar concerned, but also while the ceiling works were under way Alf White was petrified that the suffragettes would take advantage of the scaffolding everywhere to set the Court on fire. He consequently spent a lot of his time searching for tins of petrol because of the danger to himself and his family in his adjacent apartment. Later, in October, the police were asked for their advice regarding the reopening of the door. They recommended that it be kept locked, for on that very day, a large house in nearby Hampton had been burned down by the suffragettes. [11]

With the outbreak of the war in 1914, Agar, along with many of the members, joined up. Although the Court was not closed, there was virtually no play — only four or five games were played during the

66. CHARLES T. AGAR

Honorary Secretary from 1913 to 1934
and Treasurer from 1915 to 1934

entire war. [12] Alf White was allowed to remain in his living accommodation at Hampton Court, but received no salary. His only source of income came from visits to the United States and a pension from his former employer, the Duke of Fife. He went to America for two of the winters, 1915-16 and 1916-17, where he helped to coach Jay Gould at his private court in Lakewood, New Jersey. Gould had become the World Champion just before the outbreak of the war, but he never defended his title. White also spent the winter of 1919-20 at Lakewood. Tennis in those days was essentially a summer game because of the lack of light in the winter months, so his absence would not have presented too many difficulties at Hampton Court.

The war ended in 1918, but Agar was not demobilised until early the following year. He returned to find that many of the old members had lost their lives fighting for their country, so he was unable to restart the Club as there was insufficient income. He inserted an appeal in May 1919, in both *The Times* and *The Field* for new members.[13] There was a good response, which enabled him to resume club activity the following month. The Court though was in a poor state. Neglect and sweating had caused the base of the walls to crumble away and there was similar damage to the floor. Bickley's advice was sought and he recommended hacking off the existing plaster to form a good key for his patent black covering, which he guaranteed would not sweat in bad weather. His estimate was for £194, which included repairing the floor, plus £29 to re-gild the crowns (figure 68).

TENNIS
HAMPTON COURT PALACE.

Mr. C. T. AGAR, hon. secretary of the Royal Tennis Court Club, Hampton Court Palace, has issued an appeal to lovers of tennis to join the club, which it is very much to be hoped may meet with a ready response, so that the court may be reopened for play forthwith.

There have been only four or five games played there during the war, but in 1914 the club was in a fairly flourishing state. The court has just been put into condition by the Board of Works, and Alfred White, the club's professional, has returned to take up his duties. The expenses of a year's working are some £120.

A good many of the former members lost their lives in the war, and unless Mr Agar is assured of a certain amount of financial support, he does not feel justified in reopening the court for play. The annual subscription is £1.

The court was built for King Henry VIII. in 1529-1530, and in the great days of tennis, in its decline and revival, it has always been a home of the game. It would be a great calamity if it was lost to tennis.

67. ADVERTISEMENT FOR NEW MEMBERS

This advertisement appeared in *The Field*, a similar one appearing in *The Times*.

Earle, now Sir Lionel, was still in charge at the Office of Works and agreed to carry out the repairs, but no money was available so soon after the war. Agar continually wrote to him over the next two years, at one time describing the Court as a 'picturesque ruin', and at other times warning that it might have to close. He applied further pressure by advising the authorities that it was unsafe for the Prince of Wales, who was expected to visit the Court, to sit in the dedans. This led to Agar being described in an internal memo as a 'persistent bugger'.[14] Although the Prince, the future Edward VIII, was occasionally seen in the dedans of tennis courts, he never played the game. He did however continue to pay his father's £5 subscription when he acceded to the throne in 1936.

At last, in May 1921, Earle authorised expenditure of £75 to patch up the walls with Bickley cement. However, Alf White suddenly jeopardised even that modest amount of expenditure, when he asked for the work to be deferred until the August. This angered Earle, who wrote to Agar demanding to know what was going on, adding that his office would 'jump at the possibility of saving the money'. The explanation was simple: the President of the Club, J.J. Freeman, had donated a prize racquet to be competed for, in order to increase the number of court hours and hence the income, and ten members were engaged in the competition until the end of July. That satisfied Earle and the work was postponed until August.[15] The Freeman Racquet was a handicap

A. Preedy. Esqre.
H. M. Office of Works
Hampton Court Palace.

Dear Sir.

I beg to submit an estimate to hack off all the painted surface of Battery Walls of Pent house & hack the stone walls sufficiently to form a a thorough good Key for my Patent Black covering, which will very much improve the play of the court. both as to the true play, & also the pace of the play.

I guarantee my work not to sweat in bad weather. Mr White informs me sweats greatly now - repairing the floor I include in the price £194 - 5 - 0 also I include repainting the lines where much worn.

refering to the crowns on the Walls I have not taken them in this estimate as I wish to suggest they should be faced with gold leaf, the large & small. done in the manner fitting the age of the court. this will give excellent effect

cost of which will be £29.

ready to put men on on receiveing your usual order to procede with the work.

always at your service.

I am Sir yours obediently.

Joseph Bickley.

68. JOSEPH BICKLEY'S 1919 ESTIMATE

112

tournament open to all amateurs. The winner that year was S. Walter, of The Queen's Club. This was the first time the racquet had been competed for, although the President had actually donated it back in 1914, but of course the war had intervened.

In September 1921 Jay Gould came over to England again and played several informal matches. He included a visit to Hampton Court to see his old mentor, Alf White. Gould had been a member of the Club for a number of years. White had unfortunately sustained a serious injury while bicycling, so was unable to play. He was however well enough to mark two games, when Gould played E.A.C. Druce (the holder of the MCC Silver Racquet), and the Oxford first string, V.A. Cazalet. Both his adversaries received half-thirty, played well and won. Gould, it was said, was suffering from having played too many matches and could not adjust to the light.[16] The accident referred to occurred when White met a motor-car head on. He was convinced tennis saved his life; in his opinion it had led to his ability to make quick decisions and as a result he was able to hand-somersault over the radiator instead of hesitating and going underneath.

Of the other great champions of the period, we know that Peter Latham and Cecil 'Punch' Fairs played exhibition matches at the Royal Court. E.B. Noel tells us that Fred Covey did too. However, no details of any matches involving Covey have been unearthed, and his match record, preserved with Lady Wentworth's papers, would appear to confirm that he never played an important match at Hampton Court.

Apart from his sterling work at Hampton Court, Agar, who lived close by in Cobham, was also the Honorary Secretary of the Prince's Club, Brighton, which he revived after it too had been struggling financially. Surprisingly the annual subscription there was £3, while at the Royal Court it was still only £1. He also served on the Committee of the Tennis & Rackets Association, where he looked after the interests of those clubs with no individual representative. He was a fine player, good enough to enter regularly the Amateur Championship and the MCC Prizes, and throughout the 1920s he played in club matches for both the Royal Tennis Court and Brighton. Assisted on the Committee at Hampton Court by Colonel George Trollope and J.J. Freeman, his hard work was beginning to put the Club into a stronger financial position, and by 1921 a balance of £149 16s. 6d. was reported. Court fees at this time were three shillings an hour and members were allowed to book two hours play. There were 110 members including H.M. The King, leading amateurs, Edgar Baerlein (the English Champion), the Hon. C.N. Bruce (at the time, second only to Baerlein) and H.J. Hill. Several of the members in the 1920s owned their own courts: Lord Leconfield (Petworth), J.F. Marshall (Seacourt), Baroness Wentworth (Crabbet Park), Aldison Horne (Ditton Place), J.O.M. Clark (Troon), W.N. McClean (Rusthall House) and the Hon. Cecil Baring, later Lord Revelstoke and future President of the Club (Lambay Island). Another notable member was E.B. Noel, the Secretary of The Queen's Club and joint author with J.O.M. Clark of the important *A History of Tennis*. He was also the tennis correspondent for *The*

Field for many years, where he wrote under the soubriquet 'Dexter'. His articles in that journal have been an invaluable source of material for this history.

Under Agar's guidance, the Club continued to prosper. Play was up by fifty per cent in 1924 and by the following year there were 160 members. The financial pressures were easing and court repairs were being carried out, prompting Agar to comment to Earle that the Royal Court now 'compares most favourably with any court I have been in this year'.[17]

In 1928 the Exchequer and Audit Department queried payments being made to the Tennis Court, the Residence of the Tennis Professional and the Members' Dressing Room. As no formal agreement with the Palace seemed to exist, their status had to be confirmed by issuing Grace-and-Favour Warrants to: 'The President and the Committee of Hampton Court Tennis Club.' One covered the court itself, the changing facilities and the workshop, and the other the remainder of the rooms at the southern end, all grouped together under the title 'Tennis Marker's Residence'.[18] This must have exasperated poor old Alf White who, as will be seen later, fought a long battle to be known as a Professional.

69. LORD REVELSTOKE
(The Hon. Cecil Baring)

President of The Royal Tennis Court
1931-33

As an occupant of a Grace-and-Favour apartment, the Club once again became responsible for the internal maintenance, with the Palace paying for refurbishment only on a change of resident. This was fine for the Marker's Residence, which they were to redecorate with every change of professional; however, the Court was never going to change hands. The Palace at first insisted on enforcing the strict Grace-and-Favour rules, but with members unable to raise sufficient funds, the condition of the court began to deteriorate again.

Meanwhile several changes were about to take place. Lord Revelstoke (Cecil Baring) had become President and one of his first acts, in 1931, was to arrange with the Lord Chamberlain's Department for members to be able to play on Sundays. Alf White was succeeded by Arthur Ashford the following year, and by the end of 1933 Agar was still administering the Club, but from a nursing home.

Early in 1934 Lord Revelstoke died and was succeeded by his son Rupert who became the fourth Baron he was invited to follow in his father's footsteps, and became President of the Club. A committee member, C.B. Gabriel, took over Agar's twin roles as Honorary Secretary and Treasurer early the following year. Charles Agar recovered and remained on the Committee until 1941, the year he died aged 69. An interview Agar gave to the *Evening News* on the occasion of his retirement from the honorary offices confirmed that George V had played many times at the Royal Court.[19]

Cecil Baring had become the third Baron Revelstoke in 1929 on the death of his brother. He was the head of the family mercantile firm, Baring Brothers, and had a home on the remote Lambay Island, just off the Irish coast near Dublin. There he built a unique open tennis court with a set of galleries along each of the side walls. He was also the driving force, together with T. Suffern Tailor, behind the construction of the Tuxedo court in the State of New York around the turn of the century.[20] His son Rupert was only 22 when he became the fourth Baron. Like his father he was a keen tennis player and was to serve as President of the Royal Tennis Court for 40 years.

70. LORD REVELSTOKE
(The Hon. Rupert Baring)

President of The Royal Tennis Court 1934-73

The circumstances of Alf White's departure from the Club were most unfortunate. The trigger was the decision to open the Court on Sundays, which White thought would allow him to close it on Fridays for his day off. Agar was not prepared to accept this because he thought that White's sons would be perfectly able to cover for him in his absence. Positions became entrenched and White was summoned to Lord Revelstoke's London residence in Bryanston Square. Lord Revelstoke told White that the Club was prepared to employ his son Harold on a salary of ten shillings a week to enable him to keep the Court open for seven days a week, but he, Alf White, had to cease 'dealing with the Club's instructions and wishes as if he was in the position of an employer, while the Committee were the employees'. White immediately dug his heels in, prompting Lord Revelstoke to comment that 'a refusal so blunt in its character as this must inevitably lead to the consideration by the Club of an alternative appointment'. Up until this point White had felt fairly secure, as he believed he could occupy the apartment at the Palace for the rest of his life, having assumed that the warrant issued by Queen

Victoria to his father, which was for life, had been renewed in his favour. In fact the warrant issued in 1910 granted the rooms to the Club, for the use of their employed marker, whoever he might be. Alf White never backed down and was consequently dismissed.[21] Ironically, when Arthur Ashford succeeded him as the Professional, he had no assistant and was allowed to close the Court on Fridays.

Rumours abound about the interest Queen Mary showed in the Club. It is said that she used the area behind the viewing window above the hazard penthouse as a private box to watch matches. She has also been credited with the decision to use the date '1531' on the first club tie, by suggesting that the preferred date, 1530, could cause confusion with the score. None of this has been verified, but what is known is that she came to the Court in 1932 when she 'listened with lively interest to the Court's romantic history'.[22]

71.　CHRIS GABRIEL

Honorary Secretary and Treasurer
of the RTC 1934-47

When the decision was taken to produce a club tie in 1936, there was a need for a logo to go on it. Chris Gabriel designed it, and although Tony Negretti improved its accuracy in 1948, it remains the logo in use today. It consists of a pair of crossed rackets with a Tudor Rose above the left racket head and a Crown above the right. Underneath the racket heads is the date. As this story unfolds, the difficulties in determining a birth-date for the RTC will become apparent. Chris Gabriel favoured 1530, but his son Kit, also a member of the club, had other ideas. Whether Queen Mary influenced the decision, who knows, but '1531' emerged on the first tie which was produced by T.M. Lewin of Panton Street, Haymarket.

72.　THE CLUB'S LOGO

Designed by Chris Gabriel

116

Gabriel was the first to suggest heating the court to prevent it from sweating. The first reaction of the Palace was that this was a matter for the Club, although they did help by preparing an estimate for the work, which came to £280. William Ormsby-Gore, the new First Commissioner of Works, took a different view. Writing to the Palace, he said: 'I attach great importance to the maintenance in good order of this, the most historic and interesting Tennis Court in Europe.' He goes on to suggest that 'Lord's, Queen's, Prince's and Oxford should be visited to see how they cope with the sweating' and concludes: 'I want to make it quite clear that I do not regard myself bound by any past decisions or existing arrangements.'[23] The Palace surveyor was duly despatched to Prince's, where he was advised that heating the court was the only solution. In his report, the surveyor also recommended that a damp course should be inserted into the west (main) wall and that the garden outside, against the court wall, should be dug out to a level lower than that of the court floor. The Treasury was asked to make a contribution towards the works, as the Club could not afford the whole cost.[24] They agreed to fund half the heating installation costs — the Club had to find the other half and pay the running costs. This was agreed, and by the end of 1934 the new heating system had been installed, the damp course inserted and the adjacent garden lowered. At the same time, four new doors were fitted in the upper corners at the outside gallery access points to prevent the heat escaping.

With the heating now on and the court drying out, the Club asked for it to be redecorated. Again the Palace refused. By now it was almost unplayable, as it had not been decorated for over ten years. The seriousness of the situation forced the Office of Works again to seek help from the Treasury, suggesting that if the club could raise £200, then the remaining £100 should be paid out of public funds. In his submission to the Treasury, the Secretary at the Office of Works wrote: 'Unless we help them out in some way, I still fear that we may have the Court abandoned by them, or rendered so unattractive that play will cease, and then we shall have the whole place on our hands. It is considered to be the most historic and interesting Court in Europe and a national monument of no little importance and we cannot look on and see it fall into decay without making some serious effort to save it. There is something also in the contention that it is difficult to apply hard and fast Grace-and-Favour terms to a tennis court.' [25]

The Club in the meantime organised an appeal to raise the £200 needed for the redecoration. With the money successfully raised, Bickley & Co. were asked to carry out the work and the court repairs were completed by the end of 1935. Apart from the total redecoration, the penthouse roofs were reconstructed and the Palace retiled the court roof again — the roof of course was their responsibility and therefore no cost fell on the Club. Lord Revelstoke and H.J. Hill generously donated £50 each and a total of £330 5s. 6d. was collected. Once the redecoration had been completed, club members were asked if they would like to see the court artificially lit and if so would they support another appeal for funds? The answer to both questions was 'yes', and another £114 was raised. The lighting manufacturers, Allom Brothers, were called in to advise. They recommended direct lighting which would cost £150 — the alternative would be to light the court indirectly using the ceiling as a reflector. This would require more power and cost £182 with a further £80 to repaint the ceiling — the Palace insisted on indirect lighting. As part of the fund-raising activities, a day's entertainment with exhibition matches was arranged. The main match was between two leading amateurs, Lord Aberdare (formerly Hon. C.N. Bruce) and H.J. Hill. That was followed by a match between the Lord's Head Professional, W.A. (Jack) Groom, and Arthur Ashford. The day raised another £18 16s. 6d. Despite the fund-raising shortfall, the decision was taken to proceed using the reserves and the new lights were in place by the end of 1936.[26]

73. THE COURT IN 1934

With the Court now in excellent condition, Gabriel informed the Palace that the Club was endeavouring to arrange for the British Open Championship to be played at Hampton Court the following season. This they did not achieve, but an invitation doubles tournament in which an amateur was paired with a professional was inaugurated. The tournament was known as the Lurgan Cup, following the donation of a cup by committee member Lord Lurgan. The winners in the first year, 1938, were Arthur Barker and Albert (Jack) Johnson (a future world champion). During the winter of 1938-39, a members' handicap tournament was started which proved very popular — it was revived soon after the war with equal success. The last national tournament played before the outbreak of hostilities was the Browning Cup (the Professional Handicap Singles), which was won on that occasion by Henry Johns.

118

Just before the war, Chris Gabriel commissioned on behalf of the Club the first translation of M de Garsault's *L'Art du Paumier-Raquetier et de la Paume* (The Art of the Tennis-Racket-Maker and of Tennis), an important book. The translation by Catherine W. Leftwich, which was published in May 1938, was limited to two hundred copies, of which numbers 1 to 150 were reserved for the members of the Royal Tennis Court. The wood blocks that were made to print the illustrations in this book are still in the possession of the club, a few of which are now displayed in the clubrooms.

With the outbreak of World War Two in September 1939, court usage dropped to less than ten hours a week. As was the case during the First World War, many of the members were away fighting for their country. Court usage continued at that level until the night of 25th September 1940, when German bombers showered the Palace with 200 to 300 incendiary bombs. About ten fires started, all of which were put out within a few hours. The only direct hit inside the palace walls was on the Tennis Professional's apartment, which ended up with a huge hole in the roof and one room completely gutted. Thankfully there were no casualties. One or two other high explosive and delayed-action bombs landed nearby causing severe damage to the court's roof and blowing out most of its windows.[27] The Court was patched up and struggled on until May 1942 when Arthur Ashford was called up to the Armed Forces; play then ceased. Although the roof was repaired in the summer of 1944, the windows remained boarded up, so when the members returned early in 1946 they found the court flooded. The Palace wanted to reglaze the windows quickly in order to stop the dissolution of the Club, but they were concerned about the political effect of carrying out such work ahead of repairs to residential accommodation that had also suffered bomb damage. By the end of the year, however, the work was completed with all the windows reglazed.[28] The first tournament staged after the war at Hampton Court was the Henry Leaf Cup in 1946, the Public Schools Old Boys Competition, when Lord Aberdare, Billy Ross-Skinner and Arthur Barker secured victory for Winchester.

Christopher Gabriel died in 1947 at the age of 71, and was succeeded by P.A. (Tony) Negretti. The members had every reason to be grateful to Chris Gabriel. He had taken over as Honorary Secretary and Treasurer in 1934 when the membership was declining and the financial position deteriorating. He had a genial personality, which helped in attracting new members, and by using sound business principles, he was soon able to reverse the situation. In business he was the Managing Director of the family firm, whose principal activity was the importation of timber for railway sleepers. He was responsible for the installation of the heating and lighting, and bringing the court into first-class condition. It was a terrible sadness that he should see his efforts destroyed by the war. The Minute Book records an appreciation following the pre-war renovation, which was signed by Lord Revelstoke and the other members of the Committee on 14th February 1936:

'The Members of the Committee wish to express their most sincere gratitude to Mr C.B. Gabriel, the Honorary Secretary, for his untiring energy he has displayed in the interests of the Tennis Court at Hampton Court Palace.

'It is entirely owing to him that all the protracted and intricate negotiations in connection with the recent repairs to the Court were so successfully concluded in September 1935.

'It would be impossible to overestimate what Mr Gabriel has done for us, and we would like him to know how deeply his efforts have been appreciated both by the Committee and by all the members of the Club.'

His successor, Tony Negretti, who took over at the end of 1947, is rightly credited with saving the Club after the war. One hundred and twelve members had stayed loyal through the war years and when he took over the membership stood at 160. He then worked ceaselessly on building up the numbers, and by the time he retired as Honorary Secretary and Treasurer in 1973, there were 941 members. In the United States he was helped in his recruitment campaign by Sammy Van Alen, who over many years has been a good friend to the Club, and by Quentin McDougall of the Hobart club, who persuaded many Tasmanians to join.

74. P.A. (TONY) NEGRETTI

Honorary Secretary and Treasurer of
The Royal Tennis Court 1947-73
and President 1973–87

After the war, petrol rationing prevented many members getting to the Court. The number of courts used had fallen from 417 in 1939, to 102 in 1946 and Arthur Ashford was becoming alarmed because he had no-one to coach for days on end. Negretti therefore decided that the quickest way to resuscitate the Club was to get as many local people involved as possible. That meant publicity. He persuaded the Palace to put up signs showing the public where the Court was, and to mention it in their guidebook. However, they would not agree to his idea of opening up the Tennis Court Lane entrance to the public, for security reasons.

In 1948 the Club found it could not afford to heat the court. Not only was there very little play and subsequent income, but also the cost of fuel had doubled since the war. Consequently, the walls and floor again began to deteriorate as the

ROYAL TENNIS COURT
HAMPTON COURT PALACE.
MOLESEY 1386

GREEN LINE BUSES

For members unable to use their cars a very good way to the Court is by Green Line Bus.

For members in the home counties Nos. 716 (Hitchin and Chertsey), 717 (Welwyn Garden City and Woking), 718 (Windsor and Epping), all pass the gates and connect with many other routes.

For members in London, unless they prefer to travel by electric train from Waterloo or by trolleybus from Hammersmith, the three buses mentioned above all pass Hyde Park Corner at 4, 15, 34 and 45 minutes past the hour all day, Sundays included. The journey takes three-quarters of an hour.

P. A. NEGRETTI,
Hon. Secretary.

February, 1948.

75. POST-WAR TRANSPORT ARRANGEMENTS

sweating returned. After Gabriel's death, it transpired that he had been paying for the fuel out of his own pocket in order to preserve what little play there was, a revelation that the Ministry of Works had been anxious to keep confidential.[29]

Negretti approached the Ministry for help with the fuel costs. They were sympathetic and put the case to the Treasury, arguing that it was the duty of the Ministry of Works to maintain an Ancient Monument. Replying to the Ministry of Works, the Treasury acknowledged that, as it was necessary to heat the court in order to preserve the structure, 'Ministry of Works must therefore provide it'. The Secretary at the Treasury, in fear of a cessation of play after more than 400 years, added to the internal memo: 'Nor will I wilfully risk being haunted by so formidable a ghost as that of Henry VIII.' On a more serious note, as a *quid pro quo*, the Treasury suggested that the Club should allow the public access to the Court.[30] The general public had been excluded following the suffragette scares of 1913, until the end of the First World War, and from 1928 it had been a matter for the Club Committee alone. When they were granted the Grace-and-Favour Warrant for the court, with it came the right to control admission, and the Court had been closed to the public since 1940. The reason the Treasury was so keen on public access was because they foresaw a potential revenue-earner by charging the public to view, which would then enable them to offset the cost of the fuel. This, of course, fitted in with Negretti's need to publicise the game. The Club agreed to a request from the palace to produce a 2,000-word booklet for the visitors, containing a brief history of tennis, the Court, the members, and how the game was played. Sixpence was charged for the booklet, which was written by Negretti and Lord Aberdare, and the Club was able to retain the profits so long as they were used for court improvements. A ticket office was erected by the garden door in the space between the passage and the garden walls. A charge of 3d. a head was made and the Court was open for three afternoons a week, Wednesdays, Saturdays and Sundays. During the first summer of operation, in 1949, the palace collected an average of £8 a day, which they regarded as a success. Four years later, the Court was opened daily in the summer, when no less than 47,164 visitors paid a total of £589 11s. 0d.[31]

On 8th January 1948, the first committee meeting for over eight years was held. At that time the Committee consisted of Lord Revelstoke as President, Ronnie Aird, Brigadier General S.V.P. Weston, Lord Lurgan (then residing in South Africa), Michael Pugh, C.S. Crawley, N.F. Railing and of course Tony Negretti. One of the first items on the agenda was Arthur Ashford's salary. It was agreed that he should not have an increase in basic pay but that, in order to encourage him to organise more play, he would receive a share of the court fees. Another item was the club tie. As recorded earlier, the date 1531 appeared under the crossed rackets and it was resolved that it should be altered to 1530. Another of Negretti's inherited worries was that Chris Gabriel, after the success of the Garsault book, had involved the Club in the production of W.W. Kershaw's translation of Scaino's *Trattato Del Giuoco Della Palla di Messer* (Treatise on the Game of the Ball) — the earliest published book on the game dating back to 1555 — and that sales were not good. In time and with much hard selling, it managed to make a small profit. The Committee was soon strengthened by the inclusion of the Honorary Secretaries of the university courts of Oxford and Cambridge, and the Master in Charge of Tennis at Canford School — their role though was largely advisory, as it would be 24 years before the Committee would formally meet again. Morys Bruce (later Lord Aberdare), Bill Cary and Sir Cecil Griffin also served during the Negretti era. Sir Cecil Griffin officially deputised for Negretti during any absence. Ronald Aird, who had been a committee member since 1935, was elected Vice-President in 1948. This new office was created because of the frequent absence from the country of Lord Revelstoke. He served in that capacity until 1973.

Something that proved useful to Negretti's recruitment drive was his list of *Tennis Courts in the British Isles*, a copy of which still hangs in the changing room. When writing to the various owners to confirm details of their courts he would always suggest they become members of the Royal Tennis Court. So once again there were several members who had their own courts: Lord Leconfield (Petworth), Sir Charles Rose (Hardwick), Major Michael Crichton-Stuart (the Hereditary Keeper of Falkland Palace), Major James Dance (Moreton Morrell), Major H.M. Martineau (Holyport) and John H. Whitney, the American Ambassador to Great Britain (Greentree). Other members were associated with 'out of play' courts: Lord Hesketh (Easton Neston), Sir Humphrey Nobel (Jesmond Dene) and P.V.F. Cazalet (Fairlawne). Negretti's target was 425 members by the 425th Anniversary of the Court, a goal achieved in 1955. Even Lord Revelstoke was asked to forego his *de facto* life membership and sign a bank standing order.

Nobody escaped! Negretti trawled through the MCC and Jesters Club membership lists looking for potential members, especially those who entered for the MCC Prizes. He was particularly keen on enrolling youngsters, and anyone he knew who had a son at either Oxford or Cambridge was pressurised. Another avenue was that those who supplied goods or services to the Club had a certain amount of leverage applied. Tennis match reports in the national newspapers were extensively examined and anyone living close to Hampton Court was approached; on one occasion he even spotted the announcement of the engagement of someone he remembered meeting at a tennis function a few years earlier. Out went a letter inviting membership of the RTC on the obscure reasoning that the individual lived closer to the Court than he did — it worked. Those who had ordered a *Scaino* were asked to consider joining and here he had many successes, including Avery Brundage the President of the International Olympic Committee. Another in the public eye who fell victim was the renowned actor, Sir Ralph Richardson, because Negretti had noticed he was occasionally playing at Leamington during his season at Stratford and 'wondered when he returned to London, if he could be persuaded to join the Royal Tennis Court'. He was.

Slowly the Club's financial position improved. In 1950 a surplus of £121 11s. 11d. was recorded; by 1955 it had increased to £231 17s. 6d.

Another means of boosting income was of course by increasing the amount of play. Ashford's incentive has already been mentioned, and another idea was to restart the handicap singles competition that had been so successful the year before the war. In 1948 the Lathom Browne competition was inaugurated. The competition was named after the Reverend R.C. Lathom Browne who had donated a cup to the Prince's Club Brighton in 1925 that was competed for by players who were unable to enter the Loder Cup, Brighton's premier competition. When the Brighton court closed in 1939 the holder was Tony Negretti. He obtained permission from the trustees to transfer the Cup to Hampton Court. In later years he would often joke that he held the trophy for longer than anyone else. In its first year at the Royal Tennis Court there were a mere 29 entries, but by the end of the millennium there were 160 competitors in ten divisions and it is now the world's biggest tennis handicap competition. The tournament was won on the first two occasions by David Warburg, who went on to become Amateur

Champion; the Cup was nearly won by Howard Angus (future Amateur and World Champion) who only failed at the last hurdle.

76. THE REVEREND R.C. LATHOM BROWNE

The Reverend Lathom Browne is seen here on the right, with Major-General F.W. Hemming at the Princes Club, Brighton. This photograph was taken eight months before he died.

The Reverend Lathom Browne was Vicar of North Curry in Somerset before becoming Rector of Hever in Kent. He first played tennis in 1868 when he was an undergraduate at Oxford, and continued to play regularly at Brighton until he died in 1928, at the age of eighty-three.[32]   For many years he was the oldest active player in the country. After his death, that distinction fell to Hampton Court's J.J. Freeman.

In 1951 Negretti suggested reviving the 'pro-am' doubles tournament for the Lurgan Cup in an attempt to help the professionals. He managed to restart the competition the following year and it ran for a further two. The winners were the same in all three years, Peter Kershaw and Ronald Hughes. It was not until 1960 that the Cup was played for again, when the winners were J.G.H. Hogben and Jim Dear (World Champion 1955-57). Ronald Hughes had an impressive Lurgan Cup record; he won it no less than five times with three different partners.

There was now growing concern over the state of the main wall, which was crumbling away, caused by the sweating after the war. The Palace surveyor recommended that three inches of the wall should be cut away, the wall waterproofed and refaced with Portland Stone to a height of seven feet six inches. The cost was £950 which the Palace accepted was its responsibility and the work went ahead in 1954.[33] Once completed, the court was redecorated and another set of blinds was put up on the west windows to control the admission of sunlight. The original set had fallen into disrepair before the war. However, the new blinds were not successful and within a short time the idea was abandoned and the windows were whitewashed.

The highlight of 1957 was a visit to the Court by the legendary Pierre Etchebaster (World Champion 1928-54). He was at the time the Head Professional at the Racquet & Tennis Club, New York, and he crossed the Atlantic to play a series of exhibition matches in the spring of that year. The first was against Peter Kershaw at Manchester — his other matches were against Henry Johns (MCC) at Lord's, John Marshall (an assistant MCC professional under Johns) at Hampton Court and the Hon. Morys Bruce (the Amateur Champion) at Holyport. The match at the Royal Tennis Court took place on May 4th and Etchebaster conceded just enough odds to make a game of it, but ensuring he won. John Marshall left the game soon after this match and nothing more was heard of him in the tennis world until some forty years later, when an extraordinary coincidence occurred. Lord Aberdare, who as Morys Bruce had been one of Etchebaster's original four opponents (at Holyport), hailed a taxicab in Central London. Upon entering the cab, the driver informed Lord Aberdare that he knew him. When asked from where, he replied: 'My name is Marshall and I once played Etchebaster at Hampton Court!'[34]

Tragedy struck later that year when Arthur Ashford collapsed and died on court. He left a wife and son, Peter. His wife was not at all well and for many years he had nursed her. On behalf of the Club, Lord Aberdare organised a successful appeal that raised enough money to give her a small income over the following years.

Without a professional, palace residents Ken Evans and his wife Betty nobly stepped in to keep the Club going, organising court bookings and opening and closing the Court as required. Ken Evans was the Propagator (Nursery Manager) at the Palace, and as such was responsible for producing annually the wonderful flowering displays in the gardens. They did this job splendidly on-and-off until the end of the 1970s. In recognition of their services, a grateful Club made both of them Honorary Members. Recently a commemorative seat has been placed in the garden beside the Court. On the playing side, Henry Johns would come over at weekends to coach members and keep the court netting in good repair. He too was made an Honorary Member. His assistant, Brian Church would come over on some Sundays. Johns had been making and re-covering balls for the Royal Court since the war. In 1951 he delegated the job to George Beton (who worked in the Lord's changing room) — Beton continued to do this work for more than twenty years. Another who gave a hand during this troubled time was Johns's predecessor at Lord's, Jack Groom.

The search for a new professional was now under way. The Committee's first choice was the former British Open Champion, Ronald Hughes, who was at the time the rackets professional at Malvern College. Too settled in the job there, he politely declined. Henry Johns then suggested Leslie Keeble, with whom he had worked at Prince's before the war. Keeble was the Squash Professional at the Lansdowne Club in central London and had expressed an interest in returning to tennis.

L.W.R. Keeble was appointed on 1st July 1958. It was agreed that he would be available on Saturdays, Sundays and any other day when there was significant play. At first he was accommodated by the palace in Apartment 30 near Clock Court, while Apartment 53 was being renovated. Keeble was to spend fifteen years at the Club, although unfortunately, as it will transpire, the latter years were not altogether happy ones.

77. KEN AND BETTY EVANS

For more than 20 years these two kept the Court functioning during the absences of a Professional.

This was a period of rapid expansion of the telephone network and the old Kingston Exchange that had provided the club's line since before the First World War had become over-loaded. The Post Office decided to build a new exchange to be known as Teddington Lock, and Negretti wrote to the Telephone Manager reminding him that, when this was first mooted, he had promised the Club the number '1530'. That promise was not honoured and the Club had to settle for '3015', the number still in use today.

An assistant for Keeble was arranged in 1963. He was Derek Barrett, who was supported by the Tennis & Racket Association's Young Professionals Fund. The arrangement was for a year. After that year was up, there was insufficient court activity to warrant a replacement and Keeble reverted to running the court by himself. Barrett however was to return to the Royal Tennis Court in the 1970s.

Following routine maintenance in 1965, some serious damage was caused to the court floor by the contractors. Several of the stone slabs were broken by the enormous weight of scaffolding they had to erect. The Club claimed that the plastic protective sheeting they had used had drawn up damp causing the paint to flake. The Palace accepted responsibility for the cracked stones which they replaced, but disputed the suggestion that the contractors were to blame for the flaking, insisting it was caused by the old paint that had acted as a sealant preventing the stones from breathing. Astonishingly, the surveyor's recommendation was to remove the paint and dye the stone with hot ox blood and soot! He also recommended a damp-proof course that would have cost the Club £2,000. These suggestions brought a rebuke from his superiors, who refused to allow a disturbance of the old floor, as it was in their opinion a straightforward case of wear and tear — the Palace therefore refused to paint the replaced stones.[35] The Club could not afford the £350 needed, so the floor was left untreated for several years leading to the curious patchwork effect that was captured in an official photograph of the Court, which was sold in the Palace Bookshop for many years (figure 109).

From 1966 onwards court usage started to fall off, having risen steadily since Negretti had taken over in 1947. The day-to-day running of the court was in the hands of Keeble and he was arguing for an increase in salary because his income was falling with the reduction in play. In 1966 his earnings from court fees were £527, but they fell each year until 1971 when they were only £407 and bookings were under ten courts a week. During this period Negretti started receiving a series of complaints about the Professional's over-familiarity with members, his failure to mark for the full hour and his muddling of the score. Relations between the two became fraught. Matters came to a head when Keeble demanded more than the customary tip from a visiting team. Negretti was outraged and demanded that the practice stop, citing his mercenary attitude to visiting teams as another reason for the drop in the number of courts. However, Negretti was by then living in Buckinghamshire — his business had moved from Central London to Aylesbury — some distance from the Court, making it difficult for him to exert complete control, and a number of the regular playing members were becoming agitated.

For four members, the final straw came when they turned up for a friendly doubles to find no Keeble, no hot water, a filthy court and balls that were so black they had to be taken outside and tossed in a blanket with chalk before they could be used. The four, who included Pat Barker and Charles Ker, met in an Esher restaurant on 15th April 1971 to decide on a course of action. Over the following months, they canvassed opinions and importantly gained the support of influential members including David Warburg, Henry Wollaston, Vernon Ely and Arden Camm. Vernon Ely organised a dinner on 23rd March 1972 held in the King's Arms, adjacent to the Palace's Lion Gate, where it was concluded that as 'the conduct of the Professional, L.W.R. Keeble, was most unsatisfactory, doing the Court no good, and unlikely to improve, he should be replaced'. Negretti was informed, and on June 21st 1972 the Committee met for the first time since 1948, at Lord's, to discuss this demand. It was decided that the matter needed careful handling because of the recently introduced employment legislation, and that therefore a sub-committee should be set up to deal with the problem and that it should contain at least one of Keeble's supporters. There were at the time a number of members who were sympathetic to Keeble, believing him to be poorly treated and underpaid. Relations between Negretti and the local members then became strained when several of them refused to serve on the sub-committee. The reason for their reluctance was the general consensus that the Club should be reconstituted with an elected committee, which could then deal with all these problems.

In the meantime, Keeble demanded that his salary be tripled and backdated three years. When told by Negretti that it was out of the question, he promptly resigned.

Without a professional, members again had to rely on Ken and Betty Evans to arrange their court bookings. Apart from this time of crisis, these two continued to help the Club out for several more years, covering for the professional's time off and holidays.

With no professional to arrange matches or service the court, the local members decided to act. A meeting was arranged at Pat Barker's office in Leatherhead on 14th October 1972 with the full knowledge and approval of Tony Negretti — there were twenty members present. Its purpose was to make suggestions to forward to the Secretary. The meeting, chaired by Sir Ronald Prain, agreed to form a local committee to assist with the day-to-day running of the Club. Mark and Pat Barker, Vernon Ely, Austen Kark, Sir Ronald Prain and Lawrence Roche volunteered, and the new Committee then elected David Warburg as its Chairman. The meeting proposed that there should be an annual election of a President, Honorary Secretary and Honorary Treasurer, and nine other committee members — that Committee would then elect its own chairman. They also concluded that the court needed a complete refurbishment and new lighting, as a matter of urgency, and that would mean increasing the subscription.[36]

Negretti agreed with most of the proposals, but felt the election should be broad-based by conducting a postal ballot of the whole membership; otherwise any new committee elected by a small group at a general meeting could result in an unbalanced locally-run club.

In the meantime, a new Committee was formed by amalgamating the new local Committee with members of the long-serving Committee. It included Ronnie Aird, Arden Camm, Nigel Bruce, Andrew Lloyd Davies, Murray Glover, Charles Ker, James Macnaghten, Michael Pugh, Michael Morton, Lawrence Roche, David Warburg, Henry Wollaston, and of course Tony Negretti. During the first seven months of 1973 most of their efforts were spent attempting to secure a new professional.

It soon became apparent that the salary on offer was not going to attract a leading tennis professional. Ten had been approached, or had applied, but none was prepared to take the job on the terms offered. Incidentally, one of those was Chris Ronaldson, who was later to play an important part in the Club's history. There was another pressure too — the Palace was threatening to take back Apartment 53, because it had been empty for nearly a year.

In July 1973 Derek Barrett applied for the vacant professional's job. Again the money on offer was too low. It was obvious that the Club could not afford to employ a decent professional unless it could generate more income. It was decided to act on the local Committee's earlier suggestion that the subscription should be dramatically increased. The proposal was for a four-fold increase from

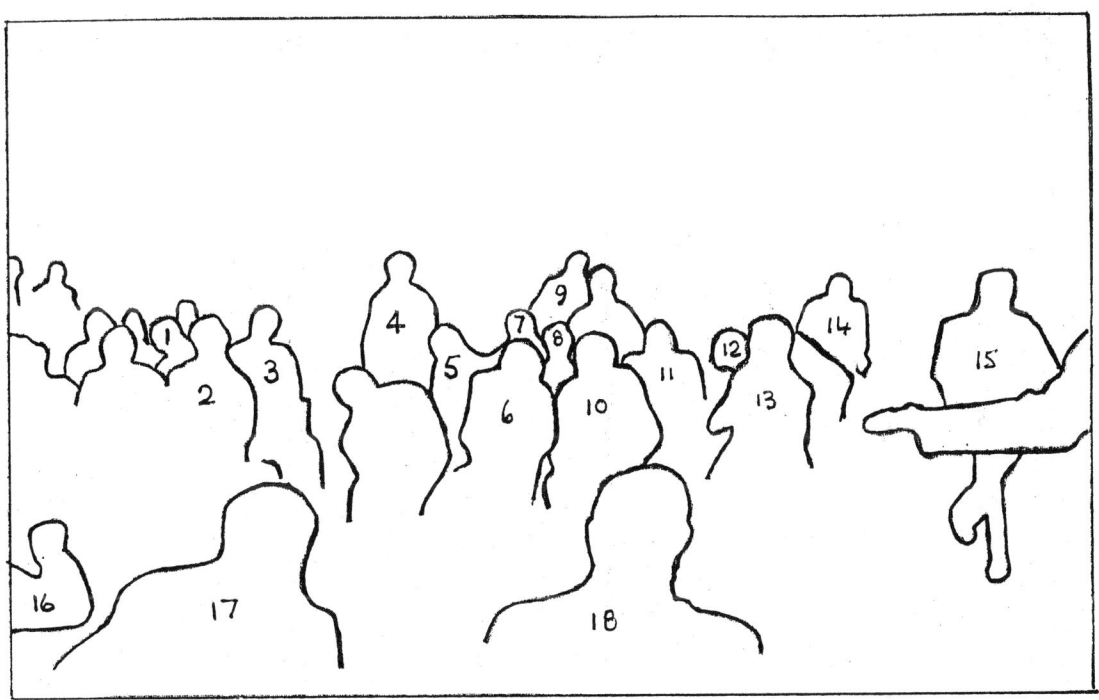

78. THE 'PALACE REVOLUTION' MEETING 4th NOVEMBER 1973

1. Vernon Ely, 2. Paul Heward, 3. Pat Barker, 4. Dr Irwin Stock, 5. Michael Morton,
6. Bill Stephens, 7. Nigel Bruce, 8. Ray Wigger, 9. Austen Kark, 10. Geoffrey Welch,
11. Stephen de Laszlo, 12. Jack Hurley, 13. Denis Hughes, 14. Howard Angus,
15. Roy Yglesias, 16. Tony Negretti, 17. David Warburg, 18. Henry Wollaston.

£1 to £4 a year — a momentous decision, as this was to be the first increase in the subscription in nearly eighty years! With the decision taken, the offer to Barrett was improved and he accepted.

A Special General Meeting was called and took place on 4th November 1973. The increase in subscription and the new committee structure were approved. There was no contested election for the President (P.A. Negretti), the Honorary Secretary (H.M.H. Glover) or the Honorary Treasurer (J.S. Macnaghten). Problems arose when the meeting struck out retrospectively those provisions which provided for the participation of all members in the election and proceeded, on the spot, to elect a general committee from amongst those attending. Twelve persons (all present) were proposed and seconded *en bloc* and elected. Negretti did not accept this, and in effect there were then two committees of management existing side by side: a new General Committee claiming to hold office immediately, on the strength of the elections on the 4th November; and the old Committee, which derived its authority from the 1928 Royal Warrant entrusting it with the management of the court.

The situation was eventually defused by reverting back to the original proposal for a postal ballot of the whole membership. Voting papers were sent out which included the names of those nominations received before the meeting, and those claiming to have been elected at the meeting. As a result of this, the nine committee places were filled by Howard Angus, Pat Barker, Nigel Bruce, Arden Camm, Charles Ker, Michael Morton, Sir Ronald Prain, David Warburg and Henry Wollaston.

This whole traumatic episode in the Club's history has become known as the 'Palace Revolution', a phrase coined by Pat Barker on the day of the fateful dinner in that Esher Restaurant back in April 1971.

Tony Negretti was the last of those faithful servants who ran the Club virtually single-handedly, having followed in the footsteps of General Lambert, Sir Spencer Ponsonby-Fane, J.J. Freeman, C.T. Agar and C.B. Gabriel. He became a member of the Royal Tennis Court in 1934. In his 26 years as Honorary Secretary and Treasurer, he increased the membership six-fold by his tireless efforts. The Lathom Browne Cup was started, the Lurgan Cup restarted and he also organised a large number of inter-club matches for all classes of player — all with the objective of increasing court use.

During the Second World War he served with the British Expeditionary Force in France, and as a major in the Black Watch in Sicily. He saw through to publication a translation of Scaino's *Treatise on the Game of the Ball* that his predecessor had commissioned. The translation was the work of W.W. Kershaw, who knew nothing of Tennis, so in 1984 Negretti published a much-improved translation of his own. He was punctilious in ensuring that club matches were reported in *The Times*, and he was also a Tennis correspondent for the magazine *British Lawn Tennis and Squash* shortly after the war, writing at a time when there was very little reporting of the game.

In business, Negretti was Chairman of Negretti and Zambra, the scientific and industrial instrument makers. In 1964 he was the Mayor of Westminster. Mayoral duties were nothing new; at one time during the War he was temporarily appointed Mayor of Lille. A good all-round sportsman, he played many sports well, most notably rugby for Harlequins, ice hockey for the London Lions and, as a member of the MCC, he played regularly in the annual cricket match against the Lords and Commons. However, his first love was Tennis and he entered the Amateur Championship and the MCC All Comers' Competition on a number of occasions. Tongue in cheek, he once recalled his best performance in the MCC Tournament, when he reached the semi-finals. In the first round he had a bye; the second round, he met the only player worse than himself; the third round, he had a walk-over; the fourth round, his opponent retired hurt; and in the semi-final he met David Warburg, then the Amateur Champion, who beat him 6-0, 6-1!

After the Palace Revolution Tony Negretti was elected President of the Club and re-elected annually for the next 14 years, finally retiring in 1987 after 40 years of service to the Royal Court. He passed away at the end of the third month of the new millennium at the age of 87.

CHAPTER 9

450 YEARS OF TENNIS!

What other pastime's cult can show
A temple such as this we know?

With its new constitution in place, an active Committee, which had elected Henry Wollaston as Chairman, was now running the Club. Lord Revelstoke, after 40 years as President, and Ronnie Aird after 25 as Vice-President, had both taken the opportunity to stand down. The November 1973 Special General Meeting had consequently elected Tony Negretti as President.

79. HENRY WOLLASTON

Chairman of the Royal Tennis Court 1973-80
President 1987-89

James Macnaghten remained as Treasurer until 1976. He was succeeded by Ronald Swash, who served in that Office until 1980, when he was elected Chairman on the retirement of Henry Wollaston. Murray Glover continued as Honorary Secretary until 1977, when Andrew Lloyd Davies succeeded him.

Of the nearly 1,000 members, a staggering 600 resigned following the quadrupling of the subscription. Of those 600, about 250 continued to pay their £1 standing orders and became known as 'Friends of the Royal Tennis Court', but they were without the full benefits of membership. There are still some 70 of these Friends, who continue to support the Club in this way nearly 30 years later.

One of the first priorities of the new Committee was to improve the playing facilities. High on the list of necessary improvements was new lighting. David Warburg was asked to investigate the possibility of installing a more efficient system. He was also asked to organise the redecoration of the Court — a task he took on with great enthusiasm. The walls were cleaned and coated with linseed oil, the old window blinds were removed and the glass whitewashed. Permission was given to paint those flagstones that had been replaced some years earlier, but a request for a ball trough was refused on preservation grounds. David Cull (then an assistant professional at Lord's) was asked to make 150 new balls and rebuild another 40. The Palace replaced the old anthracite boiler in the changing room with a new gas-fired one. This allowed the area under the hazard penthouse, that had previously served as a coal cellar, to be cleared and converted into a workshop for the Professional ten or so years later.

80.   THE 1974 COURT RENOVATION

James Macnaghten (left) and Vernon Ely working on the main wall

A well-known member of The Queen's Club and also a member of the RTC, Jack Hurley, greatly assisted the Club by providing platform scaffolding, necessary for reaching the roof and up the walls. During the war he had saved the life of Ray Wigger who, in gratitude, joined the RTC as a Life Member and took up Tennis. It happened on the slopes of Mount Etna in Sicily when Ray was hit in the head by a sniper's bullet. When stretcher-bearers refused to carry him to safety because of heavy enemy fire, Jack Hurley threatened them with court-martial if he did not find his body, dead or alive, back at the regimental aid post. Seriously wounded, Ray was airlifted out to Algiers. After he woke up, he was astounded to see Jack Hurley who had himself become a casualty when he was brought in wounded a few days later.

The Privy Purse Office was approached and asked if play could be extended beyond 8 o'clock at night. Permission was granted to continue until 10 o'clock. The Privy Purse Office was also asked if it would agree to the commercial sponsorship of the Lurgan Cup. This they agreed to and Mark Barker negotiated successfully with Harvey's of Bristol to sponsor the competition, which was renamed the Cockburn Cup after their port of the same name. However, any wine-tasting had to take place outside the Palace walls. The revamped tournament continued as a 'pro-am' doubles with the winning Amateur receiving the Lurgan Cup, and his Professional partner the Cockburn Cup. That year, 1974, the winners were Peter Kershaw and Chris Ennis of Manchester.

81.   STEPHEN de LASZLO

Another competition began in 1974 following the presentation of a rose bowl by Stephen de Laszlo. For a long time he had felt that the competitions available were too serious, and not open to players of a lesser standard — something in which an element of fun was needed! The de Laszlo Bowl has become a very popular doubles competition where the highest handicapped player is paired with the lowest, the second highest with the second lowest, and so on. Another feature of the competition is the centre line rule. This prevents a player from straying into his partner's half of the court — an offender is invariably the victim of some raucous barracking from the dedans!

Stephen   de   Laszlo,   who represented Hungary at both Lawn Tennis and Swimming, did not take up Real Tennis until he was in his mid-fifties. A great supporter of international tennis, he organised the British team's attempt to retain the Bathurst Cup in 1969. The team were all members of the RTC, Howard Angus, R.D.B. (Richard) Cooper and David Warburg. They won the preliminary round against Australia in Melbourne, but lost to the United States in New York and Tuxedo. Over the years Stephen de Laszlo has organised many overseas tours involving some 160 tennis players. The touring parties invariably included Hampton Court members, which resulted in RTC challenges at most of the clubs visited. On the same theme he has generously presented trophies to Queen's, Lord's, Paris and Bordeaux to encourage Anglo-French links.

All this extra activity was putting pressure on the new Professional Derek Barrett, so he asked to be relieved of the task of tying and re-covering the balls. By his efforts he had significantly increased court usage and this was appreciated by the Committee, so his request was agreed to. Once again, this work was sub-contracted out to Henry Johns and George Beton at Lord's. In an attempt to save money, four sets of manufactured Dunlop balls were purchased, with two of the sets presented to the Club by Sir Ronald Prain. Sadly, as other clubs had found (except for the special circumstances at Falkland Palace) they were not a success.

As the Court was open to the public, members often had to cope with disruptions from the side galleries. One professional, the fiery Keeble, was not beyond blasting a ball at an unruly member of the public in order to silence them. On one occasion he was on court with Pat Barker when he spotted someone trying to remove a ball from the winning gallery by cutting the netting with a penknife. After some strong words the young offender left. Amazingly, he returned later during the game and started cutting away at the net again. Pat Barker spotted this from the hazard end and instinctively cannoned a ball into the gallery, hitting the young man on the side of the nose. With blood all over the place, he retreated, never to be seen again! On another occasion Derek Barrett hit a ball very hard into the last gallery, striking a young woman square on in the face. After she had departed, he retrieved the ball from the gallery and found a perfect lipstick imprint on it. He kept that ball for many years, and would use it to show players new to the game 'the power of a tennis ball'! Shortly after this last incident the Palace installed protective wire grills along the whole length of the side galleries. Recently the Palace replaced these grills with clear Perspex, which has afforded better viewing and helped to reduce the disturbance to the players when the public are admitted by cutting the noise from the side galleries.

The new grills were installed early in 1975, and by the summer of the same year David Warburg had completed his investigation into the court lighting. In this he was greatly assisted by David Gaskill, a member of the Manchester Tennis & Racquet Club, who arranged for the new lighting to be installed at a favourable price. In appreciation he was made an Honorary Member of the Club. David Gaskill's recommendation was for thirty-six 400-watt high-intensity sodium floodlights reflecting light indirectly off the ceiling as before. Despite his efforts, the cost was still an enormous sum for the Club, £3,500. In addition, the ceiling had to be repainted to make the system effective, increasing the cost even further. The problem was that there was only £1,500 in the Club's reserves, so a fund-raising scheme had to be devised. Sir Ronald Prain, a man with an acute financial brain, came up with a clever idea. Three committee members and an anonymous friend lent the Club £2,500 until the end of the year. That allowed the lights to be installed before the winter season while the main plank of the fund-raising could be put into place. Twenty-five members were then asked to contribute not less than £100 each, interest-free for three years, in return for Life Membership. The scheme offered Life Membership for £45 to those over 65, and £70 for those under. The cost would be taken out of the amount loaned before the balances were to be repaid, at, or before, the end of 1978. The offer was quickly taken up, and the Royal Tennis Court became the best-lit court in the country. The other part of the scheme involved increasing the annual membership subscription from £4 to £8.

With new lighting and the Court redecorated, the Club was able to attract some important national tournaments, the first of these being the challenge for the British Professional Championship in May 1976. The defending champion Frank Willis (Manchester) had been challenged by Norwood Cripps (Queen's) and the match was held over three legs. The first two had taken place on each of their home courts and by the start of the last leg at Hampton Court, Willis was leading by six sets to two. Cripps took the next set but Willis was too strong — he then won the only set he needed to retain the Championship. The match, organised by Pat Barker, was a financial success and after the payment of prize money there was a small profit for the Club. Pat Barker's skills as a tournament organiser were noted and put to good use throughout the remainder of the nineteen-seventies, when he supervised all the major national and world championships that were held at the Royal Court.

One month after the Professional Championships an even more prestigious tournament came to Hampton Court, the British Open Singles Championship. As with the Professional Singles, it was played over three legs, the first two at Queen's and Manchester. Frank Willis had qualified for the challenge, where he met Howard Angus the holder, by beating Norwood Cripps. At the start of the third leg Angus led by six sets to two. He retained the Championship by winning the first and consequently the final set. The players then sportingly agreed to play two more exhibition sets and the spectators in the packed court were treated to some wonderful tennis.

Another two national tournaments were held at the Court towards the end of the year, the Cutty Sark Invitation Singles and the Cockburn Cup. Howard Angus and Norwood Cripps contested the Cutty Sark final, with Angus running out the winner by three sets to two. Howard Angus also won the Cockburn Cup, partnering the Club's Honorary Secretary, Murray Glover, in a popular win for the home team.

The Committee next decided to commission a new brochure for sale to the public. The old one had been a tremendous success with over 100,000 copies sold, necessitating seven reprints. Sir Ronald Prain approached the Palace and persuaded them to place a huge advance order. This not only paid for the initial publication costs, but it also guaranteed that the Club would make a profit on the venture. The new brochure was illustrated and explained in simple terms the Court, its history and how the game is played. At first it was sold for 30p: today it sells in the Palace Bookshop for £1. The original drawing used for the front cover, showing the Court from the public gardens, was sketched by Arthur Wren and presented to H.M. The Queen at Buckingham Palace by a delegation from the Committee in April 1977 in honour of Her Majesty's 50th birthday.

This was a time of rising inflation, so with increases in subscriptions expected to be more frequent, the Committee sought and obtained approval at a Special General Meeting in November 1976 for the introduction of a quarterly Direct Debit system. This, though, was again to send shudders through the membership. To many the scheme was anathema and several refused to sign up to the new arrangements. The combination of the Direct Debit and the doubled subscription resulted in the playing membership of 400 falling to 250. Fortunately 120 of those who resigned agreed to stay on as non-playing members at the old rate of £4.

For those who remained there was soon the opportunity to witness some world class tennis, as 92 years after the last and only world championship match to have taken place at Hampton Court, another was arranged for the 8th, 10th and 12th June 1977. The rules at the time gave the Champion the right to defend the title on a court of his choosing. Howard Angus was the Champion, having beaten Gene Scott following the resignation of Jimmy Bostwick a year earlier. For his first defence, Angus elected to play at Hampton Court. The challenger was again the New York-based amateur Gene Scott. Scott was a former Davis Cup lawn tennis player who, after taking up (Court/Real) Tennis, had won the US Open Championship five times. After the first day, honours were even, but the second was decisive with Angus taking all four sets for a 6-2 lead. Needing only one more set to retain the title, he took the first on the final day.

82.   1977 WORLD CHAMPIONSHIP GROUP

l to r.   Alastair Martin, David Warburg, Pat Barker (the tournament organiser),
Howard Angus, Gene Scott, Jimmy Van Alen and Alan Lovell

Harvey's, the sponsors of the Pro-Am Cockburn/Lurgan Cup, unfortunately withdrew in 1977 and the tournament was not staged for the following two years. But then the dairy product company Unigate, who were the main sponsors of

Tennis at the time, extended their financing to include the Pro-Am. The arrangement lasted for only three more years and the competition has not been played at Hampton Court since.

There was still the need to pay off the members' lighting loans and the subscription was raised again at the start of 1978, this time to £12 a year. By the end of the year all the contributors had been paid back, on or before time.

It was at this time that local schools were persuaded to take an interest in the game. Firstly, Kingston Grammar School sent some boys for tuition, late in 1977. They were followed by Hampton School early the following year. Sir Ronald Prain successfully negotiated a Sports Council grant in 1979 to help with the costs, and this continued for the next ten years. Happily, both these schools continue to enjoy the arrangement — an important one — as young blood is so vital for the future of both club and game.

Howard Angus again agreed to defend the World Championship at Hampton Court in April 1979. This time the eliminating competition was held there too. Before this could happen though, the floor had to be repainted, costing the Club £1,700. In December of the previous year Chris Ronaldson (Troon) had defeated Norwood Cripps (Queen's) by five sets to one. Ronaldson then went on in early April to meet the American challenger, Jimmy Burke of Philadelphia, whom he decisively beat by seven sets to one. However, in the Challenge Match, played on the 17th, 19th and 21st of the same month, he met an in-form Angus, who comfortably retained the title without losing a set, needing only two days.

Detailed press reports of all the World Championship Matches played at Hampton Court can be found in Appendix 12. In the 1970s and 1980s, thanks to the enthusiasm of Roy McKelvie and Christina Wood, *The Times* and the *Daily Telegraph* gave good coverage to major tennis tournaments, including a number staged at Hampton Court, at a level rarely seen since.

Howard Angus has an outstanding record at both Tennis and Rackets. He was World Rackets Champion 1973-75 and World Tennis Champion 1976-81. In addition he was Amateur Rackets Champion from 1972 to 1977, Amateur Tennis Champion and MCC Gold Racquet holder from 1966 to 1980 and again in both competitions in 1982, and won several open tennis championships. He was a member of the Committee of the Royal Tennis Court for nine years and shortly after stepping down he was elected an Honorary Member in recognition of his services to the Club. In 1981 he was awarded an MBE for services to Tennis and Rackets.

In 1979, three committee members who were at the heart of the Palace Revolution stepped down: Sir Ronald Prain who was the Chairman of the Finance Sub-Committee and had masterminded the financial recovery of the Club, David Warburg who had done so much to restore the Court itself, and Pat Barker the highly successful tournament organiser. They were all part of multi-generation tennis-playing families. Sir Ronald Prain's son, Graham, is a regular player today, and his grandson Christopher won the Club's Junior Championship in 1995. Graham agreed to organise the distribution of the new Club Brochure. David Warburg's son Thane captained Cambridge University at Real Tennis and became a single-figure-handicap player. A.R.V. (Arthur) Barker, father of Mark and Pat, represented the Club on many occasions. He was a fine all-round sportsman who represented Oxford University at Tennis, Rackets, Squash and Football, and was the first winner of the Lurgan Cup in 1938. Mark's son Simon is currently one of the leading players in the Club and both he and Thane Warburg have been successful in the Camm Cup (now the Barker Camm Cup), the Club Championship. The two of them have also represented the Club in the Field Trophy on a number of occasions. In 1998 Pat Barker celebrated the 50th anniversary of his first game of tennis and, in 1999, Graham Prain his 40th.

83. 1979 WORLD CHAMPIONSHIP GROUP

In the centre of this group are Howard Angus holding the World Championship Salver,
a bearded Chris Ronaldson, and the Marker, Derek Barrett, standing between them.

In September 1979 Derek Barrett left. He had been discontented for some time and felt that his work was not properly appreciated or adequately rewarded. Once again Ken and Betty Evans stepped in, ensuring a continuation of play. Henry Johns made himself available for marking once more. In the meantime, Ronald Swash had taken steps to secure the services of Chris Ronaldson. This time he accepted the job, but asked that an assistant be appointed from the start.

The young Australian, Rob Bartlett, who was supported by the Young Professionals Fund, started on the same day, November 19th 1979.

Chris Ronaldson's talent for filling courts is legendary. In his first year at Hampton Court over 3,000 courts were taken and the figure soon rose to over 5,000. Play at times starts at 6 o'clock in the morning and sometimes finishes after midnight. Attempts are made to ensure that no member leaves the Club after a game without having their full quota of games booked, and the professionals regularly spend time at the end of a day telephoning round whenever opponents are needed the following day. As another means of boosting play, Ronaldson persuaded the Committee to agree to the establishment of a level singles members' tournament. Three years later, following a donation of a Cup by Arden Camm, this competition became the Camm Cup. The Club Ladder was also started. At first it was a summer competition culminating in knockout phase between the top four players — a prize was also given to the player who had climbed the furthest up the ladder. Its success has led to it becoming a continuous challenge. It produces some competitive matches where the victor, if below the vanquished, jumps above his opponent, with all those in between dropping down a rung. A full appreciation of Chris Ronaldson's career is given in Chapter 13.

Quite often in the Club's history several key committee changes have occurred in a short space of time. The previous year had seen the departure of Barker, Prain and Warburg, and the 1980 AGM saw the retirement as Chairman of Henry Wollaston, although he continued to serve on the Committee for another two years. The new Chairman was Ronald Swash. This created a vacancy for Honorary Treasurer. Alan Baddeley agreed to take the role on, and was co-opted onto the Committee and formally elected the following year. Andrew Lloyd Davies stepped down as Honorary Secretary, but he too stayed on the Committee, in his case for three more years. Ray Moorman succeeded Andrew Lloyd Davies as Honorary Secretary.

Ronald Swash spent his working life in industry, commerce, professional institutions and charities. He was a Rugby Fives Blue at Oxford, played Lawn Tennis for Cambridgeshire and held office in several sports clubs. Latterly, with two colleagues, he raised funds and arranged for the building of new Fives Courts at Oxford and subsequently for the restoration of the Thames Ditton Village Hall.

The Committee now turned its attention to the 450th Anniversary. There has always been the problem of determining the date when Tennis was first played at Hampton Court. In 1980 the club tie sported the date 1530 (as it still does), but as has been noted, an earlier version used the year 1531. However, Tennis was definitely played at the Palace in 1529 and almost certainly earlier than that.

The Club's Patron, Her Majesty Queen Elizabeth II, and His Royal Highness The Duke of Edinburgh graciously accepted an invitation to a reception to be held at Hampton Court on 24th June 1980.

Only after this acceptance was it realised that 1980 was *not* the 450th anniversary of the present Tennis Court, and that Falkland Palace, and not the Royal Tennis Court, could claim to be the oldest complete court still in use. Earlier anniversaries do not appear to have been celebrated. One was considered in May 1929, but J.J. Freeman announced in *The Field*, that 'there was no intention to celebrate the 400th Anniversary as it would be difficult to arrange because the court is open to the public and the prolonged illness of Mr. C.T. Agar, the hon. secretary'. However, H.J. Inman, a member of the Club, penned some verses to mark the event, which were first published in the *Surrey Comet* in January 1929. It is these verses that appear at the head of some of the chapters in this volume (see Appendix 17).

Having established however that Tennis had been played at Hampton Court since about 1530, the necessary wording was altered to 'the celebrating of the 450th anniversary of the playing of Tennis at Hampton Court Palace'. Members had the choice of attending either an exhibition match, or the reception in the Cartoon Gallery, but not both. Unfortunately, there was a serious restriction on numbers that left many disappointed. The original intention had been to use the Great Hall, which would have allowed greater numbers to attend, but it was being renovated at the time. The Cartoon Gallery had a maximum capacity of 240, but the large number of official guests meant only 180 members and their spouses could be accommodated.

84. THE VAL ST. LAMBERT GOBLET

As part of the celebrations, two commemorative goblets were commissioned. The first was a beautiful piece of glassware by Val St. Lambert, of which 32 were made. Engraved on one side was the club insignia of crossed rackets surmounted by a rose and a crown, above which was inscribed 'The Royal Tennis Court' and below 'Hampton Court Palace 1530-1980'. On the reverse was the Monogram of William III. Two of these goblets were to be presented to the Queen; the remainder were for sale to members at £40 each. The second, a Bohemia goblet, was sold by the Club to members for £12, and 150 were made. Lord Rennell of Rodd, a keen tennis player, organised the supply and engraving of these goblets. Thanks to the efforts of Arden Camm, their sale made a handsome profit of over £500.

85. THE 450th ANNIVERSARY

Her Majesty Queen Elizabeth II is greeted at the Court by Lord Aberdare and Henry Wollaston

The Queen's visit was an unqualified success and much of the credit must go to Michael Morton who was the committee member responsible for the organisation of the greatest social occasion in the Club's history. Enquiring in advance as to what drink should be provided during the pause for refreshment, Michael was advised that Her Majesty might choose a small gin and tonic and that Prince Philip would probably ask for 'whatever you haven't got!' In the event he asked only for a small whisky! Reprinted below is his report that appeared in the Club Newsletter in September 1980:

'The long-awaited and much heralded visit by her Majesty The Queen and H.R.H. The Duke of Edinburgh to Hampton Court Palace to mark the 450th Anniversary of the playing of tennis at the Palace took place on 24th June 1980.

'Due to the inevitable traffic jams around the Palace during the evening rush hour Her Majesty's arrival at the door to the Tennis Court from the East Front was delayed – and the weather did not exactly shine for the occasion.

'The late start and the wet weather did not, however, put a damper on the auspiciousness of the event. Inside the Tennis Court, Her Majesty and His Royal Highness were first introduced to Lesley Ronaldson, Mr. & Mrs Peter Dawes and Mr. and Mrs Henry Johns.

86. THE 450th ANNIVERSARY

H.R.H. Prince Philip with Henry Johns

'The Royal Party then proceeded into the dedans where, for ten minutes or so they watched (under instruction) a four-handed game of tennis then in progress between Chris Ronaldson, Alan Lovell, David Cull and David Johnson, which was marked by Derek Barrett. By all accounts this game was splendid entertainment – hard, fast and furious – and was in particular enjoyed by Her Majesty's Private Secretary who was nearly laid low by a hard force to the dedans!

'As the game ended, Her Majesty and His Royal Highness walked onto the Court where all the professionals, who represented nearly every Court in Great Britain as well as Australia, together with the players and several members of the RTC Committee, were assembled for presentation. One professional was heard to remark that Cambridge was not the same place since the Duke's son left it – and another that he did not yet know much about the game. (This was not altogether surprising since he had only been in post for a fortnight!)

'Television cameras had whirred on the Court, both before and after the Royal arrival and departure – the B.B.C. filmed the entire proceedings including the party in the Cartoon Gallery, for inclusion in a later Royal Heritage series – and the press were present in force.

143

87. THE 450th ANNIVERSARY

Her Majesty The Queen with Henry Wollaston

Many of the professionals were photographed with either The Queen or The Duke of Edinburgh, and their wives and others watching from the Galleries had equal enjoyment from the proceedings and the party held in the Court afterwards.

'In the meanwhile, under the television lights, there had been gathering in the Cartoon Gallery some 180 members and their wives together with sundry other specially invited guests.

'Representatives from Courts in France, U.S.A., Australia and Tasmania as well as from Courts in Great Britain, the Tennis and Rackets Association, the Lord Chamberlain's Office, the Privy Purse, the game's present sponsors, Unigate, the Press and the staff at Hampton Court itself (including the RTC's own reserve "professionals", Mr. & Mrs Evans) thronged the huge Cartoon Gallery, eating and drinking whilst awaiting Her Majesty's arrival.

'On leaving the Tennis Court, the Royal Party walked along the East Front to be met at the entrance to the Palace by the Chief Steward and Lady Moore and, after pausing for refreshment in one of the many rooms adjacent to the Cartoon Gallery (where further members of the

RTC Committee including Howard Angus and Sir Ronald Prain with their wives, and Vernon Ely were presented). Her Majesty and the Royal Party entered the Cartoon Gallery, in keeping with the intention of the function, informally and unheralded.

'For the ensuing half hour Her Majesty and His Royal Highness progressed down the length of the Gallery being introduced to various official guests either by the Chairman of the Club, Henry Wollaston or by the President of the Tennis and Rackets Association, Morys Aberdare.

'What was said, what questions were asked or answered, what impressions were given or got must be the prerogative of each individual who was present. It is perhaps enough to say that the process, the first in 450 years, seemed to pass in 450 seconds.

'At the end of the Cartoon Gallery, Her Majesty and H.R.H. The Duke of Edinburgh proceeded into the Communication Gallery where, after presentation of various members of staff of the Department of the Environment to Her Majesty and His Royal Highness, she and His Royal Highness signed photographs which, when framed, will take a prominent place on the walls of the Ely Rooms.

'Before the Royal Party's final departure down the Queen's Staircase, the Chairman presented Her Majesty and His Royal Highness with engraved glass goblets to commemorate their visit and conducted them round an exhibition of pictures reflecting all aspects of the game of Tennis, which had been garnered together by Mr. & Mrs Peter Railing for the occasion in the Haunted Gallery.

'The Cartoon Gallery, meanwhile, continued to hum with conversation. Old friendships were renewed, and tennis players the world over and their wives discussed the game, and the events of an evening which the Royal Tennis Court are proud to have been offered the opportunity to arrange.

'The Court Circular on the next day read:

> *"The Queen and The Duke of Edinburgh this evening attended a reception at Hampton Court Palace to mark the 450th Anniversary of the playing of Real Tennis at Hampton Court. Having been received by the Mayor of Richmond-upon-Thames (Councillor Mrs N.J.F. Millar) and the Chief Steward of Hampton Court Palace (General Sir Rodney Moore) Her Majesty and His Royal Highness watched a game of Tennis and escorted by the Chairman of the Royal Tennis Court (Mr H.W. Wollaston) met the players and officials and attended a Reception. The Lady Susan Hussey, the Rt. Hon. Sir Phillip Moore and Lieutenant-Commander Robert Guy R.N. were in attendance".*

'Finally, it would not be right if in this report the Club forgot to express its grateful thanks to the very many members of the Staff of the Department of Environment who made many of the necessary arrangements so easy and in particular to the Superintendent, Ryan Harman who co-ordinated all the services with naval efficiency; to the caterers (both of them) who prepared and served the food and drink with practised ease, to the press and television who were far less obtrusive than had been at first feared, and lastly to Her Majesty and His Royal Highness themselves who graced an occasion which will not soon be forgotten by those who were present.'

Michael Morton
September 1980

88.   THE 450th ANNIVERSARY

The Exhibition Match played before H.M. The Queen and H.R.H. The Duke of Edinburgh.
Chris Ronaldson and David Cull against Alan Lovell and David Johnson, with Derek Barrett marking.

CHAPTER 10

RECENT TIMES

Although the 450th Anniversary dominated 1980, there were other important developments. Vernon Ely had generously donated £1,500 for the rooms at the Tennis Court Lane end of Apartment 53 to be converted into clubrooms, with a ladies' changing room on the ground floor. The work was completed by September and the benefactor officially opened the Ely Rooms in November 1980. Unfortunately the ladies' changing room suffered from persistent chronic damp and in the following year it became uninhabitable. Vernon Ely was a major benefactor to RTC and other sports clubs and charities for many years. He lived to the grand old age of 92. Since the Palace Revolution he had enjoyed using — and paying generously for — the changing-room locker bearing Prince Albert's nameplate.

The Unigate Pro-Am tournament was again held at Hampton Court in October and resulted in a popular win for the all-RTC combination of Ronald Swash and Chris Ronaldson. In 1980 the Club won the inter-club Field Trophy for the first time, under the captaincy of Murray Glover. This was the start of an extraordinary run of eleven victories in thirteen years (1984 was shared with Seacourt).

There were changes on the professional side. Rob Bartlett moved to Canford in April and was replaced by Alistair Curley, who arrived in September — he had learnt the game at Troon. Towards the end of the year, for the first time ever, pressure on court time became an issue. It was decided to introduce a £20 entrance fee for new members. This made little difference to the numbers applying so the following year a waiting list was introduced. The income from the new entrance fee and an increased annual subscription (from £12 to £20 at the start of 1981) was very welcome, as the conversion of the Ely Rooms had cost twice as much as expected.

Murray Glover and Nigel Bruce both stepped down in 1981 after nearly a decade of committee service. They had seen the Club through some very choppy waters and helped steer it into the calm and prosperity of the 1980s. However, there were now two aspects of committee work that were troubling Ronald Swash. Firstly, they were becoming bogged down with petty detail; and secondly, whenever a key member resigned there was often no natural successor. He devised a system of sub-committees to deal with minor matters and to make recommendations to the Main Committee on major issues. Each of these sub-committees was to have a chairman, another committee member, and a co-opted member. The hope was that the co-opted member would understudy the chairman, so that new blood could be brought onto the Main Committee.

Chris Ronaldson in the meantime had embarked on the most important series of matches of his life, all played at Queen's. The previous December he had beaten Frank Willis in the British eliminator for the right to challenge Howard Angus for the World Championship. In April 1981 he defeated Barry Toates, then of Boston, in the final eliminator. Later that month he gained the highest prize Tennis has to offer when he took the title from Angus. For the first time in its history, the Royal Tennis Court had a reigning World Champion as its Professional.

In playing terms, the year was a bad one for Howard Angus, who also lost the Amateur Championship to Alan Lovell. Alan Lovell was already a member of the Club and it was largely due to the new Champion's presence in the Field Trophy team that the RTC had such a wonderful run of victories during the eighties and nineties. Often the team was not the strongest on paper, but just kept on winning thanks to the loyalty of its best players and its team spirit. Many an exciting final or other tie was won 3-2 due to someone playing way above themselves on the day. For some years the unique solid silver racket-and-ball Field Trophy had gone missing, but eventually Murray Glover tracked it down, after some determined detective work, to *The Field*'s own offices.

89. RECOVERING THE FIELD TROPHY

Murray Glover receives the Field Trophy from the Marquis de Rovigny,
the General Manager of *The Field*.

The assistant professional merry-go-round continued with Alistair Curley swapping with Hobart's Wayne Davies. Although he was only at Hampton Court for four months, little did members suspect that this gifted and determined

Australian would eventually be the one to topple Chris Ronaldson as World Champion. Curley returned to Hampton Court in July and Davies moved to Bordeaux. Curley, though, had decided to emigrate and take over from Lachlan Deuchar as Head Professional at Hobart. This move brought Chris Ronaldson's great friend to Hampton Court. Lachie Deuchar agreed to become his assistant and training partner — there was of course the inducement of the top-class practice he would get with the World Champion.

So began a golden era at the Royal Tennis Court, with members benefiting from the services of the World Champion as the Head Professional, and the talents of Deuchar, who was ranked either two or three in the world throughout his six-year stay.

90. RONALD SWASH

Honorary Treasurer 1976-80 and
Chairman of the RTC 1980-88

The Club Chairman, Ronald Swash, has never been one to think of Tennis only in terms of Hampton Court. So when Hatfield approached the Club for a professional sharing arrangement, he was only too happy to recommend it to the Committee. Ronaldson and Deuchar shared these duties and were later joined by Kevin King. This assistance was needed for nearly a year, after which time Hatfield engaged King on a permanent basis. Kevin King is familiar to many RTC members; over the years he has often helped out at the Club. A similar professional sharing arrangement was also offered to Petworth, but not taken up.

The game of Tennis from time to time produces some wonderful eccentrics and for one such, Esmond Seal, the year was to end on a tragic note. This much-loved member collapsed and sadly died on court during a game with Mark Barker. By cruel coincidence, it was Mark who had found Arthur Ashford dead on court almost to the day, 24 years earlier. Esmond's wife Barbara generously donated a Salver in his name for a veteran's singles tournament. To enter this tournament a member has to be over 50 years of age — there is a handicap, but it is based on the difference in age. This sometimes results in some extraordinary matches particularly when fit 'young' players become eligible and find themselves up against wily septuagenarians, or even octogenarians. Always an enjoyable competition, the Seal Salver annually attracts an entry of around fifty.

Esmond Seal was the first to join Nigel Bruce in organising 'Hamster' matches. Back in 1969, Nigel Bruce had been concerned about the lack of opportunity for average club players to participate in inter-club matches. Up until then it was usually the better players who were called upon to represent the Club. He started the Hamster matches based on the formula used by the already established 'Angoras' at Hatfield. The Hamsters regard their role as one of upholding the best traditions of the game, with the emphasis on the highest standard of sportsmanship, dress and hospitality. They are not a formal part of the club structure and these days one has to be invited to join. Their playing membership is limited to twelve, to encourage team spirit and social ambience. Nigel Bruce was for some years the esteemed Secretary of the Tennis & Rackets Association. He retired from that office in 1981. After he died in 1997, it was found that he had bequeathed his valuable collection of tennis books to the Club.

January 1982 saw the Club hosting the inaugural Ladies Open Doubles Championships, and March the Amateur Singles. This was the first time the Club had hosted the Amateur and it resulted in another Angus-Lovell final, with Angus regaining the title. The Amateur was staged again at Hampton Court in the following two years, and in 1983 the same pair met in the final with the result reversed. This was the start of a four-year run for Alan Lovell. The tournament did not return to the Royal Tennis Court until 1996 — on that occasion another member, Julian Snow, won it for the ninth time — extended to twelve by the end of the century. Julian has also challenged for the World Championship. The outstanding play of Angus, Lovell and Snow in turn was primarily responsible for Great Britain's regular successes in the Bathurst Cup in the 1970s, 1980s and 1990s.

The time had come for Chris Ronaldson to make his first defence of the World Championship. He decided it would take place at Hampton Court in November 1982. Before that, an eliminator between Wayne Davies and Colin Lumley had to be fought out. This too was played at Hampton Court, on the 22nd and 24th October, with Davies coming through by seven sets to one. Unfortunately, the day before the Challenge proper, Davies fell ill with appendicitis. The rescheduled match took place the following March.

Towards the end of 1982, it became apparent that the Bordeaux Club was failing and facing closure. Chris Ronaldson devised a rescue plan, which he put to Ronald Swash. The problem was that it meant that an RTC professional would necessarily be away from Hampton Court for several weeks at a time. Ronald Swash, as mentioned before, was always prepared to support the game as a whole and he persuaded the Committee to back the proposal.

Ronaldson's Bordeaux team, apart from himself and Lachie Deuchar, included Rob Bartlett, who was free having left Canford; he was awaiting the completion of the new court in Ballarat where he had been appointed Professional. Jonathan Howell, seduced from Moreton Morrell, and Thane Warburg completed the resuscitation party. Jonathan Howell enjoyed himself to such an extent that he remained at Bordeaux for over seven years, eventually becoming Head Professional when the crisis was brought to an end.

91. 1983 WORLD CHAMPIONSHIP GROUP

l to r: Lord Aberdare (President of the T&RA), David Norman (Chairman of the T&RA),
Wayne Davies, Lachlan Deuchar (Marker), Cliff Chetwood and Chris Ronaldson

In 1983, and again the following year, the Club hosted the Professional Doubles and Ladies Doubles tournaments. In addition, a new Invitation Mixed Doubles competition was inaugurated for the Billy Ross-Skinner Cup. This competition has proved immensely popular and since its inception and up until 1999, was an annual fixture at the RTC. W.M. Ross-Skinner was a keen supporter of the Club. He played first string for Cambridge in 1925, represented the Royal Tennis Court in many matches both before and after the war, and was the winner of the Lurgan Cup in 1939. Maggie Wright and Colin Dean won the Cup in its inaugural year. In 1987 George Wimpey sponsored the tournament, an arrangement that was to last eight years. To his immense satisfaction, Wimpey's Chief Executive, Sir Clifford Chetwood, won the tournament three times, twice with Sally Jones and once with Alex Warren-Piper. Oracle was the sponsor in 1995, and the following year British Land extended their general sponsorship of the game to include this competition. The last time the tournament was played at Hampton Court it was won by an all-RTC combination of Fiona Deuchar and Charles Crossley. Another national competition held at the Royal Tennis Court for the first, and so far the only time, was the Bridgeman Cup in 1984. This over-50s open singles competition was won on that occasion by the former World Rackets and Amateur Tennis Champion, Geoffrey Atkins.

With Wayne Davies fit again, the postponed World Championship Challenge went ahead on the 18th, 20th and 22nd March 1983. By the end of the first day they were level at two sets apiece. On the second day Ronaldson took command winning all four sets. Davies though, came out fighting on the third and final day, winning the first two sets before Ronaldson gained the only one he needed for a seven sets to four victory.

With the Bordeaux Club now secure, Ronaldson and Deuchar were again able to devote all their energy to members. In May, a youngster who in time became one of the world's best players, Mike Gooding, joined them. Sponsored by the Young Professionals Fund, he was sent to Hampton Court for four months training prior to taking up the job of Professional at the Sun Court, Troon.

For generations the professional's accommodation had suffered from damp, and for many years the installation of central heating had been an objective, but the cost had always been prohibitive. Vernon Ely once again stepped in with a generous donation that allowed heating to be installed in Apartment 53 and in the Ely Rooms. At first the Palace insisted that one of their nominated contractors should carry out the work, but Cliff Chetwood, who had enormous experience in such matters, persuaded the authorities to allow an outside contractor of the Club's choosing to be used. This resulted in the work being carried out for £10,000, as opposed to a Palace estimate of nearer £15,000.

Until now most of the Club's social activity had centred on the various tournaments played at the Court. The Annual Dinner was born out of the success of the 450th Anniversary celebrations. Many of the members who had been unable to attend because of the restriction on numbers, felt that there should be a dinner the following year, 1981. It was held at the RAC Club in London's Pall Mall. The guests of honour were the Club's two World Champions, Howard Angus and Chris Ronaldson. The support was good so another was arranged the following year at the Fairmile in Cobham. With the dinner now established as an annual event, it was decided to hold the third in the most splendid of settings, the Great Hall of the Palace — the dinner was a resounding success and Tony Negretti was the guest of honour. It was held there again the following year, but the response was not so good. As a dinner is such a special event when held in the Palace, it was decided to use the expensive facilities no more than every third year. Since then the members have enjoyed Annual Dinners in the Great Watching Chamber, the Cartoon Gallery, the Oak Room and again in the Great Hall.

With three club singles tournaments (the Lathom Browne, the Camm Cup and the Seal Salver) attracting more and more entries, in addition to the de Laszlo Bowl, the professionals were having trouble completing the competitions within the season. Evenly balanced matches were running into third sets and they often could not be completed within the allotted hour, necessitating a return by the players on another day. It was therefore decided that a third and final set, if needed, should start at three games all. This has worked well and ten years later, with even more pressure on court time, it was agreed to start the first two sets at one game all. Subsequently 'sudden death' — i.e. one point more only to be played to decide a game — replaced deuce for handicap competitions, and is currently included in the Rules of Tennis, as an integral part of establishing individual national handicaps. Although not popular with all RTC members, the sudden death at 40-all system assisted enormously in organising court time.

This was essentially a problem in the winter and spring — there were often spare courts in the summer. Lachie Deuchar suggested that a good way of utilising the spare capacity would be to introduce a 'Night Pennant' competition, a popular format at Australian clubs. Here two teams of three would book three hours of court time. Each player would have a set of singles and two sets of doubles. Several teams compete against each other and the top two would then play in a final. The Night Pennant has been very successful and recently this formula has been used with several RTC teams battling it out with others from nearby clubs.

More silverware was added to the trophy cabinet in 1984. Following a bequest of £500 by Major G.O. Savage, the Club was able to purchase two trophies for the winners of a level doubles tournament. The inaugural competition for the Savage Trophies took place the following spring. By 2001 these trophies had been mislaid or lost and the successful pair from the two previous years, Richard Harris and David Watson, who between them had won the competition no less than eight times, donated two splendid claret jugs in their place. The jugs were consequently named the 'Harris-Watson Trophies'. Derek Steel (a future Chairman of the Club) donated a punch bowl to encourage tennis and social bonhomie between Bordeaux and Hampton Court. Unusually, all that is required to secure this trophy is for a team from the club without it, to cross the Channel and challenge the one with it. The result of the tennis match is considered irrelevant!

Towards the end of 1984, there was a small fire in the tennis workshop under the hazard penthouse. The official report concluded it was 'accidental but insoluble'. One only has to look at the devastating consequences of the 1986 fire at Hampton Court, and of the one a few years later at Windsor Castle, to realise how rigorous the authorities have to be about the enforcement of fire prevention measures. There is a no smoking rule at the Tennis Court and members were reminded that this had to be strictly enforced. As far back as 1849, the Lord Chamberlain, Lord Breadalbane, had informed William Beresford, the Master, that anyone found smoking in the Tennis Court would be excluded. Fire is a real worry for the Tennis Court; there is evidence in the roof of an earlier fire at the northern end. The Crown has a policy of not insuring its properties; therefore if the Court were to be lost in this way, it is possible it would never be replaced. One only has to see how many tennis courts have been lost in the past, because of fires, never to be complacent.

With an ever-increasing membership and the resultant congestion on the court, Ronald Swash suggested that it might be opportune to think about building a second tennis court. The negotiations that lay ahead were long and tortuous and will be dealt with in a separate chapter. Here the Second Court project will only be mentioned where it has a general bearing on the running of the Club. Suffice it to say that Ronald Swash prepared a paper on the subject for committee discussion in January 1985, but the minutes reveal that it was thought to be 'inappropriate at the present time'.

Chris Ronaldson elected to defend his World Championship for the second time at Queen's rather than Hampton Court. The decision though was not due to pressure on court time; it was because Queen's had a larger spectator capacity, was located closer to Central London, and therefore easier for people to get to. It was also easier for him to concentrate fully on the match at hand, whereas distractions could more readily arise at Hampton Court. In all of his defences, his opponent was Wayne Davies. This time he convincingly retained the title by seven sets to one, but two years later, again at Queen's, he was to lose it after a magnificent six-year reign.

Early in 1985 the Court's playing surfaces were again causing concern. Palace advice was sought and they came up with an estimate of £3,000 to grind down and repaint the floor — the walls they would attend to at their cost. Chris Ronaldson suggested he and Lachie Deuchar could carry out the floor work to save money. With permission granted, they ground off the old black paint exposing the beige Ketton Stone flagstones that dated back to 1700. Members then had the dubious pleasure of playing under eighteenth-century conditions for a few weeks. There were of course no floor lines, excepting the two black marble ones across the court central to the two end galleries (page 44) and severe difficulties were experienced in following the flight of the ball against the pale floor. A strange phenomenon appeared in the form of a ghostly '6' in the centre of the court at the service end. The explanation for this can be seen in a 1934 photograph of the Court (figure 73). The challenge of playing as their forefathers had came to an end when the new paint was applied — a dramatic change! The floor was now a terracotta colour and the change was generally welcomed. In gratitude, Ronaldson and Deuchar each received £500 from club funds for their backbreaking work. During the works The Queen's Club kindly made their courts available to RTC members.

Although the newly-painted floor was a tremendous success, the repainted walls were a disaster. The Palace works department had used a black paint, which did not harden properly, causing it to come off on the balls. The walls were repainted the following year with marginal success, but the soft paint has been an irritating problem ever since.

In past years tennis clubs had experimented with different-coloured balls, seeking an improvement on the predominant white, which too easily dirtied. The Club's President, Lord Revelstoke, had tested green ones at Lambay, and blue balls ornamented with red could be found in Venice two centuries ago. Black balls were sometimes used in white courts such as Rusthall House and Ditton

92. THE CLUB TROPHIES

Top row (l to r):
Lathom Browne Cup
Barker-Camm Cup
Harris Watson Trophies

Middle row (l to r):
Seal Salver
Wollaston Cup
Divorce Doubles Trophy

Bottom row (l to r):
De Laszlo Bowl
Steel Bowl

Place, and red ones were tried during the 1930s at Cambridge when the walls there were white. One wonders what colour balls were used at Hampton Court in the eighteenth century when its walls were white. As in Lawn Tennis most courts eventually came to use yellow balls. Yellow has certainly been found to offer the best visibility against black or red playing surfaces, such as at RTC, especially when the balls are a few days old.

Another innovation in the 1980s was the practice of RTC professionals to mark from the upper gallery at the hazard end. This provides a resting-place for the score pad and also enables the professional to continue sewing balls while marking — a more productive use of time. The marker is also in less danger of being struck by the ball. Not all UK clubs followed this lead — some courts do not have suitable galleries — and the practice in Australia continued to be to mark from the dedans.

Ray Moorman, the Honorary Secretary, decided it was time to step down after seven years and Margaret Ruffer was elected at the 1986 AGM in his place. She had been co-opted onto the Committee a year earlier when it was felt that with the growing number of female members (about 15% of the total membership) they should have at least one representative. Business commitments forced her to give up the Secretaryship in 1988 and John Edwards was then elected to the office — he worked tirelessly in that capacity for the next ten years. Since Margaret Ruffer was elected, there has always been at least one lady on the Committee.

In the spring of 1986 Prince Edward first came to the Royal Tennis Court. He had learnt to play the game at Cambridge. He came to Hampton Court for a BBC Television interview on the subject of Tennis, and while there had a lesson with Chris Ronaldson. So began an association with the Royal Tennis Court that continues to this day. He was made an Honorary Member and plays quite regularly. On court His Royal Highness is very competitive, making for an enjoyable game, as many members have discovered. Despite pressure to keep the numbers down for a smaller royal wedding in 1999, the tennis world much appreciated that Prince Edward and Sophie Rhys-Jones should invite Chris and Lesley Ronaldson, and Jonathan and Julie Howell, to their wedding at Windsor. Following their marriage their Royal Highnesses were created The Earl and Countess of Wessex.

As the summer drew to a close, a young American, George Wharton, who worked as an assistant at Newport, Rhode Island, was sent over to gain experience in the United Kingdom. He spent six weeks with Chris Ronaldson before moving to Holyport, where he worked for another six months before returning to Newport as Head Professional. There was, though, another more important change on the professional staff about to take place.

Towards the end of 1986 Lachie Deuchar decided it was time to move on. He had been offered the position of Head Professional in Melbourne, his home city. Strenuous efforts were made to keep him, but his mind was set. In appreciation of almost six years service, the Club organised a farewell party for him in the

Palace's Tiltyard Restaurant. This took place on 19th March 1987 and it is a measure of his popularity that over 150 members and friends came to bid him farewell.

As a temporary measure Jerome Fletcher was engaged for two days a week until the Club secured the services of yet another Australian, Matty Hayward. Engaged as the Second Professionàl in July, he was popular with members and was to remain at the Club for three years.

After half a lifetime of dedicated service to the Club, Tony Negretti decided the time had come to call it a day and Henry Wollaston was elected to succeed him as President. In his professional life Henry Wollaston was a barrister, working for the Home Office. He was a useful tennis player and played both Squash and Eton Fives for Cambridge in his university days. Sadly, illness forced him to resign after only two years.

A tragic death occurred in 1987. David Warburg, three times Amateur Singles Champion, who had given many years of voluntary service to Tennis in general and the RTC in particular, died while playing on the court. Always competitive, he would have taken satisfaction from having just won, rather than just lost, the first set by six games to five.

In November 1987, the Club again hosted the British Open Singles and, in addition, the Open Doubles Championship for the first time. Lachie Deuchar retained both titles — in the Singles final he met the new World Champion, Wayne Davies, who had beaten Chris Ronaldson in the semi-final. In an exciting close-fought match Deuchar, staring defeat in the face, managed to save three consecutive match points in the fourth set, go on to win it, and take the fifth for a most popular victory. He and Wayne Davies teamed up in the Doubles, beating Norwood Cripps and Paul Tabley in the final. This was a busy period on the tournament front — the following month the British Ladies Singles was staged, with Sally Jones winning through. The year also saw the inauguration of the National League and the start of yet another remarkable run. RTC won the League in the first four years of its existence 1987-1990, when Chris Ronaldson was a member of the team.

In many tennis courts the back of the grille is used to display a club insignia or identity. The Royal Tennis Court is no exception. There had long been a picture of Henry VIII there that over the years had taken a severe battering. Lesley Ronaldson, apart from being a superb tennis player, also has artistic talent. She was therefore commissioned to paint a replacement portrait. Four years later, when the back of the grille was replaced by toughened glass, a new detachable picture of the Tudor King was hung behind the glass.

After several years of near maximum capacity and full membership, the Club's financial position was strong. By the beginning of 1988 there was £32,000 in the reserves and the Committee was anxious to make good use of it. Once again the possibility of building a second court was raised and this time it found more favour. The decision was taken to set up a sub-committee to investigate further.

Ronald Swash now felt that, provided a suitable successor was at hand, no individual should remain Chairman indefinitely – and he had served eight years as Chairman, following four years as Treasurer. It was therefore decided – with the constitution amended accordingly at the 1988 AGM – to set a maximum of two three-year terms for any person to act as the Club Chairman, who should be elected not by the Committee but by a General Meeting of the members. Ronald Swash's successor was Derek Steel who was duly elected Chairman at the same AGM.

Derek Steel, a contemporary of Sir Roger Bannister and Chris Brasher, ran victoriously for Oxford against Cambridge at 880 yards and 440 yards in 1948 and 1949, respectively, and represented England at the shorter distance. He was Treasurer of the Achilles Club for twenty years. Co-founder of Steel, Burrell, Jones (SBJ), a firm of specialist reinsurance brokers at Lloyds, he served as High Sheriff of Greater London in 1987.

He was proud of being initially the highest-handicap Chairman and then, after a hip operation, the first non-playing member to hold that office. With a wry smile he considered that one of his major achievements as Chairman was persuading the Palace to fit a bolt on the door of the lavatory in the side penthouse corridor – a tiresome issue that plagued many a committee meeting. However, those that worked with him would acknowledge that his was a welcome steady hand on the tiller through an important period in the Club's history.

It is a sad feature of the modern age that terrorism threatens the country's national monuments and buildings. Hampton Court Palace is not immune to this threat. Security concerns about the IRA had stopped members parking their cars along Tennis Court Lane in 1973, but increased worries now meant that identity cards had to be issued. Access for tennis players and their guests was seen by the Palace as a weak link in their security. It later became necessary for a daily list of those visiting the Court to be submitted.

93. DEREK STEEL

Chairman of
The Royal Tennis Court 1988-95

159

94. SIR CLIFFORD CHETWOOD

President of The Royal Tennis Court 1989-2001

The summer of 1988 brought a new face to the Royal Tennis Court. It was that of Nick Wood. This popular young man later took over as Second Professional when Matty Hayward left for Hatfield. He spent ten years at Hampton Court before taking up his first senior post as Head Professional at Holyport in 1998. Just before he left Hampton Court, all the years of training and guidance from Chris Ronaldson finally paid off when he won his first major tournament, the European Open Singles Championship in Paris.

Sir Clifford Chetwood took over from the ailing Henry Wollaston as Club President in 1989. Choosing a career in the construction industry rather than in opera singing, he became Chairman and Chief Executive of George Wimpey PLC and was knighted in 1987 for services to the building industry. He particularly respected the etiquette and wonderful sportsmanship prevalent in tennis and the way women are treated as equals. For these reasons he persuaded the Wimpey Board to sponsor many national and international tournaments to the tune of over half a million pounds in eleven years. For twelve years he served as a Trustee of the Victoria and Albert Museum and as an advisor thereafter. For many years he has been a Vice-President of the Tennis & Rackets Association.

Sadly, Henry Wollaston died shortly after retiring as RTC Chairman. A year after his death, his widow Daphne donated a Cup in his memory to be competed for by the junior members. The new junior handicap singles tournament for the Wollaston Cup was inaugurated in 1991.

Another of the Honorary Officers resigned at this time. After nine successful years as Treasurer Alan Baddeley stood down. David Best was elected at the 1990 AGM in his place.

For the first time, the qualifying rounds for the British Open Singles Championship were staged at the Court in 1990. They have now become an annual fixture. On the domestic scene, the Oldhams, Richard and Richenda, who contributed much on the social side, decided to donate a trophy for a 'Husband and Wife' Weekend Doubles competition. First held in the summer of 1991, it did not take long for it to become known as the 'Divorce Doubles'. Despite this, it is an enjoyable competition and these days it is combined with a barbecue in the garden. Recently the need to be a couple to qualify has been relaxed, effectively upgrading the competition to the official Club Mixed Doubles.

The lack of social facilities had bedevilled the Club for a number of years. The Ely Rooms had, at that time, been converted for use as accommodation for the second professional. It was against this background that the Committee agreed to convert the area under the hazard penthouse into a members' mini-lounge. It was also to be partially used as a workshop in order to encourage inter-action between the members and the professionals. Chris Ronaldson had long since moved out of the old workshop there in favour of his first-floor living room. A wooden floor was put in (without a single fixing hole being drilled into the walls or the old floor, a condition laid down by the Palace Curator), the grille was converted to toughened glass to allow safe viewing of play, the whole area redecorated and new furniture purchased. Just over £11,000 was spent on this conversion, which was completed in early 1991. As things turned out, it was only a temporary solution, as developments two years later made the area redundant.

Facilities for members were now about to change dramatically. The Club had made representations to the Palace on many occasions during the nineteen-seventies and eighties in an attempt to recover the old Keeper's House, now ingloriously called Apartment 69. It had been lost to the Club when the last Keeper died in 1883. The Club had been promised it back when the occupant, a retired garden superintendent, vacated it. This happened in 1991, but the

Thatcher era had bred a new commercial attitude into government agencies. Some of the more desirable residential premises in the Palace had been let, or were earmarked for letting, as tourist accommodation for the Landmark Trust. Apartment 69 was one so earmarked. However, the Club was now deep into negotiations over the Second Court and needed to persuade the Palace Director that they should honour previous promises, as the property was now considered to be an essential part of the proposed two-court complex. The Palace agreed, but if the house was to revert back to the Tennis Court, then they insisted that it should be paid for.

The aforementioned new commercial climate had long been threatening the Club, and the Palace took the opportunity to impose a charge on items such as security, maintenance, car parking, administration, and a contribution in lieu of rates, in addition to rent for the house. The rent was assessed at £7,000, this being the profit they were expecting to make had the house been let to the Landmark Trust. The other costs to be borne by the Club were agreed at £13,000, making a total of £20,000 a year that had to be found.

As part of the agreement the Palace completely restored the building. The top two floors of Apartment 69 were separated off into a flat to accommodate the Head Professional, with the ground floor converted into a lounge and dining room for members. The adjacent two-storey annexe had its upper floor converted into a workshop for the professionals and the lower floor into a kitchen. The agreement also gave the Club the magnificent walled garden to the west of the Court. The whole of the premises was re-plumbed, rewired and redecorated. New central heating was installed, new kitchen units were fitted and the house carpeted throughout. Three members, Bill Lack, Richenda Oldham and Nigel O'Hagan, were particularly helpful at this time. Bill Lack, an architect, undertook to oversee the building works. Living locally alongside Hampton Court Green, he was well placed to carry out this task. Richenda Oldham spent many days browsing around the auction rooms of southern England looking for suitable items of antique furniture for the clubrooms. In her professional life she was a freelance journalist in the interior design field, and before she knew it, she was also given the job of choosing the soft furnishings. Nigel O'Hagan made the quality fitted units in the workshop.

The Club also has reason to be grateful to Russell Denoon Duncan. He volunteered, or perhaps it would be more accurate to say, was coerced by the Chairman, to act for the Club and deal with the Treasury Solicitor during the drawing up of the contract. As a senior partner in a firm of major City solicitors, he had immense experience in this field. The agreement took two hard years to hammer out, but was eventually concluded towards the end of 1993, allowing the clubrooms to be officially opened by His Royal Highness The Prince Edward on 16th January 1994. Over 200 members and their guests attended the opening party. They were treated to an entertaining exhibition doubles in which the Club's two ex-World Champions, Howard Angus and Chris Ronaldson, lost to the established pairing of Alan Lovell and Norwood Cripps. Alan and Norwood had won the British Open Doubles Championship six times between 1977 and 1982.

A plaque to commemorate the royal opening has been mounted above the lounge door.

There was of course a price to pay! In order to meet the new Palace charge, subscriptions had been raised the previous January from £40 to £70 a year, and to £90 in January 1994. However, the new facilities were universally welcomed and the subscription increases did not on this occasion lead to a significant number of resignations. Members now have the added benefit of being able to hire these rooms for private or corporate functions.

Throughout the negotiations for Apartment 69, the house was always described as the 'Marker's Flat'. In fact the Markers had never lived there; the house was originally built for the Master or Keeper of the King's Tennis Court and was known as the Keeper's House. It was the apartment at the other end of the Court that was used by the Markers and is still occupied by the Club under the Grace-and-Favour Warrant entitled 'Tennis Marker's Residence'.

95. H.R.H. PRINCE EDWARD OPENING THE CLUBROOMS

Watched by Sir Clifford Chetwood, Derek Steel and Chris Ronaldson

While all this was going on, another dilemma had been facing the Committee: Should the Club become a limited company? In the litigious climate of these times, there is a need to protect the interests of all of the members against claims, from whatever source, and of course the Royal Tennis Court now had to enter into legally-binding contracts. There was no real choice: the proposal was put to the Membership at an Extraordinary General Meeting on 14th February 1993 and unanimously approved. At the same meeting the opportunity was taken to bring the members up to date with the ongoing Second Court negotiations. They received the same presentation that had been given to the Palace authorities and heard of the difficulties that were being experienced in the discussions, which will be expanded upon later. Those present, however, were enthusiastic and the vote to continue was unanimous.

John Mackenzie, a former committee member and now the Club's solicitor, was charged with the task of finding a way of creating a limited company that could be known as 'The Royal Tennis Court' and not The Royal Tennis Court Limited. Companies House was persuaded that the Club had a case for dispensing with Limited, but an unexpected problem arose over the use of the word 'Royal'. John Mackenzie had to negotiate with the Home Office for approval. Eventually the Home Office relented, after it was pointed out that the Club had used the title since 1818.

The Royal Tennis Court, a company limited by guarantee (£1 per member) and not having a share capital, was formed on 19th May 1994, although for accounting reasons it did not start trading until 1st July 1994.

With the creation of the new company all the members of the Committee became Directors. The first Board of Directors of The Royal Tennis Court were: Derek Steel, Chairman; John Edwards, Honorary Secretary; David Best, Honorary Treasurer; Michael Banks, Paul Covell, Barney Gibbens, James Hansford, Dîanne Ingham, Henry Macintosh, David Seelig and Jane Vaughan. Although the Articles of Association describe the Board of Directors as the Committee, as time went by the Committee was referred to, more and more, as 'the Board', and henceforth this text will reflect that.

The Club Newsletter is a considerable task for anyone to take on and the Honorary Secretary John Edwards, who had cheerfully edited it for the previous six years, decided that the time had come to hand over this responsibility. David Frost, a former rugby correspondent of *The Guardian*, who also wrote on tennis in both *The Guardian* and *Country Life*, volunteered for the job, and despite several attempts to retire he was persuaded to continue until the end of 2000. Martin Bronstein who had assisted him, and who had dramatically redesigned the layout and introduced photographs, is the new editor. Martin is a freelance squash and tennis writer. As well as these three, there is a distinguished list of former editors — Sir Ronald Prain, Murray Glover, Andrew Lloyd Davies, Ray Moorman and Ronald Swash. The Newsletter was born out of the 1973 Palace Revolution, and for the first 28 years was published biannually. Prior to that Tony Negretti used to keep members informed by a single fact-sheet sent out once a year. A decision was taken in 2001 to issue the Newsletter quarterly.

In 1995 another World Championship eliminator took place at Hampton Court. Julian Snow, the Amateur Champion, and the Petworth Professional Chris Bray, were the combatants. The match was played over the 22nd, 24th and 26th

February. Bray won by seven sets to two, and went on to defeat Lachlan Deuchar in the next eliminator in Hobart, only to succumb to Wayne Davies in the third and final eliminator. Davies then challenged Rob Fahey, but failed to recover the world title, which he had lost to Fahey the year before.

At the 1995 Annual General Meeting Barney Gibbens was elected to succeed Derek Steel as Club Chairman. Barney Gibbens OBE had qualified as a Chartered Accountant. In 1962 he and a colleague set up the first UK software company, Computer Analysts and Programmers. In 1987 CAP merged with SEMA, a French company, and Barney took early retirement three years later. He was the founding Master of the 100th City Livery Company, the Worshipful Company of Information Technologists, and first President of the Computing Services Association. A jovial supporter of the club's social activities, he was one of the Hampton Court 'Courtiers', who played at other courts around the UK and France raising funds for the Second Court project. Like his predecessor Derek Steel, he regularly travelled back from his holiday home in France to conduct RTC business.

96. BARNEY GIBBENS

Chairman of The Royal Tennis Court 1995-2001

On 8th June 1997 another important Special General Meeting was held at the Palace. Its purpose was to ask the Membership for their approval to continue with the Second Court negotiations, which had now reached a critical stage. Amid the splendour of the Banqueting House, the riverside dining room designed by Wren for William III, and surrounded by the murals of Verrio, members were given a comprehensive presentation of all aspects of the project. If the scheme were to go ahead, then there were important financial implications for the members to consider, not least a substantial increase in their subscriptions. At the meeting the vote to proceed was unanimous.

Early in 1998, John Edwards, the Honorary Secretary, decided the time had come to fulfil a long-held ambition of travelling around the world. John Yarnall agreed to join the Board and take over his work on a temporary basis, a role that became permanent when John Edwards returned towards the end of the year and decided that twelve years on the Committee/Board of Directors, ten of them as Honorary Secretary, was a reasonable contribution. He had been only the Club's ninth Honorary Secretary and the longest-serving since the fourth, Tony Negretti. His years in the hot seat were characterised by his enthusiasm and willingness to get involved in almost anything members asked of him. John Yarnall was voted onto the Board at the April 1998 AGM and officially confirmed as Honorary Secretary a year later. He is a former Director of Hampton Court Palace and therefore in the unique position of being able to understand both sides of the argument whenever the Club and the Palace are at odds. More importantly, he can spot possible areas of conflict before they arise.

97.   LEADING LAWN TENNIS PLAYERS VISIT THE COURT IN 1996

l to r: John Lloyd, Ken Rosewall, Kevin Curren, Jonathan Howell,
Stan Smith, Prince Edward, Chris Ronaldson and Sue Haswell

A major new tournament was inaugurated at Hampton Court in September 1998, the Dresdner Kleinwort Benson Classic (DKB), a sponsored invitation singles and doubles event involving eight of the world's top professional players. It was organised by Events 2000, a company set up by Sue Haswell and Lesley Ronaldson. Lesley Ronaldson has had years of experience in organising tournaments and Sue Haswell had previously run pre-Wimbledon charity events at the Club involving well-known lawn tennis personalities. In 1996, Ken Rosewall, Stan Smith, John Lloyd and Kevin Curren supported the event, and the following year the 'Two Woodies' came, Mark Woodforde and Todd Woodbridge, at the time the Wimbledon Doubles Champions.

At the first DKB Classic members were able to watch the World Champion Rob Fahey, the former World Champion Wayne Davies, their fellow Australians Frank Filippelli and Steve Virgona, along with top British players, Chris Bray, Mike Gooding, James Male the World Rackets Champion and Nick Wood. Nick had the most successful week of his career to date, when he defeated successively Bray, Gooding and Male — Male having knocked out Fahey — to claim the richest prize in tennis history. He then went on to win the doubles with Chris Bray.

There was a degree of irony in his victories, as a Channel 4 'fly-on-the-wall' documentary television series was being filmed at the Palace at the time, and they had originally planned to film Nick Wood during his training for the event and follow his progress through the competition. They were mortified when he won, as they had earlier dropped the idea from their schedules. However, they did feature the Tennis Court, interviewing Chris Ronaldson at length about the game and the proposed Second Court, and included a piece on ball-making and racket-stringing. They also featured the archaeological dig that was being carried out as part of the Second Court project.

98. THREE WORLD CHAMPIONS

Wayne Davies, Chris Ronaldson and Rob Fahey in 1998

The following year the same players returned, except that Ruaraidh Gunn replaced an injured Wayne Davies. Those who came to watch saw an awesome World Champion; Fahey swept everyone aside winning both the singles and doubles, the latter with Nick Wood. The tournament ran for another two years with Rob Fahey winning both singles competitions, and with Nick Wood able to maintain his hundred per cent record in the doubles.

In recent years the social programme has been expanded, something that over the years has not always received the highest priority. As well as the splendour of grand banquets in the Palace staterooms, members are now able to enjoy summer barbecues in the club's charming walled garden and, just before Christmas, a carol concert in the beautiful Chapel Royal. Another innovation is an annual exhibition match, which has proved very popular. Chris Ronaldson and Lachie Deuchar featured in the first of these in 1998. Subsequently members enjoyed the doubles pairing of Frank Willis and David Cull, playing against Howard Angus and Norwood Cripps. That evening was organised as a benefit for Frank Willis, the Manchester professional, who was retiring after a distinguished career. On another occasion Adam Mickelburough came over from Prested Hall to take on Chris Ronaldson, and in 2001 members experienced some spectacular tennis when Nick Wood returned to his spiritual home to pit himself against the invincible World Champion. The match went 6-5, 4-6, 6-5 to Rob Fahey.

99. THE 1999 DKB CONTESTANTS

l to r: Nick Wood, James Male, Chris Bray, Steve Virgona, Frank Filippelli and Ruaraidh Gunn
Seated in the Last Gallery – Rob Fahey and Mike Gooding

100. RICHARD STOCKS

Chairman of the RTC since 2001

In April 1999, the Ladies World Championships were held at Hampton Court. Unlike the men's event, which as seen before is played on a challenge basis, the ladies use a knockout format. Thirty ladies took part in a week of singles and doubles with RTC's Sue Haswell the World Number Two, and Holyport's Penny Lumley the World Champion, contesting the singles final. In a hard-fought match, Penny Lumley, 2-4 down in the final set, won four games in a row to retain the title. These two were the reigning Ladies World Doubles Champions and they successfully teamed up again to beat Sally Jones and Alex Garside in the final.

In January 2001 Richard Stocks took over as Chairman from Barney

101. PENNY LUMLEY

*On her way to retaining
the World Championship*

Gibbens. Richard Stocks has been a member of the Royal Tennis Court since 1980, having been introduced to tennis by his brother at Holyport, where he remains a member. Like his predecessor, Richard qualified as a Chartered Accountant, in his case with Peat Marwick Mitchell (now KPMG) in 1964. His career in the financial services industry was mainly spent on the unit trust and life assurance side, before taking 'early retirement' and becoming a financial services regulator in 1993. In 2000 he was appointed Director of Authorisation at the Financial Services Authority (FSA) with responsibility for authorising firms and individuals wishing to carry on investment business. In the spring of 2002, after two earlier attempts at 'final' retirement, he was finally persuaded to give up daily commuting to London from his home in

Weybridge. His other great sporting passion is golf. He is a member of the Royal & Ancient, Littlestone, and St. George's Hill where he was Captain in 1997. Educated at Tonbridge School he undertook the duties of Secretary of the Old Tonbridgian Golfing Society for 28 years and is now the President.

102.   1999 LADIES WORLD CHAMPIONSHIPS GROUP

Barney Gibbens had not completed his second three-year term. He resigned as Chairman as he felt it his duty when the Board decided not to proceed with the original Second Court scheme. The events that led up to the Board's decision will be dealt with at length in Chapter 14.

Almost 300 years to the day after Robert Streeter, the King's sergeant painter, had applied the last brush strokes to William III's monogram on the main wall to complete the restoration of the Tennis Court, the House of Orange returned. On 16th March 2002 the three sons of Queen Beatrix of the Netherlands visited the Court.

The occasion of their visit was the celebration of the first wedding anniversary of Prince Constantijn and Princess Laurentien. They came to Royal Tennis Court and the Palace for the day at the suggestion of Her Royal Highness The Countess of Wessex, who as a member of the Club enjoys the occasional game of tennis herself. They were accompanied by their Royal Highnesses Crown Prince Willem-Alexander of Orange, his new bride Princess Maxima and Prince Friso together with a small group of their closest friends. After lunch in the Club's garden and a guided tour of the Palace by Lesley Ronaldson, they returned to play some tennis. The Court, which apart from the glazed windows, the painted floor and the chase lines, looked exactly as William III had left it three centuries earlier. (The three royal brothers, Princess Laurentien and one or two others in the group took easily to the game, being good ball players.) Prince Willem-Alexander was given a copy of Cees de Bondt's book, written in Dutch, on the history of tennis in the Netherlands.

After the conclusion of play the royal party pronounced the day a great success and expressed a wish to return.

Towards the end of 2001, in the wider world of tennis, problems were arising over an upcoming World Championship Challenge scheduled for the following February. Only James Male, the World Rackets Champion, had qualified to make a challenge by virtue of winning the British Open Championship in 1999, but persistent injury problems had forced him to withdraw.

Prior to the nineteen-eighties the timing of any defence of the World Championship was the prerogative of the Champion. A system was then devised whereby the winner of any National Open Singles Championship had the right to challenge. The Champion had to defend within two years of the last challenge but retained the right to choose the venue. What was not foreseen at the time was the arrival of a Champion who would be so dominant that he would win all of the qualifying events, thereby preventing any challenger emerging. Robert Fahey was such a Champion.

Months of discussions between the National Associations of the four tennis-playing countries and the International Real Tennis Professionals Association (IRTPA) — following Rob Fahey's agreement to waive his privileges — resulted in a formula being devised that allowed the IRTPA to take over the running of the Championship. A series of eliminators would take place involving the next four highest-ranked players. They were Tim Chisholm (New York), Chris Bray (Petworth), Mike Gooding (Burroughs) and Nick Wood (Holyport).

The IRTPA invited all clubs to bid for the Challenge itself to be held on 29th November, 1st December and 3rd December 2002. The Royal Tennis Court was the successful bidder, bringing the Championship Challenge back to the United Kingdom after a gap of fifteen years.

The publication date of this volume has meant that details of this, the fifth World Championship Match to be staged at Hampton Court, with arguably the greatest tennis player of all time defending his title, falls to others to record.

CHAPTER 11

THE TENNIS COURT LODGINGS

Adjoining the Tennis Courts over the centuries have been various rooms for the use of the Kings, Princes, Masters or Keepers, Markers, Professionals and the Players. Both tennis court sites at the Palace had such lodgings and the present Stuart Court had them at both ends. This chapter deals with the many structural alterations and the changes of use suffered by these rooms.

Henrican Closed Play

Rooms were provided at the northern end of this Play for the Keeper or possibly the Marker. They were on two floors and linked to the Court by a winding staircase in the turret on the north-east corner of the building. As discussed earlier, it is likely that these rooms, or a passage adjacent to them, had viewing windows looking onto the playing area at the service end at first floor level. In 1537, only four years after their construction, the rooms were absorbed into the newly-built apartments for the infant Prince Edward.

The Stuart Court

There are now apartments at both ends of this Court. The rooms at the southern end were built first and have been used for a variety of purposes over the centuries — dressing rooms for the royal family, and then for other players, accommodation for the markers and professionals, and occasionally as offices for the palace administration. At the northern end is a house originally built for the Master or Keeper of the King's Tennis Courts and was known as the 'Keeper's House'. Today this house is referred to as Apartment 69 and the collection of rooms at the southern end is known as Apartment 53.

THE ROOMS AT THE SOUTHERN END (Apartment 53)

The first rooms on this site were probably the lodgings built in 1529 next to Wolsey's Open Play. These consisted of two chambers, an upper and a lower, and were built originally for the King's use whenever he played. If the earlier analysis is correct, then they would have been linked to the Palace by a gallery that ran alongside the east boundary wall (figure 12). It is likely that the lodgings are those that can be seen in the 1630 Abram Booth drawing (figure 23). When Henry VIII was forced to give up tennis, the Keeper, or possibly the Marker, may have used the rooms, as the accommodation next to the Henrican Close Play was lost at this time. If that were the case, then later Tudor keepers whose responsibilities included Hampton Court, such as Oliver Kelly up to 1543, Thomas Johns 1543-84, William Hope 1584-91 and Edward Stone, who

172

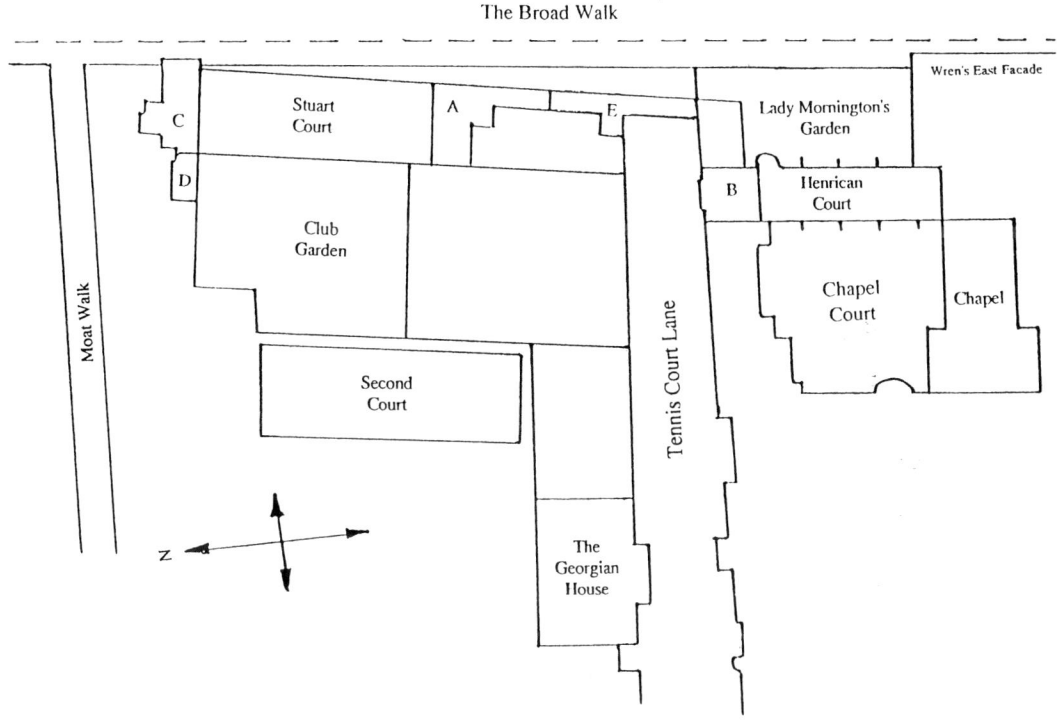

103. PLAN OF THE NORTH-EAST AREA OF THE PALACE

The Plan shows the relevant positions of the lodgings associated with the Tennis Courts.

A.   Originally built in 1529 by Henry VIII against Cardinal Wolsey's Open
      Tennis Play. Rebuilt in 1637 and substantially altered in 1660.
      (Now Apartment 53)

B.   The site of the lodgings built by Henry VIII for his Close Tennis Play in
      1533. Converted into apartments for the infant Prince Edward in 1537.

C.   The Keeper's House built by Charles I in 1637 as a two-storey dwelling.
      Third floor added in 1854. (Now Apartment 69)

D.   18th Century Scullery – additional storey added in 1849.
      (Now part of Apartment 69).

E.   The Ely Rooms located above the Whispering Gallery.
      (Now part of Apartment 53).

succeeded Hope, could have lodged there whenever their presence was required. The likely occupants during the early Stuart period would have been firstly Jehu Webb, and after 1621 John Webb (his son).

Major alterations were carried out in 1636-37 when Charles I put a roof on the Court. The wall of the lodgings next to the Court was rebuilt and taken up to the height needed to support the southern end of the new court roof. A new pitched lead roof was then provided for both the lodgings and the Whispering Gallery (the gallery that linked the tennis facilities to the Palace).

After the Restoration, the lodgings were described as the 'King's Dressing Rooms'.[1] The works accounts show that Charles II had new flooring put in and additional windows cut out.[2] As part of William and Mary's rebuilding programme at the end of the century, the projection into the park was removed to enable the new garden wall to be built — at that time these lodgings were being described as 'for the players'.[3] They were always under the control of the Keepers who had the right to let out any surplus accommodation. Although little is known about their use during the eighteenth century, the works accounts often refer to them as 'offices'.[4]

These rooms would almost certainly have been used as dressing rooms by most of the tennis-playing monarchs: Henry VIII, Edward VI (when Prince Edward), Charles I, Charles II, James II (when Duke of York), William III, Edward VII (when Prince of Wales) and George V. The brass plaque on one of the lockers in the changing room bears witness to Prince Albert's use of them.

The last Keeper, William Beresford, made good use of his rental concession and let the bulk of the rooms to Lord George Seymour, but retained control over some for his and the members' use. The Markers operated from a small workshop in the room opposite the garden entrance, which now houses the court's heating boiler. Until 1848, the players' changing facilities were on the first floor.[5] Beresford then agreed to pay for the conversion of an old ground floor storeroom into a new changing room — the one in use today. Towards the end of the nineteenth century, those rooms close to Tennis Court Lane were taken over by the Clerk of the Works.

No marker employed by the Club lived in this apartment until Tom White. Sir Spencer Ponsonby-Fane was instrumental in securing a few rooms for him after Beresford's death in 1883. As Beresford was the last person to be appointed Keeper, the status of the rooms became unclear when he died. Sir Spencer, then Comptroller of Her Majesty's Household, took up the Club's case and successfully argued for them to remain part of the Tennis Court.[6] Three years later Tom White applied for, and was granted, an additional room for his growing family, and in 1903 the Club's dressing room was completely renovated including a new stove to provide hot water to the existing bath.[7]

104.   c1880 VIEW OF THE STUART COURT

The Stuart Court just before the east side windows were glazed.

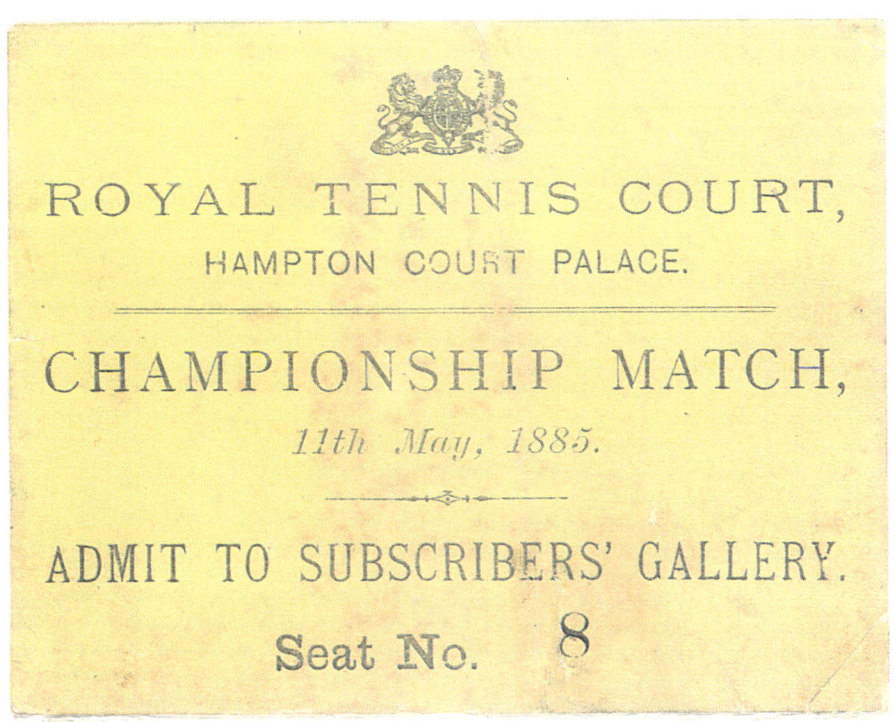

105.   WORLD CHAMPIONSHIP TICKET

106. MEMBERS' LOUNGE

Alfred White was able to move into the rooms on the death of his father in 1910, but only after the direct intervention of George V. The King, a member of the Club, granted the use of the rooms to 'the President and Committee of the Royal Tennis Club for the use of the marker'. This was despite the Palace's preference that they should have been given to their electrician, who was required to be on permanent standby in case of fire — with the introduction of electricity in the Palace, there was a constant fear of fire. The problem was solved when the electrician's house, in nearby Molesey, was connected directly to the Palace by the 'new telephonic communication' — White was then able to move in.[8] With five children, his accommodation was somewhat cramped, so in 1913 he applied to use the distant rooms near Tennis Court Lane that were at the time still occupied by the Clerk of the Works, Edwin Chart, who was about to retire. White asked The Hon. Neville Lytton if he could use his influence with Lionel Earle, the First Commissioner of Works — Lytton obliged and White was granted the use of the extra rooms.[9]

In 1928, the rooms were granted 'Grace-and-Favour' status in circumstances described in an earlier chapter. The Palace, under the terms of the Grace-and-Favour Warrant, therefore renovated the rooms when Arthur Ashford was appointed Professional on Alf White's retirement in 1932. However, they did not see the need for a bath to be installed as Ashford had requested — arguing that the players had had one in their dressing room since 1886 and that the Whites had always used it after the members had gone home. The Palace could not understand why Ashford and his wife needed a bath, when Alf White with his large family had been quite happy with the facilities below. They eventually relented after pressure from the President, Lord Revelstoke, who insisted that a

108. MEMBERS' DINING ROOM

107. THE KEEPER'S HOUSE

109. THE PATCHWORK FLOOR

This photograph of the Court was used on an official postcard
sold in the Palace Bookshop during the 1970s.

modern house in that day and age should always have a bath.[10]

Neither Arthur Ashford nor the members had any use for the remote rooms at the southern end, so once again they fell into disrepair. Their condition deteriorated further following the bombing raid in 1940 that devastated the professional's accommodation.

Leslie Keeble, Derek Barrett and Chris Ronaldson in turn occupied Apartment 53 and in 1980 the remote rooms were restored for use as clubrooms. With all of the tournament activity of the nineteen-seventies and a resuscitated club, there was recognition that some social accommodation was needed — the Club therefore approached the Palace with a request to restore the derelict rooms. Renovation costs had to be shared, so the donation from Vernon Ely, referred to previously, enabled the work to go ahead. On completion the rooms were officially named the Ely Rooms. Shortly after, with further help from Vernon, central heating was installed in both the clubrooms and the professional's apartment.

Due partly to their remoteness and partial occupation by successive assistant professionals, the Ely Rooms never worked well as club rooms. As recorded earlier, the area under the hazard penthouse was then converted for use as a clubroom and workshop. However this arrangement was quickly superseded because the acquisition of the old Keeper's House allowed both improved members' facilities to be set up there and the Ronaldsons to transfer to the living accommodation above. This left Apartment 53 available for the second professional, Nick Wood. Ivan and Ben Ronaldson moved in when Nick Wood left in 1998.

110. THE CLUB GARDEN

In 1998 the ground floor players' changing room was totally refurbished. Two new showers and a new bath were installed, and the walls battened as in Beresford's day, helping to recreate some of the ambience of a bygone era. These works were a major project for the Club, costing nearly £20,000.

THE KEEPER'S HOUSE (Apartment 69)

The Keeper's House at the northern end of the Stuart Court was built by Charles I in 1636-37. Like the lodgings at the southern end, it helped support the new court roof. At first it was a two-storey dwelling with a pitched lead roof, as can be seen in the pre-1660 view (figure 25). This house, as its name implies, was for the Keeper (or Master) of His Majesty's Tennis Courts. The first occupant was John Webb. It is open to debate whether his successor Ralph Bird resided there, for he was Keeper during Cromwell's Commonwealth, and the Protector was not keen on tennis. On the other hand, Cromwell came to love

179

Hampton Court, using it as his private residence. So he may have made the Court available to any guests who stayed there, which may have created a need for Bird to be on site.

Charles II's Keeper, Captain Thomas Cooke, lived in the Keeper's House.[11] But, before he moved in, the lead roof was replaced with a tiled one and realigned, the first floor park-side windows altered and the whole place renovated.[12] These works were carried out in parallel with the major court restoration. Whether the next Master, Henry Villiers, occupied the house is uncertain as the Court was out of play during his period in office, having been commandeered by Wren as a timber store. Villiers was appointed soon after the accession of William and Mary in 1689 when Thomas Cooke seems to have become incapacitated — he was succeeded by Horatio Moore.

111. TENNIS COURT LANE

*The entrance to the passage that leads to the Tennis Court
is the left-hand door at the far end of the Lane.*

When the Court was renovated in 1700-02, Horatio Moore, as has been seen, submitted his estimate for repair of both of the end dwellings. Although the King initially rejected the estimate, it is clear from the accounts that work was carried out to make them habitable. After Moore died the house was at the disposal of successive keepers during the eighteenth century: Thomas Chaplin 1707-28, Charles Fitzroy 1728-62 and Richard Beresford 1762-64 and 1765-91 — it would seem unlikely that William Chetwynd, who briefly held the office between 1764 and 1765, ever lived there. After Richard Beresford's death, Charles Meynell occasionally used the house. He died in 1815 and, for a short while after, his widow Elizabeth continued in occupation until the last Keeper, William Beresford, took possession.

There is some evidence that Beresford at first made little use of the house, for in 1829 it was said to be 'uninhabitable'.[13] Four years after his appointment as Keeper, he went up to Oxford and subsequently served eleven years in the Army. In 1830, after the Palace had carried out a renovation, he lent the house to Miss Eliza Stewart, an aunt of Sir Christopher Teesdale, who became the Prince of Wales's equerry and tennis partner. She occupied it until her death in 1848.[14] Beresford was then asked if he still required the property — he did — and he was to use it personally for the rest of his life.[15]

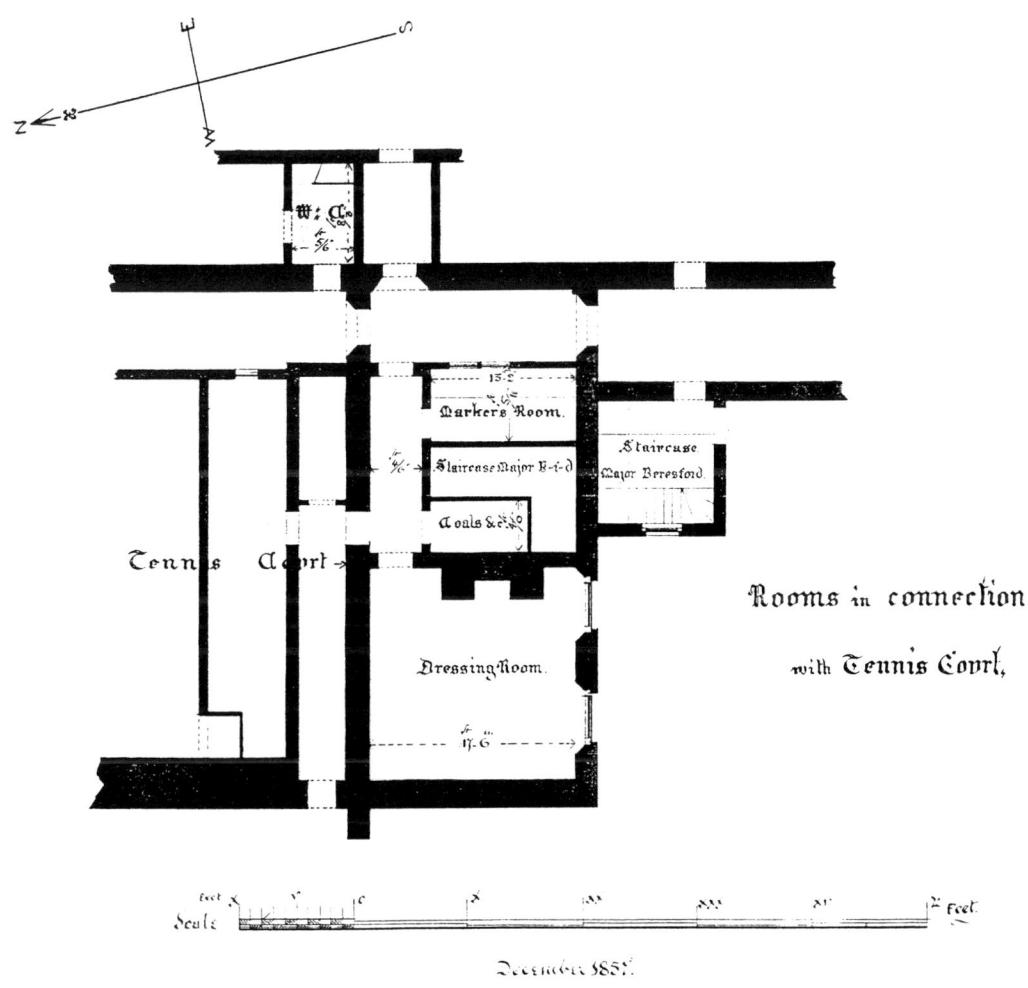

112. MEMBERS' FACILITIES IN 1848

The Right Honourable Major William Beresford, in whose time the house was known as Suite 46, carried out two major alterations. Soon after repossessing the property in 1849, he added two small rooms on top of the old detached scullery, which had itself been built sometime in the previous century — these rooms were bedrooms for his servants.[16] They were later knocked into one and today this room houses the professionals' workshop. In 1854, Beresford stripped off the old pitched roof of the main house and added another floor creating three new bedrooms — there was now a flat roof with crenellations topping off the walls.[17] That conversion cost Beresford £437 4s. 1d., an enormous sum of money for those days when one considers that new five-roomed houses in neighbouring East Molesey were being sold at the time for £150.[18] The external appearance of the building following the completion of this work has not changed since. As mentioned before, when Beresford died in 1883, the office of Keeper of the King's Tennis Courts lapsed. The house was then given over to Archibald Graham, the Superintendent of the Parks and Gardens, and he and his successors occupied it until 1991. They were, in turn, Messrs. Gardiner (from 1897), Marlow (1907), Hepburn (1931) and Fisher (1949). Mr. Fisher retired in 1974 but continued in residence until his death in 1991.

When the Club recovered the house, in circumstances described earlier, it was completely renovated. The top two floors were converted into accommodation for the Head Professional with the ground floor and the annexe for members. Chris Ronaldson and his family moved into the new flat in 1993 and the members now have well-appointed clubrooms that include a lounge, dining room and kitchen, as well as a beautiful walled garden.

CHAPTER 12

MARKERS AND PROFESSIONALS

Until the formation of the Club early in the nineteenth century there was no resident marker attached to the Court. Those that worked there were appointed by the monarch and would have been required to attend at any court where a member of the Royal Family wished to play. Because some of the early Masters of the King's Tennis Courts appear to have had a dual role, or a confusing one, they also find their way into this chapter.

Cardinal Wolsey built the first tennis court at Hampton Court, but it is not known whether or not he had his own marker. However, when Henry VIII played at Hampton Court he would certainly have brought with him his personal marker, who at that time was Anthony Ansley.

Anthony Ansley

No direct link between Ansley and Hampton Court has yet been found, but it can be taken for granted that he attended Henry VIII there, especially as he was paid for his services during December 1531, a month when the King was known to have played at the Palace. The surviving Privy Purse expenses show Ansley receiving payments from December 1528 to December 1532 at many of the royal courts. As well as Hampton Court, he was paid for his services at Greenwich, Windsor, The More near Rickmansworth in Hertfordshire and even across the Channel in Calais.

Ansley also supplied the King with tennis balls. He, or his wife, may have made them, as there is no record in their register of him being a customer of the Ironmongers' Company, who were the principal suppliers of tennis balls at that time. How long he remained the Royal Marker is not known; it would seem he continued at least until the King stopped playing, as records show his wife was owed money for tennis balls in 1536. Amongst the debts of Sir Francis Weston, drawn up by him before his execution for his part in Anne Boleyn's alleged adultery, was the item: 'A poor woman Hanesley of the tenys play had married, for balls. I cannot tell how much.'[1] Ironically, Weston in happier times had been a regular playing partner of the King.

As mentioned in an earlier chapter, it is possible Ansley combined the role of Marker with that of Master or Keeper. Even less is known of any of the other Tudor Masters, whose duties included responsibility for Hampton Court, such as Oliver Kelly, Thomas Johns, William Hope or Edward Stone, or whether any of them had a dual role.

The Webbs

The careers of the two Webbs, Jehu and John, were dealt with earlier as they were both Masters of the King's Tennis Courts, Jehu from 1604 until about 1621, and thereafter John until 1656. They are mentioned here because they also undertook roles normally associated with the markers. They both coached the Prince of Wales before he became Charles I and supplied him with rackets and balls, and Jehu probably taught his brother Henry to play. Before his untimely death, Henry was the better of the two tennis-playing princes.

The first person thought to have held the title Marker in His Majesty's Tennis Courts was a Timothy Phesaunt. It is not known when he was appointed, or whether he ever worked at Hampton Court. His death in 1660 led to the appointment of Robert Long, about whom much more has been recorded.

Robert Long

As early as 1642, Robert Long was the royal supplier of 'long paume balloons' (balls for another form of tennis) and was paid for his attendance whenever a member of the royal family played that game.[2]

A few years later Long could be found working as a tennis marker in the St. James's Palace Tennis Court under the employ of John Hooker, the Keeper. There he came into contact with the Duke of York (afterwards James II) and by good fortune some of the Duke's tennis expenses, those covering the period December 1647 to April 1648, are preserved in the archives at Petworth House. They give an insight into the cost of playing in the mid-seventeenth century. The Duke was charged three shillings for each set played, whether 'hand-to-hand' (singles) or four-handed, and an additional sixpence for each set that Long marked. For every dozen balls 'tossed' by Long in practice, the Duke paid 1s. 6d. The same accounts tell us that the Duke purchased rackets at five shillings each, socks for 2s. 6d. a pair and paid sixpence for the loan of a pair of drawers for one of his guests. His Royal Highness appears to have paid the expenses of his companion players — how much of this money filtered down to Long is not known, but amongst the manuscripts is a receipt for £45, money he received from Hooker for services over the same period.[3]

Following the Restoration, Long petitioned Charles II for the post of Groom of the Chamber, describing himself as 'Clerk of the Chapel to the late King and keeper of balloons and paumes and of tennis shoes and ankle socks to his Majesty when Prince'. He was not successful, but, as compensation, was appointed Marker in the King's Tennis Courts on 24th December 1660. Long's salary was £30 0s. 10d. a year and he received additional payments whenever he attended the King.[4]

As described earlier, he was entrusted with overseeing Charles II's renovation of the Tennis Court at Hampton Court and with the construction of the new Court at Whitehall, after the King had granted Thomas Cooke, the Master, a

113.   VARIOUS RACKETS WITH HAMPTON COURT ASSOCIATIONS

Top left:: A John Case racket
Top right:: The rackets used by George Lambert and Tom Pettitt
during the 1885 World Championship
Bottom left:: An Alfred White racket
Bottom right::   Chris Ronaldson's 1981 World Championship racket

185

**114.   THE ORIGINAL 1531 CLUB TIE AND
THE PRESENT ONE WHICH DISPLAYS 1530**

115.   ROYAL WEDDING PRESENT

The Club commissioned Morris Smith, the former
production manager at Grays of Cambridge, to
make this miniature racket for the wedding of
H.R.H. Prince Edward and Sophie Rees-Jones.

**116.   THE PRINCE OF WALES
TAPESTRY**

This tapestry used to hang in the doorway of
the passage at the end of Tennis Court Lane
leading to the Court whenever the Prince of
Wales (afterwards Edward VII) was playing.

186

117. THE TENNIS COURT TODAY

This photograph of Chris Ronaldson and Lachlan Deuchar at the service end of the court was used as an official Palace postcard. The first print run had the image reversed, for the second run it was corrected.

licence to build it. All did not go smoothly at Whitehall though, because the new Court collapsed during construction due to poor workmanship — luckily there were no fatalities. However, this could not have reflected badly on Long, as he continued as supervisor, seeing the project through to completion. Because of his close association with this Court, it was commonly called 'Long's'. His son, also Robert, who was 'marker at Tennis and keeper of ye Long Paulims', was appointed in 1669 to succeed him on his death, which came to pass seven years later.

The Eighteenth Century

Nothing of any certainty is known of any royal markers during the eighteenth century. This was of course the low point in the game's history. Ironically, it was the collusion of some of the markers with the *sharpers* and *cheats* who frequented the tennis courts at this time, defrauding the nobility out of large sums of money, that hastened the decline of the game.[5] The last recorded reference to the office came in 1733, when the holder, Monsieur Latell, died. He was described as the 'King's Marker at Haymarket'.[6] Latell may have attended Frederick, Prince of Wales, the most prominent tennis player among the early Hanoverians. As to who may have served the enthusiastic Frederick, Duke of York, fifty to sixty years later, two names come to mind. Again both could be found at the James Street Court where the Duke was a *habitué*; they were Davies the Marker, or possibly John Mucklow the Keeper and lessee of the Court.[7]

118. FIRST DAY COVER

An image of the Royal Tennis Court was used in 1978 for the
'First Day Cover' of a stamp depicting Hampton Court Palace.

With the Royal Tennis Court becoming a Members' Club in 1818 we move into the era of Committee-appointed markers. John Case may have been the first of these; he is certainly the earliest we know of.

John Case   (c1820-1848)

Assisted by - Henry Case (his son)
            Joseph Case (his nephew)

John Case was born on 8th March 1800 in Teddington, Middlesex. Marriage records reveal that by the time he was eighteen he was resident in the Parish of St. Bartholomew the Great in the City of London, but three years later with the birth of the first of his nine children he was back living in Teddington and employed as a servant. His City of London address was only a mile or so from the

Courts at James Street and Great Windmill Street, either of which may have served as his introduction to tennis. On the other hand, he could have discovered the game at Hampton Court if his employment in service was in one of the Grace-and-Favour apartments at the Palace, or it may have been through his wife's connections, for she had been born there. The first mention of him as a Tennis Marker comes in July 1823, by which time the family had moved into the Palace. Three years later though, they moved across the river to East Molesey, and for the next eight years John Case appears to have had a number of jobs, at times describing himself as a milkman, a farmer and even a labourer, which could indicate that he only worked at the Royal Tennis Court on a part-time basis.[8] There was, though, the possibility of other part-time employment at the newly erected Tennis Court at Oatlands House just down the road, at which markers' facilities had been provided.[9] However, he was definitely at Hampton Court in 1835 and by 1841 he was again describing himself as a Tennis Marker.[10] On 18th April 1843, Case was given a contract to manage the Court which was renewable annually. From that moment on, he lost his salary and had to rely on court fees and coaching for his income.

He taught Henry, his third child, to play, and was assisted by him until 1843. After that his nephew, Joseph Case, helped him.

What little is known about his tennis playing ability comes mainly from the recollections of Sir Spencer Ponsonby-Fane, first published in *The Field* in 1910.[11] Sir Spencer met him in 1835 and described him as 'a queer little man, no longer young, a very fast player, but not as good as Peter Tompkins, who was his usual antagonist'. Tompkins at the time was the leading player in England. Case enjoyed talking about his matches and often played against Edmond Barre, whom he always called 'the Gaul'. He was a racket-maker too.

John Case and his son Henry partnered each other in an exhibition four-handed game in the presence of Queen Victoria and Prince Albert on the Duke of Wellington's Strathfield Saye Court in 1845. Soon after, the Consort came to play at Hampton Court. Afterwards he told Case of his intention to play regularly – but he never returned.

John Case died of tuberculosis on 27th March 1848 at the age of 48, still working at the Royal Tennis Court.

Joseph Case (Assistant to John Case c1843-9)

Joseph Case, who appears as Charles Case in most tennis books, was trained during his late teens by his uncle John Case at Hampton Court. Born in Bristol in 1829, his father, also Joseph, was a hatter in the city. His employment as an assistant at the Royal Court probably commenced in 1843 when Henry Case left. In 1849 he moved to Leamington, succeeding Edmund Tompkins as Head Marker. He remained at Leamington until 1858 – nothing is known of him subsequently.

Henry Case   (1848 1864)

Assisted by - Thomas Stone
              Henry John Case (his son)
              John Nightingale

Henry Case was born in East Molesey in 1827. He learnt his trade under his father John at Hampton Court, before moving in 1843 to the Marquess of Salisbury's recently erected court at Hatfield House. John Case had been able to secure the job for his son there through the good offices of Lord Charles Wellesley, whose family owned the Court at Strathfield Saye, which had provided Hatfield with its first marker Charles Phillips. There was however some confusion over the terms of Henry Case's employment. His salary was to be ten shillings a week with lodging and heating provided, but John Case thought the agreement included his board. Case senior wrote to the Marquess of Salisbury on his son's behalf, but received an abrupt letter back demanding acceptance of the offer by return of post, because he had another applicant for the place. Henry Case subsequently spent five years in the service of the Marquess, returning to Hampton Court when his father died.[12]

At the Royal Tennis Court he was engaged on an annual contract under the same terms as his father.

His first assistant at Hampton Court was Thomas Stone, who went on to become one of the games longest-serving professionals. Case and Stone made rackets, balls, tennis shoes and ginger beer in their tiny workshop opposite the garden entrance, in the room that today houses the Court's heating boiler. His rackets cost 30 shillings each, the tennis shoes 14 shillings a pair and the ginger beer fourpence a glass.[13] Case's rackets were said to be cumbersome compared with French ones and looked worse after a few games. However, they must have been durable because *Noel and Clark* recorded sixty years later that 'a good many are still to be seen'. The tennis shoes he made had buff soles and buckskin uppers.

119. HENRY CASE
Head Marker at the Royal Tennis Court 1849-64

According to Julian Marshall, Henry Case was 'a good and effective player but never rose to the first professional rank'. He was though, as recalled earlier, responsible for teaching the Prince of Wales to play tennis.

He married into the famous Tompkins tennis-playing family; his wife Martha was a daughter of Edmund 'Peter' Tompkins, the Brighton Marker.[14] They lived in East Molesey and the second of their seven children, Henry John, whom he taught to play, helped him out after Stone left. Henry Case died aged 36, a result of alcohol abuse.

Thomas Stone   (Assistant 1850-1859)

Thomas Stone was born on 19th June 1839 at Hampton Court Palace. His parents were at the time living in one of the two remaining Pavilions. (See Chapter 5 note 48). His mother, Mary, was a servant and cook, and his father, also Thomas, was the Lamplighter at the Palace. Thomas Stone was to serve the game of tennis for 74 years.[15]

With the Tennis Court on his doorstep he was probably captivated from an early age, for it is known he was helping out Henry Case when he was only eleven years of age. His time at the Royal Court, as mentioned earlier, coincided with the Prince of Wales's introduction to the game. By way of thanks to his doubles partner, the Prince gave Stone a tapestry which is believed to have been hung by the door in Tennis Court Lane to let people know when the heir to the throne was playing; it is now displayed at the Royal Melbourne Tennis Club.

After nine years with Henry Case, Thomas Stone left for the James Street Court, Haymarket. There he benefited from the experience of one of the game's most respected professionals, Edmund Tompkins (World Champion 1862-71). Stone was an accomplished marker and had the honour to mark the famous World

120. THOMAS STONE

Stone is seen here in the Hobart Court before the dedans wall was raised.

Championship contest between Edmond Barre and Edmund Tompkins at James Street in 1862, an extraordinary match that ended with an agreed draw, although Tompkins was ahead by six sets to four. Advantage sets (two clear games needed to win) were played and a further four were declared drawn. There were five days of play spread over a period of 26 days, after which Tompkins was recognised as the Champion.

When the James Street Court closed in 1866, Tompkins and Stone moved to Oxford's Merton Street Court. It was there that Samuel Smith Travers approached Stone. Travers, who had played tennis at James Street, built his own Court in Hobart, Tasmania, and Stone accepted an offer to become his personal professional there.

Stone arrived in Hobart in January 1875 just as the new Court was completed, or about to be. But there was an immediate problem, for the new Court, which was supposed to be based on the James Street Court, had been built using the wrong dimensions. Of most concern were the penthouse roofs and battery walls, which were far too low. Stone managed to persuade Travers to rectify them before the latter ran into financial difficulties, which prevented any further remedial works being carried out. Soon after his arrival in Hobart, Stone joined the Southern Tasmanian Volunteer Artillery, formed as a result of the perceived 'Russian threat', and in 1878 he was commissioned as a lieutenant.

After seven years at Hobart, which by then had become a club court, he moved to the new Melbourne Club on the mainland, where he remained until his death in 1924. Stone oversaw the building of Melbourne's new Exhibition Street court, which was modelled on Hampton Court. At Melbourne, Stone found himself coaching many of the State's leading politicians and towards the end of his life he was introduced to another Prince of Wales. This was the future Edward VIII (afterwards the Duke of Windsor, subsequent to his abdication), whom he met at Government House. It is said he kept the heir to the throne amused with tales of his grandfather's ruthless competitiveness on the old Court at Hampton Court. His son Woolner, another long-serving professional, was employed at Melbourne until he died in 1964. Interestingly, his successor was Chris Ronaldson after a hiatus of nine years.

John Nightingale (1864-1867)

Assisted by - Henry John Case

John Nightingale was born in Tennis Court Lane the son of a palace gardener. He was at first employed as an assistant to Henry Case, and was known to have been working at the Court in 1861 when he was 17 years of age.[16] It would therefore seem likely that he was engaged shortly after Thomas Stone left for James Street.

Following the death of Henry Case, he was promoted to the position of Head Marker on a salary of 16 shillings a week. However, he was found to be 'inefficient', and was dismissed in March 1867. He subsequently became a Police Officer and was stationed at the Palace.

Henry John Case (Assistant to Henry Case, John Nightingale and Tom White c1863-67 & 1884)

Henry John Case was born in 1853 and only ever worked at Hampton Court as an assistant marker. His name first appears in the Minute Book when John Nightingale was employed as Marker in 1864, but he had been taught to play by his father and was known to have helped out around the Court from an earlier date. His salary was five shillings a week.

He left the Royal Tennis Court in 1867, about the time his family moved from Molesey to Richmond. Young Henry John then worked as a linen-draper before moving to Hertford, where he served in the Hertfordshire Yeomanry prior to becoming the Innkeeper at *The Vine* in the late 1870s.

121. HENRY JOHN CASE

Henry John Case, seen here in the Theobalds Court, served
under three Markers at Hampton Court.

He lost *The Vine* playing cards and returned to Hampton Court for a short while in 1884 working under Tom White. This may have been something of a refresher course prior to moving back to Hertfordshire the following year, as he secured the job of professional to Lady Meux at Theobalds Park. There he described himself as a 'Professor of Tennis', while his wife Annie made the balls. Very little tennis was ever played at Theobalds and he was also expected to carry out other miscellaneous tasks on the estate. For instance he was Admiral Sir Hedworth Meux's gunman. He was obviously well thought of, as Sir Hedworth gave him a house, which was for life. He died there in 1940 at the age of 86.[17]

Henry John Case was also descended from another great tennis-playing family, the Tompkins; his grandfather was Edmund 'Peter' Tompkins, and his uncle, the fourth Edmund, was the World Champion.

George Lambert (1867-1868)

Assisted by - Edward (Ted) Johnson

George Lambert was one of the greatest tennis players of the second half of the nineteenth century. He was part of another tennis-playing dynasty. The founder, his father Joseph, had taken over at Hatfield when Henry Case left in 1849. Five of his six sons became tennis professionals. George, baptised Charles George, was his third son, and should not be confused with the youngest, another Charles, who succeeded his father as the Hatfield marker.

Born in 1842, George was sent to Oxford as Sabin's assistant at Merton Street in 1859, taking over from his older brother Thomas who had died shortly before reaching his nineteenth birthday. He moved to Hampton Court in March 1867. There he was engaged as Marker on a salary of 18 shillings a week and was assisted by Edward (Ted) Johnson.[18] He only remained at the Royal Court for 21 months, as he was unable to get the regular top-class practice he needed; most of the talented players were to be found at Prince's or Lord's. It was therefore to Lord's that he moved on the 1st January 1869, where he was to serve for 20 years.

During his time at Lord's he rose to become the best player in the world and in 1871 he challenged Edmund Tompkins for the World Championship. However, no contest took place and from that moment on he was regarded as the World Champion. He reigned unchallenged

122. GEORGE LAMBERT

Head Marker at Hampton Court
1867-68

for 14 years before losing the crown to Thomas Pettitt at Hampton Court, in circumstances already recalled.

In 1874 Major Walter Clopton Wingfield introduced a 'boxed tennis set' which enabled a form of the game to be played outside without walls. These sets proved amazingly popular and led to the establishment of Lawn Tennis. Other versions of these sets followed leading to a variety of views on how the game should be played. There was a need for an agreed set of rules, so it naturally fell to the tennis committee of the MCC (at the time Lord's was the headquarters of Tennis) to frame them. This in turn led to George Lambert's involvement, and he produced a boxed tennis set of his own for MCC members. Several of the tennis professionals saw the new game as a means of supplementing their income by providing and servicing equipment. In 1876, Lord's gave Lambert permission to market his sets to the public — they sold for five guineas. Each set contained a net, supporting poles, a plan of the court, and balls. The balls, which he made and patented, were rubber with cloth cemented on. *The Field* carried out experiments on them, and found that they were uniform in size and 'bound' (bounce), but were concerned that they would not stand severe use in all weathers. Lambert also produced a ball using 'mackintosh' instead of cloth as a cover. He manufactured rackets for lawn tennis as well.

Several of the Lamberts were good cricketers. The father Joseph and his sons William and Charles all turned out for Hatfield Cricket Club on a regular basis. Charles was a good bowler and on three occasions took all ten wickets in a match. George Lambert had his own XI, which often played against Hatfield CC. They consisted mostly of groundsmen and staff employed by the MCC and they played their home matches at Lord's. As part of the preparation for his 1885 challenge for the World Championship, held by George Lambert, Thomas Pettitt spent a year at Hatfield training, ironically, with Charles Lambert. During this period he too played several times for Hatfield CC.[19]

George Lambert left Lord's in 1889 and moved to the Wellington Court at Cambridge, where his career finished in 1891. He died in 1915, penniless.

Lawn Tennis.

**GEORGE LAMBERT,
CHAMPION TENNIS PLAYER,**

BEGS to inform the nobility and gentry that, by permission of the Marylebone Cricket Club, he supplies complete SETS OF LAWN TENNIS, from £5. 10s., including Ladies' Adjusting Nets and Racquets, also The New Covered Ball, protected by ROYAL LETTERS PATENT, which will not absorb wet and cannot come unstitched.
Rules of the Game, with Plan of Court, as revised by the M.C.C., forwarded on receipt of 6 stamps.

123. LAMBERT'S ADVERTISEMENT

George Lambert's advertisement for his boxed tennis sets appeared in *The Field.*

William Lambert   (1869-1880)

Assisted by - Edward (Ted) Johnson

The fourth son of Joseph Lambert, William, was thought to have assisted his brother George at the Royal Tennis Court before taking over as Marker himself in 1869 — the salary was again 18 shillings a week. He was 25 years old at the time and lived locally in Teddington. In 1880, he went to Lord's and again worked under his brother George. By 1888 he had moved to his last job in tennis, as private professional to the Earl of Plymouth at Hewell Grange.

Like his brother George, William became involved in lawn tennis in its infancy. On 17th May 1877, while still in the employ of the Royal Tennis Court, he and his brother Charles played in the first-ever public lawn tennis exhibition match. It took place at a skating rink in London's Maida Vale, with Julian Marshall as the umpire. Marshall had been on the MCC committee that had framed the first set of rules for the new game.

William's cricketing ability was alluded to earlier. At this he was the best of the Lamberts, and during his time at Hampton Court he was selected for the Colts of England and in 1874 played for Middlesex.

Edward (Ted) Johnson   (Assistant to George & William Lambert 1867-c1878)

Ted Johnson was a local boy from Hampton Wick, the son of a locksmith and bellhanger, who was engaged in tennis for some 60 years. He started work at the Royal Tennis Court in 1867 at the age of 13 and remained there until the late 1870s assisting George, and then William Lambert. He linked up with George Lambert again at Lord's for a short time before moving, in 1879, to the new private Court built by Sir Ivor Guest (afterwards Lord Wimborne) at Canford in Dorset. Although he suffered from a lack of match play there, he did win the Manchester Professional Handicap in 1889. He remained at Canford for over 40 years until after the First World War, when the Estate was sold and he was pensioned off. But Canford became a Public School and Johnson returned to teach the boys the basics of tennis and to mark school matches. He was the head of yet another great family of tennis professionals. Three sons followed him into the game, one, another Ted, was for 65 years the Professional at Moreton Morrell, and one of his grandsons, Albert 'Jack' Johnson, won the World Championship in 1957. Edward senior passed away in 1926.

Tom White   (1880-1910)

Assisted by - Alfred White (son)   John McCann
              Stanley Lambert   John White (nephew)
              Henry John Case   Harold White (grandson)

196

Tom White was born in 1835 in the old County of Westmoreland and brought up at Brougham Hall, Eamont Bridge, near Penrith, where his father was Lord Brougham's bailiff. At first he was employed as his Lordship's greyhound trainer, but as a young lad it was the Tennis Court that attracted him. In his late teens, Lord Brougham decided to employ him as his professional and sent him to the James Street Court for a few weeks' instruction under Edmund Tompkins. He became a very good player and it was said that he could 'make a good game' with J.M. Heathcote, the Amateur Champion, who often played on the northern circuit.

124.   TOM WHITE ON COURT AT HAMPTON COURT

Tom White was the Club's longest-serving professional.

He was, though, unable to earn a decent living at tennis, so he went to the Isle of Man, where he managed a hotel for a dozen or so years. As this was not successful he applied for the job of Marker at Hampton Court when William Lambert left in 1880.

At the Royal Court, White was at first assisted by his son Alfred, and then in succession by Stanley Lambert, Henry John Case and John McCann. McCann left in 1890 to become the first professional at the new Holyport Court near Maidenhead, and Tom White's 14-year-old nephew, John White, was employed for the next 16 years. In his latter years McCann returned, while White's grandson Harold also helped out.

At Hampton Court, Tom White's role was described as Manager, for which he was paid £1 a week plus threepence a set whenever he was required to play. He was said to be a 'good player, good teacher, true character, full of humour and determination, always at full pressure however weak his opponent might be'. As a player he had modest success. He regularly entered the early Professional Handicap Singles competitions at Manchester and in 1892 he won it. The spectators in the dedans became very excited during the final, as his defeated opponent was his son Alfred, prompting *The Times* to comment on 'a most popular victory'. Another notable success for Tom White was his defeat of George Lambert when he was nearly 70 years of age, with Lambert in his early sixties.

He was not a well man and suffered badly from rheumatism and gout. The Committee was very concerned about his health and on one occasion in 1898 gave him £5 to 'go to the seaside'. The following year the assistant's wage was increased to 15 shillings a week because of the increased workload. By 1908 he was unable to play.

125. ALFRED WHITE IN 1889

Tom White passed away on 8th April 1910 at the age of 75, having given 30 of those years to the Royal Tennis Court — at the time of writing, the Club's longest serving professional. After his death, J.J. Freeman, who had played with him once a week for more than 25 years, said: 'he was one of the keenest tennis players and one of the best of men.' [20]

An amusing remark is attributed to Tom White. The occasion is thought to have been a doubles match played at Sheen. Partnering the Duke of York (the future George V) against his father, the Prince of Wales (later Edward VII) and the Duke of Fife, the Duke of York became impatient at his lack of quick improvement. White is said to have responded: 'Ah, Sir, there is no royal road to tennis!' [21]

Sheen Tennis Court Club.

Station—MORTLAKE. *East Sheen, Surrey.*

General Committee.

H.R.H. THE DUKE OF CORNWALL AND YORK.
THE DUKE OF FIFE.
LORD WINDSOR.
SIR GODFREY LUSHINGTON.
THE HON. ALFRED LYTTELTON.
J. J. FREEMAN, ESQ.,
ROGER H. FULLER, ESQ.
J. KELSALL, ESQ.
JULIAN MARSHALL, ESQ.

Annual Subscription

TWO GUINEAS—London and Local Members.

ONE GUINEA
Naval and Military Officers.
Country Members (residing outside a radius of fifteen miles of East Sheen).
Members of Sheen House Club.
University and Public School Students.
Members of any Tennis Club.

ENTRANCE FEE.—The first hundred Members shall be elected without Entrance Fee, and shall have the privilege of joining the Sheen House Club (which is on adjoining property) without Entrance Fee at an additional Annual Subscription of Three Guineas. Country Members, Two Guineas.

The Sheen House Club Entrance Fee is Two Guineas, and the Annual Subscription Five Guineas in the ordinary way.

The Club year shall commence on the 1st January and all Annual Subscriptions shall be payable in advance on that date.

The Club being Proprietary, no other liability will be incurred.

The following shall be the charges in force at the Club.

Members—2s. an hour, each player.
1s. every additional half hour.

Non-Members—4s. an hour.
2s. every additional half hour.

When playing with, or receiving instruction from, the Professional, an additional Fee of 1s. an hour and 6d. for every half hour shall be charged.

Rackets 21s. and 25s. each.
Stringing Rackets 7s. 6d.

Repairing Rackets,—Main strings 6d. each.
Cross strings 3d.

The Court will be open on Sundays, providing it is previously booked.

All communications to be addressed to Mr. White, Sheen Tennis Court Club, East Sheen, Surrey.

126. THE TERMS AND CONDITIONS AT THE SHEEN TENNIS COURT CLUB

The Tennis Court at Sheen had close links with Hampton Court. All of those who served on the first committee were members of the Royal Tennis Court, with the possible exception of J. Kelsall. The Professional, Alfred White, was trained at Hampton Court.

Alfred White (1910-1932)

Assisted by - Harold White and another son

Alf White was 'a player of delightful style', but never of the top grade. He had been taught the game by his father at Hampton Court, where he assisted until 1883 before moving to the Duke of Fife's Court at East Sheen, near Richmond in Surrey. His wages at Hampton Court were five shillings a week. He was just 19 years of age when he moved to Sheen where he first acted as the Duke's private professional, but in 1900 when His Grace could no longer play, he gave White the Court to manage, which he ran as a semi-public club until 1906. He then accepted an engagement at the new Court at Harvard University in Boston, which he ran for two years before moving to The Racquet and Tennis Club in New York. He remained there for another two years before returning to England shortly before his father died.

He was therefore at his prime during his years at Sheen and became one of the game's most respected professionals. On at least two occasions, world championship challengers engaged him as a personal coach. In 1890, he trained with Charles Saunders at Holyport prior to his match against Pettitt in Dublin, and in 1904 Cecil Fairs asked him to assist with his preparation at the Princes Club Brighton, for his upcoming challenge to Peter Latham.[22]

Alf White was appointed Marker at Hampton Court in September 1910, on a salary of 30 shillings a week. He was allowed to employ his son Harold and in time his second son joined them, as did a daughter who helped out with the re-covering of the balls. White ran the Royal Tennis Court very well, making his own rackets and balls. The balls were made of thin strips of shirting that became very hard in use. When Henry Johns was the Professional at Fairlawne in the 1930s, he purchased a set and recalled that they were nice to play with — praise indeed from the man who for 40 years was the game's premier ball-maker. Alf White made the balls for the Covey v Kinsella World Championship match in 1922. As a racket-maker White had a good reputation — Jay Gould, Tom Pettitt and Cecil 'Punch' Fairs were among his customers. Many were exported to America, but he did not confine himself to making rackets only for tennis — he also made them for lawn tennis, and even a special small version for the game of squash-tennis played at Moreton Morrell. White's rackets bore the stamp 'Alfred White and Sons'.

Like his father, he always entered the Professional Handicap Singles, in those days held at Manchester. The competition did not take place between 1892, the year he was beaten by his father, and 1910, but he reached another final in 1911. That was the last year he entered and he produced his best ever performance, just losing in the final to Ted Johnson of Moreton Morrell.

An ingenious man, Alfred White designed and installed court lighting at both Sheen and Manchester. His system involved reflecting light off a screen stretched across the roof of the court. This meant it was shadow-free, but the resulting level of illumination was poor. To demonstrate his system, he played exhibition matches on the Courts in 1903 with Cecil 'Punch' Fairs. He also invented a net-fixing device, a version of which is still embedded in the main wall at Hampton Court.[23]

By 1914, he was becoming increasingly sensitive about being called a Marker. The last two decades had seen a move away from the use of the term in favour of 'Professional', and a series of correspondence had aired the subject in the columns of *The Field* twelve months earlier. 'Marker' was used on all official documents concerning the Royal Tennis Court. In a letter to the Secretary Agar he wrote: 'The term Marker is really only applied to a small boy attached to the court who marks the score more or less correctly, to call me a Marker is as disrespectful as calling Varden a caddie.' In fact his father had described himself as a Tennis Professional while referring to his nephew John as a Tennis Marker. Had the earlier nineteenth-century practice of calling a Head Marker a 'Manager' survived, in situations where they ran courts employing under-markers or boys, Alf White might never have become so irate.[24] Agar wrote to Lionel Earle, the First Commissioner of the Office of Works, who duly obliged, and from that moment on they referred to him as the Professional.[25]

127. ALF WHITE WITH EDWARD GRAY

This photograph was taken at Brighton shortly after Alf White (right) took over as Head Professional at Hampton Court in 1910

About this time E.B. Noel paid tribute to Alf White with these words. 'Were I a beginner at tennis there would be no one I would choose as a mentor before White, and the best players may learn much from his ripe experience. He has done as much as anyone to raise the profession to its present level, and no one is more imbued with the dignity of the game.'

There soon followed the First World War, during which there was very little play at Hampton Court and the Club ceased to function, and was therefore unable to pay him, so he went over to Lakewood, New Jersey, to help coach Jay Gould. He was no stranger to the Georgian Court, as he had worked there at times during his previous period in the United States. In total, he spent the winters of 1915-16, 1916-17 and 1919-20 at Lakewood. After the war, he returned to Hampton Court to help Charles Agar restart the Club.

In the 1920s he was able, with the help of his sons, to restart the family racket and ball-making business, which, along with an annuity from the Duke of Fife, and his salary and court fees at Hampton Court, helped to provide him with a reasonable income. The circumstances of his unhappy departure from the Club in 1932, when aged 67, were dealt with earlier. The experience left him very bitter, especially towards Charles Agar and Lord Revelstoke whom he blamed personally for bringing his distinguished career to an end. He described himself as 'the victim of the most disgraceful injustice in the history of tennis.' Despite this, Lord Revelstoke joined Lord Aberdare and Lord Leconfield in organising a testimonial fund for him.

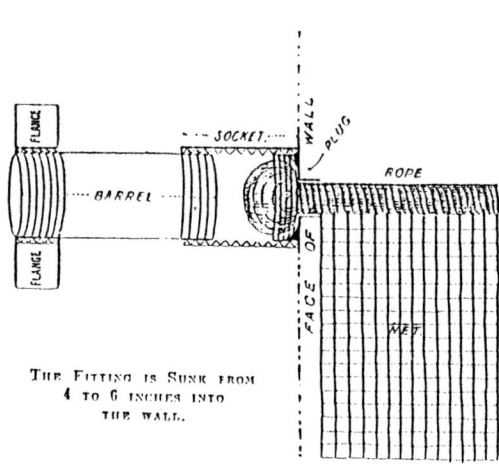

128. ALF WHITE'S NET-FIXING DEVICE

A version of his net-fixing mechanism is still embedded in the main wall at Hampton Court.

Alf White retired to a smallholding at Horncastle in Lincolnshire with his two sons. Once or twice he attempted to restart ball-making, writing on one occasion to Lord Leconfield hoping to revive his arrangement to supply balls to Petworth. He also worked with Slazengers when the New York Racquet & Tennis Club commissioned them to develop a tennis ball. Neither of these approaches brought any reward.

He was asked to write an autobiography but declined, because he felt recalling the manner of his dismissal would have brought the Royal Tennis Court into disrepute. However, he remained fond of the Club and letters to Agar's successor, Chris Gabriel, would always end with an offer of help, if the Club so desired. He also presented the Club with several framed photographs, including two of the 1885 World Championship and a

129. TOM WHITE AND STANLEY LAMBERT

202

large picture of the Honourable Alfred Lyttelton, which still hangs in the clubroom.

On the occasion of his retirement he gave an interview to the *London Evening Standard*, where he recalled an interesting doubles match that had taken place early on in his career, which involved three members of the Royal Family. In this match, which has echoes of the one involving his father, he partnered the Prince of Wales (afterwards Edward VII), against his two sons, Prince Albert Victor (the Duke of Clarence) and Prince George of Wales (the future George V). This unique match also took place at Sheen.[26]

Stanley Lambert   (Assistant to Tom White 1883-84)

Stanley Lambert was born in 1870. At the age of thirteen Tom White took him on as 'the boy'. He only stayed for a year and then left to join his father William at Lord's, before moving to Oxford and eventually America. There he worked under Robert Moore at the New York Racquet & Tennis Club and for a short time in 1908 under Alf White, finally switching to lawn tennis towards the end of his professional career.

130. JOHN McCANN

John McCann   (Assistant to Tom White 1885-90 and again 1908-10)

John McCann was twice employed as Tom White's assistant at Hampton Court, although during the second engagement he was effectively running the Court on his own because of the Head Professional's failing health.

It seems likely that McCann's introduction to tennis came through a connection with Tom White when the latter was a hotelier on the Isle of Man, for McCann, the son of a stonemason, had been born and raised in the town of Laxey on the island.

He came to the Royal Tennis Court in 1885 as a 20-year-old following the departure of Henry John Case to Theobalds. He stayed for just over four years before moving and taking up the position of Professional to Samuel Heilbut at his new Court at Holyport Grange.

Having left Mr Heilbut's service he returned to Hampton Court in 1908 and remained until Tom White died two years later. During this time he and his wife Jane, who helped to make the balls, lodged across the river in Thames Ditton. It would appear that Tom White had not only taught the young McCann the art of ball-making but he also had learnt how to make rackets. A beautiful miniature racket crafted by John McCann, along with some of the balls he made, is still in the possession of his family.

Following the death of Tom White in 1910, and the arrival of White's son Alfred as the Head Professional, John McCann retired from tennis and settled in his wife's home village of Overton in Hampshire, where they brought up three sons and a daughter. There he took a job as a postman, which has provided the only known photograph of him. He died in Overton in 1953 at the ripe old age of 87.[27]

John White (Assistant to Tom White 1890 - 1906)

When John McCann left for Holyport in 1890, Tom White decided to employ his nephew John. After 16 years guidance under his uncle, John White had become an accomplished tennis player. He then decided to join the growing number of English professionals who saw their future in the United States.

Known in America as Jack White, he arrived at The Racquet & Tennis Club, New York (then at 27 West 43rd Street) after leaving Hampton Court in 1906. While there he benefited from the training he received from the Club's Rackets Professional, George Standing, and prior to the First World War he was regarded as the best professional tennis player in the United States. As leading professionals, he and Standing were asked to open Clarence H. Mackay's new Court on his magnificent Harbor Hill estate at Roslyn, Long Island in 1909. Because of his pre-eminence, there was considerable surprise when White was defeated by Walter Kinsella in the first ever United States Professional Singles Championship in 1915. However, Kinsella was a superb player, at the time the World 'Squash-Tennis Champion', who went on unsuccessfully to challenge for the World Tennis Championship three times. Like many other New York professionals, White spent several seasons at Aiken in South Carolina and continued his association with the Club there after leaving New York in 1920. He finished his career coaching squash and lawn tennis at the Round Hill Club, in Greenwich, Connecticut.[28]

Harold White (Assistant to Tom White and Alfred White c1906-32)

Harold White probably began his tennis career in 1906 following John White's decision to emigrate to America. The Committee was never happy with him, and two years later told Tom White to consider sending him to be taught at another court and employing someone else as assistant. It is not clear if he took up this opportunity, but he was allowed to work for his father when he returned to Hampton Court in 1910. Apart from active service with the Royal Fusiliers during the First World War he remained at the Royal Court until Alf White departed in 1932. The Committee did not want him to succeed his father as Head Professional, but would have been happy for him to continue as an assistant. It was said that he inherited his father's love of mechanics more than his proficiency as a player. In the circumstances he decided to quit tennis and move to Lincolnshire, where he and his younger brother set up a poultry farming business.

131. ALF WHITE AND HAROLD WHITE

Arthur Ashford (1932-1957)

Arthur Ashford began his working life as a ball-boy at The Queen's Club in 1914. He quickly impressed and was very soon elevated to head ball-boy. While at Queen's, he benefited from the experience of the great Peter Latham.

As a youngster, he regularly entered the Young Professionals' Handicap Singles Tournament, and won it in 1930. On that occasion his opponent was the 19 year-old Henry Johns. The competition was played on Ashford's home court and he won 8-5, 8-6, giving odds of half-fifteen.

His game was said to have dramatically improved after he moved to Hampton Court in 1932, but he never reached the top flight. He was a good teacher and his pleasant personality made him popular among the members. He was initially engaged on a salary of £2 15s. 0d. a week, plus a shilling for every court taken. Despite Alf White's efforts, when Arthur Ashford's contract was drawn up, the Committee reverted back to the term 'Marker'.

In 1942 he was enlisted, serving in the Royal Air Force at Stafford, working on the bombers based there. After the war, he resumed his career at Hampton Court where he helped first Chris Gabriel, and then Tony Negretti, in their efforts to revive a seriously ailing Club.

On 3rd December 1957, he suddenly collapsed and died while alone on court, leaving a wife and son. Following this tragedy, members generously contributed to a fund to help his widow Emily, who had herself been ill for a number of years. Although he taught his son Peter to play tennis, he was not keen on him turning professional. However, Peter did so, and spent 15 years at Queen's, coaching both tennis and rackets, before moving to Winchester in 1975 as their Rackets Professional.

In his autobiography *Oh I Say!* Dan Maskell, the well-known lawn tennis commentator and his old friend and fellow ball-boy from their days at Queen's, wrote, with a little poetic licence, about the manner of Arthur Ashford's death:

132. ARTHUR ASHFORD

The Royal Tennis Court Professional
1932-57

'It is perhaps appropriate for one who had always expressed such reverence for the game's origins that Arthur should have died on that famous court, the victim of a sudden heart attack as he bent down to play a low backhand. It was the sort of end that any serious sportsman might have chosen.'

Leslie Keeble (1958-1972)

Leslie Keeble was better known as a squash player than a tennis player. His career began as an apprentice in all of the court games played at the Prince's Club in Knightsbridge in the 1920s. Jim Dear and Henry Johns were among his contemporaries. In the 1939-45 war he served in the Royal Air Force.

Before coming to the Royal Tennis Court in 1958, he had for some ten years been Squash Rackets Professional at the Lansdowne Club in Fitzmaurice Place, off Berkeley Square. Prior to that, he had for a short time worked at the International Sportsmens' Club. When Jim Dear retired from competitive squash in 1954, Keeble was his natural successor as the leading British squash professional of the day. He was Professional Champion in 1947, when he was described as 'a beautiful stroke player who exploits every shot in the game'. He was also twice runner-up in this event. But with the arrival on the scene of the Egyptian Mahmoud Karim and later the legendary Khans from Pakistan, he was unable to repeat his earlier successes.

At tennis he won the Lurgan Cup in 1963 partnered by David Warburg. His years at Hampton Court have largely been dealt with in an earlier chapter, including the strained relationships towards the end. Some members still remember him with affection although, as previously observed, he upset many others. He retired from the game and moved north to Withernsea near Hull following his abrupt resignation in September 1972, where he and his wife Ruby opened a small newsagents and confectionery shop. He died in 1996.

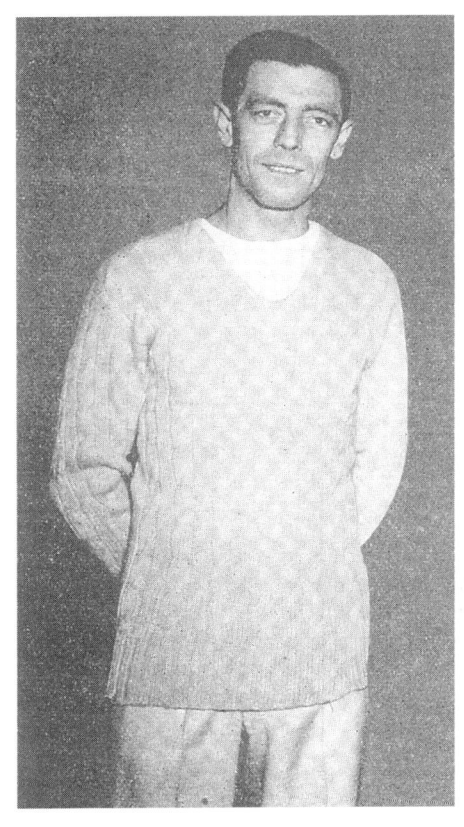

133. LESLIE KEEBLE

Professional at the Royal Tennis Court 1958-72

Derek Barrett (1973-1979)

Derek Barrett was one of the first youngsters to benefit from the T&RA's Young Professionals Fund. He had started his working life as a member of the cricketing staff at Lord's, and it was there that he was introduced to tennis. Having decided to switch games at the age of 17, his first job in tennis was as an assistant to Leslie Keeble at Hampton Court, arriving in September 1964. (He was the only assistant Keeble had during his years at the RTC). He found himself back at Lord's in July 1965, where he worked under the man who had the greatest influence on him, Henry Johns. After four years he left to take up his first appointment as a Head Professional, at Seacourt. There he coached a variety of racket sports including squash.

A native of Hull, he returned home in the summer of 1970, when the Professional's position became vacant at the Hull and East Riding Squash Rackets Club. While there he ventured into the world of Rugby League and played for Hull Kingston Rovers for two seasons. He played mainly for the 'A' team, but made the first team on a number of occasions. After a few years, though, he became disillusioned with squash and sought to return to tennis. His old friend from Lord's, David Cull, alerted him to the vacancy at Hampton Court and, with the personal recommendation of committee member Michael Morton, he was offered the job.

So it was that he started as the Professional at the Royal Tennis Court on 1st October 1973. The negotiations relating to his employment were touched upon earlier. Suffice it to say here that it was agreed that his starting salary would be £1,000 a year, plus a percentage of the court fees.

134.   DEREK BARRETT WITH THE BROWNING CUP

Professional at the Royal Tennis Court 1973-79

His appointment at Hampton Court coincided with the installation of the first fully-elected club committee, and with everybody in positive mood there was a dramatic increase in activity. While at the Royal Tennis Court, Barrett developed a personal friendship with Howard Angus, which helped in securing for the Club many national tournaments and two World Championship Challenges. He was considered to be one of the best markers of the period and marked both of the World Challenges. In fact, his years at Hampton Court, in terms of major tournaments staged, were the busiest that the Club has ever seen. He resigned in the summer of 1979, as he was not seeing eye-to-eye with the Committee regarding his working hours, and felt he was not being properly rewarded for his efforts.

Disillusioned for the second time in his career he was determined to get back to Hull and had decided to apply for a job as a bus driver in his home city. It was only the persuasiveness of John Tours at the Manchester Tennis & Racquet Club that kept him in the game; he literally talked him into taking the job of Head

Professional there. During his time at Manchester, he significantly boosted the amount of play on both the tennis and the rackets court, but it was the rackets court that saw the biggest increase in activity.

These days, the majority of rackets courts are to be found in the country's public schools, and it was his preference for working with youngsters that took him to Wellington College as their Rackets Professional in the summer of 1984. Wellington is close to the Royal Military Academy at Sandhurst, so he occasionally helped out there too. During his years at Wellington he produced several successful pairs, winning a number of the Public Schools Competitions at Queen's.

As a tennis player, he won the Browning Cup in 1975 and reached the final of the Seacourt Silver Racquet two years later.

In search of a fresh challenge, he moved to the Montreal Racquet Club in September 2001.

CHAPTER 13

THE RONALDSON ERA

Since the departure of Derek Barrett the Club has had the benefit of the services of a professional who has now been a major force in the game for more than thirty years. On 19th November 1979 Chris Ronaldson was appointed Head Professional of the Royal Tennis Court. From that moment on the Court has been virtually running at full capacity.

Chris Ronaldson

Born in Cambridge on 21st January 1950, Chris Ronaldson spent his early childhood in East Africa where his father was in the Colonial Service. The family returned to England when he was 12 and settled in Oxford.

He came into Tennis when he responded to an advertisement for the job of assistant professional to Peter Dawes at the Merton Street Court, Oxford, in September 1971. Although he was already well known on the junior lawn tennis circuit, he had never seen the parent game before. The T&RA's Young Professionals Fund funded his employment.

Two months after taking the job he married Lesley Lee who, like him, was to become a major asset to the game. They had met when they were both studying at Kent University. He had been the Captain of the University Lawn Tennis Team and also played in their squash matches, and, when looking for someone to represent the University at lawn tennis late in 1969, was impressed by her ability to beat any of the prospective male contenders. A year later they were both sent to Sheffield to play in the Inter-Universities Squash Championships. They got to know each other on the long train journey north.

Within a year he found himself running the Oxford Court on his own when Peter Dawes moved to Seacourt. Although he was only there for a little over two years, he made his mark by producing a winning team for the varsity match using three players new to tennis. They were Jonny Leslie, a talented squash player, and Alan Lovell and Peter Seabrook, the successful Winchester rackets pair who had just come up to Oxford. Alan Lovell and Peter Seabrook later became RTC members. Jonny Leslie's father, John, has been a member of the Club for many years and, in his eighties, still plays to a good standard, regularly reaching the later rounds of the Seal Salver competition.

What tempted Chris Ronaldson away from Oxford were the excitement of an important new tennis project in Australia and the enthusiasm of those controlling it. In Melbourne the first new Courts to be built anywhere in the world for 50 years were under construction.

The Royal Melbourne Club had lost its last professional, Woolner Stone (son of Thomas, ex-Hampton Court) nine years earlier and play was down to 15 hours a week. About a dozen stalwart members at a Special General Meeting took the courageous decision to sell the old city centre premises and build two new Courts

135. CHRIS RONALDSON

Head Professional at The Royal Tennis Court since 1979

in the suburb of Richmond. The move did not go smoothly as, like many building projects and particularly new tennis court developments, it suffered from delays. On his arrival in December 1973 Ronaldson found that he would have to work for a while at the old Exhibition Street Court. However, when the time came to move to the new premises nine months later, bookings had doubled.

The Ronaldsons worked well as a team. They both went out and joined the local lawn tennis and squash clubs, fertile recruiting grounds for converts to the game. Lesley Ronaldson's effervescent personality is a particularly useful asset in these circumstances. Chris Ronaldson employs simple but effective means of increasing court usage, firstly by not allowing any member to leave the premises without taking their full complement of advance bookings, and then by making strenuous efforts to match any member needing an opponent.

With his own game improving, success was beginning to come. In 1974 he reached the final of the Australian Open Championships, where he lost to his great friend Barry Toates, the Hobart Professional. In 1977, on a visit to the United States, he reached the finals of both the US Open and the US Professional Singles Championships, losing to Gene Scott and Norwood Cripps, respectively. In the same year he won the Tasmanian Open by defeating the talented Graham Hyland and won his first national championship, the Australian Open, where he gained revenge over Toates.

By 1978 the Melbourne Club was flourishing and the family — both Ivan and Ben were born in Australia — felt the time had come to move on. In order to further his career he needed more tournament play and regular top class practice, and that was more readily available in the northern hemisphere.

Surprisingly, he opted for a job at the Sun Court, Troon, the northernmost Tennis Court in the British Isles excepting Falkland Palace. The house with its Tennis Court was originally built by J.O.M. Clark, but was by that time a hotel run by Alastair and Jill Breckenridge. They had painstakingly restored the Court and it was their enthusiasm that attracted the Ronaldsons. The move took place in December 1978. The month prior to the move had been very significant, for it was then that he defeated World Champion Howard Angus in the final, to win the first of his seven British Open Singles titles, a feat still unequalled.

Troon had never seen anything like the Ronaldsons. The level of activity prior to their arrival was even less than that they had found at Melbourne. An average of just six courts a week was being taken and there were only 15 active playing members. Within three months over 70 courts a week had been achieved and by July the figure had reached 88, with 100 members playing regularly. Although he was at Troon for less than a year, he inspired three men to turn professional. The first was Walter Gregg, who had learnt to play at Falkland Palace; the others were Alistair Curley and Mike Gooding.

That previous eventful November, Ronaldson had also beaten Norwood Cripps in the British eliminator for the World Championship while Jimmy Burke had won the American eliminator by defeating Gene Scott. In April 1979 Ronaldson defeated Burke in the final eliminator at Hampton Court, before losing heavily to Howard Angus in the Challenge itself. Further disappointment came at the end of the year, when Angus again beat him to regain the British Open Singles.

After only ten months at Troon he visited Hampton Court and discussed at some length the vacancy for senior professional at the Royal Tennis Court with

212

the Treasurer, Ronald Swash. The Committee agreed the proposals for his employment, so Chris and Lesley Ronaldson set off for Hampton Court leaving Walter Gregg in charge at Troon. They found that court occupancy was only a third of that they had left behind at Troon. Court usage had dropped off during the two months the Club had been without a professional. Once again, the same tactics were employed and within a year bookings had trebled. At first Ronaldson was an employee of the Club, but concern that the Club was about to breach the Value Added Tax threshold, which would have forced up membership subscriptions, led to him becoming self-employed soon afterwards.

In 1980 he won the first of his three US Open Singles titles. There is no doubt that he would have won this title more times, were it not for his protest against the insistence of the United States Court Tennis Association that only American-made Bancroft rackets could be used. He did not enter the competition for a number of years due to the American governing body's stance. There were at the time only two manufacturers making tennis rackets, Bancrofts and Grays of Cambridge. Ronaldson had always preferred Grays, but they had just stopped making their narrower headed racket, which had previously been acceptable to the Americans. These days Grays are the game's sole supplier of rackets.

Having beaten Frank Willis and Barry Toates in eliminators he challenged Howard Angus again for the World Championship in April 1981. The venue was The Queen's Club in London, and when Ronaldson was leading by five sets to one, and 5-4 in the seventh, Angus unfortunately turned sharply and tore a calf muscle which forced him to concede the match.

So on the 19th April 1981 Chris Ronaldson began a six-year reign as World Champion. He defended his World Title three times, his challenger on each occasion being the Australian Wayne Davies. In March 1983 at Hampton Court he won by seven sets to four, in March 1985 at Queen's by seven sets to one and finally at Queen's in April 1987 when he lost by seven sets to four.

Of the major National Open Singles Championships he won an unequalled twenty — seven British, three American, five Australian and five French. He also won three World Open Singles tournaments, three Scottish Open Singles, the British Professional Singles nine times and the US Professional Singles seven. Although he never concentrated on the doubles game, he has won all four of the major National Doubles Championships, plus the World Doubles, the Scottish Open Doubles, the British and the US Professional Doubles. Usually he was partnered by Mick Dean, or his brother Steve. In addition he has won every tournament for which he was ever eligible, both in the United Kingdom and Australia. At the height of his career he went for over three years and 53 consecutive matches in competition without being defeated in any level singles tournament. In 1984 he completed the Grand Slam — all four major Open Singles Championships, the British, American, Australian and the French — the first time this had been achieved.

Chris Ronaldson retired from competitive tennis at the end of 1993 at the age of 43, having suffered for a number of months from a shoulder injury. But he still keeps himself in good physical shape and in his fiftieth year he took a group of club members to the summit of Mount Kilimanjaro in Tanzania, the second of three treks he made to the top of Africa's highest mountain. Three years later he successfully completed the 'Three Peaks Challenge' for charity, climbing Ben Nevis, Scafell Pike and Snowdon, the highest mountains in Scotland, England and Wales, respectively, all within a 24-hour period.

136. CHRIS RONALDSON
WORLD CHAMPION

David Warburg presents Chris Ronaldson with
the World Championship Salver in 1981

His playing career was characterised by intense concentration and determination. Another factor was his clever analytical brain. This was useful when he worked with Charles Wade in formulating the National Handicap System, and pioneered at Hampton Court the computerised control of it. In 1991, he and Lachie Deuchar beat the best of Britain's academics, managers and accountants, when they entered the Business and Investment Management Game run by *The Independent* newspaper. On the way to the final they beat Oxford's third-placed Keble College, and in the final, a team from the leading City accountants KPMG. More recently he has gained a First Class Honours Degree in History at the Open University, and now lectures on the subject of twentieth-century European History.

In 1985, he wrote and co-published *Tennis: A Cut Above The Rest*, the game's first comprehensive coaching manual. The book is divided into three parts: the first part deals with elementary aspects of play; the second with specific strokes and tactics; and the final part is autobiographical. In 1998 he followed it up with a video version, the game's first instructional film. He and his father, Bruce, run Ronaldson Publications (Ironbark), which has now produced a dozen volumes related to tennis, including this one.

His successful rescue of the Bordeaux Club in 1983 was dealt with in Chapter 10, but he was soon involved in yet another challenge. He was a partner in the consortium that saved the Holyport Court from the developers when they purchased it in 1985, and he now holds over fifty per cent of the shares. Holyport is now a thriving club, although he plays no part in the day-to-day management.

For many years Chris Ronaldson has worked on various T&RA sub-committees and is currently in charge of youth development. His experience and expertise are constantly in demand and he is invariably one of the first to be contacted when a new tennis court is proposed.

In 2001, at a ceremony in New York, he was inducted into the International Court Tennis Hall of Fame.

Chris Ronaldson continues to be a major influence in the game. Hundreds of today's tennis players owe their enjoyment of the game to his drive and enthusiasm, and many of those at the top regularly tap into his vast experience by employing him as a coach. There is little doubt that the predominance of world-class Australian players seen today can be traced back to his years in the Antipodes. He is a man of integrity, which has gained him worldwide respect, although his forthright support for the advancement of his fellow professionals sometimes brings him into conflict with those who administer the game. But there can be no finer example of his dedication to the game and the Club, than the sight of him painting the court floor at Hampton Court on the only day the Court closes — Christmas Day!

Lesley Ronaldson

Not content only to support her husband's magnificent tennis career, Lesley Ronaldson also has a notable one of her own.

She was four times British Ladies Open Singles Champion between 1979 and 1986, and four times British Ladies Open Doubles Champion — the first three with Gill Dean, the wife of her husband's doubles partner, and the last with Katrina Allen. She and Katrina Allen also won the Ladies World Doubles Championship in 1987. In addition, she has won the US Singles and the US Doubles titles.

In Melbourne in 1985, she came within two points of emulating her husband, when she was defeated by Judy Clarke in the first-ever Ladies World Championship, losing the third and final set by five games to six.

She was forced out of competitive play in 1988 with hip trouble and shortly afterwards had to have an operation to replace the joint. Amazingly, she came back to win the Ladies Over-40s Singles in 1991. Unfortunately the joint failed after six years and the operation had to be repeated; in 1998 the other hip joint was replaced. She has bounced back yet again and entered the 1999 Ladies World Championship Doubles, held at Hampton Court. She took part in the World Doubles again in 2001 in Washington, where she and Sally Jones reached the semi-finals. That same year, partnering RTC's Bernard Weatherill, she added the Billy Ross-Skinner Cup to her long list of successes.

Because Lesley was no longer able to play competitively there was no need to retain her amateur status, so in 1988 she turned professional and has since worked part-time at both Hampton Court and Holyport. For years she had given free lessons and hand-sewn thousands of balls. Baskets of balls were even taken in for her to sew on the occasions she was in hospital in Melbourne giving birth to her children.

137. LESLEY RONALDSON

Also active in the wider world of tennis, she was a founder member of the Ladies Real Tennis Association and its Chairman for the first ten years. Under her chairmanship many national and international tournaments were inaugurated and she also helped to establish the Ladies World Championship, which is held every two years, rotating between Australia, Europe and the United States. In recent years she has been heavily involved in the promotion and operation of the inter-club National League through her own company, Events 2000 Unlimited, which also runs the richest annual invitational tournament in the world at the Royal Tennis Court.

At Hampton Court Palace, with her interest in history, she trained and qualified as a Palace Guide, something much appreciated by visiting tennis teams. Her connection with the Palace has been invaluable when it comes to liaising with the administration over the use of the State Rooms for club functions and dinners. These contacts are also useful when arranging the hiring out of the clubrooms. Here she almost single-handedly organises the hiring, the security clearance, and at times the catering for members and outside corporate bodies.

In recognition of their contributions to the Royal Tennis Court, Lesley and Chris Ronaldson were made Honorary Members of the Club in 1993.

Ivan Ronaldson

Ivan Ronaldson is reputed to be the hardest hitter of a tennis ball in the world.

The oldest of the three boys, Ivan was from an early age a familiar face at the Club. Although not at first officially employed as an assistant, he was trained by his father and was often to be found arranging matches, repairing rackets, re-covering balls and giving an occasional lesson.

He is a fine player in his own right, the winner of the Under-12 section of the British Junior Championships at Queen's between 1984 and 1986, the Under-14 section in 1987 and 1988, and the Under-16s in 1989 and 1990. On the last occasion he beat his brother Ben in the final. In 1996 he won the French National Championship, and repeated that success two years later. He added the French Under-25 title in 1997 and was triumphant again the following year.

138.   IVAN RONALDSON

Ivan Ronaldson (centre) is seen here with Tim Chisholm and Rob Fahey before the final of the 2001 DKW Classic Tournament.

Turning professional in August 1994 at the age of 20, his first appointment was at Holyport. He moved to Fontainebleau in March 1996, where he ran the Court largely on his own and significantly increased the amount of play. In September 1998 he left Fontainebleau and joined the professional staff at Hampton Court. During his time at the Royal Court he gained a Diploma in Sports Psychology.

Towards the end of 2001 Ivan spent six weeks working under the rapidly-rising tennis talent Tim Chisholm at the Racquet & Tennis Club in New York. The following summer, wishing to run a court as a Head Professional, he moved to Prested Hall.

Ben Ronaldson

Two years younger than Ivan, Ben began his professional career at the Royal Tennis Court in 1994 as an assistant to his father. The following year he spent six months at Leamington under Kevin Sheldon, before returning to Hampton Court.

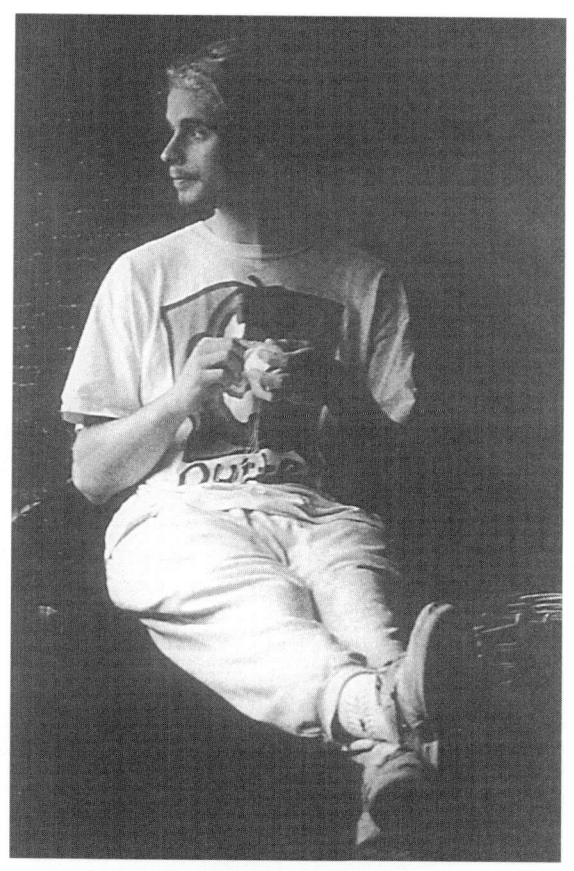

139. BEN RONALDSON

*Sewing balls whilst marking
a friendly match from the dedans.*

His first tournament success came in the 1998 Henry Leaf Cup (the Public Schools Old Boys Doubles Tournament), when he and James (Spike) Willcocks won the trophy for Canford. They successfully defended the title in 1999.

A sharp brain led to him becoming the English National 'Magic' Champion in 2001. Magic is described as a strategy game played like chess, but using cards that are forever changing. A professional circuit is funded by the company that produces the game, which has led to him being flown all over the world at their expense to compete in international tournaments.

On the tennis court there is a friendly rivalry between the brothers, and at the time of writing Ben is ranked above Ivan. They often enter doubles competitions as a pair, but success here has yet to come.

Luke Ronaldson

Born in his parents' first year at Hampton Court, Luke appears to have inherited the Ronaldson tennis ability, as in 1996 he won the first-ever National Junior Singles Handicap Tournament at the Oratory. However there is no sign of him entering the family business.

Rob Bartlett (1979-80)

Rob Bartlett was raised on land in Victoria. When he was 25 years of age the family's farming properties were sold and he left Australia to travel the world. Prior to that he had first played tennis soon after meeting Chris Ronaldson in

140. ROB BARTLETT AND FRIENDS

Rob Bartlett seen here on the left with Lachie Deuchar, Jonathan Howell and Chris Ronaldson, in a photograph taken at Canford in 1981.

1974, and continued to play infrequently until his departure in 1978. A year later when Ronaldson moved from Troon to Hampton Court, it was agreed that he should immediately take on Rob Bartlett as his assistant. The Young Professionals Fund funded his training. He spent five months at the Royal Tennis Court before moving to Canford School in Dorset. There he had the dual role of establishing the Tennis Club, and acting as coach for a variety of school sports. Apart from the pupils, only half-a-dozen masters and their friends used the Court — four months after his arrival there were 70 members. In 1982 the exciting prospect of a new Court, at Ballarat in his home country, tempted him to apply for the professional's job there. His application was successful; however there was a delay with the construction, which allowed him to join Chris Ronaldson's resuscitation team at Bordeaux and this was followed by a three-month stint at Hobart. Subsequently he spent three years at Ballarat before resigning as Head Professional, but he did not sever his links with the Club there and continued to assist them professionally. In 1999 he became the first Professional at the new Court at Romsey, in the Australian state of Victoria, where he has again been successful in building up another new Club from scratch. Finally, he has moved to Sydney where he plies his trade with great success and popularity.

Alistair Curley (1980-81)

Having been taught the game by Chris Ronaldson as a 22-year old member at Troon, Alistair Curley decided to take the assistant professional's job at the Royal Tennis Court following Rob Bartlett's departure in September 1980. He too was funded by the YPF. One of the recognised means of broadening assistants' tennis education is to swap them with their counterparts at different clubs. So it was, that after four months at Hampton Court he flew to Hobart, Tasmania, with Wayne Davies making the reverse trip from Hobart to Hampton Court.

Curley, a sociable young man, enjoyed the Tasmanian life style so much he decided to emigrate. First though, he had to return to Hampton Court to complete the last five months of his training. Once back at Hobart, he took up the position of Head Professional in succession to Lachlan Deuchar, and remained for eight years

141.   ALISTAIR CURLEY

before resigning and returning to amateur status. Today he is very active on the Australian tennis scene in his role as Secretary of the Hobart Real Tennis Club.

Whilst Head Professional at Hobart, Curley helped fashion the style of the current World Champion, Robert Fahey, whom he introduced to the game and who was his assistant for two years.

Wayne Davies (1981)

Wayne Davies's introduction to tennis was via a 6-0 whitewash by Lesley Ronaldson. Smarting at this, he decided he needed to find out more about the game to salvage his pride. As a top-grade squash player, the Ronaldsons had spotted his potential in 1978 and he was immediately asked to play in a Melbourne club match. His first job in tennis was as an assistant to Colin Lumley at Melbourne in 1979; the following year he crossed the Bass Strait to join Lachlan Deuchar at Hobart.

142. WAYNE DAVIES

He arrived at Hampton Court in January 1981, in circumstances already described. Although he only stayed for four months, members benefited greatly from his abrasive, but effective, coaching methods, and there was a bonus, in that members who arrived early, or stayed on after a game, would often be treated to some spectacular tennis when he and Chris Ronaldson went on court to practise. After his spell at Hampton Court he moved to Bordeaux. The Club there, as recorded earlier, was in desperate financial trouble and almost a year after his arrival found that they could not afford to pay him, so he had to move on. During his time in France he continued to play squash and rose to become the third-ranked player in that country. The summer of 1982 saw him move to the Racquet & Tennis Club in New York; he was to stay there for 13 years as their Head Professional. However, he very nearly lost the job before he had started! New York had expected him on the 10th January and when he failed to turn up they telephoned the following day asking for an explanation. He was under the impression that his employment would commence some nine months later on the 1st October. The confusion was caused by the American method of recording dates – '1/10/82' instead of '10/1/82'! Luckily the New York Club was sympathetic.

At New York, Wayne Davies developed into one of the great tennis champions. He earned the right to challenge Chris Ronaldson for the World Championship three times, finally capturing it in April 1987 at the age of 31. He defended it four times, three on his home Court. On each of the three occasions his opponent was Lachlan Deuchar. The fourth time he met another of his compatriots, the young Robert Fahey, and lost the title in a home-and-away match, staged at Hobart and New York in 1994. Over a 17-year period he was involved in no less than ten World Championship Challenges.

After leaving New York, he concentrated on the development of the new Tennis Court and Club in Sydney, which he also helped to finance. The new Court was built at Macquarie University and opened in October 1997; he managed it for the first four years.

Throughout his career Davies has been troubled by knee injuries and has had to cope with half-a-dozen operations, many of his matches being played with a cumbersome knee support. Although he won many national titles, the British Open was not one of them, but it might have been a different story had his injuries not prevented him from entering a couple of times. It is testament to his persistence and courage that he was always able to get back to peak fitness to defend his World Title.

He was also one half of a formidable doubles partnership with Lachie Deuchar. They went undefeated for over ten years, in which time they won no less than eight British Open Championships.

The rule whereby the World Champion had the choice of venue for the defence of the title had, in the eyes of some, long been controversial. Wayne had hoped his decision to play a home-and-away match — only the third time that a defending champion had agreed to play on an opponent's court in nearly 260 years of the Championship, and not since Covey/Gould in 1914 — would lead to a change to fairer matches for future challengers. However, arrangements for the following four challenges continued as before and it was not until the unsatisfactory situation that arose in February 2002 — when the old system failed to produce a challenger — that the more equitable system, mentioned in Chapter 10, was put in place. To highlight the issue of 'home country advantage', Wayne won the New York leg of the 1994 match by four sets to two, but eventually lost the title by nine sets to five.

Wayne Davies retired from competitive tennis in 2000.

Lachlan Deuchar (1981-87)

Within five months of losing one immensely-talented Australian, Wayne Davies, the Royal Tennis Court gained another, Lachlan Deuchar. He came to Hampton Court in October 1981. During Lachie's five-and-a-half year spell at RTC, the Club could claim to have two of the top three professionals in the world and, in Howard Angus, Alan Lovell and Julian Snow, the top three amateurs in the world.

143. LACHIE DEUCHAR

Originally engaged at the age of 16 as Chris Ronaldson's second assistant at Melbourne in 1975 — Colin Lumley was the first — he moved to take charge at Hobart in 1979. A great friend of Ronaldson, he agreed to revert back to the role of second professional in order to help the World Champion with his training. The bonus was that he developed into the world's number one ranked tennis player, although he was never able to wrest the World Title from Davies. He had five attempts, reaching the challenge round three times, all in New York, and on the third he came closest, failing by the narrowest of margins, by six sets to seven. His greatest achievement was his six consecutive victories in the British Open Singles. Of the other major national championships, he won the US Open twice, the Australian twice and the French three times. On several occasions he defeated reigning world champions on level terms in major tournaments. His doubles achievements with Wayne Davies have already been recorded.

Deuchar returned to Melbourne as Head Professional in the spring of 1987. However, like Ronaldson before him, he found he needed to be in the northern hemisphere to remain at the top of his game, so after a season he resigned and returned to the United Kingdom. He worked as an unattached professional until the Harbour Club opened in 1993, when he was appointed their Head Professional. There, his years of hard work resulted in a thriving Court requiring the employment of two assistants to cope with the increased workload. Recurring injuries persuaded him to retire from competitive play in 1998. Three years later he resigned from the Harbour Club.

144.   GREAT FRIENDS AND RIVALS

Chris Ronaldson and Lachie Deuchar
at Queen's in 1990

Lachie Deuchar became notorious for finding himself in unusual situations. One such befell him in June 1984. Two Seacourt members, Edmunds and Ault, had previously set a target of less than 48 hours for travelling to every UK tennis court in play and completing a single set of tennis on each. Having completed the obligatory set at Jesmond Dene, his and Chris Ronaldson's challenge came to an abrupt end half-an-hour later in a car crash on the outskirts of Newcastle. Lachie was in the passenger seat and mercifully no-one was seriously hurt. They set out again in September 1984 and this time completed the course in about 38 hours. However, RTC members Wally and Joy Triggs, by playing a set on every UK court in just over 34 hours, took this record from them in May 1987.

Mike Gooding   (1983)

Mike Gooding came to Hampton Court in May 1983 for a 'crash' training course, which formed part of his preparation for a career as a tennis professional. He was a Scottish Under-15 badminton player and had been playing tennis as an amateur at Troon for a couple of years when he applied for the job of professional there. Although he was only at Hampton Court for a few months, this talented young man endeared himself to many members. After his training, he spent a year at Troon before moving to New York, via Canford, to work under Wayne Davies. The years of training with the World Champion paid dividends as he developed into a world-class player himself.

Having spent five years at New York he left for Hatfield in 1993, where he and Adam Phillips shared the professional duties. After three years, he resigned to concentrate on improving his game as an unattached professional, although he did work for a short spell under Lachie Deuchar at the Harbour Club.

Gooding is a particularly fine doubles player. As a junior he won the Under-24 Doubles Championships three times with Julian Snow, and with Chris Bray he has so far won three British Open Doubles titles. In addition, he has recorded victories in the other three national Open Doubles Championships, the US, the Australian and the French. In 1995, he won his first major national Open

145.   MIKE GOODING

Singles Championship in France. He repeated that success in 1996 and added the prestigious British Open the same year. As a result he qualified for the World Championship Challenge in 1996, but was defeated by Wayne Davies in the eliminating round at Melbourne.

In September 2001 he took up the post of Head Professional at the Burroughs Club at Middlesex University.

Matty Hayward   (1987-90)

Matty Hayward came to Hampton Court in July 1987. A gifted amateur from Tasmania, he turned professional on his arrival at the Royal Tennis Court and served for three years as the Second Professional under Chris Ronaldson, before moving to Hatfield to join his fellow Australian, Jiannis Hrysicos. A little over a year later he took over as Head Professional when Hrysicos returned home.

As a player he won the 1988 Young Professional Singles (the Taylor Cup), but he suffered from a persistent hip problem which forced him to give up singles play

146.   MATTY HAYWARD

225

fairly soon after. He is, though, still a more-than-useful partner in any doubles pair. His greatest successes were with Paul Tabley in 1990, when the pair reached the final of the World Doubles Championship and that same year won the Tasmanian Doubles.

In 1993, he resigned from Hatfield and returned to the amateur ranks, resuming his pre-tennis career as a pharmacist.

Nick Wood   (1988-98)

To run the court effectively at full capacity, the Club needed three professionals, and to this end Nick Wood was appointed as an assistant in September 1988. He went on to assume the role of second professional following the departure of Matty Hayward in 1993. He had learnt the game in his native Newcastle, at Jesmond Dene. Coming from a sporting family with a squash and lawn tennis background — his father ran the nearby Northumberland Lawn Tennis and Squash Rackets Club — he initially concentrated on squash and made the National Training Squad. In 1984, at the age of 14, his father introduced him to tennis and shortly after he caught the eye of Chris Ronaldson during a visit to Jesmond.

A promising stylish young player, he won the Under-18 section of the British Junior Championships the day before starting work at Hampton Court. He went on to win three successive Under-21 Open Singles, the first in 1990, the Taylor Cup in 1991 and the Under-24 Open Singles for the next three years. In addition, he took the Under-24 Open Doubles title four times, the first two with Rob Fahey, and the last two with Jean-Guillaume Prats. He has won the Browning Cup

147. NICK WOOD

twice, in 1995 and 2002, and in 2000 he won the coveted Seacourt Silver Racket. He had his first success in a national tournament in 1995 when he won the

United States Open Doubles Championship with Julian Snow. They repeated that success in 2000, and the following year he won both the US and the British Open Doubles with Chris Bray. He collected his fourth US Open Doubles title in 2002 partnering Mike Gooding.

Towards the end of 1993 he went to Melbourne to broaden his experience, swapping with Brett McFarlane for a few months.

Just as he left Hampton Court in the summer of 1998, to take over as Head Professional at Holyport, Nick Wood broke through to the top by winning his first major tournament, the European Open Singles in Paris. He followed that up in September by winning the Dresdner Kleinwort Benson Classic, a new invitation tournament played at the Royal Tennis Court, involving the world's top eight professionals. In the doubles section of this tournament he has a hundred per cent record, partnering Chris Bray, Rob Fahey and Mike Gooding twice. He won both the British and the US Professional Singles tournaments in 2000, and in the same year he reached his first National Open Singles final, the Australian, where he was beaten by Rob Fahey.

When he left Hampton Court for Holyport a farewell party was held in the Club garden. It was a warm summer's evening in late August and Chris Ronaldson in his speech of thanks, acknowledging the affection members had for him, said of his protégé: 'I doubt whether he has an enemy in the world'. A sentiment echoed by all those present.

Several other professionals have worked for short periods at the Royal Tennis Court during the Ronaldson years. They include: Gerard Eden, Jerome Fletcher, Jonathan Howell, Kevin King, Colin Lumley, Brett McFarlane, Adam Phillips, Marc Seigneur and George Wharton. To these must be added two members of the Club, Charles Crossley and most recently Nick Hatchett.

CHAPTER 14

UNFINISHED BUSINESS!

Since the late 1980s the Club has been attempting to build a Second Tennis Court within the confines of the Palace. Although the project has recently run into problems and at the time of writing is stalled, the story is worthy of a chapter as it has been nothing short of a marathon for those involved. This chapter attempts to set into perspective the difficulties that have been encountered throughout the long negotiations with Historic Royal Palaces.

In 1984 the Stuart Court was running at full capacity due largely to the efficiency of the professional staff led by Chris Ronaldson. The Club Chairman, Ronald Swash, realised that this presented an opportunity to build a second tennis court; he then discussed the idea with Ronaldson. The Professional's considered written reply included the following: 'I believe we could fill five tennis courts if they were built side by side.' Buoyed up by Ronaldson's enthusiasm he prepared a paper for committee discussion early in 1985 but found the majority were not in favour of disturbing the status quo. Perhaps that was not surprising: after all the idea must have seemed quite revolutionary as no-one had built a tennis court in the United Kingdom for over 70 years. The last was J.F. Marshall's at Seacourt in 1912, if one discounts the unorthodox Courts at Lambay Island and Rusthall House, the former with penthouses on both side walls and the latter an unsatisfactory conversion of an old long fives court. The explosion in court-building activity at the end of the twentieth century was still to come.

That rejection might have been the death-knell for the idea had it not been for the successful financial policies of the eighties, for which Ronald Swash must take much of the credit. These had resulted in a surplus of £32,000 by the end of 1987. It was the Committee's desire to make good use of the reserves that led to the Second Court question being raised again. This time the idea gained more support and a sub-committee was set up to progress matters.

Towards the end of 1988 Ronald Swash and Chris Ronaldson went to see Lord Maclean, the Chief Steward of Hampton Court Palace and, as such, the Queen's personal representative. The late Lord Maclean, a former Lord Chamberlain, was very fond of tennis and of the Club, of which he was an Honorary Member. His was a familiar face in the dedans, where he was often to be found enjoying a game no matter what the standard of play. He therefore readily agreed to investigate, on the Club's behalf, the possibility of royal approval. The answer that came back was most encouraging; Her Majesty had no objection to the construction of a new Tennis Court at the Palace so long as there was no call on the public purse. That important letter was dated 16th February 1989.

Derek Steel, the new Club Chairman, when setting out the case for the new Court wrote: 'We represent an enthusiastic group of twentieth-century users of the historic Court, and would like to join with the "powers that be" at Hampton Court Palace to add a twentieth-century facility to continue the development of this historic game.'

It was recognised from the start that any building erected within the confines of the Palace would have to be architecturally sympathetic and necessarily expensive. In order to gain the support of the authorities, it was felt that the new Court would have to be of some benefit both to the public and to Historic Royal Palaces. Therefore a strategy had to be developed which would provide a new visitor attraction for the tourists, coupled with an increased income for the Palace. These aspects pushed up the cost of the new court considerably. It was clear that a robust business plan would be needed, because substantial borrowing would be necessary in a situation in which there was no security. The Club did not own the land on which the Court was to be built, and would never own the finished building. As a Royal Palace, Hampton Court had no powers to grant a lease. So the granting of a licence was the only legal device available to them that would allow the Club to occupy the premises. That aside, professional financial advice indicated that a strong business plan would overcome the lack of security. Members' contributions by way of subscriptions and court fees would not be enough to repay the loan; additional income streams would have to be developed. As this story unfolds, it will be seen that the reliance on these third-party incomes to repay any loan would create tensions within the Club; and would eventually lead to the abandonment of the proposed new Court as a major visitor attraction. However, that is several years down the line.

At the start of the negotiations Hampton Court Palace was administered by the Department of the Environment (DOE) and then by the Historic Royal Palaces Agency (HRPA) under the control of the DOE. As time went by responsibility switched to the Department of National Heritage, then to the Department of Culture, Media and Sport, and finally the Agency became a Charitable Trust established by the Royal Household. Historic Royal Palaces (HRP) not only looks after Hampton Court Palace, its gardens and park, but also the Tower of London, Kensington Palace, Kew Palace and the Banqueting House (the only remaining part of the old Whitehall Palace).

The chain of command led from the Secretary of State down through the Chief Executive of the Historic Royal Palaces Agency to the Director of Hampton Court Palace. There was then the Curator, the Surveyor of the Fabric, the Finance Director and the Marketing Department. The support of each of these departments would be necessary but no one foresaw the length of time that the negotiations would take and as a consequence the Club had to contend with several changes of key personnel along the way. Whenever that happened further delays always occurred, either because of the time involved in briefing a new incumbent, who would often take a different view on decisions of his predecessor, or by overcoming any scepticism.

The consent of English Heritage was also necessary. John Thorneycroft, English Heritage's representative with responsibility for Hampton Court Palace, had been kept informed from the start. However, it was clear at the beginning that Lord

229

Montagu, then the Chairman of English Heritage, would need some convincing if his support were to be forthcoming. He felt that the Court should be built in some less sensitive location elsewhere in London. Throughout the negotiations, the Club had to contend with two opposing views, those who thought the Palace should be preserved in aspic, and others who felt it had an evolving history and was a living entity. For the project to succeed, those of the latter persuasion would have to triumph over the former. The Palace's first 200 years of history had seen dramatic changes but nothing of any consequence had been built within its walls for nearly 300 years.

The key personnel at the Palace from the outset were John Yarnall, the Palace Director, Dr Simon Thurley, who was at first employed by English Heritage but was appointed Curator soon after the negotiations started, and Daphne Ford, the Archaeological Recorder. David Beeton was the Chief Executive of the Historic Royal Palaces Agency.

At the first meeting with the Palace representatives it became clear that John Yarnall and John Thorneycroft were basically supportive. They pointed out that the London Borough of Richmond upon Thames was the planning authority and would have to give planning permission. It was considered essential to the proposed development that Apartment 69 (the Keeper's House) should form a link between the two Courts, and here John Yarnall was able to confirm that it would revert back to the RTC once the current occupant vacated it, although that could be years away. The Keeper's House was, of course, originally part of the Tennis Court.

The Club wanted the new Court to be erected adjacent to the existing one. The first concern of English Heritage was the location of the Henry VIII's Close Bowling Alley. This had been demolished in the latter part of the eighteenth century, but they feared it might be partially under the proposed site. If any part of the Bowling Alley had been under the 'footprint' of the new Court, they would have opposed its construction. A geophysical survey located the approximate position of the Alley and confirmed that an archaeological dig would be necessary. With the help of Sir Clifford Chetwood, plans were drawn up for submission to English Heritage who were at once concerned about the bulk of the new building. However, with their help, adjustments were made that went some way towards alleviating their worries — but not entirely!

It was now October 1990 and the first of the many changes of personnel occurred. John Yarnall was posted back to Marsham Street to run the Department of the Environment's office estate in Central London. His successor was Crawford MacDonald, who was also broadly in favour of the project, as he too perceived a potential benefit, seeing the new Court as fitting in well with the concept of the Palace as a living history. Incidentally, both John Yarnall and Crawford MacDonald developed an interest in the game and became members of the Royal Tennis Court after their terms at Hampton Court. John Yarnall, after his retirement, took on the role of Honorary Secretary of the Club in 1998, in circumstances described earlier.

The attitude of the Curator, Simon Thurley, was very important. Although based at Hampton Court he was employed by Historic Royal Palaces and his superior,

David Beeton, was not keen on the idea of a Second Court. He felt it would be likely to lead to a Public Inquiry, which would put undue pressure on his staff. However, Simon Thurley was in favour, so long as the new Court blended architecturally with the rest of the Palace.

It was clear that the project was going to be a long haul and one person had to be given responsibility for it. That person was a newly-elected committee member, Michael Banks. As a marketing man he had the public relations skills to deal with the diverse personalities involved and as an ex-marine he was as tough as they came for the long grinding battle that lay ahead. He lived locally in Esher and, as an independent consultant working close to the Palace, he was well placed to arrange his day to enable him to attend the numerous meetings that were to come. Within a year, however, the workload began severely to affect him. As his income was directly dependent upon his own time being charged to his business clients, and with the project beginning to use up many of those available hours, he informed the Committee that he was unable to continue without some consideration of his position.

It was soon apparent that no other member was going to be found who could spend the necessary time on the project and, if it was to continue, someone was going to have to be employed, at least part-time. The option of appointing an external consultant was considered, but it was recognised that anyone coming in from outside would not have Michael Banks' experience and background. He was therefore invited to submit his proposals for continuing on a partially-paid basis. It was only the essential daytime work that would be paid for; all other time involved was to be free of charge as part of his normal voluntary committee duties. He submitted his proposal and the Committee considered his terms to be reasonable and unlikely to be bettered by an outside consultant. In addition, his heart and soul were by now in the venture and it would have cost a considerable amount for an outsider to be brought up to speed.

It was obvious that strict financial control was going to be necessary and to that end Derek Steel insisted that a Second Court Committee be formed to progress and monitor the project. It was to be composed of himself as Chairman, the Honorary Secretary, the Honorary Treasurer and Michael Banks, and it would have the power to co-opt specialist help as and when required.

It was now early 1991 and the estimated building cost had escalated to £1.8 million. James Hansford, a Committee member and the Club's auditor, was brought in to develop the business plan. Both the main and the grille walls were to be made of glass, which would have allowed seating for 350. First-class viewing facilities were essential as the entrance charge for tourists and tournament income would be important sources of finance. Other major third-party income streams would be television rights and the hiring of the Court's facilities to corporate bodies.

A list of interested parties and influential people was drawn up. The list was long and it was recognised at an early stage that a single person or body could potentially derail the scheme and, therefore, a strategy had to be developed to convince the sceptical and the downright hostile that the Second Court would be to everyone's benefit. It was agreed that Michael Banks would contact all concerned and explain the project personally. Of course with Hampton Court Palace, Historic Royal Palaces and English Heritage, there was day-to-day contact, but other organisations that needed to be consulted included:

> The London Borough of Richmond's Planning Department.
> Richmond's Director of Leisure Services.
> The local Member of Parliament.
> Local Councillors.
> The London Region of the Sports Council.
> Elmbridge Borough Council (who were responsible for Molesey on the other side of the river).
> The London Advisory Body (part of English Heritage).
> The Historic Royal Palaces Advisory Group.
> The Hampton Court Association.
> The Hampton Residents' Association.
> The Friends of Bushy and Home Parks.
> The Georgian Group.
> The Royal Fine Art Commission.
> The Society for the Protection of Ancient Buildings.
> The Historic Gardens Society.

Returning to the summer of 1991, a visitor questionnaire was prepared to gauge the level of interest amongst the general public. Tourists were asked a series of questions, and head counts were carried out. The answers, which were encouraging, were combined with known Palace data so that a realistic figure for visitor income could be included in the business plan.

Early the following year Lord Montagu stepped down as Chairman of English Heritage. His successor, Jocelyn Stevens (now Sir Jocelyn) was amenable to the idea of the new Court, and Sir Clifford Chetwood managed to secure his backing at an early stage. This was a vital breakthrough.

In March 1992, with the visitor information available and a draft business plan in place, a presentation was made to Historic Royal Palaces Agency. The Club of course stressed the benefits to Hampton Court Palace as it saw them. The new Court would accommodate up to 350 in comfort, with good sight-lines through two glass walls. The Club also proposed that there should be a museum dedicated to Tudor sport. The Palace would therefore have a new 'live' visitor attraction, which would generate additional income from tourists, television coverage, which would create more marketing opportunities, and they would derive more income from the Club itself by way of higher rent from two courts.

After due consideration, the reply from HRPA was devastating. They felt the Club was underestimating the problems involved in getting Scheduled Monument Clearance and Planning Permission. They thought the budgeted £2 million was too low and that £3 million was a more likely figure. David Beeton reconfirmed his opinion that the Secretary of State was likely to 'call in' the scheme and hold a Public Inquiry. If a Public Inquiry were held, the Club would incur crippling costs of between £100,000 and £200,000 — with no certainty of a successful outcome. Also of serious concern to the Agency was the unwanted publicity an Inquiry would bring with it. There was no chance of official status for the project and no time to let HRPA staff work on it. They confirmed that Palace-approved architects would have to be used and that if work went ahead, once all the permissions had been obtained, then only a Palace-approved contractor could be used to build it. There was still general unease about erecting the new Court alongside the existing one. However, as a means of moving forward, they agreed to a feasibility study being undertaken and recommended the appointment of Feilden & Mawson, an established architectural practice which had a good understanding of the requirements for works within royal palaces.

It was now falling to the Second Court Committee to deal with the negotiation for the recovery of Apartment 69, which was in turn raising the question of whether the RTC should become a Limited Company. This was because the issues were inextricably interlinked with the Second Court. How events unfolded was dealt with in an earlier chapter but before any final decisions could be taken an Extraordinary General Meeting had to be called. This meeting, held on 14th February 1993, was also used to bring members up to date with the latest developments and to seek their continued support. Members were given the same presentation HRPA had seen and informed of their adverse reaction to it; undeterred they voted unanimously to press on regardless. The meeting also agreed to the formation of a Limited Company.

It was obvious that the Second Court negotiation was going to be a long drawn-out affair and with the project management having to be partially paid for, some fund raising was going to be necessary. Of several schemes which were looked at, many could only be put to members if the Court were on the point of being built, but two were put into effect straight away. Firstly, a £1 levy (later increased to £1.50) on each player on each day he or she played was instituted. This was considered a fair burden on the court fee, as the new Court would primarily benefit the playing membership. Secondly, H.R.H. Prince Edward graciously agreed to host a fund-raising dinner in the Great Hall.

Early in 1993, Pat Barker hit upon the idea of playing on every Court in England and France with a view to raising money. In a Richmond pub he shared his thoughts with his regular doubles group, Barney Gibbens, David Frost and Chris Winn. As they quenched their thirsts, the embryonic idea was discussed and by the time they left they had become the founder members of the 'Hampton Court Courtiers'. Their plan was to visit various Courts as a team and ask for a donation from each player in the host team. In return each host would receive a Courtier tour shirt, and a tot of a specially produced 'Lord Dedans Gin', which would also be for sale in bottles. The tour met with a great deal of enthusiasm at the 21 Courts visited, with even the owner of Fairlawne in Kent agreeing to open his private Court for the cause. On several occasions H.R.H. Prince Edward and his equerry Sean O'Dwyer played for the Courtiers. The tour raised over £7,000, which included the sale of 96 bottles of gin — a welcome boost for the coffers.

233

Despite the negative reaction from HRPA, Crawford MacDonald was amenable to the imposition of a charge on members of the public entering the Stuart Court. The charge, 50p, which was voluntary, only applied to those who did not have a full palace ticket and the money, which was collected by the Club, could only to be used for the development of the Second Court. One may recall that the Palace had charged tourists to enter the Stuart Court back in the 1950s and 1960s, but the practice had long since ceased. The Palace Director also allowed RTC to rent out the clubrooms to help boost income, once the licence for Apartment 69 had been finalised.

The feasibility study took six months to complete with the report arriving in April 1993. Feilden & Mawson had investigated four possible sites for the new Court (figure 148):

Option 1   West of the Stuart Court, and adjacent to it.

Option 2   West of Apartment 69 in the old moat.

Option 3   At the end of Tennis Court Lane on its north side, abutting the Ely Rooms.

Option 4   In the Melon Ground on a site occupied by the greenhouses to the west of the Club's garden.

Only Options 1 and 2 were seriously considered, and after much deliberation HRPA and English Heritage went for Option 2, the Moat Site. The feasibility study had finally provided ammunition for English Heritage to squash the Club's preferred Option 1, which they had consistently opposed because of their worries over the size of the building and the way they thought it would have dominated the Stuart Court.

Wolsey's moat had long since been filled in — but there still had to be an archaeological dig. The Oxford Archaeological Unit under the direction of Daphne Ford, the Palace's Archaeological Recorder, carried it out. Plans were submitted to the Department of National Heritage in support of Scheduled Monument Clearance, which was obtained at the end of March 1994, allowing the dig to go ahead the following June. A single 12.5-metre-wide trench was dug across the moat, but its full width could not be established as the southern edge lay beyond the agreed area of excavation. It was a surprise to everybody that the moat at this point was found to have been around 20 metres wide. Nothing was found in the trench that would stop the Court being built through archaeological objections but to RTC's consternation the Curatorial Department pressed for another trench to be dug to establish the full width of the moat!

As things turned out a second dig was not needed, as English Heritage also had misgivings about the Moat Site. The Palace was at the time reviewing its garden strategy and had taken the decision to centralise plant propagation in Home Park. They therefore suggested the new Court should be sited where the greenhouses were in the area known as the Melon Ground, effectively Feilden & Mawson's Option 4.

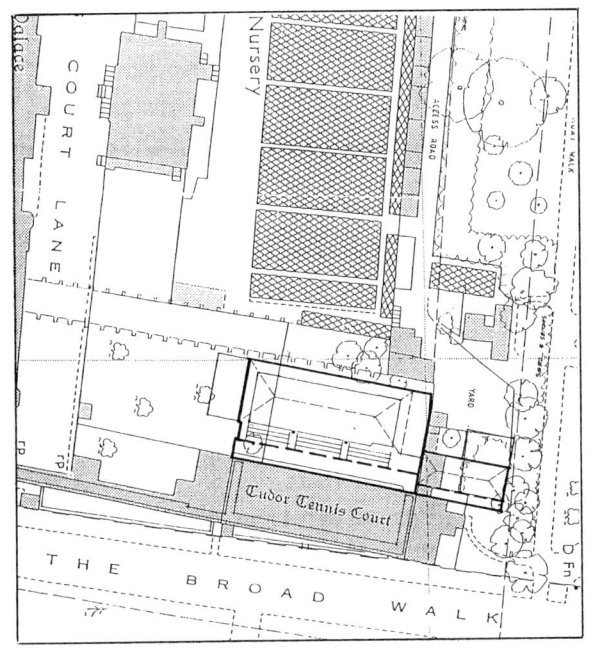
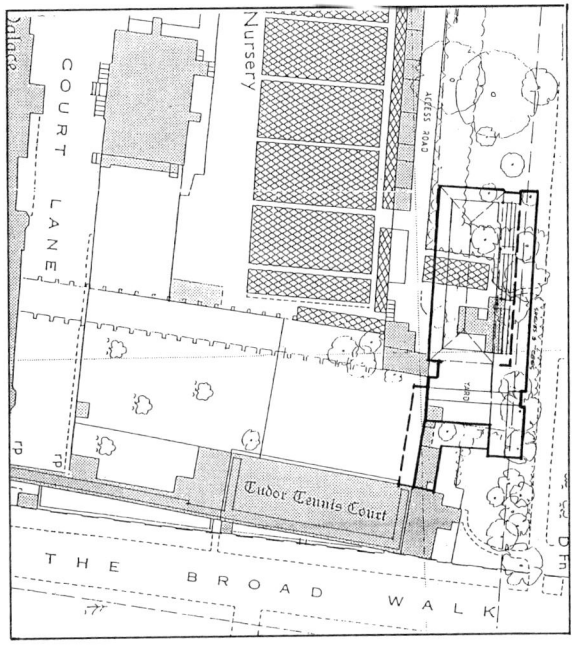
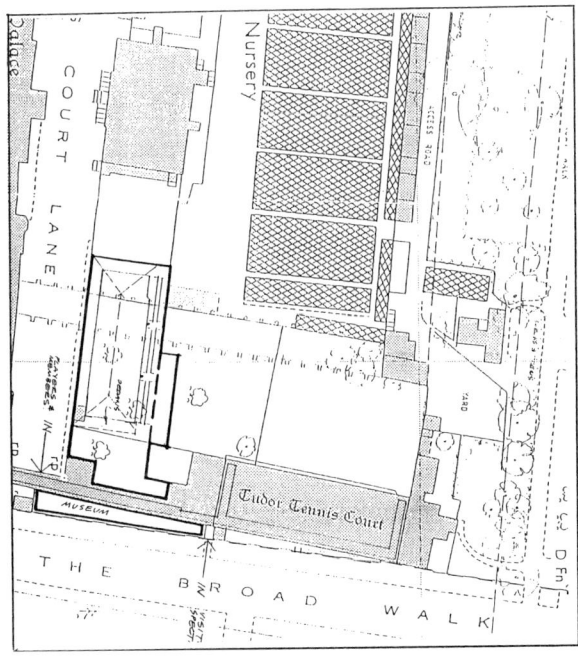
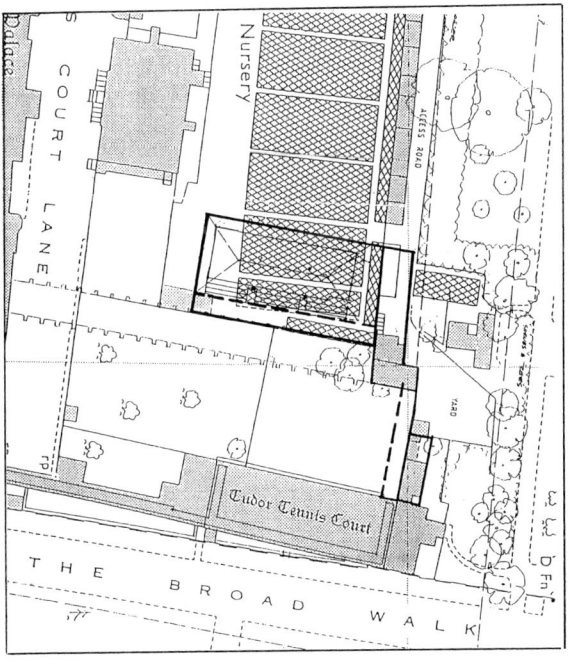

148.   THE FOUR SITES INVESTIGATED

Top left: Option 1 – Adjacent to the Stuart Court
Top right: Option 2 – The Moat site
Bottom left: Option 3 – Tennis Court Lane site
Bottom right: Option 4 – The Melon Ground site

Time was marching on, and in April 1995 the major fund-raising dinner referred to earlier took place. The evening was a great success with nearly £10,000 being raised. Those who attended joined H.R.H. Prince Edward for cocktails in the King's Guard Chamber, before moving to George II's Public Dining Room for a performance by the London Mozart Players, who afterwards combined with the National Youth Music Theatre in some comic sketches. The writer and broadcaster Richard Stilgoe acted as compère during this part of the evening. Guests then moved through the State Apartments to the Great Hall where they enjoyed a magnificent banquet.

With the Melon Ground site agreed by all parties, Feilden & Mawson were given the go-ahead to develop new plans. The bulk of the building once again worried English Heritage; the first draft plan suggested it would be seen above the tree screen from the Wilderness, the garden area leading to the Lion Gate and Bushy Park. One of the principal views of the Palace is that from Chestnut Avenue in Bushy Park. There were also concerns that the Court would dominate the Georgian House, the large detached mansion in Tennis Court Lane. A scale model was commissioned to allow the various parties to study all the implications. To alleviate anxieties it was agreed that the new Court would be sunk just over a metre below ground level to ensure that the roofline would be lower than that of the Stuart Court.

In 1995, Crawford MacDonald left Hampton Court and was succeeded by Robin Evans. He was concerned that some of the tourist income RTC hoped to derive would be to the Palace's detriment. Every source of income where there was overlap was re-examined, with the Palace insisting on reductions in the Club's forecasts of income. This resulted in a serious shortfall of anticipated income in the business plan, which meant there was only one way of maintaining a reasonable payback period — and that was to increase the amount members would have to subscribe. Detailed consideration of these matters was to set the project back another two years.

There was obviously a limit! The Club's annual subscription had traditionally been low compared with other sporting facilities and other tennis clubs, but the Royal Tennis Court faces problems others do not. With only one court, few people are on the premises at any one time unless a tournament is in progress or a social event is taking place. This, coupled with security considerations, meant that the Club was restricted in what it could organise on the social side. On the other hand the Committee, now a Board of Directors, took the view that the Second Court would bring with it not only increased playing facilities but also an opportunity to expand the social programme. The proposed new Court had been designed with a large dedans and bar and a substantial function room above. Fire doors were to be set into the main glass wall by the net to allow 160 people to dine on the court floor and there was still the walled garden between the Courts available, large enough to accommodate a marquee. It was therefore felt that, as long as the subscriptions were broadly in line with other clubs, the membership might be prepared to accept an increase.

As the project developed several specialist consultants had to be employed. It was only possible to pay for these because the Club had managed to negotiate a freeze on the amount it had to pay for its licence to occupy the premises while the project was in progress. The Committee had earlier taken the view that the Club should be in a position to pay an increased licence fee and had sought approval at three successive AGM's for above-inflation increases in the subscription. Therefore the freeze on the licence fee had created surpluses that, so long as the negotiations continued, helped to fund the project.

The negotiations had now dragged on into early 1997, and over the following months the atmosphere slowly improved as the proposals were fine-tuned in preparation for submission to the Secretary of State for approval. Before this could be done, an EGM had to be called to put the whole package to members. The meeting took place on 8th June in the Palace's Banqueting House, William III's beautiful riverside dining room, where the proposals were overwhelmingly endorsed.

After a few anxious weeks a letter arrived addressed to the President, Sir Clifford Chetwood. It was from David Beeton, informing the Club that the Minister was 'content', and therefore HRPA was also 'content' and they would be prepared to help develop the project. Unfortunately, this did not extend to supporting it publicly.

With the green light given, the Club moved to the next stage: detailed consideration of the internal features. Chris Ronaldson now became more involved as he had been given responsibility for developing the playing aspects of the Court. He had serious concerns over the likely playing characteristics of the glass walls, so sample glass panels were set up for him to test. His worries were confirmed; it was clear that more research was needed before the right balance could be struck. There were questions of the speed and angles of deflection of the balls off the walls and floor; the distraction caused by people moving around in the seating bank; the level of lighting behind the glass relative to that in the playing area; and the possible use of one-way glass. Ronaldson visited the new Washington Court in the United States, the first in the world to have a glass main wall, to evaluate its playing characteristics. Concerns were also expressed over the possible noise levels that would be experienced behind the glass grille wall, where another seating bank was planned for Club members. A *trinquet* court that had a glass main and back wall was visited in Paris, in order to carry out tests; trinquet is another form of tennis played in a similar court. The noise levels behind the end wall caused by the hard tennis ball travelling at speed were considered unacceptable. All proposed solutions had drawbacks, so the glass grille wall and the additional seating it would have allowed were abandoned.

In the meantime another bombshell was about to be dropped by the Palace. Dr Edward Impey, the new Curator – Simon Thurley had left to take over as Director of the Museum of London – raised concerns over the 'Tapestry Wash Building' during construction, as it was only one metre away from the west wall of the new Court. If the building work went ahead in the summer months, a filtered air-conditioning system would have to be installed because the windows and doors were normally left open in hot weather. The dust created during construction could damage the priceless tapestries and the loss of light would have to be compensated for. In addition he had concerns over security. Hampton Court is world famous for

237

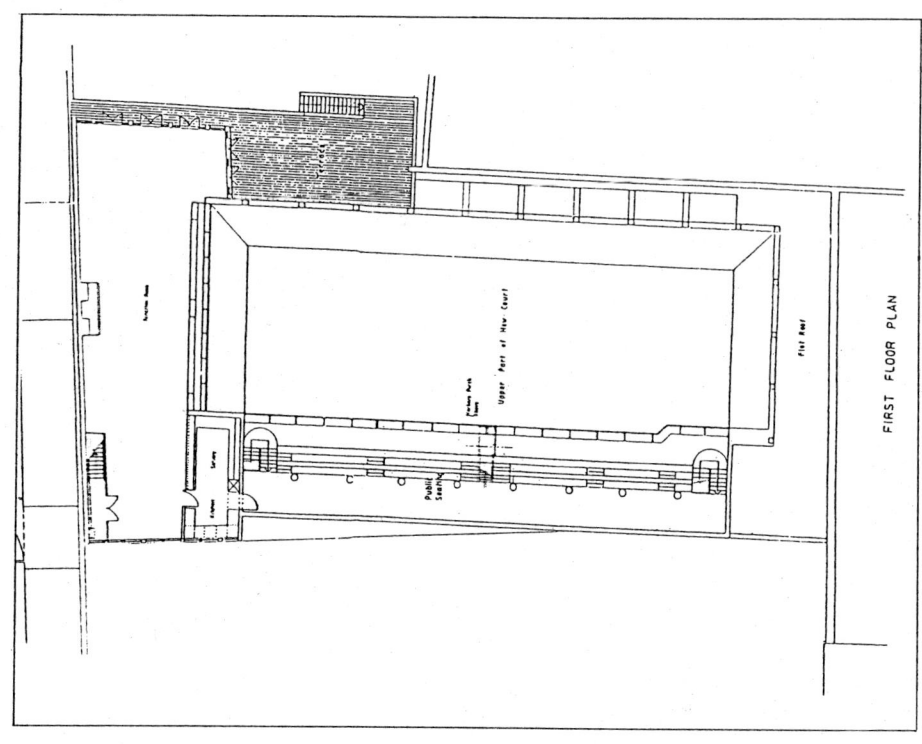

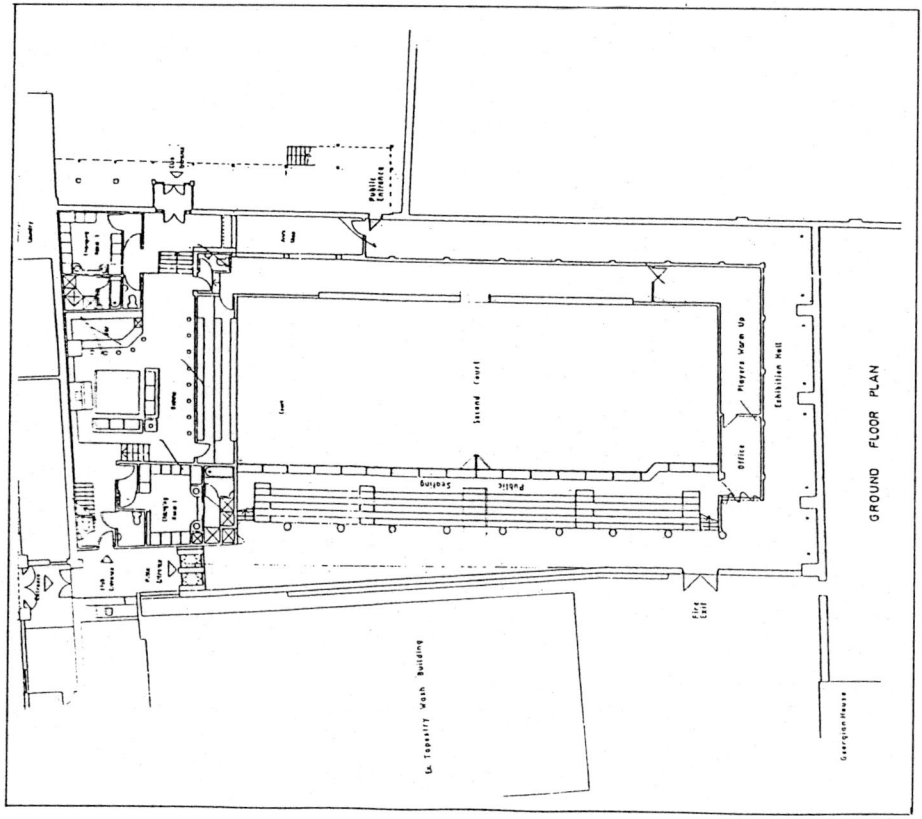

149. PLANS FOR THE PRESTIGIOUS COURT

tapestry restoration work and receives tapestries from other royal palaces and from private collections; it is a very important source of income for the Palace and provision would have to be made in the budget to address these concerns.

The Curatorial Department was now involved in yet another archaeological dig, consisting of a series of test pits. They found that the east wall of the Melon Ground (the west wall of the Club's garden) had been built directly on top of the west wall of Henry VIII's Close Bowling Alley! This was not considered a problem so long as extreme care was taken during construction. As far as the site itself was concerned, it was known to have been the Tudor privy orchard and it was thought to have been a kitchen garden in Georgian times. The excavations confirmed it had been in garden use ever since and there was little potential for finding significant archaeological remains. The way ahead was once again clear but English Heritage insisted that a watching archaeological brief during construction would be necessary.

The possibility of obtaining funding from the National Lottery was also being explored. Both Bristol & Bath and Bridport had previously made successful applications. Club member Nigel Lester, a City Banker, put in a great deal of hard work on the scheme, but unfortunately the approach to the funding of sports proposals had changed and the application was rejected. It was felt the project as a whole had too much non-sporting content but, primarily, it was considered poor value for money; the cost per head of those who would benefit was too high.

Meanwhile, the London Borough of Richmond upon Thames kept coming back with requests for more and more detailed information before the planning application could be submitted. This was continually delaying the project but by December 1998 the proposal was ready. Richmond then requested an astonishing 31 copies of the application and support statement, which was a 100-plus-page document. For most planning applications the architects would expect to prepare about eight copies, but the Club's scheme was potentially controversial, so the document had to be sent to every interested party — of which there were many.

On 27th May 1999 the scheme finally went before the Borough's Planning Committee. Amazingly, they had only received one letter of objection, and this was despite the aforementioned 'fly-on-the-wall' television documentary series of 25 half-hour programmes that had been screened over the previous few months, exposing the project to some two million people. This lack of opposition was not only a reflection of the nine years' hard work put in by Michael Banks and the Second Court Committee but a vindication of the strategy adopted, which had transformed nearly every possible objector into a positive supporter. This removed any residual reason for the Planning Committee to refuse the application, which was subsequently passed.

By a strange quirk of fate, those who attended the planning meeting were surprised to find the very next application on the committee's agenda was for a new rackets court at St. Paul's School in Barnes. It too was passed and with the help of an anonymous benefactor this scheme soon came to fruition.

Although the achievement of planning permission was a major hurdle overcome, there was still a colossal amount to do. Many problems had been temporarily 'parked', because they required expenditure on specialist consultants and that money would have been wasted had permission been refused. These included architectural advice on internal work and finishes, and specialist financial advice. The Club's licence from the Palace still had to be finalised before the business plan could be worked up into a presentable document that could be taken to the banks. Every aspect of the business plan had to be re-examined and subjected to a 'risk analysis'. The finished document and every revenue stream within it were going to be under the microscope of any potential lender. Richard Stocks had taken over from James Hansford the responsibility for developing the financial plan and internal fund-raising was back on the agenda. There was considerable pressure from the financial advisers that the banks should be asked for a loan of no more than two-thirds of the total amount required. That meant that a large contribution would be required from members. A questionnaire was sent out to gauge members' support for a number of schemes. The response was magnificent, suggesting that the members of the Club might be prepared to put up around £650,000.

Hanging over the project like the Sword of Damocles was the question of Value Added Tax on the construction cost — around £400,000 — as the estimated cost of the Court had by now escalated to more than £2.5 million. The Club was partially exempt from VAT as a non-profit making sports club, which meant it was not liable for the tax on members' subscriptions, but conversely it could consequently only recover a small percentage of the tax on its expenditure. Further financial advice was sought and a scheme was devised whereby a new company would be set up which would develop and operate the new Court. This scheme was thought to have the best chance of reclaiming the tax without sacrificing the Club's exempt status. The Board decided that it was in the members' interest to set up a new company without delay, which could be done at minimum cost, and which would hopefully test the VAT position fairly quickly. The new company, RTC New Court Limited, was incorporated on 22nd May 2000.

Frustrating the Club at this time was the lack of progress in the negotiations with the Palace. Robin Evans had left in the summer of 1999. This led to a year's hiatus until the new Director, Hugh Player, was appointed the following summer. David Beeton had also retired, so the new Chief Executive of Historic Royal Palaces, Alan Coppin, had to be fully briefed: from this point on it would be he who would take control of the negotiations.

With attention refocused on the financial aspects, fears that had in the past been raised by some members resurfaced. The main concern was the over reliance on the third-party income — palace visitors, corporate entertainment and television revenues. The business plan called for half a million pounds per annum from these sources and a shortfall in any one area could potentially have disastrous consequences on the Club's ability to repay any loan. These fears were brought into sharp focus when it became clear that HRP (now a Charitable Trust), far from insisting on the Court being a visitor attraction, had now become lukewarm about this aspect. Events in the country were not helping; the Government was being crucified over its handling of the Millennium Dome at Greenwich and several other high-profile new visitor attractions were in trouble. HRP accordingly advised RTC of official thinking and at the same time re-emphasised that they would require firm control over which sponsors would be allowed into the Palace and what would be allowed to go out on television. The Club had known from the outset that the Palace would require some control over these aspects but it became apparent that the controls likely to be imposed would make it extremely difficult for the Club to find acceptable sponsors. The heightened risk of this potential veto over corporate income weighed heavily with the Board.

With no requirement for the new complex to be a major visitor attraction, there came the possibility of a more affordable Court; for without the tourists there was no need for a glass wall, the seating bank behind it, the museum, or the security that went with them. Substantial construction and running costs could be saved. At the same time HRP had imposed an ultimatum because of the length of time the negotiations were taking, seeking a guarantee that the Club could raise the money and get the support of the members. Concerns over the Club's ability to bring in the third-party revenue had for some time also been causing strains within the Board and with a cheaper option on the agenda, which did not have to rely on those disputed incomes, a decision was made to recommend to the membership that the original concept should be abandoned and a more traditional Court be built.

This decision shook the Club to its foundations. Michael Banks, who was wedded to the concept of a prestigious Court that would have opened up the game to many more people, felt he had no option but to resign. Sir Clifford Chetwood, who had worked closely with Banks behind the scenes over many years, and who shared Banks' views, followed him. Barney Gibbens returned from an extended stay in France to learn of the decision and also resigned. At one fell swoop the Club had lost its President, its Chairman and the man who had been the driving force behind the project for ten years.

An emergency members' meeting was convened, and because of the large number who wished to attend, it was held in the Queen's State Apartments. On 12th March 2001 members were invited to discuss all the options. They were: to carry on with the prestigious Court; to develop the more modest option suggested by the Board; to look at the possibility of building a much cheaper court, or courts, outside the palace walls; or to scrap the whole idea — all through the development years there had been a few members who expressed concern that a Second Court would change the character of the Club. After much heated debate the Board was asked to work up its proposal, so that it could be properly assessed to enable members to make an informed decision at an EGM.

The bulk of the savings in the scaled-down Court had been achieved because it would be built on a greatly reduced footprint. With the abandonment of the glass main wall and the seating bank behind it, and a slightly smaller dedans, which did not utilise archaeologically sensitive walls, the estimated cost was brought down to £1.8 million. There was still to be a glass wall above the dedans penthouse, and the room behind was to have tiered seating for spectators, which would be used for conducted tours. This, it was hoped, would satisfy the requirement for the new Court

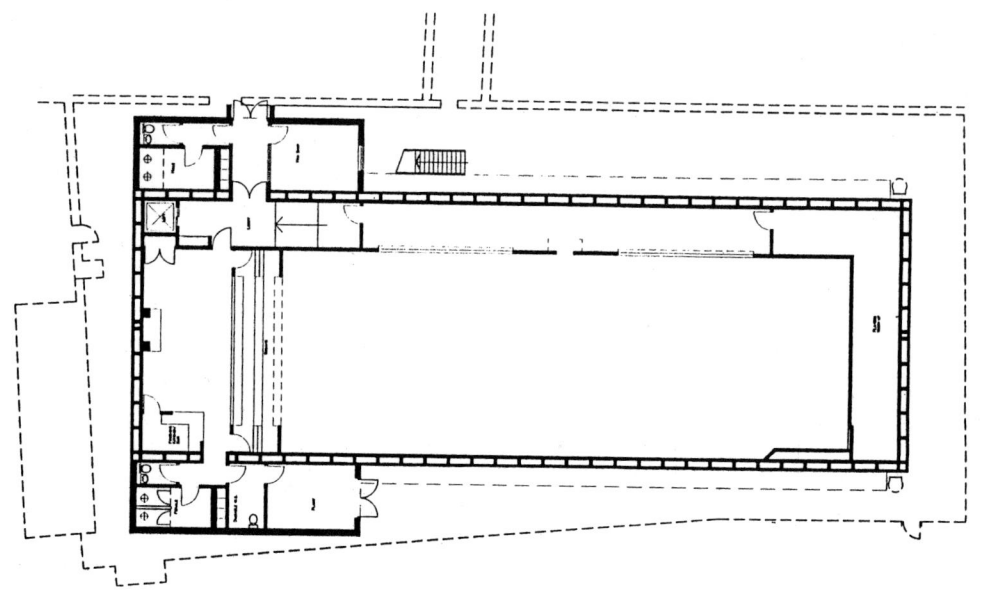

GROUND FLOOR PLAN

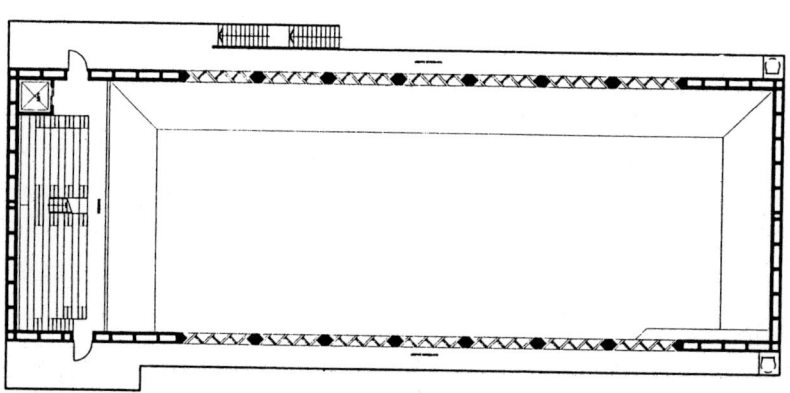

FIRST FLOOR PLAN

150. THE SCALED DOWN PLANS

to be of benefit to visitors, but at the same time it dramatically reduced the security problems and hence the associated costs, because large numbers of tourists would not now be milling about behind the main wall, in the passages, or the garden between the two Courts.

The new proposal, after internal funding had been taken into account, would leave the Club with around a £1 million borrowing requirement, a much more acceptable ratio to a commercial bank.

Development costs had now virtually ceased, as the redesigning of the Court was being undertaken, at no cost to the Club, by board member Jamie Ingham, an independent architect. The only fees that were being incurred were for the occasional item of outside specialist advice.

Following the resignation of Barney Gibbens as Chairman in early 2001, Richard Stocks was asked by the Board to assume that role until the Club's Annual General Meeting two months later. At that meeting he was unanimously confirmed as the new Chairman of the Board.

The policies adopted by HRP were under the control of trustees. The Trustees of Historic Royal Palaces are an august body, which at the time included the Lord Chamberlain, the Keeper of the Privy Purse and several other luminaries with specialist expertise; their Chairman was Lord Airlie. The Trustees had for some time been pressing, through Alan Coppin, for the Club to finalise its proposals. With the decision taken to work on plans for the scaled-down Court, the Board was confident that a fully viable scheme could be put to the Trustees by the end of the year.

Suddenly without any warning the Trustees, at a routine meeting in July, took a decision not to approve the Second Court on the planned site. Two reasons were given. Firstly, 'on careful reflection, they considered the scale of the development and its location so close to the Georgian House and the Palace was inappropriate', and secondly, 'they wished to pursue other potential uses for the site which would afford wider public use, such as a garden centre.'

The RTC Board was aghast! It had been at HRP's insistence that the Club should develop its plans for the new Court on this site: this following their rejection of two earlier sites. They had also known of the scale of the building for over ten years and now it was only two-thirds of the previous size. As for using the site as a garden centre: the proposed Court was not going to take up the whole of the area HRP were considering for the centre, so it might have been possible for the two activities to have existed side by side, and in any event the Club would have been prepared to discuss matching through rent any reasonable figure HRP might have gained through profits.

Passions were running high. Delays had been caused by changes in management at HRP, with their resultant learning curves, and reversals of positions from those previously understood by the RTC. Members were fuming over twelve wasted years and the loss of more than a quarter of a million pounds on development costs, and many were calling for compensation. There were however counter arguments, the principal one being the fact that the licence fee had been frozen since 1996 pending the outcome of the negotiations, which had in some measure made the project self-financing.

151. ARTIST'S IMPRESSION OF THE SECOND COURT

It soon became apparent that the official reason for rejection masked a deeper concern, the subject of the earlier ultimatum, the belief that the Club could not raise the money and that members' consent would not be forthcoming. In the first respect they had good reason to believe it because, in the intervening months following planning approval for the grander scheme, lenders had become less keen to advance money on unsecured projects following the collapse of several high-technology companies. Throughout the development years the Club had always been advised that a strong business plan would overcome the lack of security. HRP had never been in a position to grant a lease that could have been assigned to a third party if the Club had found it could not repay the loan; so there was never any question of security from that source.

With the advent of the Internet and the subsequent 'e-boom', banks had for a number of years been accepting that 'security' could lie in performance, and therefore they were not necessarily demanding traditional asset backing for their loans. By 2001 that was all over and the loan now had to be guaranteed. The irony was that the scaled-down project had been well received by the banks and would have easily met the earlier criteria. The second point, that members were not behind the project, the Board could not accept. At the three special meetings that had been called to review progress over the years, the project had received overwhelming support, and within the last year the membership had given assurances of support indicating willingness to provide loans amounting to nearly half a million pounds.

Despite the gloomy news the Board felt duty bound to explore every remaining avenue open to them. There was felt to be no point in attempting to persuade the Trustees to reverse their decision until the scheme was at a stage that would satisfy all their concerns.

Spreading the guarantee across the whole membership was clearly not acceptable to the banks. If the project were to come to fruition, the Club needed to find a person, or a small group of people, or an organisation, prepared to back it. Unfortunately, no-one has so far come forward.

CHAPTER 15

IN CONCLUSION

Oh! Visitor to this resort,
When in the precincts of this Court,
Canst picture the historic throng
Passing this corridor along,
Or neath the Pent House wend its way
To watch a King and courtiers play?

The old Tennis Court at Hampton Court Palace is so steeped in history that it is the one court on which most tennis players aspire to play. Whilst the structure as a whole is not the oldest, the site it occupies can without doubt claim to be where the ancient game of tennis has been played longer than anywhere else in the world. In spite of the many alterations and restorations the Court has faced over the centuries, tennis players fortunate enough to have enjoyed the facilities it offers can rest assured in the knowledge that the service wall at least has been in constant use since 1529, or even earlier!

When a visitor to Hampton Court sees the Palace for the first time, the sight is awe-inspiring. As one passes through the Trophy Gate, under the gaze of the lion and the unicorn, the whole of the magnificent West Front of the Palace looms large. The long walk down Tennis Court Lane, past the old Tudor kitchens on the right and the grand Georgian House on the left, conjures up thoughts of tennis players of a bygone era. Anticipation is heightened by the gloomy walk through the old dank corridor, once known as the Whispering Gallery, between the Lane and the Tennis Court. As one goes through the second of the three old heavy wooden doors, the first faint sound of impacting tennis balls is heard, and on passing though the third door one is immediately bathed in light streaming through the Court's side galleries. When one finally enters the playing area and stares at the stark black walls, one can only begin to imagine what secrets they harbour – if only the walls could talk!

They could tell tales of the red-robed Cardinal surveying his new court, of Henry VIII contemplating the futures of his various queens, of Charles I weighing up the risks of ruling without Parliament and later pondering his fate while under house arrest, of Charles II's mistresses chattering in the dedans as the Merry Monarch worked up a sweat, and of the obscene gambling culture of Frederick, Duke of York's circle. On other occasions the walls might have wondered whether they would ever see a tennis ball again. They had to cope with Sir Christopher Wren's vandalism when he needed somewhere to store his timber, of George I's conversion of the Court into a drawing room, and with the damage caused by Hitler's bombs during the Second World War.

They would remember some of the personalities of the past: great champions such as Barre, Tompkins, Lambert, Latham, Fairs, Gould and Etchebaster. What did they make of Pettitt's unorthodox style, and more recently Howard Angus's fleet-footed athleticism, or Chris Ronaldson's relentless determination, during their successful championship matches? Then there were the antics of others: the man who so nearly became Prime Minister, Charles James Fox, running around the Court with no clothes on, and the English champion Charles Taylor, playing a game mounted on a pony. They would have been proud of a few, and two in particular: John Lambert, who as Treasurer ran the Club single-handedly for nearly half of the nineteenth century and Tony Negretti, whose tireless efforts, recruiting hundreds of new members after the last war, laid the foundations for the successful Club of today.

Little wonder then, that the Royal Tennis Court is foremost amongst the Courts visited by lovers of tennis. That most respected of tennis historians, E.B. Noel, held the Court in such high esteem that he wrote: 'Every tennis player should make a pilgrimage to this shrine of tennis.'

And as for the future: Whatever the outcome of the attempt to build a Second Court, the Club will continue to thrive providing there is a good working relationship with the Palace. Too often in the past the Club has been brought to its knees by unrealistic demands on its limited resources – commonsense needs to prevail. There is a partnership: the members keep the Court alive, which in turn helps the Palace by providing an additional tourist attraction and income. Happily the Club is now in a strong position, the last 20 years having seen almost as much play on the Court as the whole of the previous 450.

After a long and colourful history, the Club, together with the game of Tennis in general, is now poised for even greater success. The next major milestone is its 500th Anniversary – and who knows what tales the next historian of The Royal Tennis Court may be able to tell!

BIBLIOGRAPHY

ABST   Lord Aberdare, *The Story of Tennis*, London 1959.

ABTR   Lord Aberdare, *Tennis and Rackets*, London 1980.

AD   Arthur Irwin Dasent, *Piccadilly in Three Centuries*, London 1920.

ADD   Additional Manuscript (BL).

AE   Averyl Edwards, *Frederick Louis Prince of Wales 1707-1751*, London 1947.

AH   Alderson B. Horne, *Musings in Commonplace Lane*, Edinburgh 1910.

AN   Allardyce Nicoll, *A History of Early Eighteenth Century Drama 1700-1750*, Cambridge 1925.

AO   Audit Office Declared Accounts (PRO).

BB   *The Black Books* (The Records of the Honourable Society of Lincoln's Inn.)

BBA   The British Biographical Archive.

BL   British Library/British Museum, London.

BLG   Burke's Landed Gentry.

BOD   Bodleian Library, Oxford.

BP   Burke's Peerage & Baronetage.

BW   L.St.J. Butler and P.J. Wordie, *The Royal Game*, Stirling 1989.

C   Records of the Chancery (PRO).

CD   Charles Dalton, *English Army Lists & Commission Registers 1661-1714*.

CDB   Cees de Bondt, *Heeft yemant lust met bal, of met reket te spelen...? Tennis in Nederland tussen 1500 en 1800*, Hilversum 1993.

CH   Charles William Heckethorn, *Lincoln's Inn Fields and The Localities Adjacent*, London 1896.

CJR   Chris Ronaldson, *Tennis, A Cut Above the Rest*, Oxford 1985.

CLK   Charles Lethbridge Kingsford, *The Early History of Piccadilly, Leicester Square, Soho & their Neighbourhood*, Cambridge 1925.

CP   *The Complete Peerage*, edited by H.A. Doubleday & Lord Howard de Walden, London, 1929.

CPR   Calendar of Patent Rolls.

CRES   Surveyor General and Land Revenue Records (PRO).

CSPD   Calendar of State Papers Domestic.

CSPV   Calendar of State Papers Venetian.

CTB   Calendar of Treasury Books.

CTP   Calendar of Treasury Papers Domestic.

CW   Charles Wade, *The History of The Leamington Tennis Court Club 1846-1996*, Oxford 1996.

DF   D. Foster, *Inns, Taverns, Alehouses, Coffee Houses, Etc. In and Around London, c1900*. (A series of hand-written volumes, located at the Westminster City Archive.)

DIL   George Smeeton, *Doings in London*, c1820.

DL   Albert de Luze, *La Magnifique Histoire du Jeu de Paume*, Paris 1933. English translation by Richard Hamilton for the Tennis & Rackets Association and the United States Court Tennis Association, 1979.

DNB   Dictionary of National Biography.

DNH   Department of National Heritage.

DU   David Underdown, *Start of Play (Cricket and Culture in Eighteenth-Century England*, London, 2000.

DW   David Williamson, *Debrett's Kings & Queens of Britain*, Exeter 1986.

E   Exchequer Records (PRO).

EH   English Heritage.

BIBLIOGRAPHY

EJHC	Edward Jesse, *A Summer's Day at Hampton Court*, London 1839.
EJT	Edward Jesse, *A History of Tennis*, published in *Bentley's Miscellany*, Vol 34, 1853, pp.443-451.
EL	Edith Lyttelton, *Alfred Lyttelton an account of his Life*, London 1917.
ER	Edward Rutter, *Cricket Memories: Rugby – Middlesex – Free Foresters*, London 1925.
FWP	F.W. Pledge, M.A., *Crawley: Glimpses into the Past of a Hampshire Parish*, 1907.
GC	George Cavendish, *Thomas Wolsey late Cardinal his Life and Death*, Edited by Robert Lockyer, London 1962.
GCT	*A Georgian County Town: Ashbourne, 1725-1825*, Vol. 1, Edited by Adrian Henstock, Ashbourne Local History Group, c 1989.
GHG	Stephen Glover, *History, Gazetteer and Directory of the County of Derby*, 1829-33, Derby 1831.
GS	Francois A. de Garsault, *L'Art du Paumier-Racquetier et de la Paume (The Art of the Tennis- Racket-Maker and of Tennis)*, Paris 1767, translated by Catherine W. Leftwich, B.A., 1938.
GSA	Giles St. Aubyn, *Queen Victoria (A Portrait)*, London 1991.
Hall	Edward Hall, *The Lives of Kings: The Triumphant Reign of Henry VIII*, edited by C. Whibley, London 1904.
Harl	Harleian Manuscript (BL).
HCP	Hampton Court Palace.
HG	Heiner Gillmeister, *Tennis: A Cultural History*, London 1997.
HKW	Howard Colvin, *The History of the King's Works*, London 1962-83.
HRP	Historic Royal Palaces. (As a Charitable Trust).
HRPA	Historic Royal Palaces Agency. (As a Government Agency).
HT	*Hampshire Treasures*, Hampshire County Council, 1979.
HWC	Hester W. Chapman, *The Last Tudor King — A Study of Edward VI (Oct 12th 1537 — July 6th 1553)*, London 1958.
HWY	Hilary Wayment, *The Windows of King's College Chapel*, Cambridge 1972.
IRTPA	International Real Tennis Professionals Association.
JL	John Latimer, *Annals of Bristol in the 18th Century*, 3 Volumes, Bristol 1887- 1900.
JM	Julian Marshall, *The Annals of Tennis*, London 1878.
JN	John Nichols, *The Progresses, Processions, and Magnificent Festivities of King James the First*, London 1828.
JO	June Osborne, *Hampton Court Palace*, HMSO 1984.
JP	Jeremy Potter, *Tennis and Oxford*, Oxford 1994.
JPM	James Peller Malcolm, *Anecdotes of the Manners and Customs of London during the Eighteenth Century*, London 1810.
L&P	*Letters and Papers Foreign and Domestic of the Reign of Henry VIII*, edited by J.S.Brewer, London 1876.
LAB	Lieut-Colonel Alfred H. Burne, D.S.O., *The Noble Duke of York*, London 1949.
Law	Ernest Law, *History of Hampton Court Palace*, 3 Volumes, London 1885-91.
LC	Lord Chamberlain's Records (PRO).
LCH	Bryant Lillywhite, *London Coffee Houses*, London 1963.
LD	*Fifty Years of Sport at Oxford, Cambridge and the Great Public Schools*, Arranged by Lord Desborough of Taplow, edited by A.C.M. Croome, Oxford and Cambridge – 2 Volumes, London 1913.
LK	Robert Lukin, *A Treatise on Tennis*, London 1822. Second edition, Oxford 1991.

LR   Land Revenue Records (PRO).

LS   *The London Stage 1660-1800*, edited by William Van Lennep,
            Carbondale, Illinois, 1975.

MEB   *Modern English Biography*, Frederick Boase, Truro 1892-1921.

MG   Michael P. Garnett, *A Chase Down-Under*, Romsey, Victoria, Australia,
            1999.

NC   E.B. Noel & J.O.M. Clark, *A History of Tennis*, 2 Volumes, London 1924.
            Reprinted as one volume 1991.

NHN   Nicholas H. Nicolas, *The Privy Purse Expenses of King Henry VIII*,
            November 1529 to December 1532, London 1827.

N&Q   *Notes and Queries*.

OM   Oliver Millar, *The Pictures in the Collection of Her Majesty the Queen*,
            Part 1, The Tudor, Stuart and Early Georgian Pictures, London 1963.

ONB   Österreichische National Bibliothek, Vienna.

PB   Pierre Barcellon, *Règles et Principes de Paume*, Paris 1800. (Rules and
            Principles of Tennis), English translation by Sir Richard Hamilton, Bt.
            Oxford 1987.

PCC   Wills proved by the Prerogative Court of Canterbury.

PD   Samuel Pepys, *Diary*.

PE   Pierce Egan, *Boxiana*, edited by John Ford, London 1976.

PHA   Petworth House Archive.

PL   Pepys Library, Magdalene College, Cambridge.

PRO   Public Records Office, London.

PW   Sir Pelham Warner, *Lord's 1787-1945*, London 1946.

Rawl   Rawlinson Manuscript. (Bodleian Library).

RG   Allison Danzig, *The Racquet Game*, New York 1930.

RMC   Roger Morgan, M.D., *Real Tennis in Cambridge: the first six hundred
            years*, Cambridge 2001.

RML   Roger Morgan, M.D., *A Fifteenth-Century Tennis Court in London*, The
            International Journal of the History of Sport, Vol.13, No.3 (Dec 1996),
            pp.418-431.

RMM   Roger Morgan, M.D., *Tudor Tennis, A Miscellany*, Oxford 2001.

RMT   Roger Morgan, M.D., *Tennis — The Development of the European Ball
            Game*, Oxford 1995.

RTC   The Royal Tennis Court.

RWH   R.W. Heinze, *The Proclamations of the Tudor Kings*, London 1976.

SAL   L.F. Salzman, *Building in England down to 1540*, Oxford 1952.

SB   *Officials of the Royal Household, 1660-1837*, Part 1, Department of the
            Lord Chamberlain and Associated Offices, compiled by J.C. Sainty and
            R.O. Buckholz, London 1997.

SC   Antonio Scaino da Salo, *Trattato Del Giuoco Della Palla*, Vinegia 1555.
            English translation by P.A.Negretti, London 1984.

SD   Saul David, *Prince of Pleasure (The Prince of Wales and the Making of the
            Regency)*, London 1999.

SHC   Surrey History Centre.

SL   The Survey of London. A series of volumes published by London County
            Council and its successors since 1900.

SM   Sir John Soane's Museum, London.

SO   Signet Office Records (PRO).

SRO   The Scottish Records Office, Edinburgh.

STE   Clara and Hardy Steeholm, *James I of England*, London 1938.

STHC   Simon Thurley, *Henry VIII and the building of Hampton Court*,
            Architectural History, Vol.31, 1988.

BIBLIOGRAPHY

STRP	Simon Thurley, *The Royal Palaces of Tudor England 1460-1549*, Yale 1993.
T	Treasury Records (PRO).
T&RA	Tennis & Rackets Association.
TBTF	Yves Carlier and Thierry Bernard-Tambour, *Jeu des rois, roi des jeux*, Musée National du Château de Fontainebleau, Catalogue produced for the Tennis Exhibition of 2nd October 2001 – 7th January 2002.
TBTV	Thierry Bernard-Tambour, *Versalia (Revue de la Société des Amis de Versailles)*, No. 3, 2000, *Sport Royal Les maîtres paumiers du Roi au XVIIIᵉ siècle*, pp 64-75.
TCB	T.C. Banks, *The Dormant and Extinct Baronage of England (Banks' Baronage)*, London 1807.
TF	Trevor Fawcett, *Bath entertain'd, amusements, recreations and gambling at the 18ᵗʰ Century spa*, Bath 1998.
ULU	University Library, Utrecht.
WG	Allison Danzig, *The Winning Gallery*, Philadelphia 1985.
WH	*Transactions* — London & Middlesex Archaeological Society, Volume 38, 1987. Excavations on the West Side of Whitehall 1960-62, Part 1, pp.59-130.
Work	Office/Board/Ministry of Works Records (PRO).
YPF	The Young Professionals Fund (T&RA administered).

---ooo00ooo---

NOTES

Some of the chapters include reference digits within the text: listed below are the reference sources. For the full titles of the abbreviations used in the Notes, see the preceding Bibliography.

NOTES for CHAPTER 2

1. NC, p.562. For a complete list of the Court's measurements.
2. STRP, p.179. For some of Henry VII's tennis expenses see — JM, pp.60, 61 and HG, pp.21, 22.
3. HKW, Vol. IV, p.173; STRP, p.45. A plan of New Hall (later renamed Beaulieu), the King's house near Chelmsford in Essex, shows the Tennis Court.
4. HWC, pp.58, 59.
5. E351/3326; WH, pp.102, 103.
6. STE, p.52; SRO, E21/62, f.167r.
7. HKW, Vol. IV, pp.264, 267.
8. LR1/56, f.226.
9. Hist. MSS. Comm. 5th Report, pp.2, 3, 113; ABTR, p.55.
10. There is a great deal of confusion surrounding the various Tennis Courts in the Haymarket area and it is often said there were two in James Street. The rate books, which can be traced right through the history of Tennis in the street, from c1673 to 1866, do not bear this out. Whenever the Tennis Court is mentioned it is always in the singular.[a] The James Street Tennis Court was erected shortly after the street, now known as Orange Street, was laid out in 1673 and was possibly a replacement for the nearby Shaver's Hall Court. It came perilously close to suffering the same fate as many of the French courts, namely permanent conversion to a theatre. At various times during the first half of the eighteenth century a theatre was set up inside the Court, but there is no indication that the premises were ever sub-divided with a tennis court and a theatre (in say a second court) operating independently.[b] Thomas Higginson took possession of the property in 1757. Higginson was something of a tennis entrepreneur. In the early 1740s he built Tennis Courts in Holborn, Great Windmill Street and St Martin's Street. The latter was originally a fives court, but adapted to Tennis on occasions in the *jeu quarré* format.[c]

    When Thomas Higginson took over the James Street Court he continued to allow it to be used as a theatre and on at least two occasions it staged championship-boxing matches. Despite being patronised by the royal family — the Duke of Cumberland for example, lost thousands of pounds on a fight in this Court — they were unlicensed affairs. This led to Higginson being brought before the bar of the King's Bench in 1761 and convicted of 'encouraging this species of brutality'. These great pugilistic battles were fought bare-fisted and to the finish, which sometimes ended in death.[d]

    Shaver's Hall was the nickname given to the notorious gambling house, Piccadilly House, which was built by the gentleman barber Simon Osbaldeston in 1635 at the top of the Haymarket close to the Piccadilly Circus of today. In the garden of the house he erected a Tennis Court and laid out two bowling alleys. The Tennis Court, which is sometimes referred to as the Piccadilly Tennis Court, was sited north of the present Panton Street. This Court was used a great deal by the nobility and was almost certainly the one visited by Charles II and his brother James. They are said to have entered the Court through a house in James Street; such a house might well have existed at the bottom of the Shaver's Hall garden where James Street ran.[e]

    Adding to the confusion is an error in one of the rate books where James Street appears as 'St James's Street', which was in fact half a mile to the west where the St James's Palace Tennis Court stood. The existence of the Great Windmill Street Court, which was located only a few hundred yards north and advertised as 'facing St James's, Haymarket', and the St Martin's Street Court which was even closer, about 100 yards to the south-east, clouds matters still further. Both these courts were later used to stage sparring exhibitions, but these bouts were licensed and the combatants used gloves.[f] The St. Martin's Street Court was pulled down in 1826 to enable the area to be redeveloped, and the Great Windmill Street Court was permanently converted to a theatre in 1830. After several changes of owner the latter court was fitted out in 1882 as a music hall called the

Trocadero Palace, a name that survives to the present day. References to a second theatre in James Street do not help either. It was set up in Hickford's Dancing Room and was often identified as being against the Tennis Court in James Street.[g] The James Street Court closed in 1866.

PRESENT DAY MAP SHOWING THE
POSITIONS OF TENNIS COURTS

1. Great Windmill Street Tennis Court

2. Shaver's Hall Gambling House

3. Shaver's Hall Tennis Court

4. Hickford's Great Room

5. James Street Tennis Court

6. St. Martin's Street Tennis Court

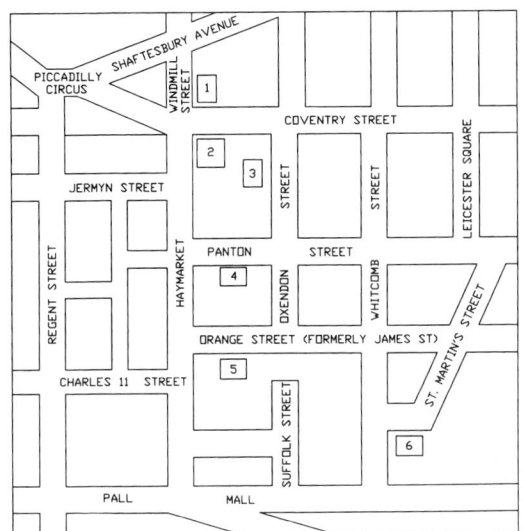

It is possible that for a short period the Shaver's Hall and James Street Courts were standing at the same time, in which case they would have been less than a hundred yards apart. The Shaver's Hall Court was in play until at least 1666 and probably remained so until 1669 when Colonel Panton acquired the property, but it had definitely been lost to tennis by 1686.[h] However, the shell of the building may have survived for a number of years after that, as it is thought it was used to store scenery for one of the neighbouring theatres before its demolition. This could account for the conflicting descriptions of James Street in the continuation of Stow's *Survey of the Cities of London and Westminster*. Strype's 1720 edition describes James Street as 'of chief Note for its tennis courts, which takes up the South Side of the Street', but in 1755 only one court is mentioned. Another explanation could be that 'courts' was a misprint, as 'court' makes more sense grammatically and the 1755 version had simply been corrected.[i]

a. Both the Street and the Court first appear in the rate books in 1675, but a plaque on the Tennis Court bore the inscription 'Iames Street 1673'.

b. AN, p.272; LS, 22nd April 1734; 23rd May 1734; 20th February 1741; 11th May 1741; 25th January 1750.

c. ABTR, pp.66, 67.

d. JPM, Vol. 1, p.335; DU, p.79.

e. CLK, pp.79-86; SL, Vol. XX, pp.101-103; JM, p.89.
    Colonel Panton acquired Shaver's Hall in 1669 for redevelopment and although James Street was just beyond its southern border it is thought he was responsible for setting it out.
    Piccadilly House was often confused with Piccadilly Hall, which stood on the opposite side of the road close to Windmill Street and had been the first house to be built, some twenty years earlier, in the open fields on the road to Reading. (AD, pp. 8-28)

f. *Daily Advertiser*, 23rd February 1744; PE, pp.33, 127.

g. SL, Vol. XXXI, p.46, 47: LS, 9th December 1697; 2nd April 1707.
    Hickford's Great Room on the south side of Panton Street was the principal auction house of the time and often used for entertainment. Whether it was this building, whose back door was described in a 1728 sale-catalogue as 'facing the Tennis Court in James Street', or an annexe next to the Court itself, which was used as a theatre, is not clear.

h.   The tennis expenses of Lord Percy, afterwards the 11th Earl of Northumberland. (PHA).
In a petition to Sir Christopher Wren, the Surveyor General, in 1671, Colonel Panton, whose redevelopment had been stopped by a proclamation against unauthorised buildings, applied for a licence to continue. His submission mentions he purchased a parcel of ground at Piccadilly on which there was a tennis court.

i.   *Survey of the Cities of London and Westminster*, 1720 edition, p.68; 1755 edition, p.646.

11.   CDB, p.89.

12.   In London the two tennis Courts in Lincoln's Inn Fields, and that in Great Windmill Street, were permanently converted to theatres, as was the one in Foregate Street, Chester. The last three Courts in Oxford, in Blue Boar Lane, Oriel Street and the surviving Merton Street Court, were also used to stage plays. The St Martin's Street and Great Windmill Street Courts were used as boxing arenas. One of the Courts in Bristol, that known as Barton Hundred, and the Court built by Richard Scrace in Bath, were also used for pugilism. (N & Q, 7th Series, Vol. 5, p.187; DIL, pp.193-195; DL, pp. 96,97; JL, Vol. II, pp.313, 359; JP, pp. 61,73; *Felix Farley's Bristol Journal*, 1st February 1755; TF, pp.18, 79.)

13.   *The Times*, 21st March 1789. The Duke of Cumberland had taken up temporary residence in The Pavilions in the House Park (later Home Park) while his apartments at Kew were being renovated.

14.   28th March 1788.

15.   FWP, p.144; HT, p.77.

16.   Work 19/1095, 20th July 1950; ABST, p.90.

17.   SD, p.65.

18.   *The Times*, 21st February 1789. This caustic comment appeared in one of a series of articles, some of which were libellous to the Duke of York and the Prince of Wales, that appeared in *The Times* during the Regency crisis. George III had suffered his first bout of madness and Parliament was debating the Regency Bill, which would have enabled the Prince of Wales to act as Prince Regent, something he was keen to achieve as he saw it as a means of securing more money to settle his ruinous debts. The Whigs and the Duke of York supported the Prince, whereas *The Times* backed Pitt and the Tories, who opposed the Bill. When the King suddenly recovered, the Regency Bill was abandoned. The Prince and the Duke then attempted to salvage their reputations by suing the Editor of *The Times*, John Walter, for libel.   The Duke's case came before the court first and was successful: Walter was sentenced to one year in Newgate Prison and one day in the pillory at Charing Cross, the last part of the sentence being commuted by the King. The Prince's prosecution followed and Walter received a further year in Newgate. (SD, p.125.)

19.   LAB, p.30; *The Times*, 28th February 1789; T&RA Annual Report 1995-96, p.92,   (Article by Lord Aberdare)

20.   14th December 1797.

21.   *Evening Standard*, 28th July 1932 - Recollections of Alf White.

22.   WG, p.69.

NOTES for CHAPTER 3

1.   HKW, Vol. IV, p.128.

2.   E36/237, pp.406, 483; E36/243, p.607.

3.   E36/237, p.272.

4.   E36/242, p.95.

5.   1596-97 - AO/1/2416/27; 1602-03 - AO/1/2417/35.

6.   E36/242, p.262.

7.   HCP Archaeological Survey 1978 - Daphne Hart.

8.   E36/237, p.85.

9.   E36/242, p.8.

10.   E36/237, p.105; E36/241, p.409.

11.   Law, Vol. I, p.68.

12.	RWH, pp.88-94.

For the complete text of the 4th December Proclamation see *Tudor Royal Proclamations*, No. 121, edited by Paul L. Hughes and James F. Larkin. London, 1964.

Closh, or ring ball, was a game played on the ground where balls had to be struck with a bat and sent through an iron ring. The game was often mentioned in prohibition orders. (RMT, pp.169-173.)

13. 1519 — L & P, Vol. III, Part 1, p.51; 1530 — NHN, p.37; 1532 — L & P, Vol. V, p.757.
14. NHN, p.180.
15. RMT, p.181.
16. Hall, Vol. I, p.255; Lord Edmund Howard was the father of Anne Boleyn.
17. CSPV, Vol. II, 1509-19, 10th September 1519, p.559, #1287.
18. CSPV, Vol. IV, 1527-33, 7th May 1527, p.61, #105.
19. RMT, p.100; Harl, 2284, f.31.
20. Law, Vol. I, p.231; Geraldine was Lady Elizabeth Fitzgerald who had been in the service of both Princess Elizabeth and Queen Catherine Howard.
21. AO/1/2412/8.
22. HKW, Vol. IV, p.129.
23. Chapter House Accounts.
24. HKW, Vol. IV, p.132.
25. E36/241, p.633.
26. E36/241, p.650.
27. RMC, p.5; RMT, p.124.   Recent research by Roger Morgan has shown that many courts of this period had floor tiles around nine inches square.
28. E36/237, pp.62, 124, 146, are examples.
29. STRP, p.188.
30. E36/237, p.170; HCP Archaeological Survey 1978 — Daphne Hart — remains of a winding staircase found.
31. E36/237, p.86.
32. E36/237, p.127.
33. EH, AS3/20, Nov. 1985.
34. E36/237,p.117.
35. WH, pp.81, 97.
36. Rawl, D775, f.51; E36/237, p.172.
37. E36/237, p.302.
38. WH, pp.80-83.
39. HWY, p.7.
40. E36/237, p.169.
41. E36/237, p.195.
42. E36/237, p.268; SAL, pp.107, 108.
43. E36/237, p.194; E36/238, p.496; STHC, p.25; SAL, p.144.
44. E36/242, p.98.
45. E36/243, p.77.
46. E36/243, p.20.
47. SAL, pp.242, 250.
48. RMT, pp.98-101; Pillared galleries, a term coined by Roger Morgan, can be seen in a series of drawings of tennis courts at French chateaux by the renowned sixteenth century architect Androuet du Cerceau. Several are reproduced in RMM, pp.64-89. More than a dozen courts of this type, which were incorporated into some of the most important houses in France, are described.
49. ABTR, p.48; GS, p.26, #95.
50. E36/243, p.39.
51. E36/240, pp.86, 89.
52. EH, AS3/20, Nov. 1985.
53. HKW, Vol. IV, p.16, for the internal measurements of the building. For the floor see the Petworth List — a list of London Courts and their measurements compiled by the Clerk of the Works at Petworth House in Sussex. JM, p.79.
54. E36/244, p.405.
55. 1606-07 — AO/1/2419/39; 1614-15 — AO/1/2421/45; 1621-22 — AO/1/2423/52.
56. AO/1/2424/55.
57. Hist. MSS. Comm. 5th Report, pp.168, 169.
58. Work 5/7, f.174.

59.   HKW, Vol. V, p.154.
60.   Work 5/13, *Extraordinary Account.*
61.   HKW, Vol. IV, p.137.

NOTES for CHAPTER 4

1.   AO/1/2417/35.
2.   E351/3259.
3.   ULU, MS 1198, f.143v.
4.   E36/241, p.409.
5.   RMT, pp.118, 119.
6.   RML.
7.   STRP, p.187.
8.   Law, Vol. II, p.4.
9.   Law, Vol. II, p.46.
10.   JN, Vol II, pp.53-95; Law, Vol. II, pp.49-51; *England's Farewell to Christian IV the King of Denmark*, 1606.
11.   E351/3259.
12.   RMT, p.108.
13.   Law, Vol. II, p.120.
14.   E351/3270.
15.   DNH, HRP. Neg. 3.0801002/18.
16.   EJHC, p.61.
17.   LC5/137, p.106.
18.   Work 5/1, f.408v; Harl.1656, f.224.
19.   Work 5/1, ff.399r, 408r; Harl.1656, ff.216, 224.
20.   Work 5/1, f.389v.
21.   Work 5/1, f.393r.
22.   Work 5/1, f.398v; AO/1/2433/85.
23.   Work 5/1, ff.393v, 400v; Harl.1656, f.217.
24.   Work 5/1, f.411v; Harl.1656, f.229.
25.   Work 5/1, f.408r; Harl.1656, f.224.
26.   Work 5/2, f.269r.
27.   Work 5/1, ff.414r, 414v; Harl.1656, ff.231, 232; AO/1/2433/85.
28.   Work 5/2, f.263r.
29.   Work 5/1, ff.400v, 408v; Work 5/2, f.258r; Harl.1656, ff.217, 224.
30.   Work 5/1, f.399r; Work 5/2, f.257v; Harl.1656, f.241.
31.   Work 5/1, f.389v.
32.   Work 5/2, f.257r; Harl.1656, f.241.
33.   Work 5/2, f.253r; Harl.1656, f.236.
34.   Work 5/2, ff.257r, 263r; Harl.1656, f.241.
35.   Work 34/599; RTC — Ministry of Works letter — 31st August 1953.
36.   RMT p.94.
37.   Work 5/2, f.269r.
38.   Work 5/2, f.263r.
39.   LC5/65, p.77; LC5/143, p.99.
40.   JM, p.39.
41.   Work 5/2, f.271r.
42.   LC5/60, p.211; LC5/137, p.34.
43.   Work 5/1, f.414r; Work 5/2, f.261v.
44.   LC5/137, p.150.
45.   PD, 22/1/1669 & 31/3/1669; OM, Catalogue Number 397.
46.   ONB, AZ.1172/1/96.
47.   Thomas Cooke received £1,500 to erect a new Court at Whitehall in 1662. (CTB, 1600-67, p.512).
48.   LC5/137, pp.410, 411.
49.   JM, p.86.

50. The original c1670 Plan of Whitehall Palace has been lost. There are several copies.
    i.   BL, Crace Plans, XI65.
    ii   Society of Antiquaries Library, MS196G.
    iii Engraved version by George Vertue 1747, on display in the Banqueting House, Whitehall.

    The plan is usually ascribed to John Fisher and dated c1680. However, there is considerable doubt as to both the attribution and the date. G.S. Dugdale in his *Whitehall through the Centuries*, p.66, sets out the case for a date closer to 1670 and suggests the plan may have been the work of Ralph Greatorex.

51. SM, Drawing Number 57/7/1. Sir John Soane gained a great reputation as the architect of the Bank of England in 1788. He was also responsible for several of the buildings erected at Whitehall over the following forty years.

52. Department of the Environment, Conservation Library, Hampton Court Drawings attributed to Thomas Fort, f.24.

53. LK, frontispiece pullout — plan of the James Street Court.

54. GS, p.6, plate 1.

55. Work 5/2, f.257v; Harl.1656, f.241.

56. PD, 28th December 1663; 4th January 1664; 2nd September 1667.

57. Harl.6271, ff.6, 7, 20.

58. LC5/141, p.532.

59. Calendar of Manuscripts of The Duke of Rutland, Vol. II, p.81.

60. Work 5/2, f.297r.

61. Work 5/3, f.319r; AO/1/2434/86; Work 5/32, f.234r.

62. Work 5/41, f.211r.

63. From research carried out by Dr Philip Lewin for an updated DNB entry.

64. Work 5/55, f.20r.

65. Work 5/55, f.40r.

66. Work 5/55, f.282v; Work 5/55, f.376v.

67. Work 5/49, f.321r.

NOTES for CHAPTER 5

1. Work 5/50, ff.273r, 279r. The buttresses on the east wall had by this time fallen into decay and only three remained. They had never formed part of the original wall and were only added as a precaution to strengthen the wall when the first roof was put on in 1636-37.

2. Work 6/2, p.103.

3. Work 6/2, p.104.

4. T1/68, p.193; Work 6/2, p.115.

5. PB, p.4.

6. LK, p.105.

7. JM, p.39.

8. Floor — Work 5/51, ff.292r, 302v; Walls — Work 5/51, f.303v; Work 5/2, f.274v; Ceiling — Work 5/52, f.351v; Nets & Curtains — CTB, Vol. XVI, p.134.

9. Work 5/50, ff.315v, 317v.

10. Work 5/51, f.302v. Ketton Stone is an *Oolite* (a form of limestone) and came from the Jurassic ridge just south of Stamford in Lincolnshire.

11. Work 5/51, f.303v.

12. LC5/70, p.51; LC5/152, p.283.

13. Work 5/51, f.326r.

14. Work 5/51, f.403v.

15. Work 5/52, f.274v.

16. Work 5/52, f.277r.

17. LC5/153, p.99.

18. Work 5/52, f.351v.

19. Work 5/52, f.419v.

20. Law, Vol. III, p.228.

21. Work 5/52, f.463r.

22. Work 5/52, f.467r.

23. LC5/70, p.51; LC5/152, p.283.

24. Work 5/51, f.312v.
25. Work 5/52, f.428r.
26. CDB, p.89.
27. Harl. 5010, f.24, *Establishment of the Household of King William III and Queen Mary AD1689.*
28. CSPD, 1700-02, Ash Wednesday March 1698.
29. LC5/154, p.453.
30. AO/1/2448/146.
31. Law, Vol. III, p.176.
32. HKW, Vol. V, p.180.
33. T56/18, p.63; Work 6/7, p.54.
34. AO/1/2449/152.
35. T56/18, p.72; CTB, Vol. XXXII, 22nd July 1718; RMT, p171-173 deals with the development of billiards from closh; see also Chapter 3 note 12.
36. AO/1/2450/154.
37. Work 4/2, f.13r.
38. Work 5/79, Xmas Qtr. 1790.
39. Work 4/3, 9th March 1724.
40. AE, p.115.
41. *Charles James Fox*, by L.G. Mitchell (Oxford 1992); DNB.
    Hampton Court — EJT, p.449. Recounted by Lord Holland (the third Baron) who had been brought up by Fox, his uncle.
    Eton — Castle Howard MSS., J14/65/5, p.54. I am indebted to Andrew Steven for the Windsor Castle information.
    Woburn — *Memorials and Correspondence of Charles James Fox*, edited by Lord John Russell (London 1854), Vol. III, p.85.
42. J. Gerard Turner was paid £11 13s. 6d., for supplying '116¾ yards of strong canvas yard wide' for covering the penthouses. It took two men four days to carry out the work and they were paid £1 4s. 0d. (Work 5/69, March 1781). The supply of canvas is again mentioned in connection with the penthouses in 1862. (RTC Minute Book, 10th May 1862).
43. Work 5/69, June 1781.
44. Work 3/3, f.25v.
45. Work 3/3, f.26v; Work 4/7, 29th August 1788.
46. Work 19/66, 2nd October 1788; Work 3/3, f.27v.
47. Work 5/77, Xmas Qtr. 1788.
48. The Pavilions were originally a group of four buildings, one set in each corner of a bowling green, and located beside the river in what is now Home Park. They were erected as part of William III's grand vision of the Palace and later designated Grace-and-Favour residences. For a while they were used to accommodate members of the Royal Family. George II's daughter Princess Amelia resided there for thirteen years from 1748, and three of George III's brothers were in occupation at various times. In 1764 they were refurnished for Prince William, the Duke of Gloucester, and for Prince Henry. Henry (afterwards created Duke of Cumberland) left soon after, but William stayed until his death in 1805 when another brother, Edward, the Duke of Kent and Queen Victoria's father, moved in. In 1792 a building was constructed linking the easternmost pair. The two Pavilions to the west were demolished in 1820, and in 1855 one of the east pair and the linking building were taken down. The remaining Pavilion still stands and is now a private dwelling under the control of the Crown Estates.
49. *The Times*, 4th August 1788; 28th February 1789; 21st March 1789.
50. 28th March 1788.
51. Work 5/81, *Extraordinary Account*, Ladyday Qtr. 1792.
52. Work 19/66; Work 1/8, p.384.

NOTES for CHAPTER 6

1. Work 19/66, 5th February 1818.
2. Work 4/23, p.63.
3. NC, p.495. Joseph Case is referred to as Charles in most tennis histories (see Chapter 12).
4. *The Field*, 3rd December 1910; 4th November 1911.

5. *Oatlands and the Golden Ball*, Michael E. Blackman, Walton and Weybridge Local History Society, Paper No. 22.

Lord Granville Leveson-Gower, who pulled down the Oatlands House Tennis Court, was a leading player at the James Street Court in his younger days (see Appendix 15).

6. *The Field*, 3rd December 1910.

7. EJT, p.449.

8. *The Field*, 3rd December 1910.

9. Law, Vol. III, p.328. It was to John Case, the Hampton Court Marker, that the Duke turned when he organised an exhibition match as part of the entertainment laid on for a visit to Strathfield Saye by Queen Victoria and Prince Albert (see Chapter 12).

10. *The Field*, 2nd December 1911.

11. Work 19/66, 22nd November 1858; 18th August 1883.

12. EJT, p.449.

13. Work 19/66, 27th April 1848; 29th June 1848; Work 1/32, p.353.

14. *The Field*, 4th November 1911.

15. JM, p.109.

16. NC, p.19; CW, p.16.

17. Marriage — 18th November 1850 — Parish of St. John, Waterloo.

18. Work 34/600; 601.

19. Work 19/66, 22nd November 1858.

20. Work 19/66, 18th August 1883.

21. The letter, dated 8th November 1858, from White Lodge, Richmond Park, was sent to Henry Case with a cheque enclosed for £11 15s. 0d. It was in payment of a bill raised by Case for £8 12s. 0d. for the Prince's tennis expenses, and included the cost of a racket. Added to Case's bill was the Prince's subscription for membership of the Club, £3 3s. 0d. The letter and the original bill are in the possession of Sue Marley, a great-great-granddaughter of Henry Case.

22. *The Field*, 2nd December 1911.

23. Messrs. Shrubsole & Co. was for 70 years the 'Kingston Bank'. Parr's Banking Co. and the Alliance Bank acquired it in 1894, and through a series of amalgamations it is now part of the Royal Bank of Scotland. In 1896 the Club's account was transferred to Coutts & Co. (now itself owned by the Royal Bank) — that account still operates today. Between the wars C.T. Agar opened an account at Barclays in Cobham for ease of access, which operated for some 40 years. During the late 1980s and early 1990s the Club's reserves were split between Coutts, the Bank of Scotland and Tyndall & Co. of Bristol.

24. Work 19/66, 27th May 1862; 4th June 1862 (copied in Work 1/71, p.211). Some restoration work on the penthouses clearly went ahead. On 10th May 1862 the Minute Book shows that Henry Case was ordered to pay for 'painting the penthouses, wire and canvas'.

25. Work 19/66, 1st June 1870 through to 13th October 1870; Work 1/92, p.82; Work 1/93, p.914.

26. Work 19/66, 14th August 1874; 18th August 1874.

27. Work 19/66, 12th July 1876; *The Field*, 17th February 1877.

28. JM, p.36.

29. JP, p.98.

30. *The Field*, 10th March 1877.

31. Work 19/66, 3rd August 1883; 18th August 1883; 14th January 1884.

32. *The Field*, 3rd December 1910.

33. Work 19/66, 28th March 1898; 4th April 1898.

34. *The Field*, 21st June 1884.

35. Work 19/66, 30th April 1884; 12th May 1884; 25th May 1884; 25th July 1884.

In order to get the blood to spread evenly over the floor it had to be warm, and the only way of achieving that was to slaughter the animal on court. In conversation with Chris Ronaldson the late Henry Johns confirmed that he had witnessed the process. He also commented that the court stank for two months afterwards.

36. *The Field*, 16th May 1885.

37. EL, p.87; LD, Vol. I, p. 303.

38. Various letters from Pettitt, Saunders and other interested parties were published in *The Field* between 2nd November 1889 and 5th April 1890.
   The black Galway marble used in the Dublin Court in its polished form was later found to be unsuitable and the polish was removed by sand rubbing, leaving the Court dark grey in appearance. (This information was kindly supplied by Andrew Steven).
39. The RTC Minute Book 1844-1948.
40. *The Field*, 1st June 1889; 29th June 1889; 3rd August 1889.
41. Work 19/66, 3rd December 1896; 16th December 1896; 12th September 1903.
42. *The Field*, 4th November 1911; 18th April 1929.
43. AH, p.56.
44. PW, p265; ER, p.6. I am grateful to Charles Clive-Ponsonby-Fane, a great-great-grandson of Sir Spencer; to Tony Stedall, Curator of the Somerset Cricket Museum and to Ronald Swash for much of this information.
45. NC, p.53.
46. *The Times*, 5th October 1924; PW, p.271; RMM, p.169.
47. *The Field*, 18th April 1929.
48. The Archives of Coutts & Co.
49. RTC Records — A book containing a list of members in 1895 shows those who agreed to pay the new subscription and those who did not.
50 *The Field*, 25th April 1929; Entries in a playbook retained by Alf White — now lost.
51. *The Times*, 27th February 1899.
52. *The Field*, 22nd October 1898.
53. BBA; DNB; MEB; Law, Vol. III, Apx. G; Work 19/67; *The Field*, 28th July 1877 (C.E. Boyle v G. Lambert); The Heath Archive (The Bowling-Green Pavilions at Hampton Court); Hampton Court Palace, List of Occupants of Private Apartments from 1891 to 1989, Ian Gray.

NOTES for CHAPTER 7

1. NHN, pp.134, 183, 193, 283; L & P, Vol.V, pp.305, 312, 749, 754, 757, 761.
2. E36/235 to E36/245. The Chapter House Accounts.
3. RML.
4. L & P, Vol. VI, 1533, #578/24, 25.
5. L & P, Vol. X, 1536, #226/33.
6. Calendar of the Manuscripts of the Marquess of Bath, Vol. V, p.149. (The Dudley Papers arrived at Longleat by way of inheritance through the wife of the first Viscount Weymouth.)
7. STRP, p.54. In 1536, Whitehall received official recognition by Act of Parliament of its administrative role and was named the 'King's Palace at Westminster'.
8. L & P, Vol. XVIII, 1543, Part II, #529/24.
9. E403/2453, f.122.
10. SO3/1; CSPD, Addenda, 1580-1625, p.343.
11. SO3/2; CSPD, 1603-10, p.75.
12. CSPD, 1603-10, pp.379, 383.
13. *The Reports of Sir Edward Coke*, London 1776 (English Transcription) Vol. IV, Part VIII, pp.45r-50r; ABTR, p.53.
14. Pell Records, 1610 (Issue of the Exchequer during the Reign of King James I), p.116; CSPD, 1603-10, p.647.
15. E101/435/5.
16. SO3/6; C66/2133, m.24.
17. CSPD, 1661-62, pp.32, 33; PCC 1656.
18. LR1/56, f.226.
19. ABTR, pp.54, 55; PCC 1631.
   During Thomas Hooker's tenancy, Charles I became concerned for his privacy when relaxing in St James Field. As a result he blocked off all entrances to the field leaving only the route through the Tennis Court 'which is to be for the king's private use & ye addmittance of whom his Ma^tye shall please'. (LC5/132, p.192.)
20. C9/31/67, 15th November 1664.
21. C9/31/67, 31st October 1664.
22. SL, Vol. XXIX, p.323.

23.   E403/2523, f.112.
24.   CSPD, 1660-61, p.208.
25.   CTB, 1660-67, Vol. I, p.512.
26.   LC5/137, p.150.
27.   CTB, 1675, p.734.
28.   CTB, 1676, p.380.
29.   SO3/19; CSPD, 1689, pp.83, 96, 137.
30.   SO3/17; CSPD, 1676, p.380.
31.   CD, Vol. 1, p.283; Vol. 2, pp.38, 139; Vol. 3, pp.99, 128; CTB, 1689-92, p.1358; CSPD, June 1687 – February 1689, p.296, #1606; *The Villiers Family as Governors of Tynemouth Castle and Owners of the Lighthouse*, by Horatio A. Adamson, published by The Society of Antiquaries, 30th March 1898, and a supplementary paper by the same author published 29th July 1903.
32.   BP; CP.
33.   CTB, April 1697-September 1697, p.247; October 1697-August 1698, pp.13, 14;   CSPD, 1697, p.58.
34.   CTB, 1702, pp.476, 965.
35.   SL, Vol. III, pp.12, 39, 48; BB, Vol. II, pp.414-416, 421, 466; CWH, pp.111, 136-139, 150-152.
       James Hooker was probably a member of the Hooker family who ran the St James's Palace Court. The Duke of York's tennis expenses, preserved at Petworth House (PHA 648), record a James Hooker partnering the Duke at St James's Palace in January 1648.
36.   SB, p.51.
37.   SO3/21; LR1/65, f.50; LC5/166, p.213.
38.   CTB, 1708, Vol. XXII, Part II, p.185; 1714-15, p.326.
39.   DF, Vol. 65; LCH, pp.570-572; Work 4/17, 3rd February 1792. The Master of the King's Tennis Courts requesting repairs to the Coffee House floor.
40.   SO3/22.
41.   LC3/64, p.83; SO3/23; C66/3569, m.2.
42.   SO3/25, June 1743; LC5/161, p.148.
43.   PCC 1782; TCB, Vol. III, p.196.
44.   C66/3684, m.14; C66/3705, m.24; N & Q, 24th February 1923.
       Additional information kindly supplied by Malcolm C. Beresford of the Beresford Family Society.
45.   SO3/27; C66/3696, m.11.
46.   BP; CP.
47.   SO3/30; C66/3869, m.6.
48.   GCT, pp.18-44; GHG, Vol. 2, part 1; BLG; PCC 1815.
49.   LC5/163, p.141.
50.   The family link was traced with the help of Anne Lenihan of Waterford Library and local historian, William Eraher, to whom I am indebted.
51.   Law, Vol 3, p.476.
52.   LC1/43, p.43; C66/4170, m.3; MEB.
53.   Recollections of Sir Spencer Ponsonby-Fane, *The Field*, 3rd December 1910.
54.   *The Illustrated London News*, 3rd April 1852.
55.   Details of the background to the corruption scandal were supplied by Dr. David A. Male, the Honorary Archivist of Harwich Town Council, to whom I am most grateful. The other MP was John Attwood, a Railway Promoter.
56.   Work 1/35, f.182.
57.   T53/68, pp.299-301. His principal addresses can be found from the parliamentary records of the six elections he fought, and from correspondence with the Office of Works preserved in Work 19/66.
58.   Work 19/66; 4th August 1883; 11th August 1883.

NOTES for CHAPTER 8

Much of the information for the latter part of this chapter has been gathered from the extensive correspondence of Tony Negretti, his personal recollections and those of other members.

1. RTC Minute Book 1844-1948; Negretti Papers – 1st August 1952; correspondence between Tony Negretti and Lord Revelstoke.
2. *The Field*, 4th November 1911.
3. *The Field*, 7th March 1914.
4. Work 19/66, 12th September 1903.
5. *The Field*, 2nd December 1911. Recent T&RA rulebooks describe these nets as fly nets; the term wing net is reserved for the net used to protect the marker in front of the net post.
6. ADD, 54149; 54150.   (Lady Wentworth's Bequest)
   The Crabbet Park Tennis Book (1909-1919) is amongst these papers. The match results provide an insight into the quality of Lady Wentworth's game, which appears to have been of a high standard. Between 1917 and 1919 she claims she was giving Edward Gray, the Brighton Professional, fifteen and was beating him regularly. At the same time Gray was giving fifteen and a beating to Captain Price, who went on to win the MCC Gold Racquet in 1920. She describes her game as 'excessively terrifying but embracing'. The same document also reveals that she took over from Gray as the Brighton Professional for a month in 1917, when he became ill.

   The papers include a partially written manuscript for a book on Tennis, which she never completed. Here, she comments about her father, who was upset with her for working as a professional in a public court. He became even more agitated when she publicly humiliated her cousin Lord Leconfield, the Lord Lieutenant of the County and the owner of Petworth House, by beating him by five sets to love (30 games to 2) on the Brighton Court, in an 'unpardonably unladylike reprisal' after he had allegedly insulted her.

   Lady Wentworth was a somewhat eccentric character, and her papers contain some extraordinary allegations about the 1914 World Championship. Fred Covey, the Champion, and an employee of the Lytton's at Crabbet, agreed to defend his title against Jay Gould in a home-and-away match; the first leg in Philadelphia, and the second at Princes Club, Knightsbridge. Covey was heavily defeated in Philadelphia, but the return match was never played because the war intervened. Gould resigned the title two years later, which Covey then reclaimed. At the time controversy raged over whether Gould had actually become World Champion, because the second leg had not been played — subsequently it was generally accepted he had. The documents however, clearly reveal that Lady Wentworth never accepted this; she alleged that Covey was drugged before the match, and that Charles Sands, a former American amateur champion, had warned her that it might happen, but Covey refused to believe it. She further claimed that a forged copy of the match articles was substituted for the real one that did not contain the 'home-and-away' clause. This could be proved, she wrote, because the document was signed 'George' Covey instead of Geoffrey, his real name.
7. Committee Minutes, 15th July 1909.
8. *The Field*, 13th June 1908.
9. NC, p.56.
10. Work 19/66, 26th March 1913.
11. Work 19/66, 12th May 1913; Work 19/435, 4th October 1913; *The Field*, 25th April 1929.
12. *The Field*, 24th May 1919.
13. *The Times*, 16th May 1919; *The Field*, 24th May 1919.
14. Work 19/807, 2nd March 1921.
15. Work 19/807, 29th June, 2nd & 8th July 1921.
16. *The Field*, 17th September 1921.
17. Work 19/807, 27th September 1925.
18. Work 19/807, 29th May 1928. The original Grace-and-Favour Warrants are in the possession of the RTC.
19. RTC Record Book.

20. RG, p.44.

Cecil Baring married the youngest daughter of the American tobacco magnate Pierre Lorillard, who was the man responsible for setting out the luxurious residential development, Tuxedo Park.

The Baring family had other tennis connections. Edward Baring, the first Lord Revelstoke, built a Tennis Court at his home, Membland Hall, near Plympton in Devon, in the 1880s. It was later converted into flats. (T&RA Annual Report 1993-94, p.14). Rupert Baring, the fourth Baron, married a daughter of Sir Thomas Fermor-Hesketh, who owned Easton Neston, where there was another Tennis Court.

21. RTC Records — Lord Revelstoke's memorandum of the meeting, 28th April 1932.

22. *Squash Rackets, Fives, Tennis & Rackets*, 22nd October 1932. Article by H.M. Wallbrook — RTC Committee Member 1928-34.

23. Work 19/807, 28th July 1933.

24. T226/70, 23rd February 1934.

25. Work 19/807 & T226/70, 5th June 1935.

26. *The Chronological Scrapbook of Tennis* (Vol. 11, 1935-36), The Racquet and Tennis Club Library, New York.

27. Work 19/1161, 26th September 1940.

28. Work 19/1095, 27th April 1946.

29. Work 19/1095, 11th May 1948.

30. T226/70, 28th February 1949; 5th March 1949.

31. Work 19/1095, Memo at the end of the file.

32. *The Field*, 16th August 1928.

33. RTC Records, Ministry of Works letter, 8th February 1954.

34. I am indebted to the late Lord Butterfield, who helped to organise this match, for bringing this story to my attention, and to Lord Aberdare and John Marshall for confirmation of their roles.

35. RTC Records, Ministry of Works letter, 1st July 1965.

36. I am grateful to Pat Barker, who gave me a copy of the minutes of this meeting.

NOTES for CHAPTER 11

1. Work 5/10, ff.275v, 283r; Work 5/11, f.214v.

2. Work 5/2, ff.257r, 257v; Harl, 1656, f.241.

3. Work 6/2, p.103.

4. Work 5/103, Michaelmas 1814.

5. Work 34/598; Work 19/66, 27th April 1848.

6. *The Field*, 4th November 1911.

7. Work 19/66, 7th September 1903.

8. Work 19/66, 1st July 1910 to 12th July 1910.

9. Work 19/66, 26th April 1913 to 13th June 1913.

10. Work 19/807, 16th September 1932.

11. Work 5/21, f.257r.

12. Work 5/1, f.405v; Harl, 1656, f.222.

13. Work 1/17, p.428.

14. LC1/49, p.114; Law, Vol. III, p.487.

15. Work 1/33, pp.421, 422.

16. Work 19/66, 5th November 1849.

17. Work 1/44, pp.148, 149.

18. *The Book of Molesey*, Rowland G.M. Baker, Buckingham 1986, p.28.

NOTES for CHAPTER 12

These short biographies have been compiled from information contained in the major published tennis works along with articles and match reports from *The Field*. Details of employment conditions, salaries, etc., are from committee minutes. Much of the history of the Cases has come from family documents and research carried out by a descendant, Sue Marley. That of the Whites comes from the RTC archives, which include some of Alfred White's letters. Other specific references are listed below.

1.   L & P, Vol. X, #869.

2.   LC5/136A, p.35.

3.   PHA 648. (The information is reproduced by permission of Lord Egremont, the owner of the Archives)
        These accounts are in the Petworth House Archives, because the owner, the 10th Earl of Northumberland, had the trust of Oliver Cromwell and was given charge of three of Charles I's children: James, Duke of York; Henry, Duke of Gloucester; and Elizabeth. The tennis expenses relate to St James Palace.

4.   ABTR, p.59; LC5/140, p.366.

5.   Stories detailing the methods used by the sharpers to swindle the nobility can be found in:
        The Covent Garden Magazine or Amorous Repository — Annals of Gaming, 1775, p.46;
        Tricks of the Town, Letter IX — edited by R. Straus, London 1927.

6.   *The Daily Courant*, 7th February 1733.

7.   T&RA Annual Report 1995-96, p.92.

8.   Baptism Records of the Parishes of Hampton, Teddington and East Molesey.

9.   SHC, 2784/51/1/92(2), the Ball-Hughes Papers.

10.   1841 Census.

11.   3rd December 1910.

12.   Preserved in the Hatfield House Archives are the letters from John Case to the Second Marquess of Salisbury, and his reply (ref. 2M/Hat. 31st March 1843). I am grateful to Robin Harcourt Williams, the Librarian and Archivist at Hatfield House, for drawing my attention to this correspondence.

13.   Tennis accounts of the Prince of Wales and Captain Hudson. (In the Case family collection).

14.   Within the extended Tompkins family of tennis professionals were four generations of Edmunds. The first Edmund ran the Merton Street Court in Oxford from 1758 until his death in 1763. He was succeeded by his son, also Edmund, who later moved to the Great Windmill Street Court, although he retained the lease of Merton Street. His son, the third Edmund, was generally known as Peter. He took over the Merton Street lease having started at Great Windmill Street, but sold it in 1836 and went to manage the new Brighton Court. The fourth Edmund, son of Peter, became World Champion having started as the first Marker at the new Leamington Club, before moving to James Street and finally Oxford, buying back the lease from Thomas Sabin. (JP, pp.82-88.)

15.   MG, pp.24-28, 84, 85.
        I am indebted to John Stanley-Rogers, a great-grandson of Thomas Stone, for new information that has recently come to light relating to the family's Grace-and-Favour residency at the Palace.
        Thomas Stone's mother Mary was in the employ of Major-General James Moore and his wife Cecilia. The Major-General, who was Equerry to the Duke of Kent, was given the Pavilions in recognition of his bravery when the Duke's life was under threat during the 'Pigtail' mutiny at Gibraltar. The Pavilions became uninhabitable following Mrs Moore's death in 1852 and it is thought the Stone family moved into an apartment within the main Palace. Apartment 57 is described in twentieth-century documents held at the Public Records Office, as the 'Lamplighter's Apartment'. (Work 19/819; 19/1324.)
        The Lamplighter's Apartment was situated amid the Tudor kitchen complex on the ground floor of the Palace. Although it has not been possible to trace occupancy of this apartment back to the Stones, it is known that Thomas the Lamplighter died in 1884, and that another lamplighter, probably his successor who died in 1891, amusingly named Oliver Cromwell, definitely resided in the apartment. It is therefore almost certain that the apartment was granted to Thomas Stone senior when he moved out of the Pavilions.

16.   1861 Census.

17.   *Tivy-side*, 4th November 1983. Recollections of his daughter Mary.

Sir Henry Meux, the brewing magnate, built the Court at Theobalds in 1840. Sir Henry died in 1883. Hedworth Lambton, third son of the second Earl of Durham, was a close friend of Lady Meux, and she agreed to transfer the Estate to him after her death, on condition he changed his name to Meux.

Theobalds came close to having a Court in Stuart times. James I had plans drawn up in 1624 for one, for the benefit of Prince Charles. James died soon after, but Charles as King cancelled the project. (HKW, Vol. III, Part I, p.275.)

18.   The salary at Hampton Court appears to have been poor. John Phillips, who was appointed as the Manager of the new Clare and Trinity Court at Cambridge when it opened in 1866, was paid 25 shillings a week. (RMC, p.33.)

19.   *Cricket in Hatfield in the 18th and 19th Centuries*, H.J. Gray, 1993. (Typed manuscripts bound into two volumes and lodged at Hatfield Library.)

20.   Obituary - *The Field*, 16th April 1910.

21.   RG, p.24.

The Duke of Fife was a prominent member of the Royal Tennis Court. In 1883 as Lord Fife, he commissioned the building of a Tennis Court in the grounds of his home Sheen Lodge, near Richmond in Surrey. He married Edward VII's eldest daughter Princess Louise in 1889 and received the Dukedom as a wedding present. Known as 'Macduff' he was said to be excellent company when he chose, but had 'the language of Billingsgate' (the fish market). He was a particular favourite of Queen Victoria. Social gatherings at Sheen Lodge led to the occasional appearance of members of the Royal Family on the Tennis Court there. (GSA, p.570.)

22.   *The Times*, 11th April 1890; 14th May 1904.

23.   *Westminster Gazette*, 14th September 1921; *The Field*, 2nd December 1911.

24.   1891 Census; CW, p.12.

25.   A series of letters on this subject is filed under Work 19/435, July 1914.

26.   The *London Evening Standard* article is dated 28th July 1932.

27.   I am most grateful to Reg Chaplin, a grandson of John McCann, and his wife Beryl, for sharing the benefit of research into their family history, which has helped to create this profile. They kindly provided the photograph of John McCann and generously donated to the Club an original version of the framed photograph of the Hon. Alfred Lyttelton (figure 52) that hangs in the clubrooms. The copy in the clubrooms, which was given to the Club by Alf White on the occasion of his retirement, has been re-touched. There is evidence to suggest that the photograph was taken at Brighton.

28.   RG, p.52; WG, p.270.

----oooO0ooo----

APPENDIX 1

THE COURT AND THE GAME

THE COURT

The game of tennis is played in a court of two halves, the service side and the hazard side. The *service* side is so called as it is the only side from which a ball can be served to start play. The *hazard* side derives its name from the various hazards that players have to contend with in that half of the court.

This appendix will only deal with the dedans courts as they now dominate the game – the difference between *dedans* and *quarré* courts is described in Chapter 2. A dedans court has penthouses (sloping roofs) with openings beneath, around three of its walls (see the plan of the court).

The penthouse that runs along the back wall on the service side, the 'dedans penthouse', has one huge opening underneath known as the *dedans* – behind this is a viewing area. Any ball played ('forced') into the dedans wins a point. Running along the rear wall on the hazard side is the 'grille penthouse' which has a small opening known as the *grille*, about three feet square, located in the upper right-hand corner as seen from the service side. As with the dedans, any ball entering the grille wins the point.

The two side walls also have their own unique features. The *service wall*, that on the left as viewed from the dedans, has another penthouse running along its entire length, with a series of galleries underneath. Counting from the service end, they are known as: the *last gallery*, the *second gallery, the door* and the *first gallery*. Then comes the players' entrance to the court, with the net post central to it. The area between the first gallery and the net post is known as *the line*. (Centuries ago, the players entered each half of the court through a door positioned between the first and second galleries. The only two surviving courts with that arrangement are those at Falkland Palace and Fontainebleau.) The galleries are repeated on the hazard side and are referred to as *hazard galleries*. Any ball struck from the service side that enters the end gallery on the hazard side (the *winning gallery*) wins the point outright. Balls played into all other galleries either set a *chase* or determine the outcome of a chase being played off, when struck from the opposite side of the court. The chase (a point played twice) is a complex feature of the game and is fully explained in Appendix 2.

Opposite the service wall is the *main wall*, the end section of which on the hazard side is thicker. This projection is called the *tambour* and has a vertical bevelled edge that deflects balls hit from the service side at awkward angles across the court. The tambour is one of the 'hazards', along with the grille and the winning gallery, which gives this end of the court its name.

On the floor, there is a series of lines known as *chase lines*. These help pinpoint the position of chases. At the service end they are set out at one-yard intervals from the back (dedans) wall for the first six yards and normally have half-yard subdivisions. (In France this area is marked out in French feet.) After the six-yard line, they become designated gallery lines – the 'last gallery', 'second gallery', 'the door' and the 'first gallery'. In addition there is a line one yard past the last gallery, this is a *yard worse than the last gallery*. On the hazard side there are fewer chase lines because this side is divided into

PLAN OF A TENNIS COURT

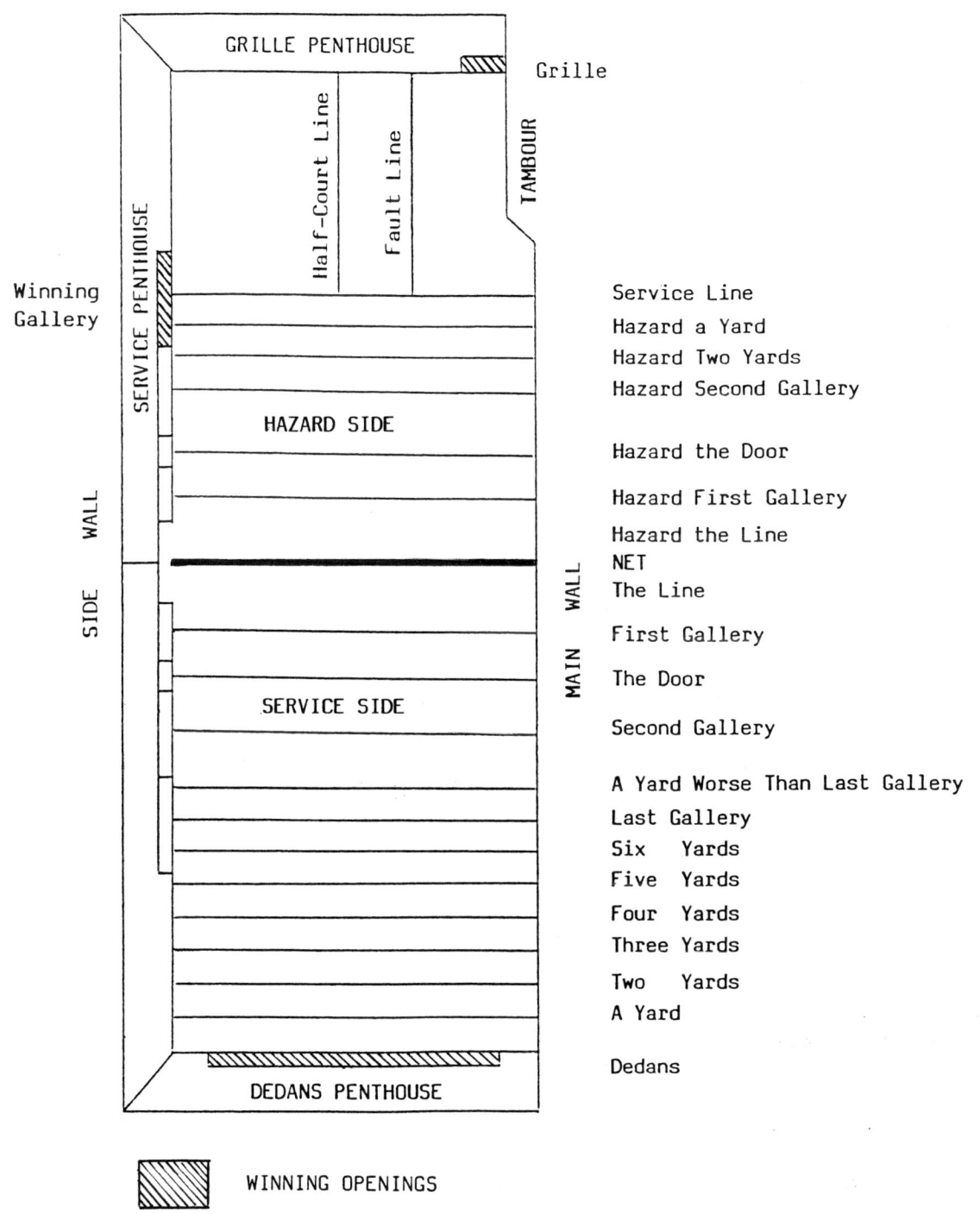

WINNING OPENINGS

two sections by the *service line* (the line across the court centred on the winning gallery). Moving towards the net from the service line the chase lines are 'hazard a yard', 'hazard two yards', 'hazard second gallery', 'hazard the door' and 'hazard first gallery'.

The floor behind the service line on the hazard side is further subdivided by the *fault line* and this defines the *service court*. For a service to be 'good', the ball must bounce at least once on the *service penthouse* (the section of the side penthouse on the hazard side) and must drop into the area bounded by the service line and the fault line. There is also a *half-court line*, parallel to the fault line, but this is only used in doubles play.

At a height of about 18 feet at the top of the side walls (higher on the end walls), there is the *play line* — a ball touching the play line or any part of the court above, including the roof, is 'out of court'.

There are however, exceptions to these generalisations and these are covered by local rules at the courts concerned. Although nearly all courts have roofs these days, they are not a requirement.

THE GAME

To win a match one must win a majority of *sets* played. There are usually three sets, five for major championships and thirteen (played over three days) for the World Championship. Ladies World Championship rules differ; these are referred to in the main text. The first player to win six *games* takes the set. (Although six-game sets are the norm, internal club competitions often vary the number for expediency, and eight-game sets were common in yesteryear.)

Each game consists of a series of *points*. A game is won by a player who has gained a minimum of four points, and who is ahead by two. The points are scored '15', '30', '40' and 'game'. Should both players reach 40, *deuce* is called, the next point being *advantage*: play then continues until one of the competitors wins a point whilst at advantage, thereby gaining the necessary two clear points. This part of the scoring system has been carried through to the modern game of Lawn Tennis.

A point is won (or lost) in a number of ways. Play starts with the server standing anywhere between the dedans and the second gallery floor line. If the service is 'good' and not returned, the server gains the point. If it is returned, a *rest* (rally) ensues. During a rest, a point is lost when the ball is struck into the net or out of court, or if one is unable to return a ball that has fallen (on second bounce) beyond the service line at the hazard end. The receiver gains the point in the event of a double service fault. A point can also be won by striking the ball into a winning opening (the dedans, grille or winning gallery), or by winning a *chase*.

As players only change ends after a chase has been laid, it is always the player who won the previous point whose score is called first. Thus the score will be called   '15-love' whichever player wins the first point in a game.

In doubles play additional rules regarding the service apply. At the start of each set the serving pair decide who is to serve first; the receiving pair then decide which of them will receive first. The designated receiver's partner is allowed to return the serve only if the ball drops (on first bounce) in the strip between the half-court line and the fault line.

----ooo00ooo----

APPENDIX 2

THE CHASE

A *chase* is a point held in abeyance until it is resumed at a later stage in the game. A chase is made when, without being hit by the player, the ball falls on the floor for a second bounce — even if it has hit a side or end wall, or a penthouse, first. A chase can also be set by striking the ball into any side gallery, except the winning gallery (the last gallery on the hazard side). The floor line pertaining to the gallery the ball entered, marks gallery chases.

When a chase is laid the score does not immediately change. If the players are at, or when they reach, *game point* (i.e. 40-love, 40-15, 40-30, or advantage), they change ends and continue to play the point. The player who originally set the chase — and is now 'defending' the chase — will generally win the point unless his opponent can cause the ball to fall (on its second bounce) behind the marked chase, that is, closer to the back wall. Alternatively either player can win a chase by striking the ball into a winning opening (dedans, grille or winning gallery), or by forcing an error. If a ball falls on, or enters the same gallery as the marked chase, then 'chase off' is called, the score does not change, and the game continues. The galleries also can be used to determine the outcome of playing off chases. A ball hit into any side gallery will win the point if a chase is being defended on the side of the court from which the ball was struck, or the gallery into which the ball is played has its floor line closer to the back wall than the chase being defended.

If a second chase is laid before game point is reached the players change ends immediately. The two chases are then played off in the order in which they were laid. The laying of chases is the only way players can change ends; therefore it is good tactics for the receiver to lay a chase as soon as an opportunity arises, as it is generally disadvantageous to be playing on the hazard side of the court. The receiver will then have the comfort of knowing that he or she will, at least, have the opportunity to serve before the end of that game. Great skill is needed when laying and playing off chases, particularly those on the service side — the closer the receiver can lay a chase to the back wall, the harder it will be for the opponent to beat it. Care also has to be taken with the serve when a chase is being played off. As mentioned above, balls can be struck into the side galleries to beat certain chases. Therefore balls veering off the service penthouse, or the grille wall, into the centre of the court, make that task easier for the receiver.

In the courts of today one sees a series of chase lines on the floor; these allow the chases to be recorded accurately. Prior to the eighteenth century, chases were marked using either a chalk mark, or by the placing of an object at the edge of the court floor. Earlier still they were marked at the point where the ball stopped rolling, or where a stopper had stopped it — someone specially employed for the purpose. When the game was played in the streets, chases were set when balls entered windows or doorways.

When marking chases, the terms *better than* or *worse than* are used to describe chases laid by balls that do not fall exactly on a floor line. *Better* denotes chases on the back wall side of the floor line, and *worse* those on the net side. Chases exactly halfway between the yard lines are marked by referring to both distances, e.g. a chase 2½ yards from the back wall is called '2 and 3'. Chases close to the net are called *chase the line*.

Chases seriously complicate the scoring and, with the practice of calling the score of the player winning the previous point first, the game can be difficult to follow for those new to it. The 'laying' and 'playing off' of chases requires a high level of concentration and a modicum of cunning — they are, though, one of the components that make this fascinating game such a delight to play.

----ooo00Oooo----

APPENDIX 3

WOLSEY'S OPEN TENNIS PLAY

Set out below is a series of references to Cardinal Wolsey's Open Tennis Play that appear in the Chapter House Account Books and the Exchequer and Audit Office Annual Account Pipe Rolls.

The Chapter House Accounts are held at the Public Records Office under the references E36/235 to E36/245. They are not bound in chronological order and many of the accounts are duplicated in other volumes. Where entries were copied it was usually by a different scribe; the form of wording often differs, as does the spelling. Typed transcripts were produced by M. Biddle for *The History of the King's Works* and these are held by English Heritage.

The declared Annual Accounts of the Exchequer and Audit Office were produced on single sheets of parchment, about three feet by two feet, bound together and rolled up as a Pipe Roll and tied with ribbon.

Costs and quantities in the original accounts are shown in Roman numerals. Matters are further complicated in that mediaeval methods of recording the numerals were still being used. Therefore for ease of interpretation figures are shown throughout these appendices in the Arabic form used today.

Amounts of money were pre-decimal, when twelve pence made one shilling and there were twenty shillings to the pound.

Apr 1529	Freemasons wourking aswill in Caen and in Reigate uppon Doris, Wyndoes, and Stoncyons to be sett in all suche lodgyngs as the Kings grace hathe apoynted. That is to sey for 2 chambres whiche shallbe next the tenys playe. (E36/239, p.5)
	Carpenters — framyng of a flower of oon of the Chambers next the tenys playe. (E36/239, p.18)
	To John van Guylders Smyth of the weke for a payre of stoon hokes servng the newe lodging next the tenys play. (E36/239, p.29)
May 1529	Freemasons wourking uppon all suche dorys, wyndoews and stouncyons for the newe lodgings besyedes the tenys playe. (E36/239, p.34)
	Carpenters lyke wourking uppon all suche flowers and Rouffe for the seid lodginges besyedes the Tenys play. (E36/239, p.34)
	Bricklayers wourking uppon the newe lodgings besydes the Tenys playe wth others. (E36/239, p.35)
Jun 1529	To John van guylders smythe for 4 stayebarris, 8 locketts, 16 standardes waying ten score 12 li whiche are bestoed in the newe lodginges besyde the tenys play. 26s. 6d. (E36/239, p.76)

Jul 1529   Tylers covryng the newe lodgings on the tenys playe.
(E36/239, p.117)

Aug 1529   Plommers wourking on pipes for the conveyaunce of water from and of the newe lodginges over the tenys playe. (E36/239, p.146)

Casting of leade. Thomas Acon employed uppon the gutters over the tenys playe. (E36/239, p.152)

Payd to John van guylders for 6 payre of tynnd henges servyng for 6 doris bytwyn the tennys playe and the galerie. (E36/239, p.163)

Sep 1529   Dieu to John van guylders smyth for 8 doble cases w[t] handylls servyng in the wyndoews of the newe lodging besydes the tennys playe. (E36/239, p.174)

Joyners wourking setting up newe batens for garnysshing the Rouffes of the newe llodgings besides the tennys play. (E36/239, p.182)

Mar 1530   Garnisshyng the newe Rouffes of the Kings Chambr next the tennys playe. (E36/237, p.406)

Aug 1530   Garnisshing of the Kings Chambrs as folowethe fyrst the uttermost chamber next the tennys playe in battons of antyqe wourke sett in waynysott. (E36/237, p.483)

Oct 1531   Payd to Galion the Kynges Glazier for 12 fotes of new glas sett in the tennys play a 5d the fote. 5s. (E36/241, p.409)

Mar 1533   Payd to John A guylders smith for a key for the store hows dore besyde the old tennys play. (E36/237, p.85)

Apr 1533   Also payd to John A guylders Smyth for a stapull servyng for a ston dore in the old Tennys play. 2d. (E36/237, p.105)

Jul 1533   Also payd to John A guylders Smyth for a standard and a lokett serving for a window in the vice of the new galary between the Kynges new Tennys play and the olde tennys play. (E36/237, p.170)

Nov 1533   Payd to John A Guylders Smyth for 3 payre of henge tynned wth revettes servyng the same 2 payr servyng the dubbyll dore at the stayre fote at the Est Ende of the new galary betwyxte the tennys playes the other servyng the utter dore goyng into the garden at the west Ende of the same galary. 6s. 8d. (E36/237, p.272)

Jan 1534   Also payd to John a Guylders Smyth for 6 Casements servyng the Syde of the new galary next unto the bowlyng allee betwyxt the tennys playes att 3s. 4d. the pece. 20s. (E36/242, p.8)

May 1534   Also payd to John aguylders Smythe for 6 shorte standards servyng above the casementes uppon the northe syde of new galary betwyxe bothe the tennis playes. 3s. (E36/242, p.95)

Oct 1534   Also payd to Ric^d Welche of London payntr and gylder for gyldyng and payntyng of 4 vanys servyng for the north syde of the new galary betwyxte the tenys plays at 16d. the pece. 5s. 4d. (E36/242, p.262)

Apr 1537   Payd to John Johnson of the weke for 71 sodlettes servyng the chamber wyndowes belongyng unto the open tennys play. 8s. 10d. (E36/243, p.607; E36/236, p.527, Ironwork Account)

1576-78   Paving wth paving tyles the Tennys Courte and sundry galleries. (AO/1/2412/8; E351/3212)

1596-97   Mendinge the stone windowes in the little Tenes Courte. (AO/1/2415/27; A351/3231)

1602-03   Takeinge downe and newe alteringe the Tennys Courte. (AO/1/2417/35; E351/3238)

1625-26   Ripping and taking downe the bourded walles round about the Tennis courte. (AO/1/2424/56; E351/3259)

The last reference then goes on to describe the building of a new brick open court — see Appendix 5.

----ooo00ooo----

HENRY VIII's CLOSE TENNIS PLAY

Listed below is a selection of entries from the Chapter House Accounts, which deal with the construction of Henry VIII's Close Tennis Play, and latterly, the Exchequer and Audit Office Annual Accounts Pipe Rolls and the Account Books of the Office of the King's Works, which give details of repairs to the same Court.

Oct 1532	Payd to John A Guylders for 4 payre of ston hookes serving for the new Tennys play. 4s. (E36/241, p.633)
Nov 1532	Payd to John Budd of Chesilhurst for 4000 and a hundrithe pavyng Tiles for the Close Tennys play at hampton Courte of hym bought and delyverd at Hampton Courte at 16s the 1000 by Convencion. 65s. 7d. (E36/241, p.650)
Mar 1533	Payd to John A Guylders Smyth for 2 staybarres 12 standards and 9 locketts for the Closes Tennys play. (E36/237, p.62)
	Payd to John A Guylders for 9 lokkettes serving for the lodgynge with in the new Tennys play. (E36/237, p.63)
	Itm for 3 staybarres serving for the upper transome in the same lodgynges. (E36/237, p.63)
Apr 1533	Also payd to Ric^d bracy John maybanke and Cristfor style for dikgyng of a new foundacion in the new galary betwix the tennys plays. (E36/237, p.86)
	Also payd to John beryman Henry Williams and Lionel bronell for workyng in their howre tymes and drynkyng tymes uppon the new tennys play. (E36/237, p.86)
May 1533	Payd to John a Guylders for 64 standards for wyndows in the new Galarie betwix the new tennys play and the olde tennys play. (E36/237, p.124)
	Wyre drawers for the wyndows of the new tennys play. William heyton paid 16d. the day. (Five others are listed at 8d. the day.) (E36/237, p.117)
	Playsterers workyng uppon the new tennys play for the hasty Expedycion of the same. (Six names and payments listed at 7d. the day.) (E36/237, p.127)
	Gagers to the said playsteres. (Seven names and payments listed at 5d. the day.) (E36/237, p.127)

Jun 1533   Also payd to John A Guylders Smyth for 100 leade nayle servyng for the pipes about the new Tennys play. (E36/237, p.146)

Itm for 251 sodeletts for the wyndows of the new tennys play. 101s. 6d. (E36/237, p.146)

Also payd to John Wilkenson plaisterer of London for 4 potts to carry the colers in for to lay over the barres of the new tennys play at the wire gratid of the same tennys play. (E36/237, p.148)

Jul 1533   Also payd to Thomas Acon the Kynges sergeunt plumm for castyng and laying of leade 4 fother 1700 di at lyke pryce layd upon the Gutters of the Kynges new tennys play and the new galary. (E36/237, p.169)

Also payd to Henry blankston of london paynter for 9 dosyn 3lb Redde leade at 18d the dosyn for to Coller the barres and wyers of the wyndows of the tennis play. (E36/237, p.172)

Aug 1533   Also payd to Robt mannyng for a lb of verdegrese servyng to painte Chymnes in the Chambers at the Ende of the Close tennys play. (E36/237, p.194)

Also payd to John wylkynson for 200 Redde ocker for pensellyng of the new tennys play and the new galary at 20d the 100. 3s. 4d. (E36/237, p.194)

Also payd to John A guylders smyth for 4 irne pynnys servyng for the ston typis at the gabull Ende of the of the new tennys play and the new galary. (E36/237, p.195)

Itm to the same for a vayn servyng for the ston type in the gabull Ende of the close tennys play. (E36/237, p.195)

Sep 1533   Payd to John a Guylders Smyth for 3 payre of ston henges Tynnyd one payre for the dore in the myddes of the tennys play and 2 payre servyng the nether lodgyng to the same play. (E36/237, p.245)

Oct 1533   Stone Reddy wrought and delyvdyd at baryngton quarry. (E36/237, p.268)

Also payd to William Johnson Freemason for 500 fote of corbell tabyll servyng the new hall, tennys play wyth lodgeyng adionyng to the same. (E36/237, p.268)

Also payd to same Willm for 180 fote of vente and Creest for the new tenys play at 8d. the fote. £6 (E36/237, p.268)

Nov 1533	Also payd to Galyon Hone the Kynges glasier for 11 wyndows of newe glasse sett in te newe tennys play Every wyndow of 3 lyhgts the myddyl lyght conteying 39 fotes pryce the fote 5d. and Every side lyght cont 36½ fotes di at 5d. the fote whiche dothe amont to 112 fotes in Every wyndow amountes in all 1232 fotes In the lesser wyndow ye 3 lyghtes cont 50 fote di whiche amountes in all 1282 fote di at 5d. the fote. £26 14s. 4d. (E36/237, p.302)
	Itm in the over lodgeyng adioynyng to the said tennys play ye 3 armes of the Kynge and the quenys pryce the pere 4s. 12s. (E36/237, p.302)
	Empcion of Bristills to pensill the walls of the new tennys play — servyng for the Briklayers to pensell the walls. (E36/238, p.496)
Apr 1534	Also payd to Henry blankston for payntyng and gyldyng of the vane uppon the type of the tennys play the Kynges armes wrought w^t fyne golde in oyle. 4s. (E36/242, p.98)
Jan 1535	Also payd to John yerlye of kyngston for a 100 of playnche bowrdde sesnyd — servyng for the close play dorys of hym bowght and delyvryd at kyngston. (E36/243, p.20)
Feb 1535	Also payd to Nycholas Homys of Rychemonde for mattyng the galary betwyxt bothe tennys playes wyth the lodgeyng adyoyng to the Close play. (E36/243, p.39)
	To John Van for 4 payre of henges and 4 payre hookes servyng 4 dorys wyth in the closse tennys playe. (E36/243, p.63)
Mar 1535	Carpenters Workyng In makyng the hasserds in the close tennys play a gaynst the kyngs comyng. (E36/243, p.77)
	5 men are listed — Carpenters at 8d the day Ratyd after Every 9 owrs 8d. 10 more listed — Nett carpenters at 7d the day Ratyd af^ter every 9 owrs 7d.
Nov 1535	Payd to John Van Smyth for 2 payre of ston henges tynnyd servyng for 2 dorys in the south side of the Close tennys play. (E36/240, p.86)
	Itm to the same for vernysshyng and tynnyng wth makyng of new wardds for oon of the kyngs locks servyng the dore at the stayre foot by the chappell goyng in to the close tennys play. (E36/240, p.89)
Jun 1537	To John Johnson for 10 mattokkes stelyd servyng to breke the grownde jn takyng the fondacion of the gallary goyng out of the quenys lodgyng to the close tennes play. (E36/236, p. 531; E36/244, p.229)
Jul 1537	Also payd to Rychard Rydgedale of the weke tanner for gatheryng of 122 lode of pybbylles in Epsom Comon for the pavynge of the lyttyll cowrtt betwyxte the quenys lowng gallary and the Close Tennys play at 1d.the lode gatheryng by convencenjon. 10s. 2d. (E36/244, p.405)
1592-93	Newe pavinge pte of the Tenes Courte. (AO/1/2415/22; E351/3227)

1596-97 — Tilinge on the Tenes Courte in maine places where the nede was. (AO/1/2416/27; E351/3231)

1602-03 — Mending ye frame of a dorecase gonnge to ye Tennys Courte. (AO/1/2417/35; E351/3238)

1606-07 — Paveinge the Tennys Courte wth pavinge tyles. (AO/1/2419/39; E351/3242)

1614-15 — Tyling the Tennys Courte roofe. (AO/1/2421/45; E351/3249)

1621-22 — Wirewoorke 495 foote for the Chappell windows and Tennis courte att 6d. the foote. £12 7s. 6d. (AO/1/2423/52; E351/3255)

1624-25 — To John Decreete Sergeannte Painter for priming stopping and painting of lead rofes in oyle the Cornishes of three Turretts at the end of the hall and Tenniscourte. (AO/1/2424/55; E351/3258)

May 1662 — Carpenters — settinge upp a shedd under the wale of the Ould Tennis Courte 15: foote square; and ioistinge; and bourdeinge itt in the bottoms for dineinge roome for the Maids of Honno^r; to the Duchesse of Yorke. (Work 5/3, f.332v)

Nov 1663 — Bricklayers imployed — mending a Butterice at the Old Tenis Court. (Work 5/4, f.303r)

Nov 1665 — Carpenters — making 2 troughs 15 foot long apiece, and putting them up through the Roofe of the Old tennis Court and making a Door and Doorcase there. (Work 5/7, f.154)

Feb 1666 — Carpenters — making 5 partsions wth slitt deale ---------- the old Tennis Court being 11 squ^r: and making 6 new Doors and doorcases and boarding up the windowes there. (Work 5/7, f.174)

Nov 1667 — Masons imployed — taking downe all the upright barrs of ye windows of ye Old Tennis Courte. (Work 5/10, f.275)

Feb 1669 — The Accounts of the conversion of the Henry VIII Closed Court into lodgings for the Duke of York.

Labourers imployed in helping in with ye timber boards and poles to ye tennis court and helping to make ye Scaffolds there and takeing up ye paveing tiles and takeing downe ye partitions of boards and pulling downe ye penthouse there. (Work 5/13, f.411r. Extraordinary Account)

There follows an enormous amount of detail of the reconstruction and supply of material, none of which is relevant to tennis.

1674 — Second Book for His Royal Highness (Duke's Building at Hampton Court).

These are the final accounts for the completion of the conversion of the Henrican Close Court. (Work 5/23, Extraordinary Account).

APPENDIX 5

CHARLES I's TENNIS COURT

A few sparse references are preserved in the Declared Annual Account Pipe Rolls of the Exchequer and Audit Office during the reign of Charles I; they are set out below. At first the Court was open, but in 1636-37 a roof was put on.

1625-26   Ripping and taking downe the bourded walles round about the Tennis courte, and bringing upp a brickewall there for the inlargement of the same squareing, and woorkeing of blackstone for the hazard of the Tennis courte and setting of a stone in the middle of the sayd courte and yoltinge of an jron hooke into it for to hould the lyne there. (AO/1/2424/56; E351/3259)

1627-28   To John Howell Stone Sawyer for sawinge of a stone for the hazarde of the Tenis Courte. 4s. (E351/3261)

1636-37   William Hancke and Thomas Oreake Masons for working and setting the archt doore in the outlett of the Teniscourte and fitting twoe windowes there and one windowe by the Teniscourte doore cont 96 foo: twoe inches at 12d. the foo. £4 16s. 2d. (E351/3270)

                James Carver turning twoe Piramides. 4s. 6d. (E351/3270)

                James Bayes for woorkeing and setting upp the firste Pyramides and taking them downe againe from the top of Teniscourte with other Carpentrywoorke. 63s. (E531/3270)

                Wm Dodson for paving with Bricke a passage from the old bouling alley to the Teniscourte yard and for digging a vault and bringing upp with Brickes and arching it over one bricke in thicknes and for other Bricklayers woorke. £11 9s. (E351/3270)

1637-38   To Wm Symons Labourer for finishing a Causeway from the newe Teniscourt. (E351/3271)

----ooo00ooo----

REFURBISHMENT WORKS BY CHARLES II

The entries below are taken from the Account Books of the Office of the King's Works, Audit Office Pipe Rolls and the Record Books of the Lord Chamberlain's Office. These extracts contain details of the refurbishment of the Stuart Court by Charles II in 1660-61.

Oct 1660	To Nicholas Batch: for land car (carriage) of: For 9 lo: of paveing tiles from the wharfe to the Tennis Courte att 12d. the lo: For car of 3 loads of sands from the wharfe to yᵉ Tennis courte att 12d. the lo: (Work 5/1, f.389r) To Long — for 1000 of foote square paveing tiles at 32s. 6d. p 100. £16 5s. and for money laid out for sands and his Charges for workemen to make choice of the tiles. 75s. (Work 5/1, f.389v)
Nov 1660	Carpenters imployed in makeing of duble scaffold all the length of the tennis courte on that side next to the parke. (Work 5/1, f.393r) Bricklayers imployed — workeing upp wᵗʰ brick part of the brickwale belonging to the tennis court on the parke side; and underpinninge all the plateing after the Carpenters; hewinge; squareinge; scimontinge; and peecinge of paveinge tiles for the tennis Courte. (Work 5/1, f.393v) Labourers imployed helping the Carpenters to draw upp their timbers att the tennis courte. (Work 5/1, f.395r) To Simon Basill — for car of 1000 of foote square paveing tiles being: 9 loads from the wharfe round to the Tennis Courte att 10d. yᵉ load. 7s. 6d. (Work 5/1, f.397r) To Izak Corner bricklayer for his taske of bricklayers worke in tileing of the New Tennis Court. £63 12s. 11d. (Work 5/1, f.398v; AO/1/2433/85)
Dec 1660	Masons imployed in squaring; workeinge; and fittinge of stones to make the damboes (tambour) in the Tennis courte: Saweinge parte of the black marble for the line cross the Courte. John Ashlee — 17 daies £2 2s. 6d. William Fitch — 17 daies £2 2s. 6d. (Work 5/1, f.399r; Harl.1656, f.216) Bricklayers imployed in; tileing the Long Gallerie goeing out of the privie Lodgeings to the new tennis Courte; on that side next the parke; wourkeinge upp wᵗʰ bricks; pte of the new Tennis Courte walle, and underpinninge all the plateing after yᵉ Carpenters on that side next the garden, heuinge; rubbing, squareinge, peeceinge, and scimontinge of tiles for to pave the Tennis Courte. (Work 5/1, f.400v; Harl.1656, f.217)

Jan 1661   Bricklayers imployed in; Lathing; and tileing of the Tennis Courte Keeps house; att the further end of the Tennis courte next the high wall; and mendinge the ranges in the kitching; makeinge of a new boyling place there: Reynold West — 14 daies £1 6s. 7d. Nicholas West — 15 daies £1 10s. 3d. (Work 5/1, f.405v; Harl.1656, f.222)

Feb 1661   Masons — squareing, and wourkeinge of free stone for the tumboes belonginge to the Tennis Co^{rt}. Moyses Bramton 9 daies £1 2s. 6d. Giles Fines 6½ daies 16s. 3d. (Work 5/1, f.408r; Harl.1656, f.224)

Carpenters — takinge downe the gallery att the Tennis Co^{rt}. and the roofe of the end gallerie where the hazard is; plaininge all the timbers; and settinge them upp againe; makeing a ------ Doorecase there; plaininge, and shootinge of bourds, new rafteringe one of the end galleries.
(Work 5/1, f.408r; Harl.1656, f.224)

Bricklayers — takinge downe all the brickwale of the Gallery in the Tennis Courte; takeing upp some of the paveing tyles out of the Tennis courte; and wourkeinge upp pt of the brick wale againe.
(Work 5/1, f.408v; Harl.1656, f.224)

Mar 1661   Carpenters imployed in plaineinge, and shooteinge, of deale bourds to cover the galleries att the Tennis Co^{rte} over the side gallerie; and both the ends; wourkeing, and frameinge the timbers for the whole frame of the side gallerie, and ends, and settinge itt upp; new ioystinge the roofe of the side galleries, and both ends; bourdeinge the gallerie over head; makeing of frames for the netts to catch the balls.
(Work 5/1, f.411r; Harl.1656, f.228)

Bricklayers — wuorkinge upp the brickeworke of the gallerie att the Tennis Courte; hewinge and squaring of bricks, and mendinge the butterisses att the Tennis Co^{rte}, next the Parke side, cuttinge of a waie for three windows in the brickwales in the little roomes belonginge to the Tennis Co^{rte}. (Work 5/1, f.411v; Harl.1656, f.229)

To John Phillipps Turner for turneing 9 Collumes for the Tennis Courte at 6d. the peece, 4s. 6d; and for turneing fower other Colloumes for that place allsoe att 12d. the peece, 4s. In all.
(Work 5/1, f.414r; Harl.1656, f.231; AO/1/2433/85)

To John Miles Smith for 18 great thimbles for the Curtaine rodds for ye tennis Co^{rt}, for mendinge, peeceing; and alteringe of 5 great Curtaine rodds there. 3s. 4d. (Work 5/1, f.414r)

Mar 1661
To Simon Basill — for takeing of some deale timber to the turners in the wicke by kingston to turne into Colloumes; and for taking them back againe: 2s. (Work 5/1, f.414v; Harl.1656, f.232)

A Warrant to pay unto Robert Long Master of his Maties: long Paulines for his Expences and attendance in supervising the Workmen in his Maties Tennis Court at Hampton Court after the rate of five shillings by the day. (LC5/137, p.106)

Apr 1661
Plaisterers imployed in burninge of plaister of parris; and laieinge of a great pte of the walles of the Tennis Co^rt therew^th. (Work 5/2, f.253r; Harl.1656, f.236)

May 1661
Masons: imployed in takeing downe the indan (dedan) att the Tennis Courte; and for setting itt upp againe; hueinge, squareinge, and wourkeinge of freestone to finish itt; wourkeinge black marble for the line to goe cross the tennis Co^rt: makeinge new the Grill by the Tamboe. (Work 5/2, f.257r)

Carpenters — takeinge upp: 200: foote of ioysts and planck from topp of the wale on both sides the Tennis Co^rt: takeinge upp; the floore of a small roome belonginge to the Tennis courte. (Work 5/2, f.257v; Harl.1656, f.241)

Bricklayers imployed — howeinge, squareinge, peeceinge, scimontinge and pollishing of paveinge tiles. (Work 5/2, f.258r)

To John Miles — Smith (Work 5/2, f.261v)
For 26: great iron thimbles for ye courtaine rodds in ye tennis Co^rt. £1 8s. 8d:
For 4: great long courtaine rodds for ye tennis Courte. £1 8s. 0d.

Jun 1661
Masons: imployed in finishinge the stonewourk of the indan att the Tennis Co^rt; — cuttinge the stone of the wale in the Tennis Courte and yoteinge in the iron to hould the line that goes crosse the Tennis Co^rt. (Work 5/2, f.263r)

Carpenters imployed — puttinge upp of bourds on the topp of the wale on both sides the Tennis Co^rt: to keepe in the balles cout: 223: fo: long: putting upp of poles att each end of the Tennis Co^rt; to carrey the blackcloth; setting up 22: bourds; att the fower Corners of the Tennis Co^rt; to hould in the balles; and settinge upp bourds in the galleries and the indan to leane on: 90: fo: in length, makeinge two coubourds to laie racketts, and balles in. (Work 5/2, f.263r)

Jul 1661
Carpenters imployed in putting up of boards like deskes upon ye walls of ye upper galleries at both ends of ye Teniscourt and making a grill by ye Tambor there. and making a doore for the Judan; making window in a little roome at ye end of ye Teniscourt. (Work 5/2, f.269r)

Jul 1661   Plaisterers imployed in blacking of ye Teniscourt twice over, and redding the nett that goes cross ye Court. Making of ye Marks and Figures in the Court, lathing and plastering the Judan and the blacking of it containing 32 yards. Plastering with plaster of Paris upon ye walls by the plates on both sides of the teniscourt cont. 67 yards. (Work 5/2, f.271r)

Aug 1661   These are to signify unto you his Maties pleasure that you forthth cause to bee covered wth Crimson velvet & garnished wth gilt nails A long remooving Seate about six or seaven foote in the Tennis Court at Hampton Court. A long Cushion and a foote cushion of Crimson velvet a small turkey worke Carpett as Robert Long his Maties Marker shall direct. (LC5/60, p.211; LC5/137, p.34)

Another identical dedans cushion was ordered under a similar warrant dated 19th March 1661. (LC5/60, p.126)

----ooo00Oooo----

RENOVATION OF THE STUART COURT BY WILLIAM III

Listed below are a selection of entries from the Account Books of the Office of the King's Works and the Record Books of the Lord Chamberlain's Office. They cover the renovation of the Stuart Court carried out by William lll between August 1699 and March 1702 under the direction of Sir Christopher Wren.

Aug 1699	Carpenters Imployed in helping to pull down the roofe of the Portico by the Tennis Court. (Work 5/50, f.273r)
Sep 1699	To Robert Webb: For Pulling down the Portico and 3 Buttresses belonging to the Tennis Court, clearing out the stones and Bricks, laying them up in heapes and Basketting out the Rubbish. £3 14s. 0d. (Work 5/50, f.279r)
Mar 1700	For 452ft: of Boarding with whole deale plained on both sides for to save the balls att 3d. ft. £5 13s. 0d. (Work 5/50, f.315v)
	For 949ft of firr plained and sett up in severall posts to fasten their netts to att 2½d. ft. £9 17s. 8d. (Work 5/50, f.315v)
	For 202ft of slitt deale lining for the plasterer to finish too att 3d. ft. £2 10s. 6d. (Work 5/50, f.315v)
	For 50ft of weather Boarding. 7s. 0d. (Work 5/50, f.315v)
	For 3 whole Deale Doors att 3s. each. 9s. 0d. (Work 5/50, f.315v)
	To Stephen South: For 8 load of Boards from the store yard to the tennis Court att 14d. the load. 9s. 4d. (Work 5/50, f.317r)
	Labourers imployed in taking up the tiles in the tennis Court. (Work 5/50, f.317v)
Apr 1700	Masons imployed in squareing and laying of 10ft of water table att the Tennis Court. (Work 5/51, f.284r)
	Bricklayers imployed in paving the passage under the Whispering Gallery. (Work 5/51, f.284r)
	To Stephen South: For 20 tun ½ of Ketton Stone from the waterside to the tennis Court. £2 11s. 0d. (Work 5/51, f.291r)
	For digging 13yds ½ of foundations for the new wall att the tennis Court and other places att 4d. yd. 4s. 6d. (Work 5/51, f.291r)
	To Thomas Hill Mason — for 1997ft of Ketton stone squared and laid in Courses att the Tennis Court att 14d. the ft. as by agreement. £116 9s. 10d. (Work 5/51, f.292r)

May 1700	WARRANT — from the Lord Chamberlain, Lord Shrewsbury, to the Master of the Great Wardrobe, the Earl of Montague.

These are to signify his Maties Pleasure, that you. Provide and deliver to Horatio Moor Esqr. Master of his Majesties Tennis Courts, Canvas Curtains, and Netts, four Yards deep, & to reach forty Yards in length, wth Curtain Rings and Staples, necessary for his Majesties Tennis Court att Hampton Court. And a line and a Nett to reach across ye middle of ye Court. (LC5/152, p.283; LC5/70, p.51)

Carpenters imployed — in boreing a hole through the Brick wall att the tennis Court. (Work 5/51, f.301r)

May 1700	To Thomas Hill — mason — for squareing, working, and setting 1070ft of Ketton stone in the tennis court laid in courses. £62 8s. 4d. (Work 5/51, f.302v)

For 42ft runing of black marble (list) 2in broad cross the tennis court. £2   2s. 0d. (Work 5/51, f.302v)

For 22ft 4" of old black marble (list) new squared and rubbed there. 11s. 0d. (Work 5/51, f.302v)

To John Grove — Master Carpenter — for 124yds ⅓ of lathing and plastering of the inside covering with oak lathe and the inside top walls of the tennis court. £10 7s. 2½d. (Work 5/51, f.303v)

For 1210yds ⅔ of ------- washing, stopping and pointing with plaster of paris the plastered walls of the tennis court and the stone ashler 8ft high and whiteing and blacking the same at ------- and scaffoling the same. £50 8s. 10½d. (Work 5/51, f.303v)

Jun 1700	To Josiah Key — smith — for 2 round rods 24ft long to fasten into the wyrer grate to stand before the King in the tennis court. 10s. 0d. (Work 5/51, f.312v)

Feb 1701	Day Bill — For repairing tileing over the Tennis Court. (Work 5/51, f.403v)

A bricklayer and labourer 17 days.	£3 10s. 10d.
An hundred of lime and a load of sand.	12s. 6d.
For 2m of plain tiles.	£2 16s. 0d.

May 1701	To John Grove — Ms Plasterer — for 829yds of cleaning and blacking the walls and mending the same att 6d. yd. £20 14s. 6d. (Work 5/52, f.274v)

To Thomas Hill — mason. In the yard leading to the Tennis Court.

For squareing and laying 1723ft of new Purbeck pavin. £53 16s. 10½d.

For 7ft 6in of new Portland astragall step 15 inches broad. £1 6s. 3d

21/7/1701   Warrant — from the Lord Chamberlain's Office (Lord Jersey) to Sir Christopher Wren

These are to pray and require you to give Orders for ceiling of ye Tennis Court att Hampton Court with Slit deal And this shall be your Warrant. Given under my name this 21st day of July in ye 13th year of His Maties Reign. (LC5/153, p.99)

Sep 1701   Labourers imployed — in carrying slit deals and uffers to make a scaffold in ye tennis court. (Work 5/52, f.336v)

Oct 1701   To James Grove — carpenter — for 53(sq) 02ft of flooring att the foote of the roofe. £26 18s. 2d. (Work 5/52, f.351v)

For 598yds of boarding the ceiling with slitt deale plained and shot. £29 18s. 0d. (Work 5/52, f.351v)

To Stephen South — for 6 load of deals from the barge to the court for the tennis court. 4s. 6d. (Work 5/52, f.357r)

Feb 1702   To John Grove — Ms Plasterer — for 1061yds ½ of brushing, mending, pointing, and blacking the tenniscourt and scaffolding ye same. £46 10s. 9d. (Work 5/52, f.419v)

For 442yds of washing, stopping, whiteing, sizeing and blacking in the gallery to ye tennis court. £3 13s. 9d. (Work 5/52, f.419v)

To Henry Wise — for trees planted by the tennis court. (Work 5/52, f.428r. Garden Account)

12	standard cherries	9s.	0d.
6	peaches	15s.	0d.
16	plums	16s.	0d.
12	pears	12s.	0d.
11	apricots	11s.	0d.
8	dwarf cherrys	4s.	0d.

Mar 1702   To Robert Streeter — Serjt. Painter

For 121yds of flatt colour in several posts and boards.	£4	10s.	9d.
For 10 casements.		5s.	0d.
For 11 window lights on both sides.		5s.	6d.

(Work 5/52, f.463r)

For painting & gilding 3 cyphers and crowns, for the gold used there. £3 10s. 0d.

For painting the wyre and marking the lines.	£1	0s.	0d.
For painting 4 trophys on the peers att 10 shilling each.	£2	0s.	0d.
For japaning a cupboard black with indian figures painted for Mr.Verrio.		5s.	0d.
For varnishing 2 frames black for Mr.Verrio.		5s.	0d.

(Work 5/52, f.467r)

APPENDIX 8

CONVERSION WORKS OF GEORGE I

Listed below are extracts from Treasury, Works and Audit Office records, that deal with the conversion of the Stuart Court into a Drawing Room during the reign of George I.

1718   Warrant from the Lord Chamberlain to the Treasury — 1st April 1718. (T56/18, p.63; Work 6/7, p.54; CTB 1718 p.295)

Tennis Court at Hampton Court to be fitted up for a Drawing room.

Warrant from the Treasury to his Grace the Duke of Montague — 9th May 1718. (T56/18, p.72; LC5/157, p.110; CTB XXXII 22/7/1718)

These are to Signify unto your Grace his Ma.ts pleasure, that you provide and deliver to the Hon.ble Grey Maynard Esqr. Yeoman of his Ma.ts Removing Wardrobe the following pticulars for his Ma.ts Service Vizt a Billiard Table cover'd with fine broad green Cloth & c. green Silk Pocket Netts, Ivory Balls and Round Irons for the said Table placed in the Tennis Court at Hampton Court, with Saile Cloth and making it up for the said Court.

Carpenter Mathew Churthill — for making a Gallery for the Musick in the Tennis Court. (AO/1/2449/152)

To Robert Weatherhelt Plaisterer — for scraping the Black of the Tennis Court and washing stopping and whiting the same. £31 10s. 0d. (AO/1/2449/152)

1720   John Spicer — Carpenter — for repairing some Floors, Doorcases and Partitions in the Tennis Court. (AO/1/2450/154)

Ordered that Mr. Fort be writ to — Ordered a new doore to be made against the Tennis Court & the breach there made good. (Work 4/2, f.13r, 25th May 1720)

----ooo00ooo----

APPENDIX 9

HONORARY OFFICE HOLDERS OF THE CLUB

PATRONS

1903-1910	H.M. King Edward VII
1910-1936	H.M. King George V
1936	H.M. King Edward VIII
1936-1952	H.M. King George VI
1952-	H.M. Queen Elizabeth II

PRESIDENTS

1896-1915	Sir Spencer Ponsonby-Fane
1915-1931	J.J. Freeman
1931-1933	Lord Revelstoke (Cecil Baring)
1934-1973	Lord Revelstoke (Rupert Baring)
1973-1987	P.A. Negretti
1987-1989	H.W. Wollaston
1989-2001	Sir Clifford Chetwood

CHAIRMEN

1973-1980	H.W. Wollaston
1980-1988	R.P.C. Swash
1988-1995	D.G. Steel
1995-2001	B.J. Gibbens
2001-	F.W.R. Stocks

HONORARY SECRETARIES

1896-1913	J.J. Freeman
1913-1934	C.T. Agar
1934-1947	C.B. Gabriel
1947-1973	P.A. Negretti
1973-1977	H.M.H. Glover
1977-1980	A.J. Lloyd-Davies
1980-1986	R.A.G. Moorman
1986-1988	Margaret E. Ruffer
1988-1998	J.P. Edwards
1998-	J.M Yarnall

HONORARY TREASURERS

1844-1887	John A. Lambert
1887-1896	Edward Rutter
1896-1915	J.J. Freeman
1915-1934	C.T. Agar
1934-1947	C.B. Gabriel
1947-1973	P.A. Negretti
1973-1976	J.S. Macnaghten
1976-1980	R.P.C. Swash
1980-1990	A.R.W. Baddeley
1990-	D.G. Best

The Office of Honorary Treasurer is the Club's oldest. In Victorian times the Treasurers undertook the duties that are now carried out by the Honorary Secretaries, therefore effectively running the Club single-handedly. In 1896 the Office of Honorary Secretary was established, but with one minor exception the Treasurers and the Secretaries were one and the same until 1973.

No committee minutes survive prior to 1844 so it has not been possible to ascertain who, if anyone, fulfilled the role of Treasurer before this date.

----ooo00Oooo----

APPENDIX 10

MEMBERS OF THE COMMITTEE OF THE ROYAL TENNIS COURT

No club records prior to 1844 have survived; therefore it has not been possible to identify anyone who served on the Committee between 1818 and 1843. Some of those shown from 1844 might have been committee members earlier. In 1994 the Royal Tennis Court became a Limited Company and consequently committee members became Board Directors.

General John Arthur Lambert	1844-87
General Sir Edward Bowater	1844-60
Capt. James Cuthbert	1844-58
Capt. Charles Corkran	1844-65
Charles V. Bayley	1844-49
Geoffrey Nightingale	1845-48
Major-General Lord Charles Wellesley	1846-50
Lt-Colonel Frances H. Seymour	1847-50
H.J. St. John	1848-56
Vice Admiral Henry Seymour	1848
Capt. J. Davidson	1852
Capt. Robert Lambert	1854-67
Sir Archibald McDonald Bent	1854
General Sir Henry Ponsonby	1859
R. Coe	1859
Capt. W.N. Seymour	1860
Lt-Colonel Arthur Ponsonby	1861
Capt. G.H. Seymour	1861
A.C. Vesey	1863-96
Rev'd. F. Champion de Crespigny	1863-84
C.N. Wilde	1864-66
Lt-Colonel Edward M. Beresford	1867-81
Reverend F.J. Ponsonby	1867-89
Berkeley Paget	1874-1907
Lt-Colonel Seymour Corkran	1874-96
Capt. the Hon. Adolphus Graves	1878
Edward Rutter	1882-1908
A.F. Byas	1883-87
John J. Freeman	1885-1932
Sir Courtney E. Boyle	1887-96
A.D. Chapman	1887-88
A.E. Kennedy	1887-96
Sir Spencer Ponsonby-Fane	1895-1915
W.A. Cockerell	1896-1913
Ernest Law	1896-99 & 1925-27
General Lord W. Seymour	1896-98
Major Lambert	1898-99
Sir Guy Campbell	1910
C.T. Agar	1913-41
Colonel George H. Trollope	1921-27
E. Hicks Beach	1925-32
C. Martineau	1926-34
C.B. Gabriel	1927-47
H.M. Wallbrook	1928-34
Lord Revelstoke (Cecil Baring)	1931-33
Hon. W.G. Brownlow (afterwards Lord Lurgan)	1931-73
Lord Revelstoke (Rupert Baring)	1934-73
Capt. W.R. Berry	1934-42
M.R. Lubbock	1934-42
Ronald Aird	1935-73

Brigadier S.V.P. Weston	1946-69
M.A. Pugh	1946-73
C.S. Crawley	1946-73
P.A. Negretti	1947-73
N.F.H. Railing	1947-73
C.W.E. Cary	1949-73
The Hon. Morys Bruce (afterwards Lord Aberdare	1949-73
Sir Cecil Griffin	1954-61
L.P.R. Roche	1973
C.M. Ker	1973-75
J.S. Macnaghten	1973-76
F.P.V. Barker	1973-79
Sir Ronald Prain	1973-79
D.J. Warburg	1973-79
H.M.H. Glover	1973-81
R.N.D.B. Bruce	1973-81
H.R. Angus	1973-82
H.W. Wollaston	1973-82
M.M. Morton	1973-82
A.J. Lloyd-Davies	1973-83
D.A.L. Camm	1973-83
R.P.C. Swash	1976-88
G.C. Welch	1979-80
R.A.G. Moorman	1979-86
M.M. Gilmore	1979-85
C.J. Ronaldson (co-opted)	1980-
A.R.W. Baddeley	1980-90
B.O. Prowse	1981-87
W.D.N. Vaughan	1981-87
I.T. Grimble	1982-87
R.C. Harris	1982-94
J.R. Mackenzie	1982-91
Y.L.I. Adam	1983-86
B.R. Weatherill	1983-90
Margaret E. Ruffer	1984-87
D.K. Watson*	1986-89 & 2001-
J.P. Edwards*	1986-98
D.G. Steel*	1987-95
H.G. Macintosh*	1987-
Jane E. Vaughan*	1987-96
J.V. Hansford*	1987-95
M.J.W. Banks*	1989-99
A.J.W. Page	1989-93
Maggie R. Henderson-Tew	1990-92
D.G. Best*	1990-
R.H. Oldham	1991-94
D.F. Seelig*	1992-
B.J. Gibbens*	1993-2001

* became Directors of The Royal Tennis Court

289

Board Directors

Dianne E. Ingham	1994-97
P.H. Covell	1994-2000
A. Larkin	1995-97
S.L. Brook	1995-99
Nicki M. Faircloth	1996-2002
J.M. Yarnall	1998-
A.J. Clarke	1998-99
J.H. Clark	1999-
F.W.R. Stocks	1999-
Helen Crossley	2000-
J.G. Ingham	2000-
J.R. Maddison	2000-01
P. J. Linacre	2001-
M.M.G. Bronstein	2002-

Note:

Between 1947 and 1973 the Honorary Secretaries of the Oxford and Cambridge University Clubs, and the Masters-in-Charge of Tennis at Canford School, were *ex-officio* RTC Committee Members. Their names are not listed here as their role was largely advisory and they were never called upon to attend a committee meeting. Some of them were never members of the Royal Tennis Court.

----ooo00Oooo----

WINNERS OF CLUB COMPETITIONS

THE CAMM CUP (The Club Championship - level singles)
(Since 2001 The BARKER CAMM CUP)

1981	A.C. Lovell	1988	J.D. Ward	1995	M.D. Ward
1982	A.C. Lovell	1989	M.J. Happell	1996	S.F.M. Barker
1983	A.C. Lovell	1990	M.J. Happell	1997	M.D. Ward
1984	A.C. Lovell	1991	T.D.J. Warburg	1998	N.J. O'Hagan
1985	J.P. Snow	1992	M.J. Carter	1999	M.D. Ward
1986	A.C. Lovell	1993	A.J.A. Curley	2000	S.F.M. Barker
1987	J.P. Snow	1994	M.D. Ward	2001	S.F.M. Barker
				2002	S.F.M. Barker

THE LATHOM BROWNE CUP (Handicap Singles)

This Cup was originally presented to the Prince's Club Brighton by the Reverend R.C. Lathom Browne for a handicap competition there. The Brighton winners appear first.

1925	Maj. C.D. Aubuz	1929	E.L. Gandar Dower	1934	W.G. MacGregor
1926	S.H. Foot	1930	S.H. Foot	1935	W.G. MacGregor
1927	S.H. Foot	1932	N.B. Manson	1937	St.J.B.V. Harmsworth
1928	Capt. F. Purchas	1933	Capt. F. Purchas	1938	P.A. Negretti

Royal Tennis Court winners

1948	D.J. Warburg	1966	Mrs. R. Deloford	1985	D.B. Wormald
1949	D.J. Warburg	1967	J.C.M. Campbell	1986	D.G. Best
1950	S.M. Robertson	1968	C.B. Lyster	1987	J. Bliss
1951	R.G. Dowell	1969	J.D. Ward	1988	A.R.W. Baddeley
1952	R.B. Hill	1970	I.D.J. Jones	1989	Sheila Macintosh
1953	E.N. Evans	1971	J. Gordon	1990	J.S.P. Gibb
1954	E.N.C. Oliver	1972	Gp. Capt. R.L. Lees	1991	N.J. Geere
1955	P.A.J. Truelove	1973	G.B. Todd	1992	P.R. Squire
1956	H.N.E. Alston	1974	J.C. Hubbard	1993	R.M. Trenowden
1957	N.J. Redmayne	1975/76	A. Osmond-Evans*	1994	T.J. Kendall
1958	A.C.S. Tufton	1977	F.C.R. Robinson	1995	D.C. Ganson
1959	A.C.S. Tufton	1978	D.E. Pearmain	1996	Carolyn Nicholls
1960	E.N. Harris	1979	A.R. Stallard Butcher	1997	J.S. Hepburn
1961	J.H. Lipscombe	1980	W.D.N. Vaughan	1998	P.S. Cobb
1962	R.J. Potter	1981	Carolyn Armstrong Smith	1999	Carolyn Nicholls
1963	P.M. Dagnall	1982	M.D. Seymour	2000	P.M. Wright
1964	C.P.C. Bradshaw	1983	P.W. Eldridge	2001	R. Hird
1965	N.W. Johnstone	1984	Jane Burrage	2002	S.A. Seymour

* Prior to this date winners are shown in the year the competition started; subsequently they are shown in the year it was completed. The 1975/76 winner's name is not engraved on the Cup.

THE SAVAGE TROPHIES   (The Club Level Doubles)

1981 M.R. Evers & R.C. Harris	1991 I. Hird & T.D.J. Warburg
1982 M.R. Evers & R.C. Harris	1992 J.V. Hansford & F.C. Satow
1983 M.R. Evers & R.C. Harris	1993 M.R. Evers & R.C. Harris
1984 D.K. Watson & B.R. Weatherill	1994 J.V. Hansford & F.C. Satow
1985 D.J. Warburg & T.D.J. Warburg	1995 I. Hird & T.D.J. Warburg
1986 D.K. Watson & B.R. Weatherill	1996 S.F.M. Barker & N.J. O'Hagan
1987 A.C. Lovell & H.B. Weatherill	1997 J.V. Hansford & F.C. Satow
1988 J.B. Cook & J.P. Snow	1998 S.F.M. Barker & N.J. O'Hagan
1989 J.B. Cook & J.P. Snow	1999 R.C. Harris & D.K. Watson
1990 I. Hird & T.D.J. Warburg	2000 R.C. Harris & D.K. Watson

THE HARRIS-WATSON TROPHIES   (The Club Level Doubles)

2001 S.F.M. Barker & N.J. O'Hagan
2002 M.C.J. McMurrugh & B.R. Weatherill

THE SEAL SALVER   (Over 50 Handicap Singles — handicapped by age)

1983 D.J. Warburg	1990 W.D.N Vaughan	1997 J.R. Partridge
1984 D.J. Warburg	1991 W.D.N. Vaughan	1998 B.C. Rich
1985 D.J. Warburg	1992 W.D.N. Vaughan	1999 B.C. Rich
1986 E.G. Danby	1993 W.D.N. Vaughan	2000 J.R. Partridge
1987 W.D.N. Vaughan	1994 W.D.N. Vaughan	2001 J.D. Ward
1988 W.D.N. Vaughan	1995 J.A.K. Leslie	2002 J.D. Ward
1989 W.D.N. Vaughan	1996 W.D.N. Vaughan	

THE de LASZLO BOWL   (Handicap Doubles)

1974 R.P.C. Swash & H. W. Wollaston	1988 Jill St. Aubyn & J.S.P. Gibb
1975 C.B. Lyster & R.A. Wigger	1989 Maggie Henderson-Tew & E.C. Butterworth
1976 R.L. Brown & R.A. Wigger	1990 P.F.D. Trimingham & H.J.O. Tudor
1977 M.J. Dix & J.W.R. Larken	1991 Tanya Fabbri & T.F. Marsh
1978 I.T. Grimble & G.C. Welch	1992 P.D. Rowell & R.F. Todd
1979 R.W. Higgins & E.F.S. Seal	1993 G.B. Claridge & J.P. Edwards
1980 Jill St. Aubyn & G.W.H. Rowbotham	1994 N.E. Carew Hunt & R.T.J. Webb
1981 R. Denoon Duncan & R.C. Harris	1995 A.E.L. Horrocks & J.G. Ingham
1982 A.E.L. Horrocks & G.W.H. Rowbotham	1996 T.H.R. Church & J.H. Clark
1983 Marilyn Haydon & S.M.C. Scowcroft	1997 M.M. Gilmore & K.A. Smith
1984 Jean Buggy & E.C. Butterworth	1998 B.C. Rich & M.R.H. Webb
1985 Jean Buggy & J.M. Wilson	1999 N.E. Carew Hunt & N. Lawson-Smith
1986 Joanna Page & D.G. Steel	2000 Susie Falkner & M.R.H. Webb
1987 Fiona Macintosh & R. Travis	2001 J.N.I. Edwards & P.D. Rowell

THE WOLLASTON CUP   (The Club Junior Singles)

1991 R.J. Burrage
1992 R.J.S. Abraham
1993 S.A. King
1994 R.J.S. Abraham
1995 C.W. Prain
1996 B.N. Palmer
1997 J.S. Hepburn
1998 T.H. Carew Hunt
1999 T.H. Carew Hunt
2000 M.R.H. Webb
2001 J.K. Watson
2002 T.O. Leith

THE LURGAN CUP   (Professional-Amateur Doubles)

1938 A.R.V. Barker & A. Johnston
1939 W.M. Ross-Skinner & E. Ratcliffe
1952 P. Kershaw & R. Hughes
1953 P. Kershaw & R. Hughes
1954 P. Kershaw & R. Hughes
1960 J.G.H. Hogben & J.P. Dear
1961 M.M. Jones & R. Hughes
1962 Lord Ronaldshay & R. Hughes
1963 D.J. Warburg & L.W.R. Keeble

THE COCKBURN/LURGAN CUP   (Professional-Amateur Doubles)

1974 P. Kershaw & C. F. Ennis
1975 H.R. Angus & M. F. Dean
1976 H.R. Angus & H.M.H. Glover

THE UNIGATE PROFESSIONAL-AMATEUR DOUBLES

1979 P.N.R. Jenkins & N.A.R. Cripps
1980 R.P.C. Swash & C.J. Ronaldson
1981 A.C. Lovell & M. Ryan

THE DRESDNER KLEINWORT BENSON CLASSIC

	SINGLES	DOUBLES
1998	N.C. Wood	C.J. Bray & N.C. Wood
1999	R.L. Fahey	R.L. Fahey & N.C. Wood
2000	R.L. Fahey	M.H.J. Gooding & N.C. Wood
2001	R.L. Fahey	M.H.J. Gooding & N.C. Wood

In 2001 this competition was run as the Dresdner Kleinwort Wasserstein Classic.

BILLY ROSS-SKINNER CUP   (Invitation Mixed Doubles)

1983 Maggie Wright & C. Dean
1984 Jane Vaughan & J. Wilson
1986 Sheila Macintosh & J. Mackenzie
1987 Jane Vaughan & P. Newsom
1988 Sally Jones & Sir Clifford Chetwood
1989 Sally Jones & Sir Clifford Chetwood
1990 Alex Warren Piper & Sir Clifford Chetwood
1991 Charlotte Cornwallis & C. Dean
1992 Fiona Macintosh & A. Sawyer
1993 Margaret Allen & D. Colquhoun
1994 Sheila Macintosh & T.D.J. Warburg
1995 Clare Southwell & J.A.N. Prenn
1996 Katrina Allen & G. Grundy
1997 Gill Dean & N. Lloyd
1998 Sue Haswell & M.W. Corby
1999 Fiona Deuchar & C.J. Crossley

There have been other handicap singles competitions; one ran for several years during the latter part of the last century and another ran spasmodically before the Second World War. Press reports have only revealed the following:

1891 G.A. Rimmington beat J.J. Freeman
1933 General S.V.P. Weston beat C.B. Gabriel
1939 M.A. Pugh beat P.W. Johnson

----oooOOooo----

WORLD CHAMPIONSHIP MATCHES AT HAMPTON COURT

Set out below are a series of match reports covering the four World Championship Challenges that have taken place at Hampton Court.

The first deals with the 1885 Championship. Tennis was often reported in great detail in late Victorian times. *The Field* for example described the match almost stroke for stroke running to over 6,000 words, and an article in *Land and Water* was only a couple of hundred words shorter. These are too bulky to be reproduced here, so the piece that appeared in *The Saturday Review* on 23 May 1885, of some 1,900 words, is used. It still gives the reader a flavour of the occasion.

THE 1885 CHALLENGE

THE CHAMPIONSHIP OF TENNIS

The glory has departed. The great match for the championship is over, and England has been vanquished. England's representative player, George Lambert, had held the undisputed supremacy at tennis for the last fifteen years. In this position he was the successor of Edmund Tompkins, who gained in 1862 a victory over the greatest of French players, *Papa* Barre, then in his sixtieth year, who had been for 35 years the champion of tennis. That encounter, however, was hardly better than an ordinary exhibition-match; it was played on several days, at irregular intervals, and it ended in a most unsatisfactory manner. Barre, on the fifth day, was dead beat, and gave up the attempt to win. In 1871, Lambert succeeded to the championship without a struggle, for it was found impossible to arrange a set match between him and Tompkins, who was unable or unwilling to meet his youthful rival. Lambert, indeed, had already claimed the title of champion for a year or more. Before that time there had been other great players, both English and foreign, — the latter chiefly French, — who played in London for pride of place; a long list, including the names of Masson, Marchisio, Charrier, and Barcellon, all illustrious in the records of the game. It does not, however, appear that in any of their contests articles were drawn up, or any formal conditions imposed, other than the usual rules of the court in which they played, whether at Hampton Court, or in the old court in Windmill Street, or in James Street, Haymarket. Victory conferred the title, scarcely more than a courtesy title, of champion on the victor; nor was this ever disputed until the holder in his turn had been conquered in a similarly informal but equally conclusive fashion. The manners of the golden age were simple; so were also the customs of tennis in those golden days.

Autres temps, autres mœurs! With new players, from a new country, we have received new ideas; and for the most recent contest for the highest honours in tennis, we are told, regular articles were drawn up, a sum of money (100*l*.) was staked and deposited on each side, and all other conditions of the match were definitely arranged and precisely set forth in a formal document, duly signed, sealed, and delivered. Hampton Court was selected as the venue, and the contest was arranged so as to extend over three or four days, not consecutive, a days repose being allowed between two days of play, and the match was 'the best of thirteen sets,' the winner of the first seven sets to be declared the winner of the match and the champion of tennis. This was to be, therefore, a severe test of strength, condition, and endurance, as well as a trial of judgement and skill. To play four hard sets of tennis twice in one week is enough to try the powers of all but the exceptionally strong men; to do so thrice within the same limit of time is almost more than may be fairly demanded of the most robust.

Thomas Pettitt, the challenger, hails from America, the land of his adoption. Born in Beckenham, Kent, in 1860, he is now only twenty-five years of age; while Lambert is all but eighteen years his senior. To this great advantage of youth Pettitt unites extraordinary activity and far more strength than his slight form, all wiry and muscular as it is, would seem at first sight to promise. The length of the match, therefore, and the shortness of the time in which it had to be concluded according to the conditions, told on him much less severely than on his opponent; and, indeed, at the end of the third day he looked as if he could have begun again and played away for another week without much trouble or distress to himself. Not so, however, his antagonist, who appeared somewhat stale at the beginning of the last day's play, and perceptibly flagged and failed before its conclusion.

Pettitt, who is said to have been picked up some ten or twelve years ago, a poor English lad, in the streets of Boston, U.S.A., without a visible profession in life, was appointed to the responsible, but not too lucrative, post of under-marker in a racket court, the sweeping out of which was his chief duty. When a tennis-court was built there, — the first we believe, in America, unless the athletic exercises of the Aztecs may be reckoned as early expositions of tennis, — Pettitt received the rudiments of the game from a marker named Hunt, who had exchanged Oxford in the old country for the Western Athens, and whom he promptly excelled at his own game. Not long afterwards, Hunt made a fresh start in search of a more congenial situation, and his pupil took his place, and soon reached a point at which he could give long odds to the best players, amateur or professional, procurable in those regions. This, indeed, is the surprising matter in the story of Pettitt's career; not that his style of play, when we first saw it here, was strange, and wild, barbaric, untutored, and apparently developed out of inner consciousness, or acquired in contests with

> The hairy-faced baboon,
> In the mountains of the moon;

but that it should have been as good as on trial it proved to be.

In 1883, longing for new worlds to conquer, he came to England, where, though warmly welcomed in his character of foreigner, he met with but small favour from the cold eye of criticism, which was offended by his eccentricities of play, some of which clashed irreconcilably with the pure traditions and classic canons of taste in tennis. 'What matter?' asked his apologists; 'his style is effective,' they observed, and with some reason, as he won match after match against amateurs and professionals in almost unbroken succession. In 1884 he came again to the scenes of these triumphs, and again played, with much the same results, against all but our best player. The only disappointment was that Lambert, who had been suffering from severe indisposition for some time, was unable to try conclusions with this brilliant visitor. Naturally enough, the younger player, full of ambition and elated with success, was impatient to bring matters to an issue; and he strove hard to force the *de facto* champion to defend his right to the title. In the end, Lambert's health having improved somewhat since last year, and after much correspondence, the match was arranged. That it was played at Hampton Court, and not at Lord's or elsewhere, seems to have provoked criticism in some quarters; but where else could the match have been played with equal fairness to the players and convenience to the spectators? The Marylebone Court would evidently have given an advantage to Lambert, who plays there constantly. The Manchester Club, with ready liberality, offered the use of their admirable court, which Pettitt would have liked, but which is inconveniently far from London. The choice eventually fell on Hampton Court, Lambert having won the toss and chosen that court, which could certainly be considered neutral and equally fair for both players. It has, moreover, this advantage, in addition to its proximity to London, that it has two wide galleries, one near the top of each end wall, capable between them of accommodating nearly one hundred spectators. Thus, with the help of the *dedans* and the side-galleries, about 170 eager amateurs, on each day of the match, were provided with seats; a result which could not have been attained in any other court in England. Never before, perhaps, in the history of tennis has such a gathering been seen as that which watched each game intently, and hung expectant on the issue of each stroke of this great match. The excitement throughout was intense, and at times almost painful. It was not so because the play was more brilliant than such as many present there had seen before; but the match was terribly even, and the games were fearfully hard-fought. Pettitt played for much; Lambert stood to lose, in reputatation and position, far more.

Old Barre, however, and the other ghosts of the great departed, if they were permitted by the laws of the unseen world to be on-lookers, must have shuddered with horror at some of the strokes they saw, and must have wept not seldom over faults of omission and commission which could not fail to cause them pain and indignation. They, in their day, played better, — some of them within the memory of living man; and so, we may add, did once George Lambert. There can be no doubt or question but that he has lost more than half-fifteen from his best game of six or eight years ago; else he had never lost this match. Some, indeed, of his strokes on the floor, some of his 'forces' for the *dedans*, were in the old grand style and impossible to return. His service, especially on the first day and part of the second, was even more difficult than that of his opponent, hard as that undoubtedly is. But 'all round' his play showed a loss of that fire, vivacity, and crushing severity which it once possessed to an unapproachable degree. He seemed often now to hesitate in his attack, to 'play safe,' as it were. In other times he would have 'killed the ball' a hundred times where he now appeared to be glad to return it at any cost. Increasing age, — though he is not yet old, if compared with Barre while that inimitable player was still supreme, — and bad health, which has attacked him during the last few years; these are the main causes to which his defeat must be ascribed. These laid him open especially to the onslaught of a young, extremely quick and active, never-tiring assailant, such as Pettitt showed himself, who wearied him out. Thus on the first day Lambert won with some difficulty three of the four sets; on the second day two; on the third day none. As he tired and gave way the other improved, and learned to return the heavily-cut strokes, to stop the severe 'forces,' and to assume the attack instead of the defence. The challenger gained as fast as the challenged player lost ground. It is only fair to say that Lambert had decidedly the worst of the luck, particularly on the last day of the match; and that, of the errors of marker and umpires, in the opinion of some good judges, by far the greater number were scored to his disadvantage.

The most instructive point of the student of tennis, and that which was also the most diverting to the philosophic onlooker, lay with the fact that Pettitt gradually discarded the wildest features of his style as the match proceeded; he played more and more steadily on the floor, and less in the air with exuberant and unnecessary violence; and he eventually won in a manner which resembled that which, rightly or wrongly, has come to be regarded as correct. This is a very satisfactory result. Foreigner as he now is, he is, after all, by birth English. It is some consolation to feel that our champion has only been defeated, when past his prime, by a young man of English birth, taught by English players. But it is still more gratifying to think that this young man has now at least begun to correct his style by better English models than he had hitherto studied, and has already felt the advantage of this step. We may, therefore, look forward to seeing him play better and better for many years to come, and, if with diminished activity, yet with a style purged of its former ugly defects, and more elegant though not less effective than before. Let us hope that we may soon have another worthy champion to oppose him. In a year or two Charlie Saunders may be good enough. Till then we must sit in sackcloth, and mourn the glory which is departed.

The match statistics were as follows:

Pettitt won by 7 sets to 5.
Pettitt's score first: 2-6, 6-1, 1-6, 5-6; 4-6, 4-6, 6-4, 6-3; 6-2, 6-3, 6-3, 6-5.
                                365 strokes to 352.

THE 1977 CHALLENGE

The following report was published in the Club Newsletter.

THE WORLD TENNIS CHAMPIONSHIP 1977
THE ROYAL TENNIS COURT, HAMPTON COURT PALACE, JUNE 8th, 10th & 12th.

Howard Angus retained his title by beating Gene Scott of the U.S.A., the Challenger, by 7 sets to 2 in a three-leg match. This was a fascinating match between two top class players of contrasting styles. Angus fantastically fast on his feet, returning almost impossible shots which must have been heartbreaking to his opponent. In general he made the most of his strokes off the back wall, cutting them severely. However, when returned he volleyed strongly and used his knowledge, as he would put it, of 'the geometry of the court', perhaps sometimes to excess when boasting on to the main wall. He used the railroad service consistently throughout with great success.

Scott with his tall athletic figure and long reach, took the ball easily, hitting rather than cutting it into the corners. His volleying was strong and accurate and was rewarded by many winning openings particularly into the grille. His tactical use of the side galleries to obtain service or defeat chases was admirable. His service, again a railroad, was somewhat inconsistent with too many faults, a disadvantage as his second serve was weak and gave Angus every opportunity to attack it. The match was played in a very good spirit and was extremely well marked by Derek Barrett, the resident professional. The score in detail was 6-2, 5-6, 3-6, 6-1; 6-5, 6-4, 6-2, 6-1; 6-4. Angus's score first.

1st Leg

This was the most exciting as fortunes fluctuated throughout. If it had not been that Scott began to tire, he might have been in the lead at the end of the day. In the event honours were even at two sets all. In the second set Scott led 3-2, lost the next game, but then led again at 4-3. The eighth game was crucial, Angus was leading 30-15 but Scott laid down chases 1 and 2 and worse than a yard but due to Angus's magnificent play Scott lost both and Angus drew level at 4-4. By this time Scott was tiring and lost the next game, but drew level again at 5-5. The final game was vital and three deuces were called before Scott got home by 6-5 after one hour's play.

Although Scott took the first game in the third set he was tiring and served a number of faults, but at this stage Angus seemed to lose concentration and Scott playing intelligently and not being afraid to make side gallery chases to regain the service side, moved ahead relentlessly from 2-2 to win the third set 6-3.

Angus had showed no sign of fatigue and in the fourth set showed his best form. His railroad services were all to a length, he cut the ball into the corners, going for the base of the tambour and the grille. The inevitable result was a quick set of 6-1, which left the scores level at 2-2.

2nd Leg

It was all to play for and Scott started in his best form and led 3-1, 40-15 in the first set. One further point and he would have been in a commanding position but this was not to be, the game just slipped away. The heart of the whole challenge match rested in the next two games. Against a normal opponent the game was his but Angus running for everything, retrieved almost impossible shots to reach deuce, but Scott realising the climax had come, saved four game points before Angus equalised at 3-3. Angus relaxing to regain his wind lost the next to trail 4-3, but then laid two short chases and won the eighth game and ended this vital set in his favour 6-5, with a shot to the grille.

Angus had now got his eye in and was moving his opponent from side to side of the court and making a number of winning openings. Finally, and with some luck on his side, he galloped away to 4-0. His enthusiasm however, got the better of him and his boasting off the main wall did him no good. Scott had recovered his wind and played admirably winning four games in a row to equalise. However, he could not sustain the pace and Angus won 6-4 taking a heavy fall in winning the final point.

In the last two sets there was little doubt as to who was the fitter and this was obvious in the rests. It would not be unfair to say that Angus coasted to 6-1 leaving him with a lead of 6 sets to 2 on aggregate, an almost impregnable position.

3rd Leg

With only one set needed for victory for Angus, it was essential for his opponent to make a good start and it looked as if it might be so. Scott led 40-15 but failed to win the first game. He recovered, making it 1-1 and then 2-1. Angus then led 40-15, but Scott, pulling up to deuce, might once again have achieved a useful lead, but Angus finished the game with a superb winning gallery to square the score at 2-2. However, Angus was not at his best, showing some lack of concentration. Scott showed great determination and his attack was still powerful, but the score advanced 3-2, 4-2, 4-3, 5-3, in Angus's favour. Scott won the next game to love by beating an easy gallery chase, to make it 5-4. Would there be a repetition of the first set of the second day? This was not to be. Angus, the master, probably played his most imperious shots of the match in this game, no one could have lived with him, and he finished with a game to love with two masterly grilles.

Scores	Games	Sets
1st Leg	6-2, 5-6, 3-6, 6-1	2-2
2nd Leg	6-5, 6-4, 6-2, 6-1	4-0
3rd Leg	6-4	<u>1-0</u>
		7-2

The Royal Court was honoured to be asked to stage this Championship and virtually all seats were sold. A magnificent trophy was presented to Howard Angus on the Sunday evening. Finally, all thanks are due to Cutty Sark for once again sponsoring tennis so magnificently.

THE 1979 CHALLENGE

The following report first appeared in the 1978-79 Tennis & Rackets Association Annual Report and was written by Christina Wood, for so long the Real Tennis correspondent of the *Daily Telegraph*.

WORLD CHAMPIONSHIP

Howard Angus retained the World Championship, sponsored by Unigate, which he has held since 1976, when he beat his challenger, Chris Ronaldson, who returned from Melbourne and is now professional at Troon, by seven sets to nil at the Royal Court, Hampton Court, on April 17 and 19, 1979. The match, the best of thirteen sets over three legs, was already decided before the end of the second leg, the score to Angus then being 6-4, 6-4, 6-5, 6-5 after the first leg and 6-2, 6-3, 6-2 in the second leg.

Once again the left-handed Angus showed what a fighter he is on the big occasion. The tall, powerful Ronaldson had defeated him narrowly in the Cutty Sark singles at Queen's Club in the previous December, and had played consistently well in the eliminating competition.

The match, between two players of contrasting style, although both played in the modern idiom with more volleying and few long rests on the floor, was extremely close in the first leg and Ronaldson really deserved to have taken one set. Angus, however, served his railroad very well, getting a splendid length. He scored repeatedly off the tambour and was particularly accurate with his attack on the grille.

Angus, mainly holding the service side, took a 3-1 lead in the opening set, but Ronaldson, beating several short chases, came to 3-all. Two very close games followed, Ronaldson reaching 4-all at his fourth game point with a shot that died under the winning gallery. Angus, retaining the service side, then served so well that he got Ronaldson tied up in the corner and took the next two games to love for the set.

In the second set Ronaldson led for the first time at 2-0, but Angus went from 2-3 to 5-3 and Ronaldson could rarely dislodge him from the service side despite laying some short chases. A desperate struggle earned Ronaldson one more game and he saved a set point when Angus failed to beat chase better than three, but Angus was quickly back at the service side and took the set.

Ronaldson again led 2-0 in the third set, then Angus, playing very well on the floor, raced to 4-2. Ronaldson, now holding the service side more often, had a splendid spell. He levelled at 4-all after Angus had been 40-30 with a dedans, followed by chase worse than a yard, which Angus failed to beat, and won a love game for 5-4. Angus, however, gave nothing away. A grille made him 40-love and although Ronaldson regained the service side and put a perfect shot into the winning gallery it was of no avail. Angus, back on the service side, got the grille for 40-15, two set points. Ronaldson managed to get back with a shot into the last gallery, but could not stay long and Angus took the set with another grille.

The fourth set was neck and neck to 4-all. Angus was now scoring most of his points on the floor and Ronaldson by volleying and attacking the winning openings. Again Ronaldson got in front at 5-4 but Angus replied with a love game and reached three set

298

points at 40-love in the final game. Ronaldson fought back to deuce, then had a bad bounce which gave Angus a fourth set point and Ronaldson put down his next shot. The tally of winning openings was Angus 13 grilles, 2 dedans, 1 winning gallery; Ronaldson 5 grilles, 8 dedans, 1 winning gallery.

Angus therefore began the second leg two days later in a commanding position with Ronaldson knowing he must win two sets to keep the match alive. Under tremendous pressure he did not play as well as in the first leg, and Angus was very confident.

Ronaldson won the first game although Angus had beaten chase half a yard with a dedans. Then Angus, again serving well and laying short chases went to 3-1. Ronaldson played well to take the next game, then Angus was off again. Ronaldson got the winning gallery to hold a point for 2-all but Angus regained the service side and forged ahead. He reached 5-3 with a winning gallery, then held three set points at 40-love and beat Ronaldson with a winner on the floor.

Angus, dominating the play, went to 5-love in the second set. Ronaldson fought back with some good winners, including two grilles and a winning gallery, reaching 3-5 but again Angus took a love game for the set. By now Ronaldson must have been feeling desperate with all his shots being returned and with added pace. He got as far as 2-3, and after Angus had won the next game to love, Ronaldson held three points for 3-4 only to be denied. In the last game Ronaldson got the grille but a dedans gave Angus match point at 40-15 and, crossing to the service side he took the match with a service that made the ball fall dead off the back wall. The difference in winning openings was small: Angus had four grilles, four dedans and two winning galleries; Ronaldson had four grilles, three dedans and two winning galleries.

THE 1983 CHALLENGE

The report on the 1983 Challenge comes from the Tennis & Rackets Association Newsletter No. 10 – Autumn 1983 and was written by Editor, William Stephens.

TENNIS WORLD CHAMPIONSHIP CHALLENGE

Chris Ronaldson defended his World Champion's title for the first time on March 18, 20 and 22 at Hampton Court in a Championship over the best of 13 sets sponsored by George Wimpey P.L.C.

The Challenger was Wayne Davies, Professional at the New York Racquet and Tennis Club, holder of the U.S. Open title and the first Australian to challenge for the World Championship. He had earned the right by decisively defeating Colin Lumley, former Australian Open Champion, in the final eliminator in October last year before succumbing to appendicitis causing the postponement of his Challenge.

In that encounter he exhibited his strength of forcing shot particularly on the volley, which, however, was shown initially to be susceptible to nerves, particularly on receipt of service when the ball would fly up on to the penthouse roof, setting up an easy kill. However, when he countered Lumley by playing on the floor he showed his excellence in this department.

Ronaldson, Professional at the Royal Tennis Court (a post which, when a Royal Appointment, used to be known as 'The Marker in his Majesties Tennis Court') had won the World Championship by defeating Howard Angus in 1981. He relies on a composite game notable for the variety of service employed and the severity of his floor shots, and is also a County Lawn Tennis player, while Davies was a ranked Squash player in Victoria and threatened to have the edge on Chris for speed around the court.

The contest was awaited with keen anticipation, and had built up considerable expectancy; needless to say it was a sell-out. Furthermore it attracted television coverage by ABC, NBC and German television.

The defending Champion started the firm favourite – having remained unbeaten in any Open Competition since January 1981 – however, once engaged in battle the Challenger dispelled any notion that it would be a one-sided affair. Ronaldson won the first set 6-0 – a score that does not suggest the robust duel fought at a cracking pace where the premium was on absolute precision. Davies was occasionally prone to indiscretion – blasting shots at the dedans with his aim awry – but was unlucky, with a remarkable number of forces hitting the surrounds of the winning openings.

Winning the second and third sets 3-6, 4-6, the Challenger probed at the Champion's growing fatigue, needing to press home his advantage before his opponent, fresh again on Sunday, could reassert his authority. Knowing Ronaldson's strength in the variety of his services in his home court and the threat of the high cut serve, Davies took every available service volley off the penthouse roof, getting on top of the ball and savagely laying fine chases on the main wall side, and on the floor his cocked wrist disguised direction. Leading two sets to one he looked confident, but suffered lapses in concentration and Ronaldson found the necessary resources of energy to fight back to win the final set of the First Leg. 6-2.

Thus the contestants went into the Second Leg level at two sets each. The tension was still apparent – Davies struggling with his nerves and admonishing himself: 'Don't bash!' (the modern equivaent of Prince Talleyrand's exhortation 'Plus fait douçeur que violence et surtout pas de zèle'). Having admitted that the slightly larger court suited him, Wayne continued to bound about like a gazelle, exploiting the Holder's occasional lapses into error through losing his usual assiduous attention to correct footwork. Chris, however, maintained cool command and took the fifth set 6-3. The sixth set was fiercely disputed, with the opponents locked in contention through many relentless rests at crucial points. Ronaldson showed deft touch and unflustered calm, beating a hazard chase the first gallery by delicately guiding a ball into hazard the second and recording successive grilles. He ran out the winner 6-5.

Davies was particularly unlucky to lose the seventh set 6-4, having led 4-2 with a game point for 5-2. The result of these two sets was of crucial influence to the outcome of the match, and took a severe toll on the loser. In this war of attrition it was the Challenger who suffered; clearly in some discomfort, his response grew progressively weaker as he lost the remaining set 6-0.

Entering the final leg six sets to two down and plagued by an injury to the right sacroiliac joint which restricted bending forward on the backhand, and needing to win all five sets, Davies tried pluckily to fight without aggravating the injury in the rallies by taking care to position himself correctly before playing a shot, and he was very effective with the boasted force into the dedans. The Champion, needed to win only one more set, played in the first two sets as if knowing his opponent was trapped like a snake in front of a mongoose waiting to pounce, and as Davies fought gamely to apply technique within his restrictions, and won the sets 6-4, 6-5, his dogged resistance brought to cricketers' minds the dangers of an injured Greenidge or Richards at the batting crease. Ronaldson sensed this in the eleventh set, and reasserted his authority in a cool controlled finale to take the set 6-2 and win the Championship by seven sets to four.

Very rarely since the days of the first acknowledged World Champion, Frenchman Clergé around 1740, has a player succeeded in his first challenge – in fact only twice this century – but Wayne, having strengthened his floor game very considerably, has all the credentials and most impressive prospects for one day becoming the first Australian to be entered on this élite Roll of Honour. Meanwhile, Chris Ronaldson demonstrated his current supremacy in a masterly exhibition of precision and command of 'All the Talents'.

----ooo00ooo----

CHRIS RONALDSON'S PLAYING RECORD

WORLD CHAMPION 1981-87

BRITISH OPEN SINGLES

1978
1980
1981
1982
1983
1984
1985

UNITED STATES OPEN SINGLES

1980
1984
1986

AUSTRALIAN OPEN SINGLES

1977
1978
1982
1984
1985

FRENCH OPEN SINGLES

1981
1982
1983
1984
1986

WORLD INVITATION SINGLES

1980
1981
1986

SCOTTISH OPEN SINGLES

1980
1981
1986

BRITISH PROFESSIONAL SINGLES

1980
1981
1982
1983
1984
1986
1987
1989
1992

UNITED STATES PROFESSIONAL SINGLES

1978
1981
1984
1986
1987
1988
1991

----ooo00ooo----

WORLD CHAMPIONSHIP

YEAR	WINNER	RUNNER-UP	SCORE	VENUE
c1740	Clergé			
1765	Antoine-Henry Masson†			
1785	Joseph Barcellon			
1816	Jean Marquisio	Philip Cox		James Street
1819	Philip Cox	Amédée Charrier		James Street
1829	Edmond Barre	Philip Cox		James Street
1862	Edmund Tompkins	Edmond Barre	6-4*	James Street
1871	George Lambert	*claimed* (Tompkins resigned)		
1885	Thomas Pettitt	George Lambert	7-5	Hampton Court
1890	Thomas Pettitt	Charles Saunders	7-5	St. Stephen's Green, Dublin
1890	Charles Saunders	*claimed* (Pettitt resigned)		
1895	Peter Latham	Charles Saunders	7-3	Brighton
1898	Peter Latham	Thomas Pettitt	7-0	Brighton
1904	Peter Latham	Cecil 'Punch' Fairs	7-5	Brighton
1905	Cecil 'Punch' Fairs	Peter Latham	5-1	Queen's & Prince's
1906	Cecil 'Punch' Fairs	Ferdinand Garcin	7-4	Brighton
1907	Peter Latham	Cecil 'Punch' Fairs	7-3	Brighton
1908	Cecil 'Punch' Fairs	*claimed* (Latham resigned)		
1908	Cecil 'Punch' Fairs	Edward Johnson	7-2	Brighton
1910	Cecil 'Punch' Fairs	Fred Covey	7-6	Brighton
1912	Fred Covey	Cecil 'Punch' Fairs	7-3	Prince's
1914	Jay Gould	Fred Covey	7-1	Philadelphia
1916	Fred Covey	*claimed* (Gould resigned)		
1922	Fred Covey	Walter Kinsella	7-3	Prince's
1923	Fred Covey	Walter Kinsella	7-3	Prince's
1927	Fred Covey	Pierre Etchebaster	7-4	Prince's
1928	Pierre Etchebaster	Fred Covey	7-3	Prince's
1930	Pierre Etchebaster	Walter Kinsella	7-1	Prince's
1937	Pierre Etchebaster	Ogden Phipps	3-1*	Tuxedo
1948	Pierre Etchebaster	Ogden Phipps	7-2	New York
1948	Pierre Etchebaster	Jim Dear	7-4	New York
1949	Pierre Etchebaster	Ogden Phipps	7-1	New York
1950	Pierre Etchebaster	Alistair Martin	7-0	New York
1952	Pierre Etchebaster	Alistair Martin	7-2	New York
1954	Pierre Etchebaster	*resigned*		
1955	Jim Dear	Albert 'Jack' Johnson	11-10	New York & Queen's
1957	Albert 'Jack' Johnson	Jim Dear	7-3	Queen's
1959	Northrup Knox	Albert 'Jack' Johnson	7-2	New York
1966	Northrup Knox	Ronald Hughes	7-0	New York
1968	Northrup Knox	Pete Bostwick	7-3	New York
1969	Northrup Knox	*resigned*		
1969	Pete Bostwick	Frank Willis	11-8	New York & Manchester
1970	Pete Bostwick	Jimmy Bostwick	7-1	New York
1972	Jimmy Bostwick	Pete Bostwick	7-2	New York
1974	Jimmy Bostwick	Howard Angus	7-5	New York
1975	Jimmy Bostwick	*resigned*		

YEAR	WINNER	RUNNER-UP	SCORE	VENUE
1976	Howard Angus	Gene Scott	11-4	New York & Queen's
1977	Howard Angus	Gene Scott	7-2	Hampton Court
1979	Howard Angus	Chris Ronaldson	7-0	Hampton Court
1981	Chris Ronaldson	Howard Angus	6-1*	Queen's
1983	Chris Ronaldson	Wayne Davies	7-4	Hampton Court
1985	Chris Ronaldson	Wayne Davies	7-1	Queen's
1987	Wayne Davies	Chris Ronaldson	7-4	Queen's
1988	Wayne Davies	Lachlan Deuchar	7-1	New York
1991	Wayne Davies	Lachlan Deuchar	7-4	New York
1993	Wayne Davies	Lachlan Deuchar	7-6	New York
1994	Rob Fahey	Wayne Davies	9-5	Hobart & New York
1995	Rob Fahey	Wayne Davies	6-2*	Hobart
1996	Rob Fahey	Wayne Davies	7-1	Melbourne
1998	Rob Fahey	Julian Snow	7-4	Melbourne
2000	Rob Fahey	Wayne Davies	7-0	Hobart

* Retired

† Antoine-Henry Masson is often referred to as 'Raymond'. Recent research by Thierry Bernard-Tambour has shown that Raymond was a cousin of Antoine-Henry and was never a great player. (TBTV, pp. 71-74. For profile of Antoine-Henry; TBTF, pp. 83-102.)

----ooo00ooo----

APPENDIX 15

JESSE'S HISTORY

Because of Edward Jesse's close association with the Palace, his little known *History of Tennis* is reprinted here in its entirety. Jesse's history was first published in *Bentley's Miscellany* in 1853.

It not only contains references to tennis at Hampton Court, but it also has some interesting information relating to the 'invasion' of English shores by the leading French players in the early part of the nineteenth century, even though 150 years of subsequent research has rendered some of his conclusions invalid. In addition, it gives details of the formation of a club at the James Street Court*, which happened at about the same time as the members' club at the Palace was established.

Jesse was the Surveyor of the Royal Parks and Palaces during the early Victorian period, and as such was responsible for Hampton Court Palace. He is rightly credited with the successful major restorations of the time. He organised the replacement of the unsightly sash windows and ugly old Georgian chimneys with ones more in keeping with the original Tudor style. Jesse was also responsible for the restoration of the interior of the Great Hall, the Chapel roof, and the gardens. His signature is to be found on many documents authorising works on the Tennis Court and the associated lodgings.

He had other talents too. He was a well-known naturalist and author, and a regular contributor to the *Gentleman's Magazine* and *The Times*. His published works included several on rural life, *A Summer's Day at Windsor, and a Visit to Eton*, and the delightful *A Summer's Day at Hampton Court*.

Although it has not been possible to link Jesse with membership of the Royal Tennis Court, it is obvious from his writing he was a tennis player. It was Jesse who first introduced the young Spencer Ponsonby (later Sir Spencer Ponsonby-Fane) to tennis when he took him to see Edmond Barre play at Hampton Court. Jesse was also a member of the 'Toy Club', an influential group who dined once a month at the Toy Inn, which was situated between the Trophy Gate and the River. Several members of the Royal Tennis Court were also members of the Toy Club, which boasted the Duke of Clarence, afterwards William IV, as its President.

The author is indebted to the Racquet & Tennis Club, New York, who provided a copy of this work.

---

* A copy of the minutes of the meeting that drew up draft proposals for the formation of this club early in 1819 were found amongst the contents of a trunk discovered in a bank vault a few years ago, which is now on loan to the British Library. (BL, Loan 70, Vol. 2, f.171.) The trunk belonged to Scrope Beardmore Davies, a Regency dandy and close friend of Byron and Beau Brummell. Scrope Davies was a very good tennis player. The same trunk contains other interesting information including a notebook of his expenditure with the James Street professionals, and his gambling activity during the 1818 season.

A HISTORY OF TENNIS

EDWARD JESSE

If history may be considered as the key to the knowledge of human actions, so may our national sports be found to illustrate, in some degree, the character of the people of this country. In earlier histories of it, there can be no doubt that much low buffoonery, as well as rude games, were practised, and even rewarded by persons of high rank. Indeed, ancient records are still in existence which will serve to prove that lands were held by royal charters, under such conditions and for such feats as, in the present day, would scarcely be heard of in the purlieus of St. Giles'. In searching some of these early records we shall find that many of our kings amused themselves in a way which was not thought unworthy of their regal dignity. Thus, among the private expenses of Edward the Second, there is a charge of twenty shillings as paid at the lodge in Wolmer Forest to Morris Ken, when the King was stag-hunting there, because he amused his Majesty by often falling from his horse, "at which the King laughed exceedingly." He also gave a sum of money with his own hands to James de St. Albans, his painter, because "he danced before the King upon a table, and made him laugh heartily."

Bear and bull-baiting, as well as dog and cock-fighting, were considered as royal sports, and ladies of the highest rank frequented these barbarous exhibitions, which were occasionally varied by hawking, archery, racing and wrestling. Even in later days, we find Sir Richard Steele, in the 134th number of "The Tatler," reprobating the cruelty practised on animals in the sports at the bear-gardens; and others are detailed by Strutt, in his "Sports and Pastimes," of the people of England, which show but little sympathy for the suffering of animals.

Of all games, however, ball-play appears to have been one of the earliest, and to have continued in vogue to the present time. Herodotus attributed the invention to the Lydians, and Homer restricted this pastime to the maidens of Corcyra. Ball-play was a fashionable game in France from the earliest times, and in England we had bowling-alleys and bowling-greens, as well as football, at least as long ago as Henry the Second. Coles, in his Dictionary, mentions the ball-money, which, he says, was given by a new bride to her old play-fellows; and Bourne informs us, on the authority of Belithus, a ritualist, that in ancient times it was customary in some churches for the bishops and archbishops to play with the inferior clergy at hand-ball, even on Easter-day. During the Easter holidays also hand-ball was played for a tanzy-cake.

Fives, probably, came into vogue in more recent times. Mr. Nichols, in his "Progress of Queen Elizabeth," vol. ii. p.19, informs us, that "when that Queen was entertained at Elvetham, in Hampshire, by the Earl of Hertford, after dinner, about three o'clock, ten of his lordship's servants, all Somersetshire men, in a square green court before her Majesty's windowe, did hang up lines, squaring out the forme of a tennis-court, and making a cross-line in the middle; in this square they (being stript out of their doublets) played five to five with hand-ball at bord and cord, as they terme it, to the great liking of her Highness."

It is difficult to fix the time when tennis was first introduced. When it was so, it was probably a very different game to what we see it at present. Indeed the very appellation of it in the French language (*la paume*) would serve to prove that the ball was originally struck with the naked hand. Thick gloves were afterwards in use, to defend it, and at a later period cords or tendons were fastened round the hand in order to enable the player to give a greater impulse to the ball. The racket was finally introduced, "telle," says Pasquier, "que nous voyons aujourd'hui en laissant la sophistiquerie de Gand." This anecdote tends to fix the date of modern tennis. Pasquier was born in 1528, and supposing the fact to have been communicated to him when he was about twenty, by an informant of seventy-six, the result will lead us to ascribe the invention of the racket to a period not many years antecedent or subsequent to 1500.

Shakespeare, in a celebrated passage in his historical play of Henry the Fifth, may have led some of our readers to suppose that the terms now used at tennis must have been about a century older than the date above assigned to them. In the answer which the hero of Agincourt gives to the ambassadors who brought him a tun of balls from the dauphin, Shakespeare makes him say –

> "When we have match'd our rackets to these balls,
> We will in France (by God's grace) play a set
> Shall strike his father's crown into the hazard.
> Tell him! He hath made a match with such a wrangler,
> That all the Courts of France will be disturbed
> With chases."

Holinshed, however, who furnished Shakespeare with some of his historical details, simply relates that the ambassadors "brought with them a barrel of Paris balles, which from their mayster they presented to him for a token that was taken in verie ill part, as sent in scorn to signifie that it was more meet for the King to pass the time with such childish exercise than to attempt any worthie exploit. Wherefore the King wrote to him, that yer long he would tosse him some London balles that perchance would shake the walles of the best court in France." Thus it would appear, that of the technical phrases used by Shakespeare, Holinshed only supplied him with the term *court*. These Paris balls are by Caxton, in his Continuation of Higden's "Polycronin," printed in 1842, called "tenyse balles," that term, though apparently unknown in France, having at this early period been brought into use in England.

Whatever, however, the antiquity of the game may have been, it is certain that the adoption of the racket gave rise to various other improvements, till at last it has settled into the present interesting, and it may be added, scientific mode of playing the game, and from which, most probably, there will be no deviation.

Tennis may with truth be said to combine a portion of the excellence and beauty of all other games of manual skill, while at the same time there is, perhaps, no game in which a man can more readily exhibit a combination of strength, skill and activity, as well as of perseverance and adroitness. Those only who understand the game can form an idea of the fascination of it, or the extreme interest produced by it when a fine match has been played in the tennis courts of Paris or London. Nor has the game been confined to the male sex. St. Foix, in his "Essai historique sur Paris," vol. i. p.160, says, that there was a damsel named Margot, who resided in Paris in 1424, who played at hand-tennis with the palm, and also with the back of her hand, better than any man, and, what is most surprising, adds the author, at that time the game was played with the naked hand, or at best, with a double glove. She must have been a sort of Joan of Arc of tennis, and was contemporary with that heroine. According to Pasquier, Margot was a native of Hainault, and went to Paris in 1421, where she played "de l'avant train et de l'arrière très habilement."

James the First, if not himself a tennis-player, speaks of the pastime with commendation, and recommends it to his son as a species of exercise becoming a prince, and it became in consequence a favourite game with Henry Prince of Wales, the Marcellus of his age. Codrington, in his life of Robert Earl of Essex, the prince's early companion, mentions, that Lord Essex, in a passion of being called the son of a traitor, struck the prince with his racket, so as to draw blood. The King on hearing it sent for Lord Essex, but, on being made acquainted with the real circumstance of the affair, dismissed him unpunished.

Charles the First certainly played at tennis the day before he finally quitted Hampton Court, and Charles the Second was a constant player at the same place, and had particular kinds of dresses made for the purpose. The tennis court at Hampton Court was built, as already stated, by Cardinal Wolsey, and it is, we believe, allowed to be the most perfect one in Europe. The fine polish of the stone floor is only to be acquired by age, and the proportions of the court are known to be very exact. The following is a list of tennis courts in England:-

In London, 2 – one in James's Street, Haymarket, the other at Lord's Cricket-ground; Hampton Court, 1; Oxford, 2; Cambridge, 1; Strathfieldsaye, 1; Hatfield, 1;

Woburn, 1; Lord Craven, 1; Theobalds, 1; Brighton, 1; Leamington, 1; Goodwood, 1; Petworth, 1; - total 15.

It may be remarked, that neither Ireland nor Scotland can boast of possessing a tennis court, and we believe that there are not more than four of five on the Continent.

In the year 1821 a tennis Club was formed in London, consisting of fifty-eight members; amongst others, were the late Duke of York, the Duke of Argyle, Lords Anglesey, Jersey, Thanet, & c.; and of which, by the way, the late Duke of Wellington was an honorary member. During the existence of this club, many interesting matches were played, and most of the eminent French tennis players came over to this country to join in these matches.

That the French excel us at this game cannot be doubted, although, at the present period referred to, one Englishman, Philip Cox, had greatly distinguished himself. As far as the records of tennis are known to us, he was the first who could boast of having beaten the best French player of his day without receiving any odds. This player was Amédée Charier. Two public matches were played between him and Cox. The first was sharply contested, and Cox won by only the odd set in five. The other match was for three sets only, of which Cox won the first two.

In June 1823 a fine match was played. Cox and Marquisio, of whom an account will presently be given, against Barre and Louis, both fine French players, no odds being given on either side. The first two sets were set and set. They then agreed to play a third in order to decide the match, but this arriving at games all, they recommenced the set, which, after a hard contest, was won by Cox and Marquisio. It should be mentioned, that Barre was then considered as a most promising young player, and is now, most certainly, the best tennis-player in Europe. The following year the same match was played, and won by Barre and Louis, the latter at that time certainly but little inferior to Barre, perhaps only half-fifteen, or, at the most, fifteen.

One of the finest French players at this time in England was Barcellon. Whether we consider him as unrivalled as a teacher of the science of tennis, or recollect his unrivalled performances in the tennis-court in James's Street, Haymarket, we cannot but look upon him as a master of the art. It was in this court that we once saw him play a match with Monsieur, afterwards Charles the Tenth, giving high odds; nor can we forget the pleasure and surprize with which we witnessed his performance.

This justly celebrated French player died of cholera at Paris in the eightieth year of his age. His long residence in this country, embracing the greater part of the French revolutionary war, and continuing, with but a short interruption, up to the period of the return of Louis the Eighteenth to Paris in the year 1814. His celebrity as a player, and his almost daily exhibitions in James's Street, with almost every amateur of the day, would entitle him to a short notice from us.

Barcellon was a native of Montpellier. He had a swarthy complexion, with fine dark eyes. His form was slender, but well proportioned, and his height about five feet eight inches. At the age of twenty, and about the year 1769, he first came over to this country, having been backed to give John Mucklow, a fine English player, then eighteen years of age, *half thirty*. This match, high as were the odds, ended in favour of Barcellon. Before, however, he returned to Paris, subsequent matches between these two took place at much lower odds, and frequently to the advantage of Mucklow. Indeed, not only to his advantage, for he won many of them, but because he had thus early in life an opportunity of forming his play from the most perfect model.

In the thirty-second year of his age, Barcellon, and his brother-in-law, Bergeron, played a match in the fine tennis-court at Fontainbleau, before the then Queen of France, the unfortunate Marie Antoinette, against the celebrated, and, up to that time, unrivalled Maçon and Charier. This may be considered the grandest match on record, for the French declare that there has never been a tennis player equal to Maçon, and Charier is admitted to have been but little inferior to him. They however lost the match, though, it should be mentioned, that the two latter had passed their prime, and were obliged to yield the palm of victory to their pupils, now become their rivals. In consequence of Barcellon's success on this occasion, he was made on the spot *Paumier au Roi*, which appointment he held for forty-five years, so that this celebrated match must have been played about the year 1782.

As a tennis player, Barcellon could not well stand higher than he did at this time; but what chiefly distinguished him was the gracefulness of his manner, enhanced by the peculiar gracefulness and symmetry of his form. In fact, he did nothing awkwardly, and we may feel warranted in saying, that had he gone upon the French boards he would have been the Vestris or De Hayes of his time.

We have heard it asserted that his brother-in-law, Bergeron, was a superior player, and perhaps it was so; but the rudeness, not to say brutality, of his manners, left him few admirers. He came over to this country but once, at which time his powers were extraordinary, and he was as formidable an antagonist, from his temper and violence, as from his skill. He was a dissipated character, corpulent, and drank to excess, and, what is curious, could play best when excited by wine. When questioned as to their comparative strength, Barcellon would answer, that he could always beat his brother-in-law when he caught him sober, but that when half drunk he was invincible.

Barcellon, as compared with our own players, was always about half-fifteen above John Mucklow, his contemporary, and perhaps equal to Cox, taking them both at their best.

Marchisio was another extraordinary fine player, and generally accompanied the French markers, Barre and Louis, in their annual visits to this country. In fact, he might be called their companion, guide, and nurse. He died at Paris, after a short illness, on the 7th of December, 1830, aged 52.

Marchisio was an Italian, and originally a marker in the tennis-court at Turin. He was brought up there under his father, who was the master or proprietor of that court. When the French overran Italy, and gave peoples' minds other matters to think of than tennis, Marchisio was either pressed into, or voluntarily joined the French army, and was at the battle of Marengo; there he received a gun-shot wound in the left arm. Sometime after this event he went to Paris, and endeavoured to better himself by entering into some mercantile speculations. Failing in these, he had again recourse to tennis, and, by practice in the courts at Paris, he soon recovered his play, and showed himself but little inferior to Amédée Charier, the admitted best performer of the day.

Marchisio first came over to this country in 1815, where his style of play was much admired, and, consisting, as it did, of quick, easy, and certain return, without any overpowering force, almost every amateur of the day was disposed to try his strength with him. In these matches, he reaped, no doubt a good harvest. He contrived, through the favour of Monsieur, or the Duc de Berri, to get appointed *Paumier au Roi*, this being the first instance of a foreigner obtaining that distinction in France. The appointment excited great envy and jealousy among the French tennis players, who never entirely forgave him this piece of good fortune.

Of his play, it may be observed, that in what are called "*cramp*" matches, he was able to give the amateurs of moderate force, the most incredible odds, and such as neither Charier and Cox would offer. For instance, he gave Lord Granville, no mean defender of the half-court, the following odds. Half court – that is, he had only half the court to play in – 30, or two certain strokes at the beginning of each game – barring all the openings, so that he could not force for the *dedans* when he had to win yard or half-yard chases – and, moreover, he was restricted from *boasting* against either of the side-walls. Amédée Charier endeavoured to give these very odds to Lord Granville, but certainly failed.

Marchisio succeeded in this description of match partly by good management and patience, but chiefly by the power he possessed of dropping the ball so short over the high part of the net, as to render it difficult to be *vollied* with effect or certainty, however forward in the court his adversaries might stand. The late Mr. Cuthbert used to declare that of all the markers he had ever played with (and he had played with them all), Marchisio was the most difficult to beat, not because he gave less odds than he fairly ought, but because he managed his *force* so well, and wearied out his opponent by his unceasing and indefatigable *return*.

It must, however, be admitted that in a single match against a superior player, Marchisio was not seen to advantage. There was a want of force and decision in his stroke. He, indeed, placed his ball admirably, and having an excellent head, was sure to find out the most exposed or undefended part of his adversary's court, but he had at the same time but little power of *cutting* a ball in so decisive a manner, as to make the return of it almost impossible. In James-street, therefore, where the walls and floor are so lively, he could not, frequently, decide a ball against such a player as Cox, except by masking his intension, or catching him out of his place.

Upon the whole, though Marchisio never attained the highest degree of excellence; there was much in his play to be admired. His *half-volley* was inimitable – his return certain – his judgement accurate – and his style good. His place as a tennis-player will seldom be met with.

But it is time to give some notice of Barre. This extraordinary player exhibited his skill in the James-street tennis court, about the year 1820, where he played, then being a very young man, in several matches with varied success, and where he still plays perfectly unrivalled. Louis XVIII made him *Paumier au Roi.* As his play improved, he became invincible, and will give incredible odds to any antagonist. As a proof of this, he would readily be backed to give Tompkins, our best English player, and the master of the Brighton tennis court, thirty in each game for a *bisque.* He would also give the same odds to Monsieur Monneron, one of the best of the French tennis players. In fact, it is no easy matter to calculate the odds which Barre could not give. His chases are so close – his force so great and certain – his return so quick – his judgement and calculation so extraordinary, and his service so difficult to be met, that we have watched his play both at Paris, in London, and at Hampton Court, with no small degree of pleasure and astonishment. Some few years ago he played in a *show-off* match at Hampton Court before Queen Adelaide and a large party, with Louis, Monneron and Cox, and nothing could be more brilliant than the play.

In addition to what has been said of him as a player, it would be doing Barre an injustice not to mention that he is a general favourite in this country, where he is a regular visitor, and, indeed, almost a resident.

Louis was another player of the same stamp, but never equal to Barre, who could give him half-fifteen in his best day. An accident, some years ago, rendered Louis unable to show his skill in a tennis-court. He was, at one time, celebrated for what are called *cramp* matches. He distinguished himself in one at Paris, when he played Mr. Hughes Ball with a boot-jack instead of a racket. He also played one match with a man on his back, and another with a donkey fastened to him, and won them both. He was a stout, thick-set man, of great strength and activity, and a perfect master of the game of tennis.

While speaking of *cramp* matches, we may mention that Mr. Charles Taylor, so celebrated as a cricket player, played a match of three sets at Hampton Court, he riding on the back of a pony, and won it. We have also the authority of the late Lord Holland for saying that his great relation, Charles James Fox, when a young man, played a match, in the same court, for a considerable wager, the condition of which was that he should be perfectly naked. The match was played, and he won it.

Among the French gentlemen players, we should not omit to mention Monsieur Bonnet, an Avocat, and the translator of Sheridan's plays, a work which did him much credit, considering the difficulty of the task, especially in the "Rivals." He was a fine player, and we had the pleasure of seeing him in several matches at Paris, with Barre, Louis, and Monneron. Lauret, a Pompier of the guard, was another good player, but Barre could give him half-thirty.

We will now proceed to describe some of the terms used at tennis, for the information of such of our readers who are not tennis players.

The size of a tennis court is generally 96 or 97 feet in length, by 33 or 34 wide. A line, or net, hangs exactly across the middle, and is one yard in height at the centre, but rises at each end, so that it hangs in a slope. Over this net the balls are struck with a racket. Upon entering a tennis court, there is a long gallery, which goes to the *dedans.* This *dedans* is a kind of front gallery, where spectators usually stand, and into which, if a ball is struck, it tells for a certain score.

The long side gallery is divided into different galleries, or compartments, each of which has its particular name; viz., first gallery, door, second gallery, and last gallery. This is called the *service* side. From the *dedans,* to the last gallery, are figures 1,2,3,4,5,6, at a yard distance each; by these, the *chases,* which form a most essential part of the game, are marked.

On the other side of the net, are also the first gallery, door, second gallery, and last gallery. This is called the *hazard* side. Every ball struck into the last gallery on this side, reckons for a certain stroke, as in the *dedans*. Between the second and this last gallery, are the figures 1,2, to mark the *chases* on the hazard side. Over these galleries is a covering, called the *pent-house*, on which the ball is played from the service side, in order to begin a set at tennis. This ball is called a *service*, and must fall upon or strike the side pent-house on the other side of the net, and drop within certain lines on the hazard side. If the ball fails to do this, it is called a *fault*, and two faults, consecutively, are reckoned a *stroke* lost. If a ball should roll round the end pent-house, at the opposite side of the court, so as to fall beyond a certain line described for that purpose, it is called a *passe*; - reckons for nothing on either side, and the player must serve again.

On the right hand wall of the court, from the *dedans*, but on the hazard side, is the *tambour*, a part of the wall which projects so as to alter the direction of the ball, and make a variety in the stroke.

The last thing, on the right hand side, is called the *grille*, and, if a ball is struck into it, it is a certain score.

If a ball falls, after the first rebound, untouched, it is called a *chase*, and the chase is determined by the galleries and figures. When there are two chases, the parties change sides, and each party tries to win, or defend the chases, and this trial of skill forms one of the most interesting features of the game.

A game consists of four strokes, which, instead of being numbered 1,2,3,4, are reckoned in a manner somewhat difficult to understand.

For instance, the first stroke or point is called	15
The second	30
The third	40 or 45
The forth, and last	Game

Unless, indeed, the players get three strokes each, when, instead of calling forty all, it is called *deuce*, after which, as soon as any stroke is gained, it is called *advantage*; and, in case the strokes are equal again, it is deuce again, and so on, till one or the other gets two strokes following, when the game is won.

The following may be called the odds given by superior to inferior players. For instance, a *bisque*. This is one point to be scored whenever the player, who receives this advantage, thinks proper. Suppose a game of the set to be 40 to 30, he, who is 40, by taking his *bisque*, secures the game.

The next greater odds are *half-fifteen*, a term difficult to be understood by persons who are not acquainted with the game. In these odds, nothing is given, in the first game, but one point (viz. 15) to the end, and so on, alternately, for as many games as the set may last.

The next greater odds are *fifteen*, that is, a certain point at the beginning of each game.

Half-thirty is fifteen one game, and thirty the next, and so on alternately.

Thirty is two certain strokes at the beginning of each game.

Forty is three stokes given in each game.

Round service is another odds given. To constitute it, the ball must strike both the side and the end penthouse, which renders it easy to be returned.

Half-court is when a player is obliged to confine his balls to one half of the court lengthways, at his option, while his adversary plays his balls where he pleases. If the ball is struck out of the defined half-court, it is the loss of a point.

When a player gives *touch no wall*, he is restricted from playing his balls against any of the walls, except in the service. The openings are barred by these odds.

We have now endeavoured to enable our readers to form some idea of this ancient, manly, and most interesting game, which has been in great and deserved estimation, in the most enlightened countries, for ages past. We have often had many questions asked of us by persons in a tennis court, who have seen the game played for the first time. To such persons the foregoing remarks may be of use, while to those who have a knowledge of, and admire the game, the preceding account of the most celebrated tennis player cannot fail to be an interesting record.

ROYAL TENNIS PLAYERS

Those members of the Royal Family known to have played the game are shown in bold type

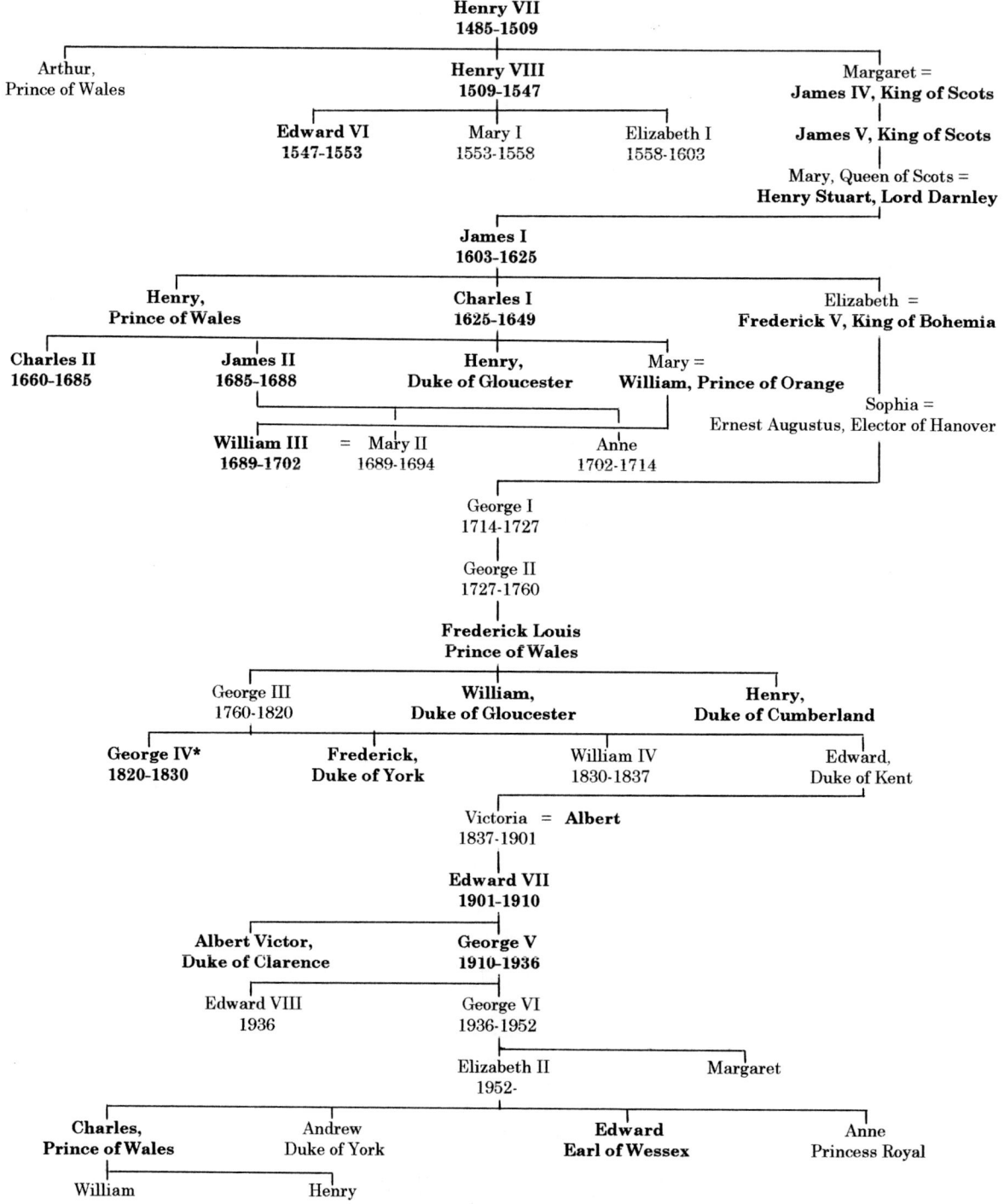

Note - Not all of the children are shown; those that are, are listed in order of succession

* see Chapter 2

APPENDIX 17

400th ANNIVERSARY CELEBRATORY VERSES

The verses below were written by H. J. Inman in celebration of the 400th Anniversary of the Court in 1929. They were first published in the Surrey Comet.

The silvery Thames embraces
Hampton Court's wide open spaces
Of Park and Lawn and Garden fair
And Tilt Yard kept in good repair.
Hard by the stream stands Wolsey's pile,
With Gothic arch in Tudor Style;
Wren's ruddy brickwork in the east
Gives architects a varied feast.
Here within this Court of Hampton
By the broad walk that you've trampt on,
There's another Court still standing,
Tribute at your hands demanding.
It is King Henry's Tennis Court
For sport of Kings and King of Sport.
Yes tribute asking at your hands
To strike a ball in the Dedans,
Or in the Grille, or lay a chase,
Or play upon the Tambour's face.
What other pastime's cult can show
A temple such as this we know?
Four hundred years its walls four square
Have stood 'gainst Time for Tennis here,
And most tenacious in its hold,
Has cast from out its sterner mould
A game that's played with softer balls
In open space without its walls.
Perchance a parallel we'll find
Betwixt this game and Henry's mind,
For in affairs of state he'd get
His rivals tangled in a net.
These through various hazards chased,
By definite defeat were faced.
With skill he served them all the same
And loss of head oft marked the game.
And other Kings and Queens they say
Were good at love games in their day
Within these Courts; Ah! Who can tell
How love set in those hearts could dwell.
Oh! Visitor to this resort,
When in the precincts of this Court,
Canst picture the historic throng
Passing this corridor along,
Or neath the Pent House wend its way
To watch a King and courtiers play?
Features we know from Holbein's brush
From Lely's, Kneller's, seem to blush
And bloom by the light of the moon
Late of a winter's afternoon.

----ooo00ooo----

313

THE ROYAL COURT ENTERTAINS A RUSSIAN TEAM

At 7 o'clock on the evening of Saturday, May 25th 1974 when the court was undergoing refurbishing and after wiping off several layers of linseed oil, a playing member was making his way home through Tennis Court Lane when he was addressed by one of the occupants of a very large car flying a red pennant.

In the car were three Russians, one an interpreter, the other two being senior representatives of the Anglo-Soviet Joint Commission under the leadership of His Excellency Academician V.A. Kirillin, Deputy Chairman of the Council of Ministers of the U.S.S.R. They were Mr. M.A. Pertsev and Mr. V.V. Andreev. An English civil servant accompanied them.

The Englishman who was conducting the party, approached the member and asked whether they were in Hampton Court and if there was anything of interest to see! He was assured that there was much to be seen but that all of the exhibits were inaccessible at that late hour. However, if the member could be of service, then he had a few minutes to spare.

All three Russians and Mr. R.J.V. Whitehead, the civil servant, dismounted and what was to be a few minutes conversation became a tour of the palace lasting over an hour.

'This is Anne Boleyn's Walk' said the member to Mr. Frydberg, the interpreter --- 'Henry VIII cut off her head.' 'The King cut off the Queen's head here' said Mr. Frydberg to the Ministers, who conferred together with some astonishment and then nodded wisely.

A hundred yards further on they were shown the Grape Vine and told that it was certainly the largest in Europe and probably in the world. This information was conveyed to the Ministers who again conferred. 'We have larger grapes in Russia' they insisted and drew a circle on the gravel as large as a tennis ball.

A few minutes later they were shown the Thames and were informed that it was the most important river in England and flowed through London, the capital. The interpreter passed this fact on, and once more the Ministers withdrew to consider this addition to their knowledge. 'The Volga is longer, wider, greater and more beautiful' came the reply, and with this no one could argue except on the last point, which would require extensive research.

At this stage the member was asked what his fee as a guide would be, although already it had been made clear that his presence at the Palace was not connected with professionalism, but with real tennis.

The tour proceeded, the interpreter worked harder, conference succeeded conference and the member was yet again assured that his services would be fully rewarded particularly as the hour was getting late. Realising that it was unlikely that the reason for his presence would be understood, the member, therefore, conveyed the party to the tennis court.

As they passed down the passage the Ministers discussed in some details the merits of tennis as a game and an exercise. 'Mr Pertsev says he thinks the surface

314

will be red but Mr Andreev insists that in England it must be grass' announced the interpreter, but of course they were both wrong.

In a somewhat involved and curious exchange of definitions the unusual form of the game was examined and it was pointed out that as the King played he was probably watched from the dedans by one of his wives whose names were given by the member and details of the unhappy demises. 'The King he play the ball here' stated the interpreter 'and behind the net sit the Queens and they include Anne of Cleeves, Anne Boleyn and Katherine Hepburn and they all ....' He then drew the handle of his umbrella across his throat and made the noise of a well known tonic water advertisement. 'We will build tennis court in Moscow' proclaimed Mr. Andreev.

The member now asked to be relieved of his duties so that he might go home. The Ministers felt that this called for a final meeting – this time adjacent to the Winning Gallery. 'You will receive two pounds for your services' said Mr. Frydberg; but the member – still as it were defending the dedans – with a degree of inspiration stated he would much rather have two pints at the Mitre.

After the last and briefest yet of their many conferences, the two Ministers agreed to this suggestion and the large limousine waiting in Tennis Court Lane proceeded with the party, now numbering six including the lady driver, to the gate, where it stopped and the red pennant was removed.

It was now that the member laid his best chase. The road was up, there was no policeman and the traffic was heavy. He walked to the middle of the first carriageway, raised his racket and held up the vehicles for the deputation to cross; the operation was repeated for the second carriageway and Cardinal Wolsey's bar was finally achieved.

At the request of one of the Ministers, the interpreter announced with some vigour that the Commission wished 'to take the largest and best drink in the Palace' and the unanimous acceptance of this resolution suggested that the 3rd meeting of the Anglo-Soviet Joint Commission* had been a complete success.

Vernon N. Ely -   the member concerned

* Visit of His Excellency
  Academician V.A. Kirillin
  Deputy Chairman of the Council of Ministers
  of the Union of Soviet Socialist Republics
  and Chairman of the State Committee
  for Science and Technology
  and Madame Kirillina.

19 to 26 May 1974

First published in the Club Newsletter in March 1975.

----ooo00ooo----

CHANGES TO THE PRESENT TENNIS COURT OVER THE CENTURIES

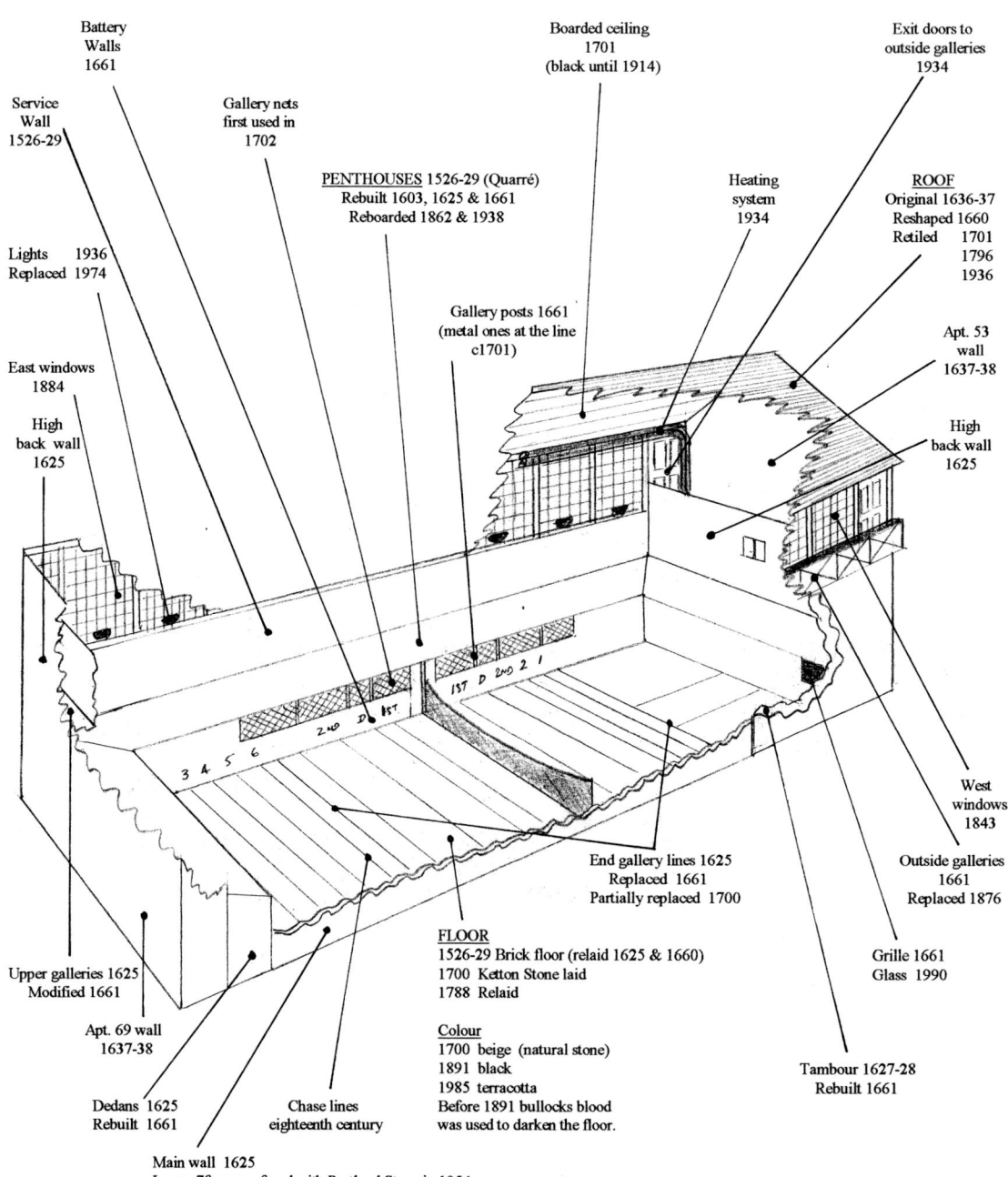

Battery
Walls
1661

Service
Wall
1526-29

Gallery nets
first used in
1702

Boarded ceiling
1701
(black until 1914)

Exit doors to
outside galleries
1934

PENTHOUSES 1526-29 (Quarré)
Rebuilt 1603, 1625 & 1661
Reboarded 1862 & 1938

Heating
system
1934

ROOF
Original 1636-37
Reshaped 1660
Retiled   1701
           1796
           1936

Lights   1936
Replaced 1974

Gallery posts 1661
(metal ones at the line
c1701)

Apt. 53
wall
1637-38

East windows
1884

High
back wall
1625

High
back wall
1625

West
windows
1843

Upper galleries 1625
Modified 1661

End gallery lines 1625
Replaced 1661
Partially replaced 1700

Outside galleries
1661
Replaced 1876

Apt. 69 wall
1637-38

FLOOR
1526-29 Brick floor (relaid 1625 & 1660)
1700 Ketton Stone laid
1788 Relaid

Grille 1661
Glass 1990

Colour
1700 beige (natural stone)
1891 black
1985 terracotta
Before 1891 bullocks blood
was used to darken the floor.

Dedans 1625
Rebuilt 1661

Chase lines
eighteenth century

Tambour 1627-28
Rebuilt 1661

Main wall 1625
Lower 7ft. was refaced with Portland Stone in 1954
William III's monogram 1702

316

CHRONOLOGICAL HISTORY OF TENNIS AT HAMPTON COURT

1514	Thomas Wolsey acquires a lease of Hampton Court Manor, starts to build the Palace.
1526-29	Cardinal Wolsey builds an open *quarré* court on the present site.
1529	Southern end lodgings built by Henry VIII.
1532-35	Henry VIII builds an enclosed *quarré* court closer to the Palace.
1603	James I carries out a major renovation of the Open Court.
1606-07	Henrican Court floor relaid.
1614-15	Roof tiles replaced on the Henrican Court.
1625	Charles I pulls down the Open Court and rebuilds it in brick (probably now a *dedans* court).
1636-37	Roof put on the Open Court, internal upper galleries included. Keeper's House built. Southern end lodgings extensively rebuilt.
1660-61	Major renovation carried out by Charles II: Roof and window structure altered. New penthouses, floor and tambour. Outside galleries replace internal ones. Central entrance to playing area introduced.
1669	Work starts on the conversion of the Henrican Court into lodgings — completed 1674.
1687	Additional support beam for roof installed.
1689-99	Court closed and used as a timber store by Sir Christopher Wren during the Palace rebuilding works.
1700-02	William III restores the Court and returns it to play: New stone floor (all previous floors were brick). Gallery nets introduced. Ceiling boarded. Roof tiles replaced.
1718	George I converts the Court into a drawing room — walls painted white.

1720	Probable date when the Court was returned to play.
1724	Roof tiles replaced.
1781	Penthouses covered with canvas.
1788	Refurbished for the Duke of Gloucester — floor relaid.
1790	Walls returned to black.
1792	Roof tiles replaced.
1818	Prince Regent orders a renovation prior to the formation of the Club.
1843	West windows glazed.
1848	Present changing room created — players previously used a room on the first floor.
1849	First floor added on top of the scullery annexe of the Keeper's House.
1854	Additional storey added to the Keeper's House.
1862	Penthouses re-boarded.
1876	Major renovation including the replacement of the outside galleries.
1883	Last Keeper dies — Keeper's House lost.
1884	East windows glazed.
1885	First World Championship at Hampton Court — G. Lambert v T. Pettitt.
1891	Floor painted black — previously the floors were darkened by bullocks blood.
1896	Club in crisis — annual subscription introduced.
1903	Edward VII grants patronage — all subsequent monarchs have done the same.
1913	Suffragettes cause the Court to be closed to the public.
1914	Ceiling painted white — previously black.
1914-18	First World War — very little play. Club ceases to function.
1919	Club revived.
1928	Grace-and-Favour Warrants issued.
1934	Heating installed in the Court.

1935	Court redecorated. Penthouses re-boarded. Roof tiles replaced.
1936	Court artificially lit.
1940	Second World War — Court damaged during a bombing raid.
1942	Court forced to close.
1946	Window glass replaced — Court returns to play.
1954	Main wall refaced with Portland Stone.
1973	Club reconstituted (Palace Revolution).
1974	Members redecorate the Court — lights replaced.
1977	Second World Championship at Hampton Court — H.R. Angus v E.L. Scott.
1979	Third World Championship at Hampton Court — H.R. Angus v C.J. Ronaldson.
1980	450th Anniversary: H.M. The Queen and H.R.H. The Duke of Edinburgh attend a reception at the Club. Clubrooms established (Ely Rooms).
1983	Fourth World Championship at Hampton Court — C.J. Ronaldson v W.F. Davies.
1985	Floor painted terracotta.
1987	The Queen gives permission for a Second Court to be built.
1990	Glass grille fitted.
1993	Keeper's House recovered and completely refurbished. New clubrooms. Walled garden acquired. New professionals' workshop. Modern flat for the Head Professional.
1997	Ministerial approval given for Second Court.
1998	Changing room restored to its former Victorian elegance.
1999	Planning permission granted for the Second Court. First Ladies World Championships at Hampton Court.
2001	Abandonment of the original Second Court scheme, cheaper option sought — mass resignations from the Board.
2002	The Royal Tennis Court to host the World Championship again.

INDEX